Mass Media and Politics
A Social Science Perspective

The *New Directions in Political Behavior* Series

GENERAL EDITOR
ALLAN J. CIGLER
University of Kansas

MASS MEDIA AND POLITICS

A Social Science Perspective

Jan E. Leighley

TEXAS A&M UNIVERSITY

Houghton Mifflin Company   Boston   New York

To Rick and Anna

Editor-in-Chief: *Jean L. Woy*
Sponsoring Editor: *Katherine Meisenheimer*
Associate Project Editor: *Shelley Dickerson*
Executive Marketing Manager: *Nicola Poser*
Senior Manufacturing Coordinator: *Marie Barnes*

Cover photograph: © Harold Burch, NYC

Library of Congress Catalogue Number: 2001133298

ISBN: 0-395-92546-0

456789-MP-09 08 07 06

Contents

Preface   xi

CHAPTER 1.   MASS, MEDIA, AND POLITICS
IN THE UNITED STATES   1

The Mass Media and Specialized News Media   3

Centrality of the Media to Today's Politics   3
Objective Importance of the Mass Media   4
Instantaneous News Delivery   5
Mass Media as a Linkage Institution   6

The Interdependence of Journalists, Politicians,
and the Mass Public   8

Models of the Mass Media   9
Reporters of Objective Fact   9
Neutral Adversary   10
Public Advocate   10
Profit-Seeker   11
Propagandist   12
Implications of the Models   12

Theories of Mass Communication   13
Media Effects on the Mass Public   13
The Public's Effect on the Mass Media   15

Studying the Mass and the Media   15

Structure of the Book   16

CHAPTER 2. THE MEDIA AS A POLITICAL INSTITUTION   20

Historical Development of the Media-Government Relationship   22
The Early Press Eras   23
Government Sponsorship of the Press   24
The Economics of the Mass Newspaper   25

The Electronic Broadcast Media   26

High-Tech Media: A New Era in Media-Government Relations?   28
The Origins and Growth of the Internet   29
New Formats in Political Communications   30

Consequences of the New Era for Mass Politics   31
The Political Consequences of Narrowcasting   32

The Politics of Regulation   33
Print and Electronic Regulation: Ownership   34
Regulating Broadcasting Content   36
Consequences of Deregulation   40

The Politics of Public and Semipublic Ownership   41

Media-Government Relationships and Models of the Press   43

CHAPTER 3. WHAT'S NEWS?   47

The News Product and Models of the Mass Media   50
Reporters of Objective Fact   50
Neutral Adversary   50
Public Advocate   50
Profit-Seeker   51
Propagandist   51

Defining What's News   52
Timeliness   53
Human Interest and Drama   53
Concrete Events   54
Defining News: A Historical Update   54

News Coverage of Politics   55
Domestic News Coverage   56
Local News Coverage   58
Foreign Affairs Coverage   60
An Update on the Content of News Coverage   61

Values Reflected in News Coverage   64

Conclusion   66

CHAPTER 4.   NEWSGATHERING: BUSINESS, PROFESSION, AND ORGANIZATION 70

Economic Influences on Newsgathering 72
Private Ownership 72
Concentration of Ownership 73
Consequences of Corporate Ownership 77

Profit, Advertising, and Ratings 78
The Ratings Game 78
Profitability 79
The Corporate Approach: Marketing to Reader Interest 80

Media Users and Audiences for the News 81
Audience Size and Media Reliance 81
Audience Interest 83
Television Viewership and Audience Overlap 84

Corporate Decision Making: Boardroom versus Newsroom 85
Corporate Cost-Cutting 85
Courting Advertisers 90

Professional Influences and Structure 91
Demographics 92
Personal Values 92
Professional Values: The Role of the Media 93
Professional Values: Objectivity 94

Organizational Constraints 95
Managerial Strategies for Marketing the News 95
News Routines, Deadlines, and Beats 96
Investigative Reporting 97

On the Media Business and Models of the Press 98

Conclusion 100

CHAPTER 5.   POLITICAL INSTITUTIONS AND THE MASS MEDIA 104

The Institutional Basis of Newsgathering 106
Accommodating the Media 107
Using the Media to Govern 110

The Presidency 113
What the White House Does 113
White House Press Coverage 115

Congress   119
What Members of Congress Do   120
Who Gets Covered   121
What Gets Covered   122

Federal Courts   124
Supreme Court and Courts of Appeal   124
Trial Courts   125

The View from Entertainment Land   126

Institutional Agenda-Setting   128
How and When Do Institutions Respond?   128
Responses to Crises   129
Responses to Exposés   132

On the Media as a Linkage Institution   134

On Models of the Press   134

Conclusion   136

CHAPTER 6. THE MEDIA, POLITICAL KNOWLEDGE, AND POLITICAL ATTITUDES   142

Theories of Media Effects   144
Hypodermic Needle Model   144
Minimal Effects Model   148
Contingent Effects Model   150

Political Knowledge as a Requisite for a Healthy Democracy   151
Findings from Survey and Experimental Research   151
Political Learning: Individual, Mode, and Message Effects   161

Political Socialization, Trust, and Social Capital   162

Political Evaluations and Policy Support   166

The Media, Political Knowledge, and Political Attitudes   169

Conclusion   170

CHAPTER 7. AGENDA-SETTING, PRIMING, AND FRAMING   175

Psychological Foundations   177

Types of Agenda-Setting   179

Public Agenda-Setting   182

Priming 184

Framing Issues 187

Individual-Level Moderators 190

Conclusion 193

CHAPTER 8.   THE MASS MEDIA AND ELECTIONS 199

The Nature of Election Coverage: Free Media 202

The Substance of Campaign Coverage   202
Bias and Tone   206
Why More Negative?   208

Political Advertising: Paid Media 211

The Substance of Political Advertisements   212
Tone of Advertising   214

Media Effects: Theory and Evidence 215

Assumptions and Theoretical Background   215
Political Learning   220
Turnout   223
Agenda-Setting   224
Vote Choice   228

The Internet as a New Campaign Medium 231

Conclusion 233

CHAPTER 9.   MEDIA MODELS, LINKAGE INSTITUTIONS, AND REPRESENTATIVE DEMOCRACY 243

Media Models: What Is Supported by the Evidence? 244

Media Models: What Should We Want? 246

Appendix: Content Analysis 251

Glossary 255

Bibiliography 267

Index 291

Preface

CRITICS FROM THE right and the left, from the traditional and the new media, from activists and the alienated all love to hate the media. Yet two critical issues are typically overlooked in these discussions. First, little systematic evidence is provided to substantiate claims of media bias, incompetence, or impact. And, second, such criticisms are made without any explicit acknowledgment of what is appropriate to expect of the media or what alternative media systems might be better than what we have. This book is intended to fill at least some of these gaps.

The central assertion of this text is that the mass media, political officials, and the mass public are interrelated, that we cannot understand the nature of one without knowing the behavior and attitudes of the others. One of the happy consequences of this premise is that it challenges simple and exaggerated claims (and those who make them) about the media and highlights them for what they are. I hope students continue to think more systematically in this manner for many years to come. In the best of worlds, readers will become better consumers of the news, regardless of what that news looks like on any given day or on any particular outlet.

I also challenge readers to assess the current media "system" in the United States in light of five alternative media frameworks that propose different roles and incentives of the mass public and reporters, and, as a consequence, different media products. Hopefully, this will allow readers to better assess the strengths and weaknesses of our current media system. It also allows us to think more broadly about media models that are so different from what we know that we look at the current system in a new, more thoughtful, way.

Beyond the substantive details and analysis of the mass media and politics, this text also conveys important aspects of my beliefs regarding teaching and learning. It is not uncommon to hear that there is a trade-off between teaching and doing research: Great teachers shouldn't be expected to be great researchers, nor should scholars engaged in publishing in the best of academic outlets be expected to be great teachers. I fundamentally disagree with this claim. I hope that this book demonstrates, in part, how doing good research is essential to outstanding teaching. I hope that it also reflects two other important aspects of my teaching philosophy: that students learn by doing, and that as political scientists we should be teaching more than civics. We should be teaching the methods and substance of political science as a science.

To this end, I have incorporated several pedagogical tools that involve students in doing political science. At the end of each chapter, I have included several exercises that instructors may assign to students. These exercises require students to practice the research skills that media scholars use in their own research: interviews, participant observation, content analysis, data analysis, and web research. I have also prepared a public opinion dataset that instructors and students may use for more in-depth research projects; this is located with codebooks on *Mass Media and Politics'* website at *politicalscience.college.hmco.com*. The dataset is a subset of the 1948–2000 American National Election Studies Cumulative File, biennial national surveys of adult Americans that are commonly used by political scientists to study the opinions and behaviors of the mass public. The files are provided in SPSS Version 10 format as well as in Excel format. The codebook includes question wording and response options. More details on these data can be accessed on the American National Election Studies web page at *www.umich.edu/~nes*.

The dataset includes all respondents from 1970 to 2000. The number of respondents per year ranges from a low of 1,281 (1998) to a high of 2,705 (1972). Year and Case identifiers are also included in the subsets to allow the merging of additional variables or additional years from the 1948–2000 American National Election Studies Cumulative File, which is also available at the web page above. Students may also use the year identifier to select respondents from one survey year. Variables in these subsets include measures of demographic information, political attitudes, civic orientations, political participation, candidate evaluations, and media use and reliance.

Also online, in the instructor's section of the website, I have made available additional exercises that instructors may choose to assign as in-class projects or homework.

In reviewing what we know about the mass media and its political roles and functions, I rely heavily on systematic research published by political scientists and communications scholars. The strength of this text surely reflects the serious and creative work done by these scholars. I hope it meets with their approval.

I have accumulated many debts in the course of writing this book. To mention just a few, my thanks go to Steve Brooks, Allan Cigler, George Edwards, Kim Hill, Patricia Hurley, Martha Joynt Kumar, Beth Leech, Dave Peterson, and Laurie Rhodebeck for helpful comments. Thanks also to Chris Owens, Christina Sutthammanont, Patrick Ellcessor, and Adam Warbler for research assistance at various stages of manuscript development. Many scholars and teachers provided me with valuable comments on the manuscript, among them Thomas Birkland, SUNY–Albany; Paul Freedman, University of Virginia; Christopher P. Gilbert, Gustavus Adolphus College; Mark Joslyn, University of Kansas; Robert Klotz, University of Southern Maine; Beth L. Leech, Rutgers University; Jerry Medler, University of Oregon; and Michael J. Shapiro, University of Hawaii. Finally, I appreciate the dedicated efforts of numerous editors (especially Melissa Mashburn and Katherine Meisenheimer) and staff at Houghton Mifflin.

Most important, Rick and Anna have kept all manner of things in perspective over the past few years, and especially the political media. From the dregs of reality TV to the simple pleasures of Teletubbies, the world of political news might not be as bad as some claim!

J. E. L.

1

Mass, Media, and Politics in the United States

The Mass Media and Specialized News Media

Centrality of the Media to Today's Politics
Objective Importance of the Mass Media • Instantaneous News
Delivery • Mass Media as a Linkage Institution

The Interdependence of Journalists, Politicians, and the Mass Public

Models of the Mass Media
Reporters of Objective Fact • Neutral Adversary • Public Advocate • Profit-
Seeker • Propagandist • Implications of the Models

Theories of Mass Communication
Media Effects on the Mass Public
The Public's Effect on the Mass Media

Studying the Mass and the Media

Structure of the Book

A LL IS FAIR in love and war—except, perhaps, for the actions of the mass media. Consider, for example, two incidents in Cuba. In 1898 U.S. newspapers portrayed horrors perpetrated by the Spanish colonial government, including starvation of women and children and imprisonment of Cubans in "death camps" on the island. Sensational headlines announced cannibalism and torture. Yet reporters and photographers sent to Cuba to cover the story found few events to report on. Frederick Remington, a reporter who later became a notable artist, wired his boss, media mogul William Randolph Hearst: "There is no war. Request to be recalled." Hearst replied: "Please remain. You furnish the pictures, I'll furnish the war."

Shortly thereafter, the USS *Maine* exploded in Havana's harbor. The cause of the explosion was unknown. In the weeks following the incident, newspaper coverage averaged more than eight pages a day. Editorials throughout the country called for war.[1] Shortly thereafter, President McKinley asked Congress to declare war on the Spanish colonial government.

Nearly a hundred years later, dozens of U.S. television, radio, and newspaper reporters joined press representatives from around the world to cover the Pope's first visit to Cuba since before the Castro-led communist regime took control in 1959. Seemingly hours before the Pope's scheduled arrival, the "real" news broke: In a tape of private telephone conversations, a former White House intern named Monica Lewinsky admitted having had a sexual relationship with President Clinton in the White House. The Pope's visit was quickly displaced in the news. Journalists on Sunday morning talk shows discussed the "crisis" in government, the possible impeachment of the president, and whether the president's immorality constrained his political leadership. Media coverage broadened to include background investigations of Lewinsky. Then the focus shifted to the media themselves: What facts were known in the scandal? Was coverage being driven by unsubstantiated allegation? Had reporters, in an effort to scoop their competitors, published without verifying their stories?

Even though these two incidents occurred nearly a hundred years apart, they raise the same fundamental questions about the role of the mass media in politics. What evidence do reporters base their stories on? Do journalists report the news—or create it? Who decides what is "bigger" news? Why are topics like torture, starvation, and sex given such prominent placement? Is this the type of news citizens prefer? And, more broadly, what are the consequences for democratic politics in the United States? Do the media provide appropriate and sufficient information for citizens to be informed and engaged? Are the interests of citizens reflected in this news coverage, or influenced by it? These questions are addressed in the chapters that follow.

THE MASS MEDIA AND SPECIALIZED NEWS MEDIA

The reporters and crews assigned to Havana in January 1998 were a diverse lot. They represented newspapers, network nightly news and morning talk shows, specialized publications, and broadcast outlets. Although all generally had the same access to news briefings and press conferences about the Pope's visit, they varied substantially in terms of the organizations they represented, the technological constraints they faced, and the nature and size of their audiences. These distinctions are important in answering questions about the role of the mass media in politics.

Widely circulated newspapers and national broadcast and cable television networks are the primary **mass media for news.** They create and distribute news to a mass audience and engage in overtly political communication. One of their key characteristics is that their messages are directed toward a large and relatively undifferentiated audience.

By contrast, **specialized news outlets** serve relatively small self-selected audiences that typically are unrepresentative of citizens in general. Some of these smaller audiences are extremely conservative or liberal, and some are especially interested in a particular issue. These specialized audiences are sometimes wealthier or more educated than citizens in general. For example, in the 1990s Rush Limbaugh's talk radio show had numerous faithful followers. For the most part they represented a relatively narrow segment of the public—67 percent were male; 95 percent were white; and 23 percent reported incomes of $75,000 and over.[2] Similarly, political magazines such as *New Republic* and *The Nation* are popular among high socioeconomic status conservatives and liberals respectively, yet circulate to substantially smaller audiences than *Time* and *Newsweek*.

This distinction between the mass media for news and specialized news outlets is not meant to suggest that the latter are of no political interest or have no effects on people's political beliefs and behaviors. Elected officials, wealthy individuals, and politically engaged citizens are likely to pay more attention to the specialized outlets than are "typical" citizens. Hence, the specialized news media may be more influential among political elites than among the mass public. These "alternative" media outlets may provide substantially different information than that provided by mass media news outlets. Their existence and proliferation are thus relevant to understanding the effects and function of the mass media more generally. The chapters that follow, though, primarily focus on the nature and political consequences of the mass media for news.

CENTRALITY OF THE MEDIA TO TODAY'S POLITICS

In the last two decades the number of specialized news outlets has increased dramatically, as has the use of entertainment media outlets for political purposes.

What used to be a large and representative mass audience for the news has become smaller, more self-defined audiences. No longer are Americans captive to the evening newscasts of the major television networks. Not only are there cable news alternatives, but citizens can also find political news on the Internet. But just because audiences have become smaller and more differentiated does not mean that the mass media are any less salient to politics today than they were several decades ago.

The mass media have political importance in several ways. First, they are "objectively" important because of their economic size, number of employees, and role in the operation of political institutions. Second, the mass media determine the rate at which political information is disseminated. Today that rate is summed up in one word—*instantaneous*. Third, the mass media are critical to contemporary politics because they are expected to play the role of linkage institution, communicating the opinions of the mass public to elected officials and vice versa.

Objective Importance of the Mass Media

By any objective standard, the media are critically important to government and politics. Most significant is the extent to which politicians use various media to communicate with their constituents. The White House Press Office, whose primary function is to provide the national media with news from the executive office, has approximately thirty employees, as does the Office of Media Affairs, which caters to "out-of-town" press covering presidential events and related topics.[3] Every member of Congress has one or more staff members devoted exclusively to media affairs.

The mass media are key elements of election campaigns as well. In the 2000 presidential election, George W. Bush spent $39.2 million on television advertising (about 58 percent of the Bush campaign's public funding) compared to Al Gore's $27.9 million (about 40 percent of the Gore campaign's public money). Spending by Bush and the Republican Party amounted to approximately $84 million in 2000, compared to about $48 million in 1996, and spending by Gore and the Democratic Party totaled approximately $63 million, compared to about $61 million in 1996. In the 1998 Senate and House elections, the major political parties, in coordination with candidate campaigns, spent approximately 73 percent of their funds on media buys.[4]

The media are also objectively important to government and politics because of their vast economic power. Approximately 375,500 individuals are directly employed in the media industry, about 220,000 of them in news production.[5] More important, a notable trend over the past several decades has been the development of huge media and communications conglomerates in which corporations own a number of interrelated media outlets. The Walt Disney Company, for example, has book publishing outlets, magazine publishing outlets, specific magazines, daily newspapers, broadcast television stations, radio stations, cable television stations, television production, movie production, and Internet groups.

This concentration of economic power is likely to be accompanied by political power because more corporate and industry resources can be devoted to securing public policies favorable to the media. In 2000, for example, the Disney Corporation employed twenty lobbyists and spent approximately $3,860,000 on lobbying activities.[6]

Instantaneous News Delivery

An even more fundamental way the media are central to politics today is the near-instantaneous delivery of political events and issues by television and the Internet. In earlier eras, people had to wait for news to reach them. For example, the Constitution formally became the fundamental law of the United States when it was ratified by New Hampshire on June 21, 1788, but Congress did not receive notice of this ratification until July 2.[7] Abraham Lincoln signed the Emancipation Proclamation, which legally freed all slaves under Confederate control, on January 1, 1863. Not until June 19, 1865, however, did General Gordon Granger and his troops arrive in Galveston, Texas, to announce to slaves (and their owners) that they were in fact free.[8]

By contrast, within three hours of the assassination attempt on President Ronald Reagan in 1981, an estimated 90 percent of people in the United States had heard the news.[9] Lewinsky's claim of an ongoing sexual relationship with President Clinton spread like wildfire through media outlets, and the television audience was saturated with the information in just a few hours.[10] During the terrorist attacks on New York and Washington in September 2001, CNN aired videotape of the second plane crashing into the World Trade Towers within minutes of its happening, and one local station actually carried it live.

This new instantaneous nature of the news has consequences for the way elected politicians govern and the way citizens use the media for political purposes. Compared to several decades ago, media coverage requires immediate reaction from and management by politicians. Political issues are legitimized by virtue of being raised in the media. Politicians must use the media to respond to these issues. The flip side is that elected officials are able to use the media to help them further their political goals.

Whether citizens have benefited is not clear. Instantaneous news delivery has likely provided citizens with more, but not necessarily more useful, information. The seemingly unending barrage of unrelated, uneven news items is difficult to comprehend and even more difficult to process so that it is relevant to politics. Some citizens feel increasingly negative about the news and the news media as well as about government. Other citizens, however, are using cable outlets, the Internet, and other media to pursue their political goals. These changes in how the news is delivered and how politicians and citizens use the media surely have implications for our democratic system.

News of the attacks on the World Trade Towers on September 11, 2001, spread within minutes on local and cable news outlets. © *Reuters NewMedia Inc./CORBIS.*

Mass Media as a Linkage Institution

In a direct democracy, citizens make policy and other governance decisions themselves. In a representative democracy, citizens elect representatives to make these decisions, and there needs to be some way to convey the interests and preferences of the mass public to their elected representatives. The organizations that perform these roles are referred to as **linkage institutions**; they provide the essential link between elected representatives and their constituents. Political scientists have increasingly come to view the mass media as a central linkage institution in the United States.

Interest groups and political parties have traditionally served as linkage institutions in American politics. Political parties represent a broad spectrum of policy preferences and seek to elect candidates to office to pursue those policies. Interest groups typically represent individuals on a limited set of issues and seek to influence elected officials to adopt their position on such issues. While both parties and interest groups are typically viewed as communicating with, and influencing, government officials, to a lesser extent they also convey information from government officials to party or group members.

"Interests" and "political factions" were central to the politics surrounding the writing and adoption of the Constitution. But none of the Framers could have imagined how important a role the media would play in politics today. The mass media provide nearly instantaneous coverage of political events to an increasingly large and diverse electorate, and when they report on citizen focus groups, public opinion polls, and election returns, they provide feedback to government officials as well.

The increasing importance of the media in linking citizens and elected officials cannot be overstated. In fact, some scholars contend that the media have supplanted party organizations and interest groups in linking citizens and elected representatives. For example, the media have been identified as a critical factor in the demise of the political party as a central electoral institution in that they provide candidates with an alternative way of reaching voters. Instead of relying on political parties, candidates can now go directly to voters via the mass media.[11]

The chapters that follow consider three key issues relating to the media as a linkage institution. First, we consider the extent to which the mass media provide citizens with basic information about elected officials, government policies and performance, and candidates in election campaigns. That is, we look at the extent and nature of coverage of day-to-day governmental affairs, asking whether the mass media provide information suitable for citizens to use in evaluating and dealing with the political system. This information function provides between-election accountability of elected officials, and it also throws light on the many actions of government that emanate from nonelected officials. The more information citizens have and the better the information, the more likely that their interests and preferences will be accommodated in the political system.

Second, we consider the extent to which the mass media provide a forum for public discussion and consideration. Beyond the compilation of political "facts," does our extensive mass media system provide an opportunity for the exchange and evaluation of ideas? For considering long-term rather than short-term solutions? For allowing diverse opinions to be expressed? This is a more demanding responsibility of a linkage institution, and political parties and interest groups carry it out, at least modestly. Technology has been viewed as a way to recreate a sense of community in today's relatively atomistic society. Instead of the town meetings of ancient Greece, where all (male) citizens debated the issues confronting the community, today's democracies can offer electronic town meetings, with public issues debated on the Internet.

Third, we consider the directionality of conveyed information. In other words, to what extent do the mass media reflect citizens' interests and preferences "upward" to elected officials, in contrast to conveying the opinions and messages of elected officials "downward" to the mass public? While both directions are important in a representative democracy, a media system that conveys more official information to the masses than messages from the citizenry to elected officials is likely to be maximizing elite persuasion or manipulation rather than democratic accountability.

THE INTERDEPENDENCE OF JOURNALISTS, POLITICIANS, AND THE MASS PUBLIC

One of the central assumptions of this book is that the public, the media, and political elites are interdependent. We cannot understand the attitudes, motives, and behavior of one without knowing the attitudes, motives, and behavior of the other two. Figure 1-1 depicts this set of relationships between the mass media, elected officials, and the public. Each influences the other, which is suggested by the two-way arrows connecting them.

The mass media influence how government officials behave, in part by raising or legitimizing issues that politicians must respond to. Government officials influence what the media do by giving them information or using them to further political goals. This reciprocal relationship is indicated by the arrow labeled "B" in Figure 1-1.

The mass media also influence the mass public by providing the vast majority of citizens' political information; this information may influence their political values, beliefs, attitudes, and even behavior. Alternatively, the mass public influences the mass media largely through the marketplace: The U.S. mass media are profit-making institutions; the larger the audience, the higher the advertising revenue that a media outlet can collect. Hence, the media are at least partially constrained by their need to maintain audience share. This reciprocal relationship is indicated by the arrow labeled "A" in Figure 1-1.

The mass public influences government officials primarily through the conduct of elections, in which citizens determine who will represent them in the halls of Congress, the Oval Office, and other elected positions. Elected officials, by virtue of their positions, can influence their constituents by convincing them of the appropriate candidate choices, policy positions, or political goals. Some call this leadership, others persuasion, and still others manipulation. Much, though by no means all, of the relationship between the mass public

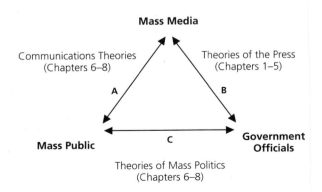

FIGURE 1-1 Conceptualizing the Mass, the Media, and Politics

and elected officials today is conducted through the media, via campaign advertising and routine news coverage, including the use of public opinion polls. This relationship is indicated by the arrow labeled "C" in Figure 1-1.

Clarifying the complexities of each of these relationships is one of the primary goals of this book. We draw on theories from the fields of political science, psychology, sociology, and communications to help evaluate the "facts" about the media and politics. Some of the theories are actually ideals about how the press *should* operate or government officials or the mass public *should* behave. Others are more abstract arguments about the nature of mass communication, the political sophistication of citizens, and the incentives that motivate elected officials and reporters.

MODELS OF THE MASS MEDIA

Models of the mass media are alternative depictions of the roles that the mass media play in society. These models are invoked by reporters, the public, and politicians to assail or defend the media's behavior. Each model makes assumptions about the nature of government, the nature of citizens as the audience or market, and the relative importance of private ownership of the mass media. Moreover, each model implies whose interests are served by the mass media, and in what way.

Reporters of Objective Fact

For decades, CBS anchorman Walter Cronkite ended the evening newscast with the pronouncement "and that's the world tonight." Cronkite was suggesting that the thirty-minute show (consisting of approximately twenty-two minutes of news and eight minutes of advertising) provided its viewers with a window on the world. The more precise metaphor for this model is that the mass media act as a mirror of events beyond viewers' direct observations. The idea is that the image in that mirror is a perfect reflection of the world, with no distortions ("the facts") and no exclusions.

A major assumption of the **reporters of objective fact model** is that the mass media play a limited role in political communication between government and citizens. That is, the mass media are merely a conduit for information, tools used by citizens and government officials to expand their scope of vision or communication, not active participants in the communication process. Beyond providing an accurate and true portrayal of the factual world of politics and society, according to this model, the media have no particular role or function to perform.

Reliance on this model of news is common. For example, reporters claim that they report only the facts, while citizens often wish that the media would "stick to the facts." One of the most basic criticisms of the model is that it is impossible to present all the facts of the world in a newscast or newspaper, whatever the length. Chapter 2 discusses the use of "facts" in the news process.

Neutral Adversary

The key feature of the **neutral adversary model** is that the mass media play an important role in monitoring government officials. In this model, the primary role of the press is to discover "truth" and act as a check on government. In the newsgathering and reporting process, various media outlets seek out the truth and report it; and the marketplace sorts out the truth from error. Government officials must carry on within full view of the press, which will question the motives, interests, and consequences of their actions.

The strongest assumptions of the neutral adversary model are those related to government officials. As did the Framers of the Constitution, this model assumes that people are motivated by self-interest and that government and society must limit the ability of elected officials to pursue their self-interest to the detriment of the public interest. The mass media play a critical, even necessary, role in limiting potential abuses by those in elected office; the news should challenge elected officials so that the truth is made known to the public. Once that truth is provided in the form of news, the neutral adversary model assumes that citizens will effectively control, influence, or communicate with their elected representatives.

Public Advocate

In the **public advocate model** of the news, journalists have a social responsibility to use the newsgathering process to engage newsmakers (government officials) and the public in debates on issues of political importance. Thus, reporting "just the facts" is a serious failure of the mass communication system. According to this model, the media occupy a unique position in the political system and should responsibly

- Provide information, discussion, and debate on public affairs
- Enlighten the public so as to make it capable of self-government
- Safeguard the rights of individuals by serving as a watchdog against government
- Provide a medium of advertising for the economic sector of society
- Provide entertainment
- Maintain financial self-sufficiency in order to be free from the influence of special interests

A small but growing number of journalists have adopted a public advocacy philosophy of journalism. This grass-roots professional movement has rejected many traditional approaches to newsgathering, mostly because the journalists felt that standard news products were failing to communicate useful information to citizens.

> Newspapers, they argued, exist so that people can participate in an effective public life, and if the people aren't participating or politics isn't effective, then newspapers have somehow failed—in the same way, say, that an airplane safety system has failed if a pilot doesn't manage to use it properly and crashes . . . [12]

The most striking feature of the public advocacy model is journalists' activist role in defining the focus and nature of public debate and consciously using the mass media to initiate and structure such debate. Public advocacy journalists also see citizens as important sources of information and opinion and as political actors. Citizens are more prominent sources and subjects of news coverage than in any of the other models, which focus attention on government officials.

Profit-Seeker

The emphasis of the **profit-seeker model** of mass communications is that the U.S. mass media are privately owned business enterprises. What becomes news—or does not become news—is a byproduct of profit generation. Unlike the previous models, the profit-seeker model sees citizens, citizenship, and other perquisites of democracy as irrelevant to press behavior; the mass media have no responsibilities other than to make profits for their owners.

That these profits are derived in part by the production of what is formally considered news is basically irrelevant. In fact, if producing news is not profitable, the news process will be modified. What is being or should be produced, according to this model, is not an enlightened or informed citizenry or more responsive government officials, but rather a profit. A fundamental difference between this model and the previous three is its assumption that the individuals who make up the news audience are first and foremost consumers who can be a target of market-like competition. The audience is not defined, as in the other models, as citizens who require certain types of information to fulfill their civic duties, nor is government or governance relevant to the news-reporting enterprise.

Since the U.S. mass media are almost entirely owned by major corporations, this model—almost by definition—is confirmed in part: The mass media are profit-seeking businesses. However, the model requires not just private ownership (or profits directed toward the public owner), but that profit-seeking—or the maintenance of audience share when media outlets compete—fundamentally influences the news process. If the profits generated by entertainment programming were used to subsidize news production, the profit-seeking model would be disputed.

Propagandist

According to the **propagandist model,** the chief purpose of the media is to support and advance the interests of those in positions of power. In doing so, the media serve the state by legitimizing its policies and interests. While this might be reflected in the media's support for government officials currently in office, it can also be interpreted more broadly as legitimizing the interests of the dominant (typically business) class. In other words, in addition to generating profit, privately owned media monopolies legitimize the social, political, and economic status quo.

One of the most celebrated proponents of this viewpoint, Noam Chomsky, contends that the media system operates as a series of filters that produce "cleansed" news that is, according to those in power, fit to print. The news filters include

- The size, concentrated ownership, owner wealth, and profit orientation of the dominant mass media firms
- Advertising as the primary income source of the mass media
- The reliance of the media on information provided by the government and business, and by "experts" funded and approved by these primary sources and agents of power
- "Flak" (excessive or abusive criticism) as a means of disciplining the media

These filters "fix the premises of discourse and interpretation, and the definition of what is newsworthy in the first place, and they explain the basis and operations of what amount to propaganda campaigns."[13] This is not to suggest, of course, that there is no diversity of opinion or conflict presented in the news.

According to the propagandist model, for the most part citizens are unaware of the media's function. Journalists understand the function and, occasionally, a few challenge the dominance of government officials and business interests, but they are easily silenced. In contrast with the other models, the propagandist view is that the only the interest of the economic and political elite is served by the current media system.

Implications of the Models

The chapters that follow link what we know about how the media function (which model they follow) with the consequences for their performance as a linkage institution. Some models of the press are likely to enhance its performance, while others will compromise it. For example, the reporter of objective fact model is consistent with the need for linkage institutions to provide information to citizens, but it does not necessarily satisfy the requirements for public deliberation. In the propagandist model of the press, the media fails as a linkage institution but can claim to convey the beliefs or interests of political elites to the masses (but not the reverse).

THEORIES OF MASS COMMUNICATION

In Figure 1-1 the double-sided arrow between the mass media and the mass public implies a reciprocal influence between the two. A critical point in evaluating these relationships is the nature of the mass audience. Simply put, what we believe about how, or how much, the media influence people's political attitudes and behaviors is tied to our assumptions about the nature of the mass public. Likewise, how much we attribute the nature of the media system to its mass audience (or, more specifically, to the size of its audience) is structured by our assumptions about the preferences and needs of the mass audience.

Media Effects on the Mass Public

Scholars have focused on two interrelated questions concerning mass communications in the twentieth century: What functions do the media play in our society? What effect does mass communication have?

Scholars have identified three functions performed by the media: **surveillance, interpretation,** and **socialization.**[14] Surveillance serves both individual and societal needs. Informing individuals of what is happening in the world beyond their immediate experience satisfies the basic psychological need to be aware of and have a sense of control over the environment. A complex and changing world seems more predictable and more livable when the media survey distant events and relay the information. At the social level, individuals in positions of social and political leadership are similarly given a broader view of the world.

The mass media also help individuals interpret the events occurring in the world around them. By their very appearance in mass communication, people, events, and issues are given legitimacy, salience, or stature. The mass media provide a political and social context within which the person, event, or issue can be understood. Some of this is driven by the current journalistic style of storytelling, which places events and issues into stories with beginnings, middles, and ends and therefore emphasizes causes and effects. Moreover, the social or political context in which an event is reported helps individuals further assess its salience.

Finally, the mass media help socialize individuals into the broader social system by portraying values and norms. Over long periods of time, individuals are repeatedly exposed to information about the behavior and attitudes of others in society and about how those behaviors and attitudes are generally received

THE FAR SIDE® By GARY LARSON

In the days before television

by society. For example, as President Clinton's public approval rating increased in the weeks following Lewinsky's allegations, commentators suggested that the U.S. public did not care about his alleged sexual dalliances. Instead, the public seemed to separate its evaluation of the president's personal behavior from its evaluation of his job performance.[15] Media reports of this "disconnect" suggested that it was appropriate.

Of course, to report that the mass media perform these societal functions does not mean that the functions were not performed prior to the establishment of the mass media in the United States. In earlier times, the functions of surveillance, interpretation, and socialization were most likely fulfilled through social interaction, either individually (one-on-one conversation or gossip) or in group settings such as schools, churches, town meetings, and voluntary associations. But when the mass media perform the functions, the size of the individual's world increases dramatically. Today, news from other continents is as readily available as news from the neighboring community was two hundred years ago. Also, despite the increasingly large scope of world news, mass media information is provided routinely and immediately—often in real time. These differences suggest important questions: How do individuals manage so much complex information? Does its immediacy alter individuals' reactions to the information or to the media themselves? Are institutional sources of information processed differently from, or in the context of, competing interpersonal sources of information?

Scholarship focusing on the effects of mass communication on individuals can be interpreted in light of the surveillance, interpretation, and socialization functions. Studies of how individuals learn from the mass media, for example, reflect on the surveillance function, while studies of framing—individuals' attributions of responsibility for social problems—easily fit into the interpretation function. Most political communication scholarship over the past several decades has emphasized the individual-level cognitive effects of the mass media with respect to political information, agenda-setting, and election campaigns. These topics are addressed in Chapters 6 through 8.

The Public's Effect on the Mass Media

To many journalists or representatives of the news media, the nature of the news is dictated by the tastes and preferences of the audience. To the public, what is on the news is merely a reflection of reporters' and editors' personal values as well as the need for high audience ratings.

In fact, communications scholars suggest that the audience has the greatest influence on media content, although some credit is given to other media-related factors. Because media distributors and producers depend on advertising revenues that are tied to audience size, the media try to attract and maintain large audiences that can be persuaded to purchase advertisers' products. Because audience members often use the media for entertainment or companionship, media content is unlikely to be morally uplifting, educational, or inspiring.[16]

It is important to carefully evaluate whether this is a fair indictment of the mass audience. Does the mass public get what it wants, or does it merely take what it is given?

STUDYING THE MASS AND THE MEDIA

One of the goals of this book is to convey what social scientists have learned about mass media and politics over the past several decades. **Social science** is distinct from historical or journalistic approaches to learning and knowing in that it relies on the scientific method. Scholars doing social science research typically identify a **theory** that explains the how and why of what they are studying. (Why do some individuals vote, while others do not? How do individuals process political information? Do individuals pay more attention to pictures in the news than they do to printed or verbal information?)

Drawing from theory, they then develop specific **hypotheses**—relationships that should be observed if indeed the theory is correct. They collect data on a sample that represents the population of interest. Studies of public opinion and political behavior, for example, typically collect data by asking questions of a group of about a thousand individuals who were selected randomly and hence are assumed to be generally representative of all adults.

Once the data (the responses to the questions) are collected, social scientists analyze them, using statistics to determine whether the relationships suggested by the initial theory were observed in the sample. If they were, there is some evidence that the theory is correct. If they were not, the original theory probably needs to be revised.

The key point is that, because the evidence is systematic (is not based on a single observation or on cases or individuals that were easy to observe), the researcher can be reasonably confident that the conclusions hold in general, beyond the cases or individuals that were observed. That yields substantive conclusions that are more compelling than those collected in a nonsystematic way.

Throughout this text, keep two points in mind. First, read the following chapters actively. Ask yourself whether the conclusions presented in the chapters are consistent with and fully supported by the evidence that accompanies them. Keep in mind that not all of the relevant evidence is presented, only the evidence that is the most rigorous and represents a fairly broad consensus among academics.

Second, while no political or social phenomena are necessarily static, the political and social behaviors we study are usually fairly stable. Social and political behaviors typically change slowly, and the findings of many research studies conducted in the 1980s are likely generalizable to the 1990s and early twenty-first century. Yet where there is reason to believe that change might be rapid—as in the case of Internet usage patterns—the temporary nature of these conclusions is noted.

Much of the empirical evidence in the chapters that follow relies on two fairly standard social science research techniques—**content analysis** and **survey research**. All research methods have limitations, and these two are no exception. More details on content analysis and survey research appear in Appendix A.

STRUCTURE OF THE BOOK

The goal of this text is to systematically evaluate the nature of the mass media and the mass public in our democratic political system. Theories drawn from the study of the mass media, the mass public, and political communication provide a framework within which to evaluate how well the mass media perform as a linkage institution in the United States.

Three broad questions are considered throughout. Do the mass media provide citizens with basic information about candidates, elected officials, and government policies and performance? Do the mass media provide a forum for public discussion and consideration? What is the direction of the information conveyed between citizens and elected officials: from the mass level to elites, or vice versa? The answers allow us to draw inferences about the nature of the mass media, the nature of the mass public, and the nature of representative democracy itself.

Chapters 2 through 5 focus on the nature of the newsgathering process and the nature of the media business. Chapters 6 and 7 discuss the nature of the mass public, including how and what citizens learn from the mass media. Chapter 8 focuses more specifically on the nature and effects of election news. Chapter 9 summarizes the findings of earlier chapters and comments on the various models as well as the larger question of how well the mass media perform as a linkage institution.

Key Terms

content analysis
hypotheses
interpretation
linkage institution
mass media for news
neutral adversary
   model

profit-seeker model
propagandist model
public advocate model
reporters of objective
   fact model
socialization
social science

specialized news
   outlets
surveillance
survey research
theory

Exercises

1. While the media were covering the Lewinsky affair in 1998, Secretary of State Madeleine Albright announced that diplomatic negotiations with Iraq's Saddam Hussein regarding arms inspections had all but stalled. President Clinton consulted with congressional leaders regarding a possible military response. Michael McCurry, Clinton's press officer, emphasized to reporters that President Clinton would make necessary military decisions independent of domestic political considerations.

   About the same time, *Wag the Dog,* starring Dustin Hoffman and Robert DeNiro, opened in movie theaters. The premise of the political satire was that the U.S. president, who was running for reelection in a tightly contested race, was accused of inappropriate sexual advances toward a young girl just days before the election. A "spin doctor" was called in to manage the crisis, and his solution was to start a war—or at least the image of a war—to distract the public from the scandal. Watch this movie, and come to class prepared to discuss how it portrays the media, politicians, and the mass public.

2. Choose a traditional news publication or news program (e.g., a daily newspaper or the evening television newscast), and investigate how the content and advertising of its affiliated Web site differs from it. What are the advantages of using one versus the other?

3. Identify your current beliefs about the nature of the mass media in the United States. What are the most important factors in determining what becomes news? In determining how the news is presented? Does the news provide relevant and accurate political information to citizens? Why do you think so?

4. Keep a media diary that documents your media habits, your recall of the news, and your reactions to it. What do you watch? Why? What did you learn? How did you feel about it?

5. Look at a news outlet you do not normally watch or read. Were any features of the news noticeably different? Better? Worse?

Notes

1. "The Spanish American War." Available from www.smplanet.com/imperialism/remember.html (accessed April 16, 2002).

2. Richard Davis and Diana Owen, *New Media and American Politics* (New York: Oxford University Press, 1998), p. 146.

3. Martha Joynt Kumar, "The Office of the Press Secretary." In The White House 2001 Project, White House Interview Program, Report No. 31. Available from http://whitehouse2001.org (released December 5, 2000).

4. Robin Kolodny and David A. Dulio, "Where the Money Goes: Party Spending in Congressional Elections" (paper presented at the Annual Meeting of the Midwest Political Science Association, Chicago, April 19–22, 2001).

5. U.S. Department of Labor, Bureau of Labor Statistics, "Occupational Employment Statistics: 2000 National Occupational Employment and Wage Estimates." Available from www.bls.gov/oes/2000/oes_27Ar.htm (accessed April 21, 2002).

6. Center for Responsive Politics. Available from www.opensecrets.org/lobbyists/client.asp?ID-248&year=2000 (accessed April 19, 2002).

7. Sol Bloom, *1937, The Story of the Constitution*. Washington, DC: National Archives, 1986.

8. Jim Hill, "African-Americans Wonder: Will Clinton Apologize for Slavery?" Available from www.cnn.com/US/9706/21/juneteenth/ (accessed March 18, 2002).

9. Walter Gantz, "The Diffusion of News About the Attempted Reagan Assassination," *Journal of Communication* 33 (1983): 56–65.

10. "Cautious Newsweek Reaps Much of the Credit," *New York Times*, January 26, 1998.

11. Martin P. Wattenberg, *The Decline of American Political Parties, 1952–1996* (Cambridge, MA: Harvard University Press, 1998).

12. Arthur Charity, *Doing Public Journalism* (New York: Guilford Press, 1995), p. 2.

13. Edward S. Herman and Noam Chomsky, *Manufacturing Consent: The Political Economy of the Mass Media* (New York: Pantheon, 1988), p. 2.

14. Harold D. Lasswell, "The Structure and Function of Communication in Society," in Lyman Bryson, ed., *The Communication of Ideas* (New York: Harper & Bros., 1948).

15. John Zaller, "Monica Lewinsky's Contribution to Political Science," *PS: Political Science & Politics* 31 (1998): 182–189.

16. Melvin L. DeFleur and Sandra Ball-Rokeach, *Theories of Mass Communication*, 5th ed. (New York: Longman, 1989).

The Media as a Political Institution

Historical Development of the Media-Government Relationship
The Early Press Eras • Government Sponsorship of the Press • The Economics of the Mass Newspaper

The Electronic Broadcast Media

High-Tech Media: A New Era in Media-Government Relations?
The Origins and Growth of the Internet • New Formats in Political Communications

Consequences of the New Era for Mass Politics
The Political Consequences of Narrowcasting

The Politics of Regulation
Print and Electronic Regulation: Ownership • Regulating Broadcasting Content • Consequences of Deregulation

The Politics of Public and Semipublic Ownership

Media-Government Relationships and Models of the Press

I N THE 1870s, to gain support for the ratification of the proposed Constitution, Alexander Hamilton, James Madison, and John Jay wrote a series of letters and published them anonymously in daily newspapers. Although writing a new Constitution had not been the stated task of the meeting of delegates called to Philadelphia, the Constitution they proposed was ratified.

Fast-forward two hundred years. The battle for public support for President Bill Clinton's 1996 health insurance reform proposal was being waged not in newspapers but instead in dueling television advertisements. In the most-discussed ad, sponsored by a coalition of insurance companies, characters named Harry and Louise discussed the likelihood that insurance reform would preclude them from choosing their own doctors. Clinton's proposal was defeated, and many observers attributed the loss to the effectiveness of Harry and Louise.

Although the pace and format of news delivery have changed, political elites have always used the media for explicitly political purposes. The media have used political elites to serve their purposes, too. Unless we understand the nature of the relationship between elites and the press, we would fail to see how the media act as a political institution.

"Harry and Louise" discussing Clinton's proposed health plan—and concerned that they would not be able to choose their own doctor if the plan were passed by Congress. *Courtesy of the Health Insurance Association of America, Washington, DC.*

In what ways do political elites use the media? How do elites view the role of the media in society? Have different media assumed different roles based on how political elites interact with them? How have elites defined the legal status of the media in our democratic society? This chapter takes a historical look at these questions, assuming that the current performance of the media as a linkage institution partly reflects ongoing relations between reporters and officials.

Four factors have structured the development of the media in the United States: markets, technology, mass politics, and the interests of political elites. Markets are a potential revenue source for privately owned media. Technology largely determines the costs—and hence the potential financial viability—of media businesses. Mass politics and the interests of political elites are in some ways two sides of the same coin. The role of the mass media in a democratic society is largely defined by the extent to which the mass public is incorporated into politics, such as through popular elections and public opinion, the public's influence on democratic elections and subsequent governance, and the way elites use the mass media to inform, persuade, or mobilize the mass public.

These four factors are especially relevant to the profit-seeker, neutral adversary, and propagandist models. The profit-seeker model suggests that the media respond to economic forces (driven by markets and technology), while the neutral adversary model suggests a certain independence of the media from government officials. The propagandist model suggests that the media are used more by government officials to legitimize their interests than by the people to communicate their interests or by the media themselves to further their goals. Consider each of these aspects as we review the historical relationships between the media and government and recent trends in government regulation.

HISTORICAL DEVELOPMENT OF THE MEDIA-GOVERNMENT RELATIONSHIP

The mass media for news and the specialized news media have played very different roles historically. Initially, the printed press served the interests of political elites. Newspapers had to be endorsed by the colonial government and were distributed to the homes of the wealthy and politically powerful.

The *Boston News-Letter,* originally printed in 1704, is generally considered the first North American newspaper, and the *Boston Gazette,* printed by James Franklin, first appeared in 1719. When James Franklin moved on to establish his own newspaper, the *New England Courant,* in 1721, he broke tradition (and likely colonial law) by not being sanctioned by the governing authorities. Compared to earlier publications, the *New England Courant* was more lively and was prone to take on social, and sometimes political, issues. When James was later jailed, his brother Benjamin took over publishing responsibilities and became a major player in the colonial press.

The Early Press Eras

Conventional analyses of the media-government relationship identify three eras: the party press, the penny press, and the modern press. The era of the **party press** was the period of the American Revolution. Newspapers were the organs of competing political factions, and the content of these papers was aimed at discrediting the other factions and strengthening their own readers' loyalties. Thus, typical stories focused on political figures' scurrilous behavior—whether political, social, or sexual—including the behavior of such illustrious leaders as Jefferson, Hamilton, and Adams. Though we have no detailed evidence on the effect of this news coverage on citizens, few papers were widely circulated, and the dominant mode of politics remained face-to-face discussions and political assemblies.[1] Thus, it is unlikely that the party press had widespread impact, even if it was influential with political and social leaders.

Soon after the Revolution, as the nation sought to develop its economic resources, another specialized use of the newspaper became more common: the publication of business and commerce news. The **commercial newspapers,** focusing primarily on shipping and trading news, had a very limited business-oriented circulation, so they, along with the partisan presses, can be classified as part of the **elite press** that dominated at the end of the eighteenth century.

By the early nineteenth century, technological and social changes allowed for a dramatic shift in the nature of news production. First, steam and water power were applied to printing presses, so the number of copies a press could produce multiplied to four or five thousand sheets per hour, compared to the two hundred sheets per hour a team of two printers could produce. Second, the size and literacy of potential audiences increased, especially in the major urban areas of the new states. But the cost of newsprint still made the price of daily newspapers too high for the typical reader.

Benjamin Day, publisher of the *New York Sun,* added the final two critical elements when he decided to write news to suit the interests of the less educated, but literate, masses and to charge advertisers to cover the costs of publication. Advertising revenue allowed Day to sell a copy of the *Sun* for one penny, and newsboys could buy a hundred copies for sixty-seven cents. Thus began the new era of the **penny press,** a **mass medium** providing news oriented toward the masses, not the elites, and subsidized by advertising revenue.

At the same time, the political system was opening up as well. The right to vote was extended to propertyless males; the election of the president and vice president had shifted from state legislatures to the electoral college; and the political elites of the Founders were being replaced by national political leaders with more diverse (less upper-class) backgrounds. The proportion of the population eligible to vote in elections expanded significantly, as did the proportion of individuals who voted.

The nature of the press and the media-government relationship reflected these changes. To grow in size, newspapers had to be more objective in their reporting of politics. Business principles prevailed; publishers realized that they would secure fewer advertisers and readers if the news reported in the paper seemed to reflect a partisan bias.

The development of the telegraph in the 1840s, which allowed for the timely dissemination of news to a larger number of widely dispersed cities, also shifted the production of news stories away from localized, and likely more partisan, reporters to reporters who wanted to sell their stories to as many newspapers as possible. With the establishment of the **Associated Press** in 1848 and its reliance on the telegraph, a more simple and direct writing style was adopted by reporters, partly to appeal to more diverse audiences from different parts of the country, but also because the telegraph system charged by the word. Hence, shorter, less rhetorical articles were more likely to be picked up by local papers.

The content of the news shifted as well to appeal to mass, rather than elite, interests. Crime and scandal became front-page news to attract the attention of the mass audience. Government officials often became subjects of media coverage when reporters tried to uncover scandal and corruption in government.

The last press era—not as well-defined as the first two—began around the turn of the twentieth century and is called the **modern press**. In this era the media system became established as big business. More specifically, ownership of media outlets was concentrated in the hands of a relatively small number of corporations; newspapers became more dependent on advertising revenue than on readership subscriptions; competition in the industry decreased; and radio and television broadcasting became dominant news and entertainment businesses.

Government Sponsorship of the Press

At quick glance, it seems that today's press is more objective than were the partisan presses of the late 1700s. The increasing corporate ownership of the media suggests that they are more independent of government officials than in earlier eras. Since economic incentives are more important than before, political influences should be of less importance. However, this description of the press has been called incomplete. According to this view, the news media have "always been and continue(s) to be intimately tied to political sponsorship, subsidization and protection . . . the change we see over American history is less *whether* the news media and news products are shaped by governmental practices and policies than *how*."[2] That is, the nature of the news and the government-press relationship are determined not only by technology and economics, but also by political elites.

During the late 1700s, specific newspapers were designated as official printers of governmental proceedings and laws. *The National Gazette,* published by Philip Frenau and designated by Secretary of State Thomas Jefferson, allowed Jefferson to respond to personal attacks being waged on him in the *Gazette of the United States,* which was supported by government advertising from Secretary of the Treasury Alexander Hamilton. "Far from being an independent institution, the political press in those days was a kept press, bought and paid for by the government, the politicians and their parties . . . nobody ever thought of the press as politically independent or objective."[3]

Moreover, Congress subsidized newspapers by charging extremely low postal rates for delivery and also allowed publishers to send newspapers to other publishers free of charge. This reliance on government subsidies continues to the present day, despite the dramatic growth and profitability of the media business.[4] However, the nature of the subsidy has changed over time. In the 1820s, for example, President Andrew Jackson appointed numerous journalists to federal patronage posts, including postmaster, clerk, inspector, and U.S. marshal. National political figures bankrolled the establishment of newspapers and continued to direct government printing contracts to their supporters.[5] Today, government subsidizes the news profession through the provision of regular and free information, a point discussed in greater detail below.[6]

Despite these various inducements to loyalty, mass politics and the competitive financial pressures on publishers eventually weakened the relationship between politicians and the elite press. Weaker party organizations and the diminished role of presidential leadership lessened the political demands on publishers, who focused on expanding circulation. As noted above, by 1890 newspapers became increasingly reliant on advertising rather than on subscription, or sales, revenue. Since advertising rates were determined by the estimated size of the newspaper's readership, the profitability of newspapers was closely tied to circulation figures.

The Economics of the Mass Newspaper

The pressure to increase circulation is one of the major factors associated with the advent of **yellow journalism,** "a genre of press attitudes and behavior highlighting sensationalism and emotion-laden copy in pursuit of more and more readers."[7] The news values associated with yellow journalism resulted in adventure stories filed by roving correspondents, reports of pseudo-scientific discoveries, stories campaigning for social justice, and an emphasis on the absurd and outrageous. This copy contrasted dramatically with the fact-based reporting of the Civil War and post–Civil War periods.

Oddly enough, news reporters during the early 1900s were developing a heightened sense of professionalism. Reporters' or press clubs were formed; trade journals such as *Editor and Publisher* began publication; and codes of ethics for reporters were developed. The establishment of schools of journalism was also critical in socializing new reporters to their obligation to serve "the public trust," much like the legal and medical professions of the time.

In addition, the office of the presidency once again increased in scope and perceived importance, in part because of the greater role the United States was taking in international affairs. Theodore Roosevelt, sworn into office in 1901 after the assassination of President William H. McKinley, courted the press and used it to enhance the power of his office. Although Roosevelt's goal was not explicitly partisan, as were politicians' goals in the earlier era, it was every bit as political: to use the press to govern.

McKinley, Roosevelt, and the presidents following them "renegotiated" the relationship between the government and the press.[8] This new relationship differed significantly from that of earlier eras in several ways. First, presidents could not expect that financial weaknesses of the media would allow them to gain control of publishers. Second, presidents could not rely on the party loyalties of journalists; the profession had adopted a norm of political independence. Third, presidents no longer interacted with editors and publishers daily, but instead interacted with reporters. And, fourth, presidents had to meet the press on its ground and respect their deadlines and news values. Hence, the role of reporters became critical, although within the constraints of organizational routines and financial imperatives.

What remained the same despite this renegotiation was that the media were still essentially political. The news became

> a coproduction of sources (usually officials) and journalists, but . . . sources cannot simply snap their fingers and make news in their own terms. Instead, not only is the news a reworking of official actions, events and statements with production values in mind. These production values favor particular kinds of news and information over others, and thereby end up endowing the news with a particular politics.[9]

THE ELECTRONIC BROADCAST MEDIA

The three eras of press-government relations described above focus exclusively on the technological, economic, and political factors structuring the relationship between newspapers and government officials. Between 1910 and 1920 radio became increasingly popular as a source of news, largely due to technological improvements in voice quality on, and dependability of, the airwaves. By the 1920s privately owned radio stations dominated as a news and entertainment source. The first commercial radio "broadcast" took place on November 2, 1920, when radio station KDKA—operating in a metal shack next to the Westinghouse plant in Pittsburgh—informed an audience of between five hundred and a thousand that Warren G. Harding had defeated James M. Cox for president.

While the technology for television broadcasting was also available in the 1920s, television did not emerge until after World War II, when electronics manufacturers stopped wartime production and turned to the civilian market.[10] The medium did not dominate American society until the cost of producing television sets decreased sufficiently to make them affordable to the middle class in the 1950s. As was the case with radios and newspapers, the introduction of this new medium increased competition for audience size and advertising dollars.

While electronic broadcasting technology has clearly revolutionized American society and politics, the scene was already set when it climbed on the political stage. Television news had to conform to the norms of an already established media-government relationship. Newspaper reporters outranked the new television reporters in seniority and had established relationships with government officials as sources.

Further, the new technology was viewed by many print reporters as lacking professional legitimacy. By the mid-twentieth century, the printed press had established a pecking order of sorts. The nationally oriented, large circulation dailies—such as the *New York Times,* the *Wall Street Journal,* and the *Washington Post*—were proud of being **"papers of record,"** news outlets that sought to provide comprehensive coverage of the national and local events of the day. These papers and their reporters were viewed as being "serious" about the news and less sensitive to the commercial pressures that affected less well-established outlets. Hence, jobs with these dailies were prestigious, and many reporters sought to write for them.

Television news, by contrast, was chided for not being a "real" news outlet, for being amateurish and having only a faint resemblance to serious news. Initially, television news shows lasted only fifteen minutes and consisted of very brief reports on the events of the day. Only with the establishment and growth

Chet Huntley and David Brinkley were popular news anchors in the 1960s and 1970s. © *Bettmann/CORBIS.*

of the thirty-minute evening newscast—with anchors such as David Brinkley and Walter Cronkite—did television news programs establish their legitimacy in national politics, largely due to their ability to attract a mass audience. With a few notable exceptions, audiences for radio news remained small, locally oriented, and homogeneous.

Television news was distinct from the printed press in two ways: its immediacy—which allowed for the broadcasting of live political speeches—and its visual content. By the late 1960s it became dominant in political campaigns, to the point of being a defining characteristic of the modern campaign.[11] By 1980, campaigns were characterized by nationally coordinated strategies run by a central campaign headquarters, a heavy emphasis on campaign management, daily press conferences, "themed" photo opportunities and television advertising, and expenses driven by political advertising.

The dominance of television news was as evident in the governance of the period as in the electoral politics. Beginning with the administration of President John Kennedy, national appeals in support of the president's legislative proposals became a common method for presidents to establish a legislative advantage over Congress. Consistent with arguments about the subsidization of the news by political elites, each president's office increasingly provided institutional support for the news media, including broadcast-friendly facilities, office space in the White House, advance scheduling of news conferences to coordinate with news deadlines, and increasing access to the president.

Hence, television news was experiencing dynamics similar to those experienced by the printed press. Because the three major networks had a virtual monopoly over evening news show audiences, competition was minimal. The main source of competition remained the printed press, whose circulation figures seemed to be stable even as the size of the television news audience was increasing. Partly in reaction to this, the printed press began to conform to the electronic version of the news, including more visuals, more abbreviated text, and more human interest and entertainment content.

HIGH-TECH MEDIA: A NEW ERA IN MEDIA-GOVERNMENT RELATIONS?

Although television news and the major national dailies were dominant by the mid-1960s, they have not remained so. Declining readership has weakened the printed press to the degree that some media critics question how long the printed press as we know it will remain in business. Network television audiences have decreased in size with the growth of cable stations. Whether in news, sports, entertainment, or educational programming, consumers now have much greater choice over which stations to watch, and advertisers have greater latitude about where and how to spend their dollars.

Two additional factors critical to understanding the new era of media-government relationships are the explosive growth of the Internet and the use of new political formats on network, cable, and radio broadcasts. Both developments are a result of technological, economic, and political factors. The use of these technologies or formats by political elites is every bit as evident as in earlier periods. However, the consequences for mass politics and governance are dramatically different.

The Origins and Growth of the Internet

The Internet developed in the early 1980s as an extension of computer networking capabilities originally developed for the Department of Defense. The first extension of these technological advances beyond military research facilities was their use in a high-speed electronic communications network of large research universities. Transmitting brief electronic mail (e-mail) messages and databases, the network gradually encompassed a wide range of research universities and teaching colleges. Additional linkages to major federal labs and agencies quickly established the Internet as a basic mode of communication in the academic and scientific communities.

With the public availability of personal computers and the development of graphics-based programming packages, the commercial potential of the Internet became evident, and the private sector responded dramatically. By the end of the 1980s, businesses developed Internet sites as marketing devices and then as sales outlets. The public sector responded as well, using the Internet to distribute information previously available only in paper versions at substantial cost.

Individual politicians reacted strategically. Many candidates for state and federal offices established official sites, which they maintained once elected to office. The Internet has also been used to encourage citizen involvement, providing a way to contact candidates and elected officials about concerns or problems via e-mail, and making available electronic "chatrooms" where people can anonymously discuss the merits of policies and candidates with others who are logged on at that time.

Of particular interest is the response of traditional media outlets to the growth of the Internet. One of the initial concerns of most media—and publishing houses in general—was how providing Web-based versions of their products might reduce the size of the audience for traditional products. Why would people purchase copies of the *New York Times,* for example, when they could access the paper at no cost on the Internet? Although newspapers and television stations at first required visitors to their Web sites to register or pay fees for access or made little information available, their concern over smaller audience sizes has abated. Today most print outlets provide additional information at greater depth on their sites. Having a Web site is believed to increase the audience for the traditional media format (newspaper or television news) by acting as a marketing tool. Advertisers pay to run their ads on the sites, so the Internet is also another means of generating revenue.

New Formats in Political Communications

The 1992 presidential campaign was, in many senses, a watershed in political communications strategy. MTV, an all-music-video cable station oriented to young adults, sponsored a get-out-the-vote campaign called "Rock the Vote." When the press reported accusations that presidential candidate Bill Clinton had had an extramarital affair with a state employee named Gennifer Flowers while he was governor of Arkansas, Clinton agreed to be interviewed on an evening newsmagazine show. With his wife Hillary sitting at his side, Clinton responded to questioning, stating that the affair was a personal issue from their past and that the media should simply stop asking about it. Later in the campaign, Clinton appeared on Arsenio Hall's late-night show to play the saxophone.

The traditional press and other politicians expressed contempt for both media strategies. Appearing on such shows was not "presidential." Moreover, it was perceived that the questions raised and issues addressed on such shows would be "easier" for the candidate to respond to than the questions or issues he would have faced on shows produced by news departments. The informal

Al Gore chats with Oprah Winfrey on her daytime talk show during the 2000 presidential campaign; George W. Bush also appeared on that show. Both candidates were also guests on the David Letterman show. © *Reuters NewMedia Inc./CORBIS.*

nature of the shows also tended to emphasize Clinton's personality rather than his stands on tough political issues. The Clinton campaign staff, however, was extremely enthusiastic about Clinton's performance and the nature of the interviews, and his staffers continued to look to these alternative formats through the rest of the campaign as well as in the years Clinton was in office.

Similar strategies were adopted in the 2000 presidential campaign. George Bush and Al Gore appeared on Oprah Winfrey's daytime talk show and on *Late Night with David Letterman*. The perceived value of these appearances is evidenced by the fact that they were scheduled when the race was seen to be close.

The 1990s also witnessed an increasing number—and, presumably, an increasing popularity—of political talk radio and television shows. Talk radio began in the 1930s. Many of the shows that debuted in the 1990s focused on national issues for national audiences; among them were shows featuring Rush Limbaugh, G. Gordon Liddy, and Michael Reagan. On television, the number of Sunday morning talk shows—using the traditional format of *Meet the Press,* in which politicians and candidates were interviewed by journalists—increased significantly as well. These outlets provided yet another alternative to the mainstream press and were quickly used by politicians, candidates, and elected officials.

CONSEQUENCES OF THE NEW ERA FOR MASS POLITICS

The move away from television network news to these newer forms of communication has been identified as the beginning of a **postmodern campaign** communications era, in which techniques traditionally associated with campaigning have become part of the governance process.[12] Thus, the political consultants and media strategists who were central to political campaigns in the 1960s, 1970s, and 1980s are now essential to governing. Beginnings and endings of political campaigns are things of the past, and survey research, focus groups, and media strategies are prominent in the daily activities and decisions of elected officials.

Political scientist Pippa Norris questions whether this era will serve the electorate well. "The multiplicity of outlets, stories and channels has undermined the sense that the network news today can ever sign off with the classic Cronkite phrase, 'That's the way it is.' The familiar authorities have gone, replaced by multiple realities, for good or ill."[13] Moreover, due to cost-cutting, news programs have replaced some **hard news** with **soft news** that costs less to produce. To attract audiences, news outlets have increasingly resorted to **tabloid journalism,** which focuses on sex, scandal, and corruption. These changes in traditional journalistic norms make it more difficult for the average citizen to make sense of the world, resulting in a more cynical and disinterested public.[14]

The Political Consequences of Narrowcasting

The development of more specialized or fragmented audiences, "**narrowcast-ing**," is probably the media system characteristic that has had the most dra-matic consequences for mass politics. More choices are available to people. If "political junkies" want detailed political news, they can find it, but sports en-thusiasts can choose to watch ESPN rather than the network news and thereby avoid politics altogether.

Historically, political candidates and elected officials have used the media to communicate persuasive messages. Mass media communication strategies were such powerful tools because they allowed a message to be conveyed to a broad, representative public. The ability to garner the support of a large public is of key importance in a democratic political system. For presidents, obtaining sup-port for programs and the legitimacy of the office as a national institution has been heavily dependent on successful efforts to engage a wide spectrum of the political community.

Since the mass media no longer deliver a mass audience, the dynamics of communication in the political system have changed. Politicians now have tools to tailor their messages to the unique interests of specialized audiences. Instead of garnering support for broad principles or general policy directions, they now have the ability—and perhaps the incentive—to offer piecemeal bits of policy proposals—a little bit for everyone. What this approach adds up to on election day or at the end of a presidential term, however, is not clear.

A second notable characterisic of the current media system is the availabil-ity of the Internet as a news source. Most observers focusing on the dramatic revolution in communications technology resulting from the Internet are over-whelmingly positive. The Internet provides instant and abundant information from diverse information sources, and it makes widespread participation in the political system possible via the use of chatrooms, electronic town meetings, low-cost communication with government officials, and, eventually, electronic voting in referenda, initiatives, and general elections.

However, some of these positive scenarios about the impact of Internet us-age on mass politics are likely to be exaggerated, if not idealistic. For example, the primary reason individuals cite for using the Web is pleasure, including seeking information about finances, travel, and entertainment, and the greatest increase in Web use between 1995 and 1996 was by individuals who were seeking entertainment-related information.[15] Furthermore, while the number of households with personal computers has increased dramatically over the past two decades, access to personal computers—and hence to the Internet—is still structured in part by class and race. Overall, 33 percent of adults report going on line at least once a week for news, but college graduates are more than four times as likely as individuals with grade school education to do so (54 percent compared to 12 percent). While 33 percent of whites report going on line once a week, only 24 percent of African Americans report doing so, and the gap between white and black usage rates was greater in 1998 than it had been in 1995.[16]

Communities may be getting "wired," but by and large they are upper- and upper-middle-class communities. As a consequence, the benefits of Internet use are likely to be limited to individuals who are the most likely to already be informed about and interested in politics. The marginal effects of Internet use on the mass public's political knowledge are likely to be small and to be concentrated within certain groups in society.

Second, and likely of less importance, politics is essentially a social enterprise. That is, politics is driven by groups of people engaged in political pursuits. It is hard to imagine political campaigns being organized solely through the Internet. Is a face-to-face discussion about politics with a classmate different from a discussion engaged in electronically in a chatroom? What is the difference between a candidate's knocking on the door to ask for support in an upcoming election and receiving an e-mail request for the same?

Moreover, relating new facts about politics to existing political beliefs or attitudes requires a context that allows the person to integrate, or make sense of, the new information. Whether that context is provided by the television news, by a friend's reaction to election results, or by discussions about social welfare over family dinners, it is needed to make electronically provided information meaningful. Thus, while electronic news sources may provide increased information, the social and political meaning of that information might well be lost in the transmission.

THE POLITICS OF REGULATION

The interrelationship of government officials and the news media is not the whole story. The way the government regulates the media and the media seek to influence such **regulation** is another important aspect of the government-press relationship. This is especially true in the case of electronic media, whose ownership and content have been much more highly regulated than has the printed press. Moreover, government regulation of the electronic press raises issues regarding the politics of the public (noncommercial) broadcast media in the United States.

Historically, **regulatory policy**—as determined by Supreme Court decisions, congressional statutes, and administrative rule-making—has been favorable toward commercial interests.[17] The dominance of commercial media ownership over public ownership as well as the lucrative financial returns attest to this. What is less clear is whether a market-driven communications system will sustain the "marketplace of ideas" that most agree is essential to democratic politics.

Discussion of the regulation of the commercial broadcast media, as well as the nature of support for public radio and television broadcasting, provides

MERGER–MANIA, UNABATED...

How much bigger can the mergers get? Especially in the media/communications business?
© *Steve Greenberg, Seattle Post-Intelligencer 1998.*

some insight into the relative validity of the five press models discussed in Chapter 1. The public media, though few in number, might effectively serve as neutral adversaries or public advocates. Also, government regulation of the media might constrain the media from acting in a purely self-interested manner, publishing anything and everything to make a profit, for example. Or such regulation could limit the way in which political elites seek to manipulate the media to further their own interests. Thus, considering the issues of public ownership and government regulation of the commercial sector is important in assessing the five models of the press.

Print and Electronic Regulation: Ownership

As noted, the printed press and the electronic press have received vastly different treatment in terms of government regulation.[18] The printed press has been protected from limitations on content under the First Amendment of the Constitution, which provides for freedom of the press. Efforts to regulate the printed press have typically taken the form of congressional laws against libel—as in the **Alien and Sedition Acts of 1798** and laws passed during World War I prohibiting stories critical of the government or the war effort. State laws banning the publication of certain types of stories—referred to as **prior re-straint** laws—were overturned in 1925 by applying the freedom of the press guarantee to the states through the Fourteenth Amendment.[19] Since the early twentieth century, though, such efforts to regulate the content of the printed press have all but ended, essentially prohibiting governmental controls over the content of the printed press.

One of the underlying assumptions of the interpretation of the guarantee of freedom of the press has been that the sphere of public debate, in which the press is expected to play an important role, is a marketplace of ideas. A democracy, by definition, must protect the right of its citizens to criticize and dissent from governmental actions, so government control of what is printed is anathema to citizens' fundamental rights. Further, the metaphor likening public debate to a marketplace suggests that if newspapers print inadequate or biased information, competitors will enter the market and provide additional information. The more news and the more news providers, the better the news product, or public information, will be. Thus, newspapers have historically escaped any government regulation of content and ownership.

This assumes, however, that the start-up costs of entering the news market are relatively low, or at least surmountable. This has become increasingly less true, at least since the beginning of the twentieth century, when ownership started to shift from single owners (usually family) to newspaper chains. Beginning in the 1970s inheritance taxes discouraged families from passing on privately owned newspapers to heirs, which made the businesses ripe for purchase by outside investors.[20] Thus, large corporate chains such as Gannett and Knight-Ridder started buying up independent newspapers.

By 1995, over 80 percent of U.S. daily newspapers were owned by chains.[21] Of cities with daily newspapers, 99 percent have only one paper.[22] Together, these trends suggest that start-up costs in the newspaper market are unlikely to be low. Partly in response to these trends, Congress passed the **Newspaper Preservation Act of 1970,** allowing newspapers facing bankruptcy to share some aspects of the production process (which would previously have been a violation of antitrust regulations).[23]

That the Newspaper Preservation Act was the first notable exception to the federal government's hands-off approach to the printed press indicates a striking contrast with its approach to the electronic media. Radio stations initially operated free from government regulation, but as the power of radio transmitters increased and the competition for radio audiences grew, stations' broadcasts often interfered with one another, sometimes causing stations to abandon their designated airwave frequencies for other, clearer, ones. In part due to pressure from manufacturers of radio sets, Congress established a temporary Federal Radio Commission in 1927. The permanent **Federal Communications Commission (FCC)** was later established by the **Federal Communications Act of 1934,** which identified the granting of broadcast licenses as the primary regulatory tool.[24]

The FCC is an independent regulatory commission with five members chosen

by the president and confirmed by the Senate. Its major responsibility is to regulate the use of the airwaves "in the public interest" by determining the channel, the power, and the hours of operation of radio stations. In addition to
these duties, the FCC was charged with regulating telephone and telegraph
services. The agency's licensing authority resulted in its granting free licenses
on a provisional basis (originally one year) or a short-term basis (three years).
In 1991 the short term was extended to seven years for radio and five years for
television.[25] Although the FCC has always had the authority to revoke licenses,
it rarely does so.[26] For example, of 2,600 requests for new commercial television licenses, only 595 were denied, mostly due to frequency scarcity.[27]

As television technology advanced and the number of individuals interested
in owning stations grew, the FCC anticipated similar congestion problems and
imposed a limit to the number of television stations that could broadcast in a
given city. With the exception of New York and Los Angeles, even the largest
cities were given only three or four VHF (very high frequency) stations in 1952.[28]

Regulating Broadcasting Content

By limiting the number of television stations that could broadcast in a local
area, or market, the FCC essentially imposed a monopoly-like structure on television broadcasting. Because the airwaves being licensed were viewed by government officials as a public resource central to structuring the marketplace of
ideas in a democratic political system, it is not surprising that the content of
these broadcasts has been subject to governmental regulation by the FCC,
Congress, and the Supreme Court. (The printed press has had no such regulation.)

The two most critical regulatory requirements were the equal time rule and
the fairness doctrine. Passed as part of the 1934 Communications Act, the
equal time rule requires stations to make broadcast time equally available to all
"similarly qualified" candidates for political office. The purpose of this provision is to prohibit stations from selling airtime only to candidates of a particular
political persuasion—whatever that might be. The provision is not applicable
to routine or live news coverage or news documentaries, only to political candidates. In the 1960s it was extended to coverage of presidential speeches, requiring stations to provide time for the opposition political party to air a
response.[29]

The **fairness doctrine**, too, was motivated by the FCC's interest in keeping
the public airwaves it had licensed to private corporations open to public debate and diverse political views. As initially implemented by the FCC in 1949,
the fairness doctrine required stations to devote a "reasonable" amount of attention to public issues and to include contrasting views about them. By 1970
the FCC expanded the fairness doctrine to require stations to contact individuals about whom controversial statements were made on television and to give
them time to respond.[30]

Though the goals of the fairness doctrine seem reasonable enough—using public airwaves as a forum for serious public issues, and making diverse viewpoints part of that dialogue—there was never unanimous agreement about its constitutionality. Broadcasting executives often portrayed it as a violation of free speech or freedom of the press because it constrained, if only marginally, what they broadcast. The Supreme Court reacted to this argument in the decision in *Red Lion Broadcasting Company* v. *Federal Communications Commission* (1969), which essentially stated that broadcasters' rights are secondary to the public's rights of debate and information on public airwaves.

Despite the Supreme Court's support for the fairness doctrine, the FCC had the task of gingerly implementing it in a political context in which industry opposition was quite vocal. One FCC response to the sensitive political environment was to make filing complaints against television stations costly and ineffective.[31] Of close to 10,000 complaints filed annually by citizens, approximately 99 percent were dismissed because they did not meet the procedural requirements, and only 0.15 percent resulted in "corrective action."[32]

One of the unintended consequences of the fairness doctrine was cited by industry executives as well as some academics as a reason that so little administrative action was generated on its behalf: that television stations simply stayed clear of meaningful, controversial issues rather than assume the costs of meeting the doctrine's requirements.[33] It is unclear, however, whether stations' minimal coverage of controversial issues reflected the fairness doctrine's "chilling effect" or were simply a result of the economic incentives faced by a medium driven by audience size and ratings. Common wisdom in the broadcasting industry is that the mass public does not want to focus on controversial political issues, and that such coverage would detract from ratings and revenues.

While it is nearly impossible to disentangle the motivations for the broadcast industry's opposition to the fairness doctrine and the relative lack of serious public affairs programming, once the fairness doctrine was officially abolished by the FCC in 1987 there appeared to be few changes in public affairs programming.[34]

The decision to formally eliminate the fairness doctrine and passage of the Telecommunications Act of 1996 provide some insight into the politics of communications regulation. These two policy decisions illustrate the basic features of the politics surrounding significant communication policy decisions, and thus are likely to provide insight into future policymaking. They also provide another perspective from which to evaluate the five models of government-press relationships.

Elimination of the Fairness Doctrine

As an administrative agency, the FCC has historically been constrained by several factors, many of which are relevant today.[35] First, it inherited a high level of industry influence from its predecessor, the Federal Radio Commission.

Second, Congress was heavily involved in the FCC's operations, and the threat of budget reductions and reauthorization hearings thus constrained the FCC to adopt regulatory policies that kept Congress happy. Third, the FCC's primary regulatory tool was control over licensing, and Congress expressly forbid the agency to control industry revenues and profit. Finally, the FCC's statutory authorization, or mission, is ambiguous, in particular its charge to regulate the airwaves "in the public interest."

Several of these characteristics are consistent with what scholars of interest group politics and the policy process refer to as "subgovernment politics," or, more extremely, a "captured agency." *Subgovernment* refers to a triangular relationship between an administrative agency, the congressional committee that oversees it, and the industry it regulates. Scholars have sometimes referred to these relationships as "iron triangles" in that they are strong and impervious to control from such "outsiders" as the executive branch and the public. When an industry lobbies committee members by providing information as well as campaign money, the committee is likely to direct the agency to act in the industry's interest. To curry favor with its oversight committee, which influences the size of its budgets, the agency may also pursue friendly relations with the industry that it regulates.

This description of subgovernment is fairly consistent with portrayals of the FCC through the 1980s. Many observers noted that the FCC consistently favored more established and profitable industries or businesses, and resisted new entrants or changes in regulatory policy that would benefit new entrants. In this sense the agency could be described as "protecting" the industry that had captured it.

The subgovernment is likely much weaker today than in the past. There has been significant growth in the number of communications groups and citizens groups lobbying Congress and the FCC, as well as greater involvement of the president in FCC policy.[36] In addition, on the rare occasion when there is unanimous support for congressional or regulatory action, the communications industry must contend with other industries affected by the decisions. Given the explosive growth in consumer-oriented communications technology over the past ten years, it is certain that the communications industry invests a great deal of money and time into having its interests represented in Congress and at the FCC, with an outcome that is not necessarily clear from the beginning.

The FCC's decision to overturn the fairness doctrine highlights the critical importance of leadership by the president and FCC commissioner. Since broadcasters had historically been opposed to the doctrine, a subgovernment model would have predicted the overturn of the provision prior to the 1980s. In fact, the possible overturn was discussed from time to time in Senate confirmation hearings of nominees to the commission.

With the election of Ronald Reagan in 1980, followed by an increasingly large Republican delegation in Congress, the rhetoric of the superiority of market forces took hold in national policymaking. By 1982 Reagan had appointed four FCC commissioners, including Mark Fowler, and by the middle of 1982 his appointees held five of the seven seats on the commission.[37] At his confirmation hearing, Fowler testified that he would be "guided by one principle and one principle alone: What is best for the people?" He said his five objectives were

- To create, to the maximum extent possible, an unregulated, competitive marketplace environment for the development of telecommunications
- To eliminate unnecessary regulation and policies
- To provide service to the public in the most efficient, expeditious manner possible
- To promote the coordination and planning of international communications which assures the vital interests of the American public in commerce, defense, and foreign policy
- To eliminate government action that infringes the freedom of speech and the press[38]

In effect, Fowler used his chairmanship to redefine the mission of the FCC as an unbiased referee in marketplace competition. That is, he redefined "public interest" to mean that which maximizes economic competition in communications. This approach to FCC policymaking has several critical implications. First, it ignores the notion that the broadcast frequency is a public good—owned by the public rather than by private interests. Second, it suggests that as long as broadcasting is unfettered by government regulation, the "public interest" is satisfied. Third, whatever information regarding public issues is provided will result solely from its value in the competition of the marketplace. Finally, and more broadly, the new market-oriented approach to communications regulation redefines the job of the agency from an active role in defining the public interest in communications policy to a focus on the structural characteristics of communications industry that will allow for maximum competition.

Passage of the Telecommunications Act of 1996

The new orientation of the FCC is evident in the politics surrounding the **Telecommunications Act of 1996**. While the act incorporated a wide range of provisions regarding telephone services, cable television, and the Internet, a key provision eliminated numerous restrictions on ownership of television, radio, and cable stations. Dropping these restrictions, supporters claimed, would make broadcast television more competitive and therefore more responsive to audience interests.

Critics of the market-oriented FCC have criticized not just the substance but also the process of the 1996 act. According to scholar Ben Bagdikian, the act completely eliminated the consumer and diversity protections included in the 1934 act, and it bypassed the public in doing so.[39] To secure passage of the act, the communications industry used "insider" connections, which is a common strategy in dealing with highly technical regulatory bills.[40] For example, the

Wall Street Journal reported that House Republicans scheduled closed-door meetings with industry executives in 1994 to develop a legislative strategy that would be supported by the industry. Donald Jones, a cable operator, was volunteering in House Speaker Newt Gingrich's office and acted as an adviser while the telecommunications bill was being written. Such traditional lobbying techniques as campaign contributions were used as well. The *New York Times* editorialized: "Forty million dollars' worth of lobbying bought telecommunications companies a piece of Senate legislation they could relish."[41]

The communications industry has also been accused of engaging in the very public strategy of disguising lobbying efforts in the form of news reports. In a segment on ABC's *20/20* in December 1989 that emphasized the benefits of government deregulation of the telephone, airline, gas and oil, trucking, and other industries, reporter John Stossel compared government regulation before Reagan's 1980 election to the centralized planning of the former Soviet Union and concluded that the benefits of deregulation were huge. At the very same time, ABC/Capital Cities was awaiting regulatory decisions from the FCC.[42] While this occurred long before the Telecommunications Act was debated, and while such forms of lobbying are likely to be rare (see Chapter 4), it is nonetheless illustrative of the potential for the large media conglomerates to secure desired levels and types of government regulation

Substantively, the Telecommunications Act of 1996 removed some restrictions on the type of activities various companies could engage in, with the justification that the changes would create more competition for older, more established industries. Once the act was passed, these new "competitors" became partners with or merged into the larger, more established corporations:

> U.S. West, one of the largest telephone companies in the country, spent $5.3 billion to acquire Continental Cablevision, the country's third largest cable system. This transaction typifies the complex—and, to outsiders, dizzying—relationships of the interlocked giants. U.S. West also owns 25 percent of Time Warner's cable properties. Time Warner is the second largest cable firm and agreed to acquire Turner Broadcasting, which in turn was 21 percent owned by TeleCommunications, Inc. (TCI), the country's largest cable company. That deal, on completion, would give TCI a 9 percent ownership of its biggest competitor, Time Warner.[43]

We return to the issue of media ownership in Chapter 4. For now, it is important to note the significant shift during the 1980s in defining the FCC's role away from a public trustee model and toward viewing the communications industry as providing a product much like automobiles or televisions—the more competition, the better the product.

Consequences of Deregulation

The consequences of deregulation can be viewed from several different perspectives. As noted above, despite the rhetoric, there has been no substantial change in network programming since the FCC abandoned the fairness doctrine. If its effect on coverage of controversial issues had been chilling, such coverage would have increased over the past decade. There is no evidence that this occurred, and one study suggests just the opposite. Today, for example, there are fewer locally produced minority politics news programs than there were prior to the elimination of the doctrine.

Deregulation has meant an increase in the number of sources of political news and a major decrease in the size of the *audiences* for network news programs and newspapers.[44] It is not clear that this competition has resulted in "better" news content. In fact, the most relevant evidence is negative. The advent of tabloid journalism—news formats focusing on sex, violence, and scandal—and the increased emphasis of local news on crime and violence are cited by many as a result of increased competition among news sources. Further, the amount of news in newspapers has decreased significantly over the past several decades, and newspapers and television news programs have responded to reader interests by increasing the number of stories on technology, business, and entertainment.[45] It appears that deregulation has not inspired a better news product, just more consumer choice among outlets providing similar content.

THE POLITICS OF PUBLIC AND SEMIPUBLIC OWNERSHIP

It would seem unfair to argue that the business of privately owned media corporations is to offer in-depth, analytical political coverage to an audience that has no interest in it. The U.S. media have historically been privately held (benefiting from government subsidies, of course). The private sector operates to maximize profits. Hence, media corporations are in effect doing what they are supposed to be doing: attracting more-or-less large audiences that they can "sell" to advertisers. The dominance of private interests in the communications sector in the United States is in fact used as a model in newly developing media markets in countries from Eastern Europe and beyond.[46] At the same time, U.S. *public* broadcasting is held to be the epitome of a failed media system.

Public broadcasting in the United States is a mixture of public and private ownership and programming.[47] The system was established by the **Public Broadcasting Act of 1967**. Nearly one-fourth of American television stations—348 of them—are semipublic entities, and 560 semipublic radio stations are linked together as National Public Radio.

The nomenclature "semipublic" is particularly appropriate in discussing these noncommercial stations. Their funding does not rely entirely on advertising revenue, as does the funding of commercial stations. In 1997, 45 percent of the revenue of public broadcasting systems came from federal, state, and local sources (including colleges and universities), while 25 percent came from subscribers and fundraisers. The remaining portion of the revenue is derived from business and industry (14 percent), foundations (6 percent), and other types of contributors (10 percent).

The approach to semipublic broadcasting reflects ambivalence, perhaps, about the role of government in controlling the nation's mass media system. The underlying assumption is that the owner can dominate, or in some ways determine, the medium's content. It is assumed that the government would use a "pure" public system, where the government retains ownership and control of the media, to further its own interests. Likewise, it is assumed (as discussed earlier) that business will use the privately held media system to further its interests.

Because of Americans' distrust of the public sector and big government, it is not surprising that the private sector has been embraced as the appropriate owner, while semipublic broadcasting is a marginal player in the media system. Yet an argument in favor of public ownership dominates most established democratic systems in Western Europe. This view holds that there is a public interest that is broader, deeper, and more enduring than can be acknowledged by the private sector. The public interest in broadcasting is that the mass media can be used to educate citizens about the history, diversity, and culture of their nation and that doing so is critical to the attainment of a fully democratic society.[48] In the United States, however, the private media sector has applied "continuous political pressure" to convince legislators as well as the public that the private use of the airwaves best serves the public interest. This pressure, along with the predominant market orientation of American society, has resulted in a small public broadcasting company "reflecting the dominance of commercial and free speech values."[49]

Recent trends suggest that corporate influence on public broadcasting has increased. The most obvious evidence is the increase in corporate donations to public broadcasting. The private sector has also been lobbying the FCC in favor of loosening restrictions on corporate advertising on public channels.[50] The dominance of corporate interests in communications policy is reflected in the attacks on public broadcasting by conservative Republicans during the 1980s and beyond. In 1994 and 1995 in particular, Speaker of the House Newt Gingrich argued that American taxpayer dollars were being used to tell the public what to think. Public broadcasting was criticized for portraying the United States negatively and homosexuality positively. Senator Larry Pressler, chair of the Commerce Committee that oversees PBS appropriations, claimed that public broadcasting was a waste of dollars, allowing "a few tricksters to get rich off of Barney dolls and lunchboxes."[51] More recently, however, the Bush administration has increased funding for the Corporation for Public Broadcasting, with a special emphasis on support for children's programming and the conversion to digital broadcasting.

MEDIA-GOVERNMENT RELATIONSHIPS AND MODELS OF THE PRESS

This chapter has demonstrated that the media are—and always have been—a political institution. They have always relied on government support in one way or another, and in this sense they are political. Since newspapers became a mass medium and U.S. politics became more democratic, politicians and reporters have needed each other to do their jobs. This suggests that the angry comments of elected officials about biased or superficial reporting are probably motivated less by the sense of what reporting should be and more by their disappointment that their expectations have not been met. Officials rarely praise reporters for getting the story right, meaning exactly as the politicians presented it.

A second way in which the media are a political institution is that their news product and business activities are regulated by government. Government regulation or public ownership of the media might counterbalance evidence presented in Chapter 1 supporting the profit-seeker and propagandist models. Commercial media could be regulated so as to encourage thoughtful and serious news coverage; or public news organizations could provide such news coverage, regardless of the decisions of commercial news producers.

Yet this is not occurring. Instead, government regulation of commercial media has always been weak, with few requirements regarding the public information provided on the public airwaves. During the 1980s this became abundantly clear when the Federal Communications Commission adopted the position that the only public interest was the guarantee to commercial media that they could pursue their economic self-interest. The assumption was that we would all be better off when the media pursued their economic self-interest. Empirical evidence, however, suggests that this is not the case. Unfettered use of public airwaves by media corporations may produce more competition for audiences, but it does not necessarily produce a better news product. More details on that news product are provided in the next chapter, which examines what the privately owned news organizations present as news and why they make certain choices in the newsgathering process.

Key Terms

Alien and Sedition
    Acts of 1798
Associated Press
commercial
    newspapers
elite press
equal time rule
fairness doctrine

Federal
    Communications
    Act of 1934
Federal Communica-
    tions Commission
    (FCC)
hard news
mass medium

modern press
narrowcasting
Newspaper Preserva-
    tion Act of 1990
papers of record
party press
penny press
postmodern campaign

prior restraint
public broadcasting
Public Broadcasting
    Act of 1967

regulation
regulatory policy
soft news
tabloid journalism

Telecommunications
    Act of 1996
yellow journalism

Exercises

1. Estimate the percentage of space in a daily newspaper devoted to political news and the percentage devoted to advertising and entertainment. What do these numbers suggest?
2. Access the Federal Communications Web site at http://www.fcc.gov/ and find a press release of interest. What is the status of current regulatory efforts on this issue? Is there any discussion of the public interest or private incentives as determinants of policy decisions?
3. Pick a country and investigate the nature of its media system. Who owns the country's newspapers and radio stations? How many are there? What types of stories do these outlets carry?

Notes

1. Lawrence K. Grossman, *The Electronic Republic* (New York: Viking, 1995).

2. Timothy E. Cook, *Governing with the News: The News Media as a Political Institution* (Chicago: University of Chicago Press, 1998).

3. Grossman, *The Electronic Republic*, p. 70.

4. Cook, *Governing with the News*.

5. Richard Davis, *The Press and American Politics: The News Mediator*, 3rd ed. (New York: Longman, 2001).

6. Cook, *Governing with the News*.

7. Davis, *The Press and American Politics*, p. 48.

8. Ibid., p. 55.

9. Cook, *Governing with the News*, p. 114.

10. Melvin L. DeFleur and Everette E. Dennis, *Understanding Mass Communication* (Boston: Houghton Mifflin, 1985).

11. Pippa Norris, ed., *Politics and the Press: The News Media and Their Influences* (Boulder, CO: Lynn Rienner, 1997).

12. Ibid.

13. Ibid.

14. Ibid. See also James Fallows, *Breaking the News* (New York: Vintage, 1996).

15. Pew Research Center for the People and the Press, online report. Available from http://www.people-press.org/medsec1.htm (accessed October 11, 1999).

16. "Public's News Habits Little Changed by September 11," accessed March 18, 2003, from http://people-press.org/reports/display.php3?ReportID=156.

17. See Wolfgang Hoffmann-Riem, *Regulating Media: The Licensing and Supervision of Broadcasting in Six Countries* (New York: Guilford Press, 1996), Chapter 1.

18. Sableman argues that the regulatory distinctions based on media types, rather than content, should be abolished. Mark Sableman, *More Speech, Not Less: Communications Law in the Information Age* (Carbondale: Southern Illinois University Press, 1997), Chapter 10.

19. Davis, *The Press and American Politics*; Sableman, *More Speech, Not Less*, Chapters 1 and 2.

20. Richard Davis and Diana Owen, *New Media and American Politics* (New York: Oxford University Press, 1998).

21. Kathleen Hall Jamieson and Karlyn Kohrs Campbell, *The Interplay of Influence: News, Advertising, Politics, and the Mass Media,* 5th ed. (Belmont, CA: Wadsworth, 2001).

22. Ben H. Bagdikian, *The Media Monopoly*, 5th ed. (Boston: Beacon Press, 1997).

23. Jamieson and Campbell, *The Interplay of Influence*, p. 179.

24. Erwin G. Krasnow, Lawrence G. Longley, and Herbert A. Terry, *The Politics of Broadcast Regulation*, 3rd ed. (New York: St. Martin's Press, 1982), Chapter 1.

25. Stephen Ansolabehere, Roy Behr, and Shanto Iyengar, *The Media Game: American Politics in the Television Age* (New York: Macmillan, 1993), pp. 16–17.

26. Robert Britt Horwitz, *The Irony of Regulatory Reform: The Deregulation of American Telecommunications* (New York: Oxford University Press, 1989), p. 160.

27. Ansolabehere, Behr, and Iyengar, *The Media Game,* pp. 20–21.

28. Ibid., p. 18; see also Krasnow, Longley, and Terry, *The Politics of Broadcast Regulation.*

29. See Hugh Carter Donahue, *The Battle to Control Broadcast News: Who Owns the First Amendment?* (Cambridge, MA: MIT Press, 1989), Chapters 4–8.

30. Ansolabehere, Behr, and Iyengar, *The Media Game,* pp. 20–21; Donahue, *The Battle to Control Broadcast News*, Chapter 5.

31. Zuckman et al., cited in Hoffmann-Reim, *Regulating Media.*

32. Hoffmann-Reim, *Regulating Media*, p. 35.

33. Davis, *The Press and American Politics*; Doris A. Graber, *Mass Media and American Politics* (Washington, DC: CQ Press, 2002). Krasnow, Longley, and Terry, *The Politics of Broadcast Regulation*, pp. 21–23.

34. Patricia Aufderheide, "After the Fairness Doctrine: Controversial Broadcast Programming and the Public Interest," *Journal of Communication* 40 (1990): 47–73. Hoffmann-Riem, *Regulating Media;* also see Horwitz, *The Irony of Regulatory Reform*, pp. 278–282, who suggests that deregulation may provide more choices in viewing—but within a restricted, i.e., narrow, range of programming.

35. Krasnow, Longley, and Terry, *The Politics of Broadcast Regulation.*

36. Ibid.

37. Donald J. Jung, *The Federal Communications Commission, the Broadcast Industry, and the Fairness Doctrine, 1981–1987* (Lanham, MD: University Press of America, 1996).

38. Cited in Jung, *The Federal Communications Commission*, p. 32.

39. Bagdikian, *The Media Monopoly*, p. xv.

40. Ibid.; Paul S. Herrnson, Ronald G. Shaiko, and Clyde Wilcox, *The Interest Group Connection: Electioneering, Lobbying, and Policymaking in Washington* (Chatham, NJ: Chatham House, 1998).

41. Cited in Bagdikian, *The Media Monopoly*, p. xv.

42. Dennis W. Mazzocoo, *Networks of Power: Corporate TV's Threat to Democracy* (Boston: South End Press, 1994), p. 111.

43. Bagdikian *The Media Monopoly*, pp. xvi–xvii.

44. Norris, *Politics and the Press*, p. 7.

45. See, for example, Phyllis Kaniss, *Making Local News* (Chicago: University of Chicago Press, 1997).

46. Hoffmann-Reim, *Regulating Media*.

47. See Graber, *Mass Media and American Politics*, pp. 34–38, for a brief discussion of completely public control, in which local or federal governments have full ownership and programming rights. The data in this and the following paragraph come from this source.

48. See Rowland Lorimer, *Mass Communications: A Comparative Introduction* (Manchester: Manchester University Press, 1994), pp. 79–83.

49. Ibid., p. 83.

50. Jamieson and Campbell, *The Interplay of Influence*.

51. "Incoherent Conservatism," accessed March 18, 2003, from http://www.cbsnews.com/stories/2001/04/11/politics/main285094.shtml.

3 > What's News?

The News Product and Models of the Mass Media

Reporters of Objective Fact • Neutral Adversary • Public Advocate • Profit-Seeker • Propagandist

Defining What's News

Timeliness • Human Interest and Drama • Concrete Events • Defining News: A Historical Update

News Coverage of Politics

Domestic News Coverage • Local News Coverage • Foreign Affairs Coverage • An Update on the Content of News Coverage

Values Reflected in News Coverage

Conclusion

NEWS COVERAGE of the Lewinsky affair (described in Chapter 1) provides an interesting example of the changing norms regarding what news is. If news is defined as "what is *new*," the national press acted appropriately in the first week of the scandal by reporting who allegedly did what, when, where, and why—the five basic Ws of news reporting. In the second week, however, the focus shifted to issues relating to journalists themselves. Some journalists criticized others for failing to verify the facts of the story, a traditional norm in the journalism profession. Did the story of sexual contact between Clinton and Lewinsky break prematurely? That is, did reporters have independent confirmation of the alleged behavior other than Lewinsky's claim in the taped telephone conversations? Is independent verification necessary in today's news environment?[1]

Contrast this with coverage of the 1970s burglary of a Democratic campaign office at the Watergate Hotel, supported by the Republican Committee to Re-Elect the President (CREEP). As recounted in *All the President's Men*, *Washington Post* reporters Bob Woodward and Carl Bernstein tirelessly searched for verifiable evidence of CREEP's involvement, a requirement imposed by their editor, Ben Bradlee, before he would allow the story to be printed.

Another notable aspect of the Lewinsky coverage is that as journalists and news organizations became part of the story, the news story itself began to shift to a discussion of the context in which the initial event occurred. Journalists emerged as authoritative sources, and more coverage was devoted to analysis and commentary than to actual events. Similarly, in the aftermath of the September 11, 2001, terrorist attacks in New York City and Washington, DC, and the resulting war in Afghanistan, journalists were the specialists, and they reported from the field on the evening news regardless of whether newsworthy events were occurring. In both cases, reporting shifted from the five Ws to commentary by journalists on the meanings of events that had transpired.

These examples are indicative of fundamental changes in the nature of the news over the past several decades. Together, they raise an important question: How often are journalists a part of news stories? This chapter documents what news is at three different levels: the criteria used by reporters and editors to define what is newsworthy; the level and nature of political coverage by the mass media; and the values that are reflected in those news decisions.

Answering these questions will help in assessing how much information, and what type of information, the mass media provide. The nature of the news product the media deliver helps determine whether they are objective reporters of fact rather than public advocates or propagandists, for example. That is, objective reporters of fact should produce different news stories than public advocates. Further, documenting the nature of the news product should help us ascertain the extent to which the media convey relevant and useful information, and whether that information is conveyed upward from citizens to elected representatives or downward from government officials to the mass public. Ex-

CNN foreign correspondent Christiane Amanpour often reports from scenes of conflict and violence in the Middle East. © *Koren Ziv/CORBIS SYGMA.*

amining the subjects and sources of news stories help to provide evidence relevant to these points.

These questions are fairly straightforward and can be answered with basic descriptive information about news shows or news publications, although such systematic evidence about the characteristics of news is rarely considered in discussions about the role of the mass media in U.S. politics. Nonetheless, politicians, journalists, intellectuals, and citizens have very strong opinions on the subject. Most discussions focus on whether the news is biased, and people's opinions often reflect their political preferences. That is, negative reporting about officials or issues that the person supports is considered biased, while positive reporting is not; negative reporting about officials or issues that the person opposes is considered good reporting, while positive reporting is not. The problem with these superficial assessments of media coverage is that they ignore the possibility that reporters determine what news is based on more justifiable principles than simply wanting to write bad things about officials they do not like.

The first, often ignored, step in evaluating the extent to which the news media are biased is to look at systematic patterns in what is defined as news. There will be exceptions to the general patterns we identify. But an evaluation of press coverage based on general trends rather than on exceptional or anecdotal cases will be more accurate in the long run.

THE NEWS PRODUCT AND MODELS OF THE MASS MEDIA

What type of news content should we expect under the five models discussed in Chapter 1?

Reporters of Objective Fact

This model implies that what is presented as news is an accurate reflection of "reality." The strictest interpretation of the model would hold that the media are unable to report all facts, which distorts what is presented as reality. To give the model a fair chance, however, we hold it to a less exacting standard based on the criteria editors and reporters use to winnow the set of infinite news stories down to what is actually delivered as news. That is, to what extent do these criteria and values produce an approximation of reality via the news?

This model also implies that the reporter's personal values and interests are irrelevant to the newsgathering process; the news reporter is a channel through which news is reported, and thus plays a passive and silent role. Finally, the model implies that news will stick closely to "facts" rather than emphasize interpretation or commentary.

Neutral Adversary

The neutral adversary model places reporters as well as editors in a more central, proactive role in determining what news is. In this view, the mass media act as unelected representatives of the people, and reporters help create the news by challenging government officials—as well as others in power. Elected officials are typically viewed negatively, as serving their own interests. (If we trusted government officials to act in the public interest, a "watchdog" press would not be necessary.) Thus, it is up to the media to question the words of government officials and serve as an official check on their actions.

This model implies that reporters' interests and values are fairly important in the newsgathering process. The model also requires reporters to independently engage in news investigation and not to use elected officials as their primary sources of information. Finally, the scope and level of political news coverage should reflect the relative importance of the various institutions of government.

Public Advocate

This model implies an even larger role for reporters in defining what news is because the reporters identify themselves as agents of the public interest. It assumes that the professional reporter can independently determine what the public interest is in a given political situation, and that he or she develops news stories that enhance the public's interest. Most importantly, the reporter not only acts as unelected representative of the public as in the neutral adversary model, but also works to engage citizens in the political process. This model effectively defines the reporter's professional responsibilities as those of a political activist.

The public advocate model thus sees reporters' views of shared societal values and political preferences (which happen to coincide with reporters' personal values) as central to the newsgathering process, and requires those values to be reflected in news stories. One feature that distinguishes this model from the others is that it places a premium on using citizens as news sources and reporting citizens' reactions to government and politics as news stories.

Profit-Seeker

By contrast, the profit-seeker model lays aside the professional and personal values of the news reporter and asserts that the primary incentive guiding the newsgathering process is economic profit. Whose incentives are at work is not entirely clear: Profit is likely to drive media owners more than editors and reporters, but the latter are competing for scarce jobs and professional status. Whoever's interests are operative, the economic incentive means that if it sells, it is news.

Evaluating this model requires paying more attention to audience interests and the extent to which media program and news decisions are based on audience size. As noted in Chapter 1, the weak form of the model rests on the fact that the media are privately owned corporations that exist primarily to increase the value of their owners' investments. A stronger version of the model is based on the extent to which the newsgathering process reflects economic considerations, as well as the extent to which news programming decisions reflect audience interest, since the size of the audience is reflected in ratings, and ratings determine profits. The model could thus be consistent with some aspects of the other models, depending on audience tastes or preferences. Because the model places economics via ratings at the center of the newsgathering process, we evaluate it in this chapter, and look at it more specifically in the discussion of the nature of news audiences, news programming, and the economics of the news business in Chapter 4.

Propagandist

The propagandist model is consistent with the profit-seeker model in its emphasis on the private ownership of the mass media, but it suggests that the incentives are both economic and political in nature. That is, the goals of the mass media are, first, to make profits for owners and, second, to legitimize the existing political and economic regimes. This legitimization occurs primarily through selective decisions about what is and is not conveyed as news, and also through the presentation of the news, which relies heavily on symbols that sustain the emotion-laden loyalty of Americans to the democratic and economic systems (despite their glaring deficiencies, scholars note).

The incentives that are implied under this model, then, relate primarily to media owners, who are likely to influence decisions about key stories by violating traditional norms regarding the professional independence of reporters and editors in determining what news is. Media owners, of course, use their influence to ensure that the legitimacy of the political and economic system is sustained. Their success in getting the type of media coverage they want will be reflected in a superficial and symbolic news product.

DEFINING WHAT'S NEWS

What the public reads or views or listens to as news is a small portion of potential news stories. Journalists choose to cover some events and activities and not others. Knowing what criteria they use to determine what is and is not **newsworthy** is key to understanding what becomes news.

Jack Fuller, a former reporter and editor who is now president of the Tribune Publishing Company, defines **news** as "the report of what a news organization has recently learned about matters of some significance or interest to the specific community that news organization serves."[2] This definition emphasizes the importance of the news organization in the newsgathering process; some news organizations will assign significance or interest to an event and report it as news, while other organizations may ignore it.

Fuller claims that this explains why the lead stories in two newspapers, even within the same geographical region, may be different. For example, he points out that the *New York Times* may report a congressional vote as the most significant event of the day, while the *New York Daily News* might lead with a deadly fire in the Bronx. These variations are often labeled as "bias," but whose bias is not specified. Based on Fuller's definition, the bias is reporters' and editors' subjective evaluations of community or audience interest.

Fuller also notes that the three critical elements of the news identified in his definition—timeliness, community interest, and significance—necessarily introduce fundamental biases in the news. **Timeliness** introduces a bias of immediacy, where recent events supercede that which is already known. Being of interest to its audience, according to Fuller, results in news that accentuates the negative and appeals to people's curiosity. Significance is typically reflected in the geographic bias in the news—if it happens close to home, it is news. Since both timeliness (in particular) and audience interest (somewhat less so) have been mentioned by other scholars writing about news definition, we look at them in greater detail.

Timeliness

News is distinguished from other kinds of information in that it is conveyed to others as soon as it is learned.[3] The expression "that's *news* to me" suggests that new information has been imparted and also that it has been gleaned recently, or is fresh. The expression "that's *new* to me," by contrast, suggests that new information that has been imparted does not have the status of news, something that is valued for its short existence.

The critical importance of timeliness necessarily limits news to information that is superficial. Bernard Roshco, citing the work of Robert E. Park, argued that "*all news can be defined as timely acquaintance-with*" rather than "knowledge-about." Unless "knowledge-about," or additional information, is included, "News . . . provides only superficial understanding of what is being reported."[4]

Human Interest and Drama

In addition to timeliness, Fuller points to the critical importance of audience interest or "curiosity." He suggests that when reporters appeal to audience interests, one consequence is the tendency to report negative developments as news: "Fear and anger operate strongly at greater distances than love, so bad news travels farther."[5] Others have argued that appealing to audience interests results in a tendency to report **human interest** stories and **dramatic events** rather than less personalized, less emotional events. A television news reporter in Philadelphia, for example, quoted her news director's instructions when she left to cover a press conference in which a city official announced plans for a major capital investment: "We don't want facts and figures for the story. We want to humanize it."[6]

On the other hand, Herbert Gans observed and interviewed journalists at *CBS Evening News, NBC Nightly News, Newsweek,* and *Time* during the late 1960s and mid-1970s, and reported that while the world had changed between the 1960s and the 1980s, the way journalists worked had not. Based on these experiences, Gans claims that the substance of stories largely determines their suitability for presentation as news, with the ideal news story being both interesting and important. Importance is determined by the actors or activities, including whether high-ranking government officials are involved, the significance of the story to the nation and the national interest, its impact on large numbers of people, and its significance for the past or future.[7] Interesting stories include

- People stories: ordinary people acting in unusual ways
- Role reversals: departures from the expected ("man bites dog")
- Human interest: people stories evoking audience sympathy or identification
- Exposé anecdotes: condemn actors and activities that violate enduring activities

- Hero stories: ordinary people overcoming villains or nature
- Gee-whiz stories: stories that evoke surprise, such as fads or freak occurrences[8]

Gans claims that interesting stories are used for two reasons.[9] First, the "important" stories often tend to be negative, so focusing on interesting stories allows the news organization to "balance" negative coverage with more positive coverage. Second, interesting stories are often "timeless," that is, not tied to a particular event that becomes "old" over time. Thus, interesting stories can be produced and held by the news organization until there is a shortage of "important" stories or other organizational or technological problems in the news system.

Concrete Events

Another criterion associated with the news is that it focuses on **concrete events**. This is partly a consequence of timeliness: If news is something that is new and recent, then the easiest way to identify "new and recent" is to look for concrete events that embody the progression of a news story begun the prior day. Hence, each day's news is an update of the stories reported the day before—or at least an update with respect to the most easily observable developments associated with that story.

Roshco contends that news focuses on specific overt events rather than on ongoing processes because of the type of information the news provides. Citing journalist and political scientist Walter Lippman, he notes that "the hardest thing to report is chaos, even though it is an evolving chaos."[10] Although Lippman was discussing the Russian Revolution, the observation still holds.

Defining News: A Historical Update

More recent, and less anecdotal, evidence suggests that these traditional criteria of news definition—timeliness, human interest and drama, and concrete events—have changed in importance over the course of the twentieth century. An analysis of news stories about crimes, accidents, and employment drawn from the *New York Times, Chicago Tribune,* and *Portland Oregonian* between 1894 and 1994 found that "stories grew longer, included more analysis, expanded from specific locations to broader regions, placed more emphasis on time frames other than the present, and named fewer individuals and more groups, officials, and outside sources."[11] Based on these findings, the researchers concluded that for a story to qualify as news, the journalist must be able to "supply a context of social problems, interpretations, and themes."[12] Their finding that more news stories **analyze** rather than **describe** events suggests that journalists today play a more central role in defining media content and are less constrained by concrete events as a news criterion.

NEWS COVERAGE OF POLITICS

Given the definitions of news discussed above, what, then, should we expect *substantively* from political news coverage? The communications scholars whose work has been discussed seem to suggest that we should not expect much. News is defined as concrete, recently occurring events that reflect human curiosity and essentially legitimize the status quo. None of these characteristics, alone or in combination, suggest that the news product will be a useful source of information with which citizens can evaluate government officials or policies or that they can use in vigorous public debate about matters of government and society.

Equally grim is W. Lance Bennett's assessment of news provided by the mainstream media. Although ideological biases might be present in the news, and although news content varies as a result of packaging differences, Bennett sees the news product as remarkably uniform. In his view, news suffers from four biases that are more fundamental than ideology: It is personalized, dramatized, and fragmented, and it creates the untenable paradox that public officials are both central to and incapable of resolving political and social conflict.[13] **Personalized news,** which focuses on personalities and the emotional meanings of events, discourages individuals from taking a broader, more socially aware view of political events, and thus trivializes matters of national importance.

Dramatized news is made up of items that can most easily be turned into stories with convenient beginnings, interesting middles, and satisfying ends. Journalists tend to focus on crisis, personality, and scandal. Political processes and complex institutions are difficult to convey in a melodramatic narrative form, so they are less likely to be news subjects. Chronic problems such as poverty and hunger are likewise difficult to present as dramatic narratives.

However, chronic problems become newsworthy when they reach exceptional levels or otherwise appear to be crises. When that occurs, the product is **fragmented news** that "comes to us in sketchy dramatic capsules that make it difficult to see the causes of problems, their historical significance, or the connections across the issues."[14] Because other stories compete for limited news space, each day's news contains dramas, with little continuity from day to day. Moreover, the lack of background information adds to the impression that the world is chaotic and unpredictable.

When news drama or crisis develops, reporters place officials at the center of the story, portraying them as uncaring, scheming politicians unable to restore order. This **authority-disorder news** bias superficially depicts social and political chaos as an evil that good politicians must do battle with, setting up dramatic tension in news stories. The stories ignore the facts that chaos in society and the polity is not that unusual and that the underlying problems are rarely readily solved by government officials. In fact, an indirect consequence of this bias is that the underlying causes of our country's problems are not raised in the news or in public debate.

From the perspective of democratic politics, then, this is a very pessimistic view of the nature of the news. It has consequences that are far broader and deeper than any ideological biases of the mass media. Yet it is one thing to claim that journalists use certain criteria to define what news is or hold certain values, and another to demonstrate that such criteria or values are reflected in the actual content of news coverage. The next part of this chapter focuses on specific details of the media's political news coverage.

Although the media content studies discussed in the next section were conducted as early as the 1970s, most scholars believe that their general conclusions still hold today. This is in part because more recent studies have confirmed their general findings. However, since most of these studies rely on data collected for especially brief time periods (a week of newspaper coverage, for example) or from likely "unrepresentative" newspapers, the discussion below focuses primarily on the original, path-breaking research.

Domestic News Coverage

One of the most systematic studies of national **domestic news coverage** was by Herbert Gans, whose analysis of network television news and weekly newsmagazines was discussed earlier. Gans analyzed samples of news stories from *CBS Evening News* and *Newsweek* in 1969, 1971, and 1975, and his findings were consistent with the news criteria discussed above. National news stories focused on national actors. Although some of these actors were ordinary people rather than government officials or political, economic, social, or cultural figures, most were either elected national leaders or other political figures. Incumbent presidents, members of Congress, and other federal officials dominated in nearly 50 percent of television stories, and state and local officials were the major actors in another 11 percent.

Approximately 40 percent of the newsmagazine coverage that did not focus on known actors focused on protesters, rioters, and strikers, while around 20 percent of the unknown television coverage focused on victims of crime or natural disorders. Other unknowns appearing in the news included "alleged and actual violators of the laws and mores," participants in unusual activities, and voters, survey respondents, and other aggregates. Thus, Gans concluded that the unknowns who appeared in the news were unrepresentative, and that ordinary people rarely appeared, except as statistics.[15]

Regarding activities in the news, Gans found that crimes, scandals, and investigations were the most commonly covered (28 percent of television news stories in 1967), followed by government conflicts and disagreements (17 percent) and natural disasters (14 percent). Newsmagazine coverage varied slightly in 1967, when the largest proportion of stories was devoted to government personnel changes, including campaigning (22 percent), followed by crimes, scandals, and investigations (18 percent) and government conflicts and disasters (16 percent).

National and local news stations provided extensive coverage of the search and rescue (and recovery) efforts surrounding the crash of John F. Kennedy Jr.'s small aircraft in July 1999. © *Boston Herald/CORBIS SYGMA.*

Since Gans' analysis relies on data from several decades ago, it is reasonable to ask whether his findings remain true today. One reason to believe that they do is that the findings are consistent with the news criteria and definitions offered above. First, the focus on the news on "knowns" satisfies the need to present news of interest to the mass audience. People's curiosity about the lives of social and political figures is well-established and is catered to by various entertainment programs. Second, the focus on crime, scandals, and natural disasters is entirely consistent with the need to focus on concrete and timely events and seems also to satisfy the "curious" mass audience.

More recent research likewise affirms Gans' findings. Stephen Hess analyzed stories written by reporters stationed in Washington, D.C., and published in twenty-two local papers around the country. He found that foreign policy, economics and finance, and scandals were the three most common subjects on television news (with 24 percent, 17 percent, and 6 percent of stories), compared to foreign policy, economics and finance, and government operations (with scandals in fourth place) in newspaper stories (12 percent, 10.9 percent, and 6.7 percent). Hess also found that 54 percent of newspaper stories focused on Congress and 46 percent on the president, while 59 percent of television stories focused on the president and 41 percent on Congress. Senators were typically the subjects of stories on foreign policy, while House members were more often cited in stories about economics and finance. Democrats, who controlled both houses of Congress at the time, were mentioned in greater proportion than their size in each chamber.[16]

Hess also provided interesting data on activities in the news, especially coverage of the policy process—that is, the broader, more complex set of activities in which lawmakers are engaged. He found that television tended to cover the policy process more as a bill moved through the policy stages, while newspapers had more evenly balanced coverage throughout the process. More specifically, 3 percent of newspaper stories, compared to no television stories, focused on the introduction of legislation; 20 percent of newspaper stories and 7 percent of television stories focused on subcommittee activity; 37 percent of newspaper stories and 24 percent of television stories focused on committee activity; 35 percent of newspaper stories and 58 percent of television stories focused on floor activity; and 5 percent of newspaper stories and 11 percent of television stories focused on conference committees.[17] This distribution of policy process news coverage is particularly interesting in light of the fact that the formulation of policy alternatives and the content of legislation, which some experts see as the most important substantive work, are done in subcommittee, while the most symbolic work is done on the floor of Congress.[18]

Finally, Hess noted that regional variations in news coverage were significant, reflecting the fact that editors took an active role in determining what was newsworthy, rather than just publishing everything that Washington reporters sent. The *Des Moines Register* was first of twenty-two papers in reporting on agriculture, while the *Seattle Times* was first in reporting on environmental and conservation issues, and the *New Orleans Times-Picayune* was first on transportation. This is particularly important because many analyses of media coverage—such as Gans'—rely exclusively on national news sources. Variations across news outlets suggest that editors and/or reporters are making distinctive news judgments. Their judgments may result from different "objective" realities they operate within; from different news values; or from variations in audience interest.

Local News Coverage

Over the past decades, few if any systematic studies on the nature of local news coverage have been conducted. In 1990 Phyllis Kaniss analyzed local evening television news programs in Philadelphia over two single-week periods.[19] She wanted to determine whether local television news was a mirror of local newspaper news coverage, reflecting the same content, but with less depth. Kaniss coded stories on the evening newscasts into five categories: government (any level), occurrences (fires, accidents, disasters, crimes, and trials), private institutions (business, education, religion), features (consumer investigations and celebrity stories, for example), and world news. Over the two-week period, occurrences received as much or more news time as government, and there were more occurrence stories than government stories. Kaniss attributed much of the emphasis on isolated events to the fact that they are more likely to provide lively visual and audio material than are routine government press conferences or meetings:

> Shots of flames billowing, cars mangled in highway accidents, or suspects being led away in handcuffs make for better television than officials standing at podiums. As one local television journalist admitted, local development issues are often dropped from the lineup on local television news because they are "more difficult to show on TV . . . all you get are people talking." In addition, crimes and fires produce more emotional sound bites than do government stories.[20]

Also, local government jurisdictions are complex; numerous government entities (city and county governments, boards, regional groups, utilities) have overlapping jurisdictions with limited authority. Thus, news about any one government entity is likely to be of interest to only a small fraction of the audience. Blood-and-guts coverage of a gory crime, on the other hand, is likely to appeal to the entire news audience in a large metropolitan area, regardless of where it occurred.

Coverage of a commuter plane that crashed into an airport hanger in Charlotte, North Carolina, in January 2003, was extensive on both national and local news programs. © *Captain Rob Brisley/ Charlotte Fire Department/Getty Images, Inc.*

News coverage of government decreased from the early television news show to the late show, according to Kaniss, primarily because government stories reported in the early show were often edited down to make room for a breaking occurrence such as a fire or automobile accident. Further, television coverage of government tended to focus on "sexy" issues (for example, crime and election stories), rather than such "sleeper" issues as housing, education, and health. Finally, Kaniss noted that the local news show tended to be used to promote network entertainment programming, either through its emphasis on celebrity and entertainment stories, or by linking supposed "news" stories to network programs scheduled that evening or in the coming week.

Overall, Kaniss concluded that television news does more than provide the highlights of the news presented in local newspapers. Technological considerations, time constraints, different professional values of reporters, and networks' entertainment interests all contribute to a news product that is quite different from (and more superficial than) that of the local printed press.

Foreign Affairs Coverage

Many of the characteristics of domestic news coverage are true of **foreign affairs coverage** as well. In 1967 about 14 percent of television news focused on foreign affairs.[21] Three types of countries dominated foreign news at the time: America's closest or most powerful political allies, their major foes, and the rest of the world, "which is reported only sporadically."[22] In 1996 Hess concluded that "most of the world's countries are seen rarely, and then only because they host an important event or person, a pope or president, or because hurricanes happen, or because a producer finds an amusing, sentimental, or ironic story that can end a program on the upbeat."[23]

Based on a content analysis of network television newscasts during the late 1980s and early 1990s, Hess reported that 6 of a total of 191 countries received "constant" coverage in 1992; 22 received "crisis" coverage, and 77 received sporadic mentions. More specifically, 21 countries were the subject of 79 percent of foreign dateline stories on television news between 1988 and 1992.[24] The differences in coverage were not necessarily driven by the relative (objective) "importance" of the regions. Asia, for example, has 60 percent of the world's population and produces 27 percent of the world's gross domestic product, yet between 1989 and 1991 Asia was the topic of only 10 percent of television news time and 17 percent of newspaper stories in the *New York Times, Chicago Tribune,* and *Los Angeles Times.*

The most distorted foreign affairs coverage involves the Middle East, which has 5 percent of the world's population and 3 percent of its gross domestic product, but 35 percent of the foreign dateline news coverage. Hess attributes the level of news coverage to several factors, including the fact that Israel is a "hospitable democracy" to news reporters; that the majority of its population

Violence in the Middle East is covered extensively on national network news. This photo shows the rescue efforts at the scene of a suicide bombing in Haifa, Israel. © *David Silverman/Getty Images, Inc.*

speaks English; and that the *New York Times* has a very large Jewish readership.

Gans categorized foreign affairs coverage into seven subject areas: American activities in a foreign country; foreign activities that affect Americans and American policy; communist-bloc activities; elections and other peaceful changes in government personnel; political conflict and protest; disasters; and excesses of dictatorship.[25] Likewise, Hess reported that combat, domestic government, human rights, and diplomacy were most often covered in television network news, while domestic government, combat, diplomacy, and economics received most newspaper coverage.[26] He also reported that violence was the defining characteristic of foreign news coverage, particularly on television, and the greater the distance, the more likely the violence would be portrayed: 40 percent of stories on countries or regions within four thousand miles of New York City focused on violence, compared to 55 percent of stories on countries or regions more than seven thousand miles away.[27]

An Update on the Content of News Coverage

The studies discussed above are based on news coverage in the 1970s and 1980s, which leads to the question of whether the findings are time-bound to those eras. To assess the generalizability of these conclusions, it is important to assess the content of news coverage over a longer time period. The Policy Agendas Project, directed by Frank Baumgartner and Bryan Jones, allows us to do just that. This project focused on collecting data on congressional hearings, media attention, and budgetary allocations of the national government from 1947 to 1994.[28] The media data provide the most reliable and accurate assessment of the nature of the news product in the United States and how it has changed over the past several decades.

Baumgartner and Jones took a sample of stories from the *New York Times Index* for each year from 1947 to 1994. Every story that was included in the *New York Times Index* in a given year could potentially have been included in the sample. Each story was coded for a topic using a system that included twenty-seven possible topics. Table 3-1 shows estimates of the topic content of news coverage in the *New York Times* from 1991 through 1994. Consistent

TABLE 3-1 Media Coverage of Issues, *New York Times*, 1991–1994 (Average percentage of stories)

News Topic	Percentage
Banking, finance, and domestic commerce	24.1%
International affairs	9.4%
Arts and entertainment	8.3%
Law, crime, and family	7.5%
Other, miscellaneous and human interest	5.6%
Defense	4.8%
Health	4.6%
State and local government	4.4%
Federal government	4.3%
Education	3.1%
Sports and recreation	3.0%
Space, science, and technology	2.7%
Environment	2.1%
Transportation	1.9%
Community development	1.8%
Death notices	1.7%
Weather and natural disasters	0.3%
Fires	0.3%

Note: Computed by the author.
Source: Frank Baumgartner and Bryan Jones, Policy Agendas Project, http://depts.washington.edu/ampol/.

with the discussion above, most news coverage focused on domestic affairs; only 9.4 percent of news stories focused on international affairs. The most prominent topics were banking, finance, and domestic commerce, which garnered 24.1 percent of news stories. The next three categories were international affairs, arts and entertainment (8.5 percent), and law, crime, and family (7.5 percent).

The next largest category is other, miscellaneous, and human interest (5.6 percent), and there are separate categories for sports and recreation (3.0 percent), death notices (1.7), weather and natural disasters (0.3 percent), and fires (0.3 percent). This seems to support the profit-seeking model of newsgathering to the extent that the mass audience is not interested in news but rather in useful information and entertainment.

Equally important are changes in content coverage over time. Comparing the average number of stories on each topic presented in the *New York Times* for multi-year periods beginning with 1946 to 1950 and ending with 1991 to 1994, the top three issues covered changed significantly. In 1946 to 1950 and 1951 to 1955, the top three topics were international affairs, defense, and banking and finance. From 1956 to 1960 through 1976 to 1980, the federal government was included in the top three, eliminating defense. In 1981 to 1985 and through 1991 to 1994, neither defense nor the federal government was in the top three, but arts and entertainment was.

To highlight the changing fortunes of various news topics, Table 3-2 lists topics for which average coverage in the 1946 to 1950 period changed by half

TABLE 3-2 Significant Changes in Average Number of Stories by Topic, 1946–1950 to 1991–1994

News Topic	Average Percentage of Stories, 1946–1950	Average Percentage of Stories, 1991–1994	Difference	Percentage Difference
Defense	12.06%	4.78%	7.28	0.60%
Foreign trade	3.0%	1.75%	1.25	0.42%
International affairs	15.06%	9.43%	5.63	0.37%
Environment	0.23%	2.13%	−1.9	8.26%
Law, crime, and family	4.06%	7.53%	−3.47	1.85%
Banking, finance, and domestic commerce	12.02%	24.13%	−12.11	1.01%
Space, science, and technology	1.48%	2.68%	−1.2	1.81%
Arts and entertainment	3.94%	8.33%	−4.39	1.11%
Sports and recreation	1.7%	2.98%	−1.28	1.59%

Source: Frank Baumgartner and Bryan Jones, Policy Agendas Project, http://depts.washington.edu/ampol/.

(either positively or negatively) compared to the 1991 to 1994 period. The table includes the average number of stories for each topic in the first and last periods (and thus ignores changes in between). Coverage increased significantly for several topics: environment; law, crime, and the family; banking and finance; space, science, and technology; arts and entertainment; and sports and recreation. During the same period, coverage of transportation, defense, foreign trade, and international affairs significantly decreased. Thus, independent of changes in the nature of news reporting, the actual topics of news coverage have changed substantially over the past several decades.

Up to this point, the analyses of news content have focused almost exclusively on the printed (typically newspaper) press rather than television news. There has been far less systematic investigation of the content of television news. One exception is a study of CNN and network news conducted in 1982 by the Media Institute. Its major finding about television news content was that the networks devoted 23 percent of their news time to business and economic news, while CNN devoted 20 percent of its general news program time to the same. This is surprisingly similar to Baumgartner and Jones' *New York Times* data.[29]

Although Baumgartner and Jones' data on media coverage are not directly comparable to Gans' earlier work, some similarities are evident. First, both research approaches find that domestic politics receives more coverage than international affairs. Second, topics such as crime rank highly, probably because of its tendency to attract a curious audience. Note that this focus on crime likely results in news coverage focusing on the unusual and deviant among "unknowns," to use Gans' term. And, third, the entertainment emphasis in the news of the 1990s—and its increasing importance over time—also affirms Gans' arguments regarding the kinds of topics that become news, in this case where coverage of "knowns" today likely includes even greater proportions of media celebrities.

VALUES REFLECTED IN NEWS COVERAGE

The newsgathering process is a collective enterprise, requiring the agreement of editor and reporter, at the least; large national organizations require even more journalists to agree on what is newsworthy. But once an event is chosen as newsworthy, how is it portrayed? Creating news stories, it is often claimed, depends on the enduring **values** of journalists.

Gans notes that values are not directly addressed in content analyses of media coverage of particular political institutions.[30] But some values are recurring themes that appear "between the lines" of media text. These values are introduced into the news at the writing stage. In his seminal work on this subject—now over twenty-five years old—Gans identified eight values in media coverage of politics:

- **Ethnocentrism:** the superiority of the U.S. political and social system over all others

- **Altruistic democracy:** democracy never fails
- **Responsible capitalism:** capitalism benefits everyone, fully and equally
- **Small-town pastoralism:** large cities dehumanize, while small towns (and the values they represent) are ideal
- **Individualism:** politics is about individuals seeking to survive threats from the political and social environment
- **Moderatism:** discourages excess or extremism in behavior or attitude
- **Social order:** society survives because we have the capability to restore order in the face of crisis or conflict
- **National leadership:** political and social authorities are responsible for restoring order[31]

Several of these values seem to be consistent with the characteristics of the news discussed earlier in the chapter, especially the biases noted by Bennett (for example, that news is personalized and dramatized). The values would seem to work nicely for reporters as they try to develop story themes for news reports. But identification of these values suffers from the same problem that claims of bias do: How do we know them when we see them?

The importance of values in presenting the news can be seen by studying ABC's "Person of the Week" feature. Beginning in 1989, this feature was included in ABC Friday evening newscasts to identify and honor one person

Although Larson and Bailey's research focused on ABC's "Person of the Week," similar features are used in other media outlets. Featured above is Tom Ridge, *Time* magazine's "Person of the Week" for November 22, 2002, who was appointed Director of the Office of Homeland Security by President Bush. © *Larry Downing/Reuters.*

who was, in the eyes of the ABC newsroom, especially "notable" that week. Stephanie Greco Larson and Martha Bailey contend that "Person of the Week" is ideal for assessing values in the news because external events do not force the choice of one person or another; but instead the news staff members have maximum freedom to choose who they want. Thus, the feature identifies the values important to news media reporters and writers.[32]

So who, according to ABC, is worthy of praise? Men were more likely to be chosen than women. When women were chosen, it was for activities consistent with traditional gender roles—women helping others and otherwise contributing to society. Men were portrayed as powerful, women as nurturing. Blacks were more likely than whites to be honored for overcoming difficult circumstances and also more likely to be honored for being first in some way. Finally, individuals were typically portrayed as benefiting society in some notable manner, and entertainment values were intertwined in the newsgathering process:

> Many profiles might be more accurately entitled, "Person of the Week Who Helps Others." . . . This theme allows "ABC World News Tonight" to end the work week on an uplifting note in contrast to the news' typical negativity and focus on conflict and violence.[33]

CONCLUSION

The important question at this point is how the general patterns of news coverage reflect on the five models of the press. As was the case in Chapter 2, the reporter of objective fact model seems to fail, given the media's tendency to emphasize particular types of facts (such as crime and accidents). True, these things do happen. But there is a much wider variety of facts that reporters could choose to cover if they were operating under an objective fact model.

Although the findings are not necessarily inconsistent with the neutral adversary and public advocate models, they do point to possible weaknesses in these models. The focus of the news on national figures, to the exclusion of coverage of state and local officials, suggests that the media are not performing either an adversarial or advocacy role in a satisfactory manner. However, this might simply reflect the fact that studies of media content focus almost exclusively on national, rather than state and local, papers. Perhaps a more careful investigation of state and local media would yield more optimistic findings. But that would require state and local reporters (and news organizations) to behave in substantially different ways in the newsgathering process.

The evidence in this chapter supports the profit-seeking model fairly well. Dramatic, personalized news provides good visuals and action, both of which are said to appeal to audience interests. The larger the audience, the greater the profit. Similarly, Hess' evidence that editors tend to choose stories of relevance to their readers suggests that the newsgathering process is motivated by the goal of securing a large, profitable audience.

Finally, the findings reflect on the media as a linkage institution in several ways. First, the value of timeliness in defining what's news suggests that there will be a bias in the news toward new, and perhaps innovative or unusual, events and individuals. This suggests that the media will not convey information regarding long-standing issues or provide a historical context within which one can make sense of the news. Yet many of our enduring social conflicts are indeed "old": poverty, racism, military aggression, ethnic conflict. As a result, the mass media are not likely to provide a forum for political deliberation—the thoughtful, ongoing discussion of political issues, interests, and alternatives. While a reasonable argument might be that these types of topics and discussions are most suitable for the specialized news media, this ignores the problem that we do not seem to have a media system that allows the issues to be discussed by a larger, more representative group of citizens.

In sum, one might be tempted to consider an alternative definition of the news: "what newsmakers promote as timely, important, or interesting . . . from which news organizations select, narrate, and package . . . and that people consume, at any moment in history."[34] This definition accurately emphasizes the interdependence of politicians, the media, and the public in determining what news is. Yet the question remains: Whose preferences or actions have greater weight than the others in this process? Chapter 4 suggests that the organizational routines and the economic and professional incentives that influence reporters as they create the news are especially important.

Key Terms

altruistic democracy
analyze
authority-disorder
  news
concrete events
describe
domestic news
  coverage
dramatic events

dramatized news
ethnocentrism
foreign affairs
  coverage
fragmented news
human interest
individualism
moderatism
national leadership

news
newsworthy
personalized news
responsible capitalism
small-town
  pastoralism
social order
timeliness
values

Exercises

1. Conduct a "casual" content analysis of the coverage of the Middle East, terrorism, or Afghanistan by searching the Internet for stories published prior to and after September 11, 2001. What did you expect media coverage to be like prior to that date? After it? What did you find?
2. Conduct a content analysis of the *Newshour with Jim Lehrer* and compare it to a network evening newscast. How are they similar? How do they differ?

3. To what extent do the visuals in the evening network newscasts matter? In a daily paper? Pick one story, describe the information provided in the story, and describe the information provided by the visual. What is the function of each?

4. Develop examples of Roshco's distinction between "timely acquaintance with" and "timely knowledge about" with respect to a current news event. What information would fall in the former category? In the latter?

Notes

1. See "Rules in Flux: News Organizations Face Tough Calls on Unverified 'Facts,'" *New York Times*, January 27, 1998, and "Clinton Pursuers Question Selves," *New York Times,* April 5, 1998.

2. Jack Fuller, *News Values: Ideas for an Information Age* (Chicago: University of Chicago Press, 1996), p. 6.

3. Bernard Roshco, *Newsmaking* (Chicago: University of Chicago Press, 1975).

4. Ibid., pp. 13–14.

5. Fuller, *News Values*, p. 8.

6. Phyllis Kaniss, *Making Local News* (Chicago: University of Chicago Press, 1991), p. 120.

7. Herbert Gans, *Deciding What's News: A Study of CBS Evening News, NBC Nightly News, Newsweek and Time* (New York: Random House, 1979), Chapter 5.

8. Ibid., pp. 156–157.

9. Ibid., p. 155.

10. Roshco, *Newsmaking*.

11. Kevin G. Barnhurst and Diana Mutz, "American Journalism and the Decline in Event-Centered Reporting," *Journal of Communication* 4 (1997): 27.

12. Ibid., p. 27.

13. W. Lance Bennett, *News: The Politics of Illusion*, 4th ed. (New York: Longman, 2001).

14. Ibid., p. 38.

15. Gans, *Deciding What's News*, p. 15.

16. Stephen Hess, *The Washington Reporters* (Washington, DC: The Brookings Institution, 1981), p. 102.

17. Ibid.

18. See, for example, Lawrence C. Dodd and Bruce I. Oppenheimer, *Congress Reconsidered* (New York: Praeger, 2000).

19. Kaniss, *Making Local News*.

20. Ibid., p. 117.

21. Gans, *Deciding What's News*, p. 31.

22. Ibid., pp. 32–33.

23. Stephen Hess, *International News and Foreign Correspondents* (Washington, DC: The Brookings Institution, 1996).

24. Ibid., p. 31.

25. Gans, *Deciding What's News.*

26. Hess, *International News and Foreign Correspondents*, p. 45.

27. Ibid., pp. 33–35.

28. Frank Baumgartner and Bryan Jones, Policy Agendas Project, accessed July 2, 2003, from http://depts.washington.edu/ampol/.

29. Media Institute, *CNN vs. the Networks: Is More News Better News?* (Washington, DC: The Media Institute, 1983), p. 21.

30. Gans, *Deciding What's News.*

31. Ibid.

32. Stephanie Greco Larson and Martha Bailey, "ABC's Person of the Week: American Values in Television News," *Journalism & Mass Communication Quarterly* (Autumn 1998).

33. Ibid., p. 496.

34. W. Lance Bennett, *News: The Politics of Illusion,* 5th ed. (New York: Longman, 2003), pp. 9–10.

4 ▶ Newsgathering: Business, Profession, and Organization

Economic Influences on Newsgathering
Private Ownership • Concentration of Ownership • Consequences of Corporate Ownership

Profit, Advertising, and Ratings
The Ratings Game • Profitability • The Corporate Approach: Marketing to Reader Interest

Media Users and Audiences for the News
Audience Size and Media Reliance • Audience Interest • Television Viewership and Audience Overlap

Corporate Decision Making: Boardroom versus Newsroom
Corporate Cost-Cutting • Courting Advertisers

Professional Influences and Structure
Demographics • Personal Values • Professional Values: The Role of the Media • Professional Values: Objectivity

Organizational Constraints
Managerial Strategies for Marketing the News • News Routines, Deadlines, and Beats • Investigative Reporting

On the Media Business and Models of the Press

Conclusion

THE NEWSGATHERING process is critical to understanding the media's role in a democratic society and thus in evaluating the five media models. The mass media for news comprise a well-established institution in society, and established institutions necessarily operate in routinized, patterned ways. Yet critics of the media often ignore the fact that newsgathering is conducted by trained professionals within particular social and corporate organizational structures. Instead, they are quick to isolate one factor (to the exclusion of others) as *the* explanation of why news is the way it is and whose interests it serves.

Not surprisingly, these claims often reflect individuals' political biases. Conservatives, for example, point to the "liberal" press—the fact that reporters are more likely to be liberal than conservative—as the explanation for the level and nature of coverage of social issues, as well as the "negative" coverage of conservative politicians and big business. Liberals, on the other hand, are likely to note the conservative influences of corporate ownership and advertising on the selection of stories, as well as the personal wealth of editors and other "media elites."

For example, just five days prior to the 2000 presidential election, a news story broke that George W. Bush had been arrested for driving under the influence of alcohol in 1976. The story had been "leaked" to a Portland television reporter by a prominent Democrat. Scores of reporters had conducted background checks on Bush for months, trying to confirm such rumors, but none of the computerized checks nor the routine reports issued in states in which Bush had resided picked up the twenty-four-year-old charge. A reporter had talked about asking law enforcement officials in Kennebunkport, Maine, but assumed that they would not willingly provide such details about the son of a prominent family. Another reporter had asked the local police chief about Bush's arrest record in July, but the reporter's editor pulled the story because it was both dated and irrelevant, since Bush had stopped drinking by 1986.

Did the story break five days before the election because the "liberal" media were biased against George W. Bush? Or had it been kept from print for four months because of the conservative ideology of an editor who was concerned about harm to his media organization? Did the values of the reporters or editors involved change over the course of the campaign? Or did the closeness of the election make the story more newsworthy in November than in July?

This chapter examines the various actors and considerations involved in the process by which news is created. If we think about the creation of news as a set of decisions made by editors and reporters, it is key to identify the decisions and influences of greatest importance. The choice process might be driven by reporters' and editors' views of their appropriate role vis-à-vis government; they might decide to report the stories that highlight their adversarial role. Alternatively, reporters and editors might be working to help those with economic and political power and so use the institution of the press to protect and enhance the interests of the powerful, including both government and business leaders. Yet another alternative is for editors and reporters to consciously seek to serve the public interest by choosing stories that they believe are critical for the public to be exposed to. Finally, reporters and editors might be motivated solely by the goal of maintaining a high level of profit for their press organizations, with no concern for any particular type of story except those that increases profits.

ECONOMIC INFLUENCES ON NEWSGATHERING

The mass media in the United States are privately owned, and most outlets are part of large media conglomerates. The mass media must make a profit to survive. This section focuses on the business side of news production, noting recent changes in corporate norms regarding the relationship between the business and news divisions of these private corporations.

Private Ownership

Most newspapers and television stations are owned by individuals or corporations whose primary goal is to make a profit from their business ventures. In this respect, media products such as daily newspapers and television programming are essentially the same as manufacturing products like toilet paper and toothpaste; if their sales do not yield a profit, they are yanked from the market. To put it more directly, the primary function of privately owned newspapers and television stations is to make a profit. Other possible roles, such as informing the public, representing the interests of the public, or acting as a watchdog over government, are of secondary importance in a privately held media system.

As noted in Chapter 2, U.S. newspapers have always been privately owned, though subsidized by the federal government to different degrees and in different ways over the past two hundred years. Historically, private ownership of printing presses was especially important in times of social unrest and revolution. If the government controlled the presses, claims of unjust governmental actions or violations of people's civil liberties could be silenced. At the time of the American Revolution, presses had to be approved by the governing British authorities, and publishers who violated the expectations of the government by printing material critical of the government were often jailed.

The early historical lesson—and one that certainly has lingered—is that a government that controls the media has the power to silence critics, so in a democracy, the government should not control the media system. In a more active vein, controlling the media system would also give the government a potentially powerful propaganda tool that could be used to sway public opinion in its favor. Thus, the private ownership of newspapers in the United States is firmly grounded in the belief about the deleterious consequences of government ownership.

Concentration of Ownership

A fundamental economic principle is that competitive markets produce the greatest social welfare; when firms compete with other firms for consumers' purchases, prices will be minimized. In terms of media competition, this principle is used metaphorically to suggest that the more news firms that are competing in a media market, the better the news product will be. For example, in **competitive news markets**, one firm will check the accuracy of another's news reporting; or competition for news will mean the devotion of more resources to "discovering" the news through investigative journalism. The assumption here is that a superior product will attract a larger audience.

Alternatively, **news monopolies** are viewed as dangerous. Single news firms have little incentive to improve their products, and might find it easier to bias the news consistent with the firm's or the owner's political biases or interests. Hence, competition has always been viewed as important to the private media system in the United States. As described in Chapter 2, trends in newspaper ownership over the past several decades have moved the system in the direction of monopoly and away from a competitive market. The trend in electronic broadcasting is not as clear. The three major networks—ABC, CBS, and NBC—typically garner the majority of the audience. But the dominance of the networks has been weakened by the establishment of a fourth, competing network—Fox—which has developed a fairly successful lineup of entertainment, news, and sports programming. The growth in the number of cable systems and channels also provides audiences with alternative programming choices.

At another level, however, ownership trends in electronic broadcasting can be viewed quite negatively. Media critic Ben Bagdikian has warned for decades of the increased **concentration of ownership** in the media sector. In 1997 he noted that the number of major media corporations decreased from over fifty in the early 1980s to close to ten by the mid-1990s. By 2001 he reported that "Six firms dominate all mass media": Time Warner, Disney, Viacom, News Corp (owned by Rupert Murdoch), General Electric, and Bertelsmann.[1]

As the number of media corporations has declined, the extent to which media own other media outlets has increased as well. This trend toward **cross-media ownership**—corporations owning newspapers, television stations, radio stations, newsmagazines, and news and entertainment production companies—is nowhere more evident than in the diversity of Disney's holdings, which include daily newspapers, magazines, books, radio stations, television stations, videos, movie studios, cable companies and programs, and record labels, along with theme parks, children's clothes, and toys (see Table 4-1).[2] Two characteristics of the Disney holdings are notable: the cross-media ownership (including

TABLE 4-1 Corporate Holdings of the Disney Corporation

DISNEY—PUBLISHING

Book Publishing Imprints

- Walt Disney Company Book Publishing
- Hyperion Books
- Miramax Books

Magazine Subsidiary Groups

- ABC Publishing Group
- Disney Publishing, Inc.
- Diversified Publications Group
- Financial Services and Medical Group
- Miller Publishing Company

Magazine titles include:

- Automotive Industries
- Biography (with GE and Hearst)
- Discover
- Disney Adventures
- Disney Magazine
- ECN News
- ESPN Magazine (distributed by Hearst)
- Family Fun
- Institutional Investor
- Jane
- JCK
- Kentucky Prairie Farmer
- Kodin
- Top Famille—French family magazine
- US Weekly (50%)
- Video Business
- Quality

DISNEY—BROADCASTING (includes the Capital City/ABC subsidiary)

Television

- ABC Television Network

Owned and Operated Television Stations

- WLS—Chicago
- WJRT—Flint
- KFSN—Fresno
- KTRK—Houston
- KABC—Los Angeles
- WABC—New York City
- WPVI—Philadelphia
- WTVD—Raleigh-Durham
- KGO—San Francisco
- WTVG—Toledo

Radio Stations

- WKHX—Atlanta
- WYAY—Atlanta
- WDWD—Atlanta
- WMVP—Chicago
- WLS—Chicago
- WXCD—Chicago
- WBAP—Dallas
- KSCS—Dallas
- WDRQ—Detroit
- WJR—Detroit
- WPLT—Detroit
- KABC—Los Angeles
- KLOS—Los Angeles
- KTZN—Los Angeles
- KQRS—Minneapolis-St. Paul
- KXXR—Minneapolis-St. Paul
- KDIZ—Minneapolis-St. Paul
- KZNR—Minneapolis-St. Paul
- KZNT—Minneapolis-St. Paul
- KZNZ—Minneapolis-St. Paul
- WABC—New York City
- WPLJ—New York City
- KGO—San Francisco

- KSFO—San Francisco
- WMAL—Washington DC
- WJZW—Washington DC
- WRQX—Washington DC
- KQAM—Wichita
- Radio Disney
- ESPN Radio (syndicated programming)

Cable Television

- ABC Family
- The Disney Channel
- Toon Disney
- SoapNet
- ESPN Inc. (80%—Hearst Corporation owns the remaining 20%) includes ESPN, ESPN2, ESPN News, ESPN Now, ESPN Extreme
- Classic Sports Network
- A&E Television (37.5%, with Hearst and GE)
- The History Channel (with Hearst and GE)
- Lifetime Television (50%, with Hearst)
- Lifetime Movie Network (50%, with Hearst)
- E! Entertainment (with Comcast and Liberty Media)

International Broadcast

- The Disney Channel UK
- The Disney Channel Taiwan
- The Disney Channel Australia
- The Disney Channel Malaysia
- The Disney Channel France
- The Disney Channel Middle East
- The Disney Channel Italy
- The Disney Channel Spain
- ESPN INC. International Ventures
- Sportsvision of Australia (25%)
- ESPN Brazil (50%)
- ESPN STAR (50%)—sports programming throughout Asia

- Net STAR (33%)—owners of The Sports Network of Canada

Other International Ventures (all with minority ownership)

- Tele-Munchen—German television production and distribution
- RTL-2—German television production and distribution
- Hamster Productions—French television production
- TV Sport of France
- Tesauro of Spain
- Scandinavian Broadcasting System
- Japan Sports Channel

Television Production and Distribution

- Buena Vista Television
- Touchstone Television
- Walt Disney Television
- Walt Disney Television Animation (has three wholly owned production facilities outside the United States—Japan, Australia, Canada)

DISNEY—MOVIE PRODUCTION AND DISTRIBUTION

- Walt Disney Pictures
- Touchstone Pictures
- Hollywood Pictures
- Caravan Pictures
- Miramax Pictures
- Buena Vista Home Video
- Buena Vista Home Entertainment
- Buena Vista International

DISNEY—FINANCIAL AND RETAIL

Financial

- Sid R. Bass (partial interest—crude petroleum and natural gas production)

(continued)

TABLE 4-1 *(Continued)*

Retail

- The Disney Store

DISNEY—MULTIMEDIA

Walt Disney Internet Group

- ABC Internet Group
- ABC.com
- ABCNEWS.com
- Oscar.com
- Mr. Showbiz
- Disney Online (Web sites and content)
- Disney's Daily Blast
- Disney.com
- Family.com
- ESPN Internet Group
- ESPN.sportzone.com
- Soccernet.com (60%)
- NFL.com
- NBA.com
- NASCAR.com
- Skillgames
- Wall of Sound

Go Network

- Toysmart.com (majority stake—educational toys)

Disney Interactive (develops/markets computer software, video games, CD-ROMs)

DISNEY—MUSIC

- Buena Vista Music Group
- Hollywood Records (popular music and soundtracks for motion pictures)
- Lyric Street Records (Nashville-based country music label)

- Mammoth Records (popular and alternative music label)
- Walt Disney Records

DISNEY—THEATER AND SPORTS

Theatrical Productions

- Walt Disney Theatrical Productions (productions include stage version of *The Lion King, Beauty and the Beast, King David*)

Professional Sports Franchises

- Anaheim Sports, Inc.
- Mighty Ducks of Anaheim (National Hockey League)
- Anaheim Angels (25% general partner ownership—Major League Baseball)

THEME PARKS AND RESORTS

- Disneyland—Anaheim, CA
- Disney-MGM Studios
- Disneyland Paris
- Disney Regional Entertainment (entertainment and theme dining in metro areas)
- Disneyland Resort
- Disney Vacation Club
- Epcot
- Magic Kingdom
- Tokyo Disneyland (partial ownership)
- Walt Disney World—Orlando, FL
- Disney's Animal Kingdom
- Disney—MGM Studios
- Walt Disney World Sports Complex (golf course, auto racing track, and baseball complex)
- Disney Cruise Line
- The Disney Institute

OTHER

- TiVo (partial investment)

Source: "Media Owner's Index: The Walt Disney Company." Available from http://www.cjr.org/owners/disney.asp (accessed March 19, 2003).

network television, cable, radio, and print media) and the vertical integration of outlets (from creation to production to distribution). One certainly can speculate how this theme-park corporate giant might have, at minimum, accelerated the promotion of entertainment values in traditional news shows.

Consequences of Corporate Ownership

Bagdikian contends that private media corporations that control the news have a dramatic advantage in determining the very substance of the news reported. Metropolitan papers around the country, he argues, typically devote entire sections to business news, which provides a valuable service "to financiers and investors with presentation of corporate leaders as heroes or exciting combatants. . . . There is no such systematic section for consumers, though most of the country's readers are not investors but consumers."[3] As another example, he notes that when Time and Warner merged, not a single sentence in the *New York Times* coverage referred to the potential consequences of the merger for the national news.

These anecdotal observations of the consequences of corporate ownership for the news are supported by more systematic assessments. Doug Underwood, along with Keith Stamm, surveyed news editors and reporters at twelve different newspapers in California, Idaho, and Washington in 1990. Their overriding conclusion was that newspapers as a whole were becoming more **market-driven** and **reader-oriented**. When these researchers asked the editors and reporters who had described their newspapers as getting worse what caused the decline, 30 percent cited management as the cause, while nearly 25 percent cited cutbacks in the newsroom. Just over 20 percent cited "content" as the reason their newspaper had gotten worse.[4] Thus, the reporters and editors who work in the country's newsrooms cite management practices and declining budgets—factors increasingly controlled by corporate owners—as why their papers have declined in quality.

Underwood and Stamm also asked the reporters and editors to rank the importance of several different management policies, including regarding the reader as customer, maintaining editorial autonomy, regarding the reader as citizen, serving the community, emphasizing profit, integrating management, and management control.[5] Editors and reporters at different types of papers ranked the values differently. Staffers at family-owned papers, for example, generally ranked editorial autonomy and serving the community as significantly more important than staffers at chain newspapers. Regarding the reader as customer was ranked significantly higher at large chains, while the profit emphasis was ranked significantly higher at both small and large chains. These perceptions of staffers at different types of papers seem to confirm the expectation that chain-owned newspapers will be motivated more by profit than by other values in producing the news. They also suggest that recent concentration of ownership and the increasing number of chains have enhanced the role of profit in the newsroom.

PROFIT, ADVERTISING, AND RATINGS

As with any business, the profit that a media corporation reports is the difference between its revenue and its expenses. For the mass media, programming costs (including salary and equipment) are the primary expense, while revenue comes from the sale of advertising time or space. The critical importance of advertising in the mass media system is highlighted by Kathleen Hall Jamieson and Karlyn Kohrs Campbell's claim that "the primary function of the mass media is to attract and hold a large audience for advertisers."[6]

Although revenue is tied to audience size for all media, each medium has a different system of ratings and revenues. A second criterion also important to advertisers—the composition of the audience—influences advertising rates. Commercial television is most appealing to national advertisers seeking large and diverse mass audiences, while newspapers are more effective for local advertisers (such as retail stores and car dealers) seeking a relatively diverse audience as well. Since, on average, newspaper readers tend to have more education and income than television viewers, it is likely that the newspaper audience will, again on average, be of higher socioeconomic status and therefore represent more buying power for advertisers.

In contrast, national advertisers on commercial television can target larger, yet more specialized audiences by choosing which shows they will sponsor. Audience demographics for a police drama such as *CSI* are quite different than for a family show such as *Touched by an Angel*. For advertisers seeking very targeted, specialized audiences, television, magazines (at the national level) and radio (at the local level) are typically the preferred media.

The Ratings Game

If the goal of advertisers is to reach the largest possible proportion of the intended audience (for the least cost), how do they decide to spend their marketing dollars? For commercial television, they make such decisions primarily by relying on ratings services such as Nielsen and Arbitron, which specialize in network and local television ratings respectively.

Beginning in the 1970s, Nielsen developed monitoring devices that record whether a television set is on and if so, which program (station) it is tuned to. To develop useful data that can be generalized to a national audience, Nielsen asks a more-or-less random sample of households from across the country to participate in the study. Families are typically asked to participate for a five-year period and are also asked to keep written diaries about who is actually watching television. The idea is to account for people engaged in other activities in the same room or a television running in an empty room, details that the electronic meters cannot provide.[7] In 1987 Nielsen began using an individualized hand-held monitoring device that requires each member of the family to sign in when they begin to watch a program and sign out when they finish. This improvement was stimulated in part by the desire to sell advertisers more accurate and detailed information about television audiences.

The most commonly reported Nielsen data are estimates of **ratings** for television programs and **shares** of the television audience. A show's rating is the estimate of the number of homes in the Nielsen sample viewing a program. Since it is based on a sample of households, however, the ratings number is an estimate and should be accurate within plus or minus 3 percentage points. A program's share refers to the percentage of the households actually watching television that were tuned into that program. "By summer 1997, the audience shares of the three major networks (NBC, ABC, CBS) had fallen to 47 percent. This meant that Fox, . . . independent stations, and cable commanded 53 percent of the viewers watching in early 1997."[8]

The Nielsen and Arbitron ratings determine the amount of money that advertising on a given show will be sold for. Thus, Nielsen and Arbitron's estimates determine the network's or station's revenue flow. Programs that fail to attract a sufficiently large audience fail to attract advertising dollars and are thus eliminated from the lineup.

Newspaper advertising rates are primarily determined by circulation estimates—that is, the number of copies sold, either by subscription or as single-issue sales, on a daily basis. Because daily newspapers attract a diverse audience of generally higher socioeconomic status, little targeting is done as part of the advertising decision.

The most appealing aspect of the newspaper audience is the proportion of the population in the community that it represents. Although newspaper circulation has been declining over the past several decades, most newspapers can rely on a large amount of advertising dollars because newspaper advertising is the most efficient way to reach a broad, yet geographically concentrated, audience. In this respect, the decreasing competitiveness of the newspaper industry (associated with the increase in the percentage of one-newspaper towns) is actually a boon to advertisers, because a monopoly newspaper has exclusive access to the entire newspaper audience. Moreover, as papers receive more advertising dollars, they are able to increase the **newshole**—the space devoted to news stories. Whether the additional space is allotted to political news, of course, is a separate decision.

Profitability

Advertising revenue—not the quality or nature of the programming or substantive content—determines the financial health of newspapers and television outlets. The content is relevant only to the extent that it affects the nature and size of the audience. Despite declining circulation, newspapers remain profitable corporate investments. Bagdikian cites John Morton, an expert on newspaper economics, as concluding that the "profit level of daily newspapers is two to three times higher than average profits of the Fortune 500 top corporations"; in 1994 the average profit for publicly traded newspaper companies was 20 percent.[9]

An important question raised by these observations is whether reliance on advertising affects the nature of the news product. One suggested answer is that corporation-owned newspapers are more responsive to advertisers than family-owned newspapers because they seek to attract the size and kind of audience that advertisers will pay the most for: middle-aged, middle- to upper-middle-income readers.[10] As a result of attracting larger audiences, more newspaper pages are devoted to advertising and fewer to actual news coverage.[11] Family-owned newspapers would be less susceptible to downsizing the news because they are motivated not only by profit, but also by a sense of community responsibility.[12]

The Corporate Approach: Marketing to Reader Interest

The push for profit, according to many observers, has led to the **corporatization** of the news organization, with publishers and editors alike seeing the television news program or daily newspaper as a "product" to be marketed, rather than a social record and an information source of political importance to citizens. Accordingly, newspaper and television outlets have devoted substantial resources to learning more about the demographics, interests, values, and attitudes of their audiences (real or potential). For newspapers, much of this investment is motivated by the long-term decline in newspaper readership.

As early as the 1970s, newspaper executives began calling for the industry to "retool" and learn more about audiences in an effort to maintain circulation. The most common changes adopted by newspaper organizations in response to readership surveys have been

- Greater use of graphics
- More, and shorter, stories
- Increasing use of news summaries
- Greater emphasis on soft news about such topics as travel, entertainment, and weather

Thus, being responsive to reader interests seems to lead to less traditional, less informative, and less analytical news.

There are problems associated with basing decisions on survey data. One problem is that news organizations might use such data selectively to justify decisions made on other grounds. Also, survey responses are sensitive to which questions are asked, in what order, and how they are worded. And then there is the matter of interpretation of the survey responses:

> Surveys can be read in any number of different ways, and that is why they have done the newspaper business so little good. The surveys consistently show that people

support investigative reporting, that they want more serious foreign and national news in the newspaper. Yet readers call in most frequently when they are insulted by a columnist or when their favorite comic strip is canceled. The readers of newspapers want their newspapers to be good—to be solid and informative and interesting—whatever that may be. They look to journalists to define for them what is interesting and important.[13]

MEDIA USERS AND AUDIENCES FOR THE NEWS

To what extent do the various media outlets and programming attract large and heterogeneous audiences, as opposed to smaller, more specialized, audiences? What are the reported uses of each medium? To what extent do individuals use multiple media outlets or specialize by using only one? The answers to these questions not only provide more details about audiences but also help define the role of the media in politics and the future of the older types of media.

Audience Size and Media Reliance

Table 4-2 presents estimates of audience size for various types of media outlets based on national survey data. Individuals were asked whether they "regularly" used various media outlets or, in the case of Internet usage, ever went online. Given the comprehensive range of news outlets included in the survey, two important patterns are evident. First, despite the rapid growth in the use of the Internet and the promotion of new television formats on cable, traditional media are still used by more individuals than any newer forms. Around 40 percent report regularly reading a daily newspaper, while 32 and 57 percent, respectively, report regularly viewing network television and local television news. Radio news is regularly used by about 40 percent of the sample. In contrast, print newsmagazines are regularly used by only 13 percent of adults.

Despite the rapid growth of cable stations, their news audiences are not particularly large compared to traditional network news audiences. Only 25 percent of the sample reported using CNN regularly. In contrast, 25 percent of the sample report going online at least three times a week, and 17 percent report regularly listening to talk radio.

Second, new formats for news on the more traditional broadcast media sometimes do better and sometimes do worse in terms of audience size. Twenty-four percent of the sample reports viewing television newsmagazines regularly, only slightly fewer than the 32 percent who report viewing network news shows regularly. This suggests that the traditional evening news format, but not television itself, is declining in favor as a news outlet. Radio news, on the other hand, attracts 41 percent of the sample, compared to talk radio shows, which attract a mere 17 percent. Thus, talk radio (as well as print newsmagazines)

TABLE 4-2 Audience Sizes for Different Media Outlets

Media	Regular Users (%)
Traditional	
Daily newspaper	41
Network TV news	32
Local TV news	57
Radio news	41
Print news magazines	13
New	
Talk radio	17
CNN	25
TV news magazines	24
Online	25*

*Online news use three days per week.

Source: Pew Research Center for the People & the Press, "Public's News Habits Little Changed by September 11." Available from http://people-press.org/reports/display.php3?Page ID=616 (accessed March 18, 2003).

are likely to draw the smallest, and perhaps most unrepresentative, audiences across the media spectrum.

It is important to note that this "snapshot" of what media audiences look like has changed quite a bit over the past decade. The biggest change is the decreasing proportion of adults who report regularly watching network news: 60 percent in May 1993, compared to only 32 percent in April 2002. The sizes of newspaper and newsmagazine audiences have also declined, with the newspaper audience declining from 58 to 41 percent of the sample between May 1993 and April 2002, and the radio news audience declining from 47 percent to 41 percent over the same time period. The most dramatic change in the demographic composition of the news audiences is associated with age. In 2002, 59 percent of individuals born prior to 1932 reported reading a newspaper the previous day, compared to only 25 percent of individuals born between 1972 and 1981.[14]

One possible interpretation of these audience data suggests that, aside from the relatively stable base of traditional newspaper readers and television news viewers, individuals with less focused interest in the news now acquire political information from different media, when they are motivated to do so. People can pick and choose the news that is most convenient, use numerous media outlets, or not acquire any news at all.

Audience Interest

What do individuals pay attention to when watching or reading the news? Respondents to a 2002 Pew Center survey reported paying close attention to news about crime (30 percent), local people and events (31 percent), health (26 percent), and sports (25 percent), followed by local government, science, and religion.[15]

As shown in Table 4–3, given the small proportion of the respondents who report following politics very closely (21 percent for international affairs, 22 percent for local government, and 21 percent for politicians and events in Washington, DC), it is important to note the nature of the audience for political news. Education, income, and age are associated with interest in political news. More specifically, individuals with higher education, with greater income, and who are older are more likely to be interested in political news.[16] Thus, the medium of television attracts the largest—and hence the most diverse—audience, while political news in all media attracts a mostly upper-class, older audience. These trends suggest that television news has the greatest potential to stimulate individuals' interest in news and to reach the broadest mass audience. On the other hand, they also suggest that television is the least likely medium to offer much political content, given the relatively low level of interest in political news expressed by the mass audience.

TABLE 4-3 Audience Interest (%)

Type of News Followed "Very Closely" . . .	
Community	31
Crime	30
Health news	26
Sports	25
Local government	22
Washington news	21
International affairs	21
Religion	19
Science and technology	17
Business and finance	15
Entertainment	14
Consumer news	12
Culture and arts	9

Source: Pew Research Center for the People & the Press, "Public's News Habits Little Changed by September 11." Available from http://people-press.org/reports/display.php3?PageID=616 (accessed on March 18, 2003).

Television Viewership and Audience Overlap

An important issue relating to both the size of news audiences and the level of exposure to political news is the extent to which audiences for the news overlap or are entirely independent. The decline of newspaper readership is often attributed to a shift from reading newspapers to watching television news.[17] The decline in the television news audience is now attributed to the Internet and to specialized cable news stations. One way to assess these possibilities is to determine whether individuals use more than one source of political information. That is, are the different news outlets substitutes for or complements to one another?

In 1996, 16 percent of Pew Center survey respondents reported using radio, television, and newspapers as news sources on the previous day, while 36 percent reported using two sources, 33 percent reported using only one source, and the remaining 15 percent reported using no news sources. The use of multiple news sources declined from 1994, when 22 percent reported using three sources, for example. Every category that included television as a news source declined somewhat between 1994 and 1996, while the categories relying on newspapers or radios, while small, either stayed the same or increased slightly. Consistent with these patterns, the proportion of respondents reporting using no television source (network, local, or cable) for news the day before increased from 14 percent in 1993 to 25 percent in 1996, and the proportion reporting using all three television sources declined from 23 percent to 13 percent.

The evidence is mixed as to whether changes in Internet, television, and newspaper audience sizes result from a "substitution effect," where individuals shift from using one news source to another. The Pew Center's 1996 study noted above suggests that the decline of television viewership is slightly greater among personal computer users than among those who do not use computers. Yet in their April 2002 survey, 65 percent of individuals who reported getting news online daily reported that they continue to use traditional sources of news about the same amount. Sixteen percent of respondents reported using traditional sources less often, and 13 percent reported using traditional sources more often. These claims would seem to dispute the claim that individuals are moving from television and newspapers to the Internet as a news source.[18]

However, in a separate report from June 11, 2002, the Pew Center headline reads "Internet Sapping Broadcast News Audience." The data show two distinct lines, with the size of the broadcast news audience declining over the previous decade and the size of the Internet audience increasing. No additional evidence is offered regarding a substitution effect. Instead, the report comments that there are two notable trends associated with these changing audience sizes: individuals are paying less attention to news in general, and, when they do so, they tend to choose outlets that allow them to quickly access their interest in the news and either switch or click to another program or story when bored. Thus, the Internet might have some advantages, but the substitution effect has not been clearly demonstrated.[19]

Details regarding online news consumers also question the extent to which Internet news is displacing traditional news media. For example, most individuals who go online do so to access e-mail or access the Web—not to access news sites. And of those who do report using the Web for news, the two leading topics that are of interest are weather (70 percent of users) and science and health (60 percent). Only 50 percent of online users report seeking out news about politics online.[20]

Further, those who seek political news on the Web tend to be "political junkies" searching for information on topics not readily covered by the mainstream media. For example, of those who went online for political news during the 1996 elections, 33 percent and 24 percent, respectively, sought information on congressional and local races—elections typically receiving little or no coverage on television news. Thus, while television news may have served, or continues to serve, as a substitute for newspaper reading, the initial evidence suggests that the Internet is being used as a complement as much as it is a substitute for traditional media sources. In their study of Internet usage during the 2000 election, the Pew Center reports that 18 percent of the general public accessed campaign news online, with convenience being the reason most (56 percent) individuals cited for doing so.[21]

CORPORATE DECISION MAKING: BOARDROOM VERSUS NEWSROOM

The previous section emphasized how advertising drives the content of television programming and provides revenue for newspaper publishing, causing publishers and programmers to consider their audiences' interests as they define what news is. While the centrality of advertising in the media system is nothing new, the appeal to viewer interests is, and so is the increased corporate ownership of news organizations. This leads to another type of corporate influence over news production—the explicit adoption of newsroom policies by corporate executives. These are policies that professional journalists would be unlikely to make. They are wide-ranging, and they illustrate how corporate management can influence the news product within the context of a profit-oriented news organization.

Corporate Cost-Cutting

In the mid-1980s outside industries took over the three major broadcast networks. The new corporate managers believed that maintaining foreign bureaus was too expensive, so they closed most of them. By 1998 network coverage of foreign affairs had declined by about half.[22] Table 4-4 shows the number of domestic and foreign bureaus operated by the major networks and CNN after the networks closed many of the foreign bureaus. Network executives contended that changing expectations of the news audience led them to increase their reliance on news footage provided by CNN, which has maintained its preeminence in foreign affairs coverage.

At the same time the number of foreign bureaus was being reduced, the salaries of foreign correspondents grew dramatically. Foreign news crews are now deployed on longer trips to develop different types of stories. Not surprisingly, the number of stories on the evening news devoted to foreign affairs has declined.[23]

Other substantial newsroom budget cuts have occurred since the mid-1980s. In 1995, when the Times Mirror Corporation, which then owned the *Los Angeles Times*, hired Mark Willis as chairman, he cut more than three thousand jobs in the papers owned by Times Mirror. Similarly

> The *Winston-Salem Journal*, once regarded as one of the country's better medium-sized dailies, ordered its news staff reduced and told surviving reporters and editors that they would be "graded" on how closely they followed new orders mandating that a page-one story should be six inches or less, and that a reporter should "take 0.9 hours to do each story" and write a minimum of forty stories a week.[24]

Staff and budget cutbacks have resulted in other cost-saving measures in newsrooms. For example, news organizations are increasingly using written and video press releases as visuals for newscasts, turning promotional pieces into "news."[25]

The major substantive consequence of these reductions in staff and resources has been to accelerate a trend toward the use of **soft news**—stories that are not keyed to specific events of the day—in domestic coverage.[26] This has been the case in the network evening news, daily newspapers, and soft news shows. The box on pages 87–89, for example, contrasts the news content of the *NBC Nightly News*, the *Los Angeles Times*, and *Time* magazine on a day in 1978 and a day in 1998. In each instance, the 1998 news stories are less focused on specific events than the 1978 stories.

The trend toward soft news is also reflected in the increasing number of

TABLE 4-4 Domestic and Foreign Bureaus Operated by the Major Networks and CNN

	U.S. Bureaus	Foreign Bureaus with Correspondents	Foreign Offices with Staff
ABC	10	5	7
CBS	5	4	5
NBC and MSNBC	7	7	6
CNN	10*	23	Not Applicable
FOX NEWS	10	5	Not Applicable

*There will be 12 by the end of 1998.

Source: "Big 3 Networks Forced to Revise News-Gathering Methods," by Lawrie Mifflin. *New York Times*, October 12, 1998, p. C1.

Changes in News Content Over Time

NBC Nightly News,
Monday, April 24, 1978

Content Primarily breaking news told in a straightforward manner. With 17 segments, the program tries to be comprehensive, not interpretive. Only one segment lasts longer than two minutes.

Lead Segment The Supreme Court's refusal to hear Patricia Hearst's appeal of her bank-robbery conviction.

Second Segment The Supreme Court upholds Henry Kissinger's request that notes he donated to the National Archives not be made public for 25 years. It also rules that a girl who was sexually assaulted can sue NBC for showing a movie with a rape scene in it just before the attack.

Other Reports An update from Italy on the kidnapping of Aldo Moro, the former Italian Prime Minister, by leftist terrorists.

A report describing a prisoner swap involving the United States, Mozambique and East Germany. "It sounds like fiction, but it's fact," sums up John Chancellor, the news anchor.

From Oklahoma City, a report about angry farmers meeting to discuss how to advance their legislative agenda a week after an important farm bill was vetoed. No interviews with individual farmers.

An interview with former President Gerald R. Ford about the decision of his wife, Betty, to seek treatment for alcohol and drug dependency.

A five-minute special report on a Korean Air Lines plane that veered off course and entered Soviet airspace before being shot at and forced to land.

Finally, a human interest feature about open tryouts for cheerleaders for the Los Angeles Rams, which attracted a die-hard 58-year-old fan. It leaves Mr. Chancellor laughing as he signs off.

NBC Nightly News,
Monday, April 27, 1998

Content More interpretive. Eight reports, but more depth and more interviews with people affected by the news. More crime and more consumer issues.

Lead Segment Three minutes on a day of turmoil on Wall Street. Tom Brokaw, the program's anchor, emphasizes that what happened is important because "an estimated 45 percent" of Americans own stock.

Second Segment A constitutional challenge to the line-item veto by farmers angry over Prresident Clinton's elimination of a tax break from the budget, with an interview with a potato farmer.

Other Reports In the series "The Fleecing of America," a segment about men and women of the armed forces being hoodwinked by unscrupulous businesses.

Another special report, on the effectiveness of small-car bumpers in low-speed collisions. The program reports that Insurance Institute tests found that the new Volkswagen Beetle performed the best while the Hyundai Elantra sustained the most damage. The segment lasts four minutes.

A roundup includes reports on students mourning the death of a teacher shot by a student in Edinboro, Pa., and a news conference by two young women who were abducted by their father 18 years ago and told their mother was dead—only to find out last week the mother was still alive.

The broadcast concludes with a report on the one-year anniversary of Colin Powell's drive to increase volunteerism in America, including an interview with Mr. Powell.

(continued)

Los Angeles Times,
Tuesday, April 25, 1978

Content   News, news and news, with foreign, national and local articles all getting plenty of play on the front page. Only in its photography, where there are offbeat pictures of people at their jobs or relaxing in the sun, is the coverage anything other than direct. Sparse local coverage inside.

Front Page   The lead article is the Supreme Court's refusal to hear Patricia Hearst's appeal of her bank-robbery conviction. There is a reconstruction of the strange episode of the Korean Air Lines flight that wandered over the Soviet Union. Other articles include the conviction of a former California Congressman on bribery charges; a purge of the P.L.O. leadership by Yasir Arafat; the Italian rejection of demands by Red Brigade terrorists holding Aldo Moro hostage; and the lawsuit against NBC for showing a violent movie that the plaintiffs say inspired a sexual assault on a 9-year-old girl.

Other Sections   On the cover of the Metro section, articles on a $4 billion budget proposal for Los Angeles County and the fallout from anti-abortion comments made by a Republican candidate for governor.

One page of business news (buried in the sports section with several pages of stock quotes) and a section called View, which is a catchall collection of articles on the arts and life styles and syndicated columns.

Los Angeles Times,
Tuesday, April 28, 1998

Content   Front page mix is not a huge departure from 1978. Inside the paper, greater emphasis on local events, health, crime and the human side of the news.

Front Page   The lead article is about Iraq's increased cooperation with United Nations weapons inspectors and the possibility that sanctions may be eased. Other articles include a murder-suicide rampage, the stock market's fall and the failure of California dairy farmers to adequately clean up after cows.

Inside the front section, a page devoted to California news has articles about the death of a toddler treated by a man impersonating a doctor and about a town divided over whether to cut down its trees. On another page, an article about a successful clinical trial that injected vaccines into fruits and vegetables as a way to inoculate people instead of using needles.

Other Sections   The Metro section front has an article about a man convicted of a sex crime who still runs a school and a feature on mail carriers in South Bay who need police escorts to make their rounds because of gang intimidation.

There is now a separate business section. Among its articles: how six people who received advice on managing their money are faring and a lawsuit by a star of the television show "Melrose Place" against Internet sites running nude photos of her.

An arts and entertainment section with a lead article on two television biographies of Ronald and Nancy Reagan, one authorized, one not.

Time Magazine,
Week of May 1, 1978

Content   A generally serious tone. The cover article is a celebrity profile, but a highbrow one. Foreign affairs, national policies and the arts get most of the attention. No scandals and little consumer news or human-interest features.

Cover Article   The renaissance in American ballet, and the coming of age of Gelsey Kirkland, "the most exciting young ballerina in the Western world."

Other Articles   With President Jimmy Carter fresh off of one of his greatest triumphs—the passage of the Panama Canal treaty that returned control of the canal to Panama—Time takes three pages to assess his performance in office and concludes that he is drifting. It also looks at the political horse-trading that went into the passage of the treaty.

A five-page spread on whether Aldo Moro, the former Italian Prime Minister, is still alive and how his kidnapping is affecting Italy.

Also: reports on the peace talks in Rhodesia and the errant flight of the Korean airliner.

Four pages of business news, led by articles on the wild week for stocks and the difficulty of finding an affordable apartment.

A piece about the prospects for a long-stalled bill on natural gas and another on the rising acceptance of solar power.

An essay on whether "Holocaust," an NBC mini-series, did more harm than good in spotlighting the fate of the Jews in World War II.

Time Magazine,
Week of May 4, 1998

Content   Still devoted to serious news, but with an everyman's touch. More about sex, scandal and crime. More interviews with ordinary people and celebrities to put a human face on the news. And "news you can use" has found a home here.

Cover Article   How Viagra, a pill from Pfizer that treats impotence, is sweeping the nation. The eight-page article has news on health, advice and sex, with celebrities and regular people saying what they think about the drug.

Other Articles   A five-page spread on a Washington State teacher who had a baby by a 13-year-old male student and is now in jail.

A three-page article about the double standard for people who have sex in the military.

Two articles on President Clinton: Should Secret Service agents guarding him be compelled to testify about his alleged trysts? And, did the White House pay off Webster Hubbell, a longtime friend of the Clintons who went to jail, to keep him quiet about what he knew about Whitewater?

On business, an article about Seagram, the owner of Universal Studios, and its young leader, Edgar Bronfman Jr. Also a piece advising investors that now might be a good time to sell because of the recent rash of insider stock sales at major companies.

Paying tribute to the growing importance of personal technology, a preview of Windows 98, and Microsoft's antitrust troubles.

New and different: A half-dozen pages at the front of the magazine on everything from people in the news to ecology and technology.

Source: "Why Today's News Is No Longer What Happened Yesterday," *New York Times,* May 4, 1998, pp. C8–C9.

nontraditional newsmagazine shows now being broadcast, partly because they cost less to produce than hard news and entertainment shows. As Figure 4-1 demonstrates, ten newsmagazines were aired on network and cable television in 1998, compared with two in 1983.

Courting Advertisers

In addition to determining what resources the news organizations have to work with, corporate managers also emphasize the importance of maintaining good relationships with advertisers. For example, Times Mirror Chairman Willis encouraged reporters to spend more time socializing with the paper's advertising sales staff.[27] His pressure to blend the advertising and news functions at the *Los Angeles Times* eventually led to a special investigation of a deal made to share advertising profits associated with the paper's editorial section with an outside business. The investigation was conducted outside the "routine channels" of newsroom reporters and editors and was reported in a fourteen-page special supplement to the December 20, 1999, edition of the paper.

In a 1992 survey of newspaper editors, 93 percent reported that advertisers tried to influence their news coverage; "a majority said their own management condoned the pressure, and 37 percent of the editors polled admitted that they had succumbed."[28] Similarly, recent Nielson survey data suggest that over three-quarters of television news directors said they used corporate public relations films as part of their news broadcasts more than once a month.[29]

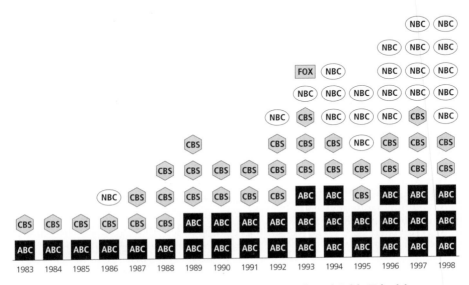

FIGURE 4-1 Trends in Newsmagazine Shows on Network and Cable Television
Source: "The Man Reshaping Primetime" by Bill Carter. *New York Times,* June 8, 1998, p. C-1.

Occasionally, more explicit pressure from advertisers—or station managers fearful of advertiser response—has been documented. For example, concerned about the possible loss of revenue from their corporate sponsors, two public broadcasting stations declined to air a documentary on advertisers' power over the media. A San Jose, California, station picked up the film, *Fear and Favor in the Newsroom*, which focused in part on an ad boycott of Knight-Ridder's *San Jose Mercury News* by automobile dealers in 1994.[30] The boycott was initiated in response to a consumer-oriented story in the business section on how to buy a car. The automobile dealers claimed they were portrayed unfairly and demanded a full-page apology that included reasons why consumers should buy cars from factory-authorized dealers. When the *Mercury News* lost $1 million in ad revenue as a result of the boycott, the paper complied, and the advertising revenue returned.

While these incidents might be exceptions in terms of the magnitude of the demands of advertisers and the responses of daily newspapers, the underlying tension over maintaining advertising revenue is very real. Doug Underwood put it in a broader context when he wrote:

> By tradition (albeit, a shaky one), daily newspapers do much of the work of extracting the information on which our Information Age depends—at least, the information that is *hard* to extract. At the same time, legions of public relations agents and corporate and government image makers are standing by eager to be the brokers of information that is *easy* to gather. Sadly, all that stands between them and the public, in many cases, are the marketing-minded editors who—working for media corporations that share many of the values of their corporate counterparts—are cheerfully participating in the corporate reshaping of the news.[31]

PROFESSIONAL INFLUENCES AND STRUCTURE

Compared to the relatively uncommon episodes of explicit advertiser threats of withdrawing advertising revenue, "implicit" corporate-ownership influences are likely to have broader, more cumulative effects on the media's coverage of politics and society. Despite this pressure, however, there have not been dramatic changes throughout the industry. Some of the most respected news outlets, as well as reporters and editors, remain dedicated to more traditional views of the nature of the news—and the proper place of corporate values. Institutional responsiveness of the media to corporate ownership has been slow in part because of the relatively stable demographic characteristics and enduring professional influences of the individuals who work within the corporate news organizations.

As noted in the introduction to this chapter, the newsgathering process is complex, involving individuals and institutions at various levels, and in different ways. No single set of individuals or institutional arrangements—such as increasing corporate ownership—fully controls the newsgathering process.

This section focuses on the demographic characteristics of journalists, as well as various professional factors that potentially influence how they do their jobs.

Demographics

The demographic characteristics of journalists may influence their choices of what stories are newsworthy and how to write about those stories. The most recent evidence suggests that journalists tend to be upper-middle class, with high levels of education and moderate income; male; white; and that they are generally reflective of the population with respect to religious affiliation.

These conclusions are based on a 1992 survey of journalists at 460 randomly chosen set of news organizations.[32] The sample is representative of radio, television, weekly and daily newspaper, wire service, and newsmagazine journalists in the United States. Eighty-two percent of the journalists were college graduates, and, not surprisingly, the most popular undergraduate major was journalism. Their median salary was $31,297, with journalists at newsmagazines generally reporting the highest salaries ($66,071) and journalists at radio stations ($20,357) and weekly newspapers the lowest ($20,865). To the extent that demographic characteristics structure a person's view of the world, we might expect journalists to reflect middle-class or upper-middle-class values.

Personal Values

Most discussions of the personal attributes of journalists do not focus on demographic characteristics that suggest a possible class bias in news coverage, but instead focus on political ideology as the major threat to journalistic objectivity and fairness in reporting: "The liberal media! There they go again!" Few presidents have considered the press allies, and Republican presidents and officials are particularly likely to blame the liberal biases of reporters for news stories they don't like. In the not-too-distant past, of course, a recurring theme of conservative radio talk show host Rush Limbaugh was bashing the liberal media for their coverage of political events and personalities.

The claim that "the media"—referring only to journalists, not to media owners—are liberal is basically true, as indicated by various surveys of journalists. In one study, 30 percent of journalists described themselves ideologically as "middle of the road," while about 46 percent reported leaning either "a little to the left" or "pretty far to the left." Only 23 percent placed themselves to the right of the ideological spectrum.[33] In contrast, the figures for the U.S. population in general are 41 percent middle of the road, 34 percent leaning to the right, and only 18 percent leaning to the left. Compared to the U.S. population, journalists are more likely to be liberal.

The left-leaning tendency is not distributed equally among all journalists.

Those at prominent news organizations were much more likely to be liberal than were those at nonprominent news organizations. In fact, journalists at nonprominent news organizations were more likely to lean toward the right.[34] This suggests that liberal leaning journalists are likely to be in news organizations that get more exposure, although their actual numbers may be smaller.

Consistent with their self-reported ideology, journalists were much more likely to identify with the Democratic Party (44.1 percent) than with the Republican Party (16.4 percent), and a large proportion (34.4 percent) identified as independents.[35] By comparison, in 1992 the general public divided almost equally across the three partisan categories: 34 percent Democratic, 33 percent Republican, and 31 percent independent.

Professional Values: The Role of the Media

At least as important as journalists' perspectives on the political world are their views about the proper professional roles of journalists and media organizations. When asked how important various media roles were, journalists perceived two roles to be extremely important: getting information to the public quickly (69 percent) and investigating government claims (67 percent).[36] Technological changes such as satellites, cellular phones, and faxes make the competition to be first in reporting the news particularly intense.

The journalists ranked avoiding stories with unverified content, providing analysis of complex problems, and letting people express views next in importance, but they were ranked as extremely important by only 49 percent, 48 percent, and 48 percent of journalists, respectively. The only other role that over 25 percent of journalists ranked as "extremely important" was discussing national policy. Their least valued roles were concentrating on the widest audience (20 percent), developing intellectual/cultural interests (18 percent), providing entertainment (14 percent), serving as an adversary of government (21 percent) or business (14 percent), and setting the political agenda (5 percent).

When asked what factors influenced their sense of newsworthiness, the most commonly cited factors were their journalistic training (73 percent) and supervisors (51 percent). Other influences included sources (40 percent), staff peers (41 percent), readership/audience research (35 percent), and network news and prestige papers (27 percent).[37]

Rather than relying solely on journalists' self-reported perceptions, the investigators asked survey respondents to send in samples of their best work, which they systematically coded. The stories tended to be about personalities and celebrities, social problems, and general human interest features. In the early 1980s, stories about crime and local government had been most common.[38] When the stories were coded for the values they reflected, the findings were consistent with Gans' earlier work (see Chapter 3) as well as with a 1990 study of British, French, and U.S. journalists.[39] Of the stories,

- 35 percent reflected impact
- 24 percent, conflict
- 13 percent, timeliness
- 10 percent, proximity
- 8 percent, unusualness
- 8 percent, prominence[40]

Finally, journalists' best work also seemed to be somewhat shorter than in the previous decade, possibly reflecting newspapers' eagerness to emulate the shorter, livelier format of television.

Professional Values: Objectivity

Many criticisms of the press center on the media's lack of objectivity, most commonly claiming that objectivity is sacrificed to the ideological biases of journalists. In this respect, objectivity is a highly valued journalistic practice, and deviations from it are viewed as compromising the role of the media in our democratic political system.

Although the common definition of **objectivity** has to do with presenting "only facts" and not inserting political beliefs into the content of a news story, journalists define it slightly differently. Communications scholar John Soloski views objectivity as the practice of seeking facts "from all 'legitimate' sides of an issue, and then . . . report[ing] the facts in an impartial and balanced way."[41]

Not all scholars view objectivity as a positive journalism norm. According to W. Lance Bennett, the norm of objectivity was a response to newspapers' competition for increasingly large audiences in the late 1800s and early 1900s.[42] Because such audiences were politically diverse, newspapers wanted to avoid overtly political (Republican or Democratic) slants. Reporters writing for these papers or for the newly developed wire services, which provided much of the news to competing papers, could no longer use a "partisan" framework to develop stories. As a consequence, journalists adopted objectivity as a professional norm to secure larger audiences, and therefore larger profits, for their newspapers.

Rather than "saving" the news from being biased, according to Bennett, the objectivity norm actually introduces bias to news coverage in two ways.[43] First, objective journalistic practices result in heavy reliance on government institutions and officials for information about and interpretation of political events. This reliance produces a news product that is "narrow" and favors "official" perspectives. That is, government officials are the basis for most stories, which necessarily provides them an advantage in news coverage.

Second, the use of objective practices suggests that "the news" is the best possible news product. What could be better than a news story that presents both sides of the story? When both sides are presented, the reader assumes that the reporter did his or her best in developing the story, and it must be good.

Bennett's argument is a good reminder that the news can be biased in any number of ways. While the most commonly noted bias is partisan, the more fundamental bias, according to Bennett, is that in favor of government officials.

ORGANIZATIONAL CONSTRAINTS

Were journalists able to choose the events they wanted to cover and write about them any way they preferred, we would easily be able to confirm that their personal and professional values influence what becomes news. But it doesn't work that way. Like other big businesses, the news media are highly complex bureaucratic organizations, and the news delivered on the evening television broadcast or the front page of the morning paper reflects several organizational constraints on reporters' values and beliefs.

Managerial Strategies for Marketing the News

With newspapers facing declining readership over the past several decades and the major networks seeing their prime-time audiences slowly eroding, it is perhaps not surprising that during the 1980s both electronic and print media began developing new strategies to market the news. Before then, the concept that news was a product to be marketed was in many respects unheard of. But with new corporate ownership stressing the importance of profit, media corporations turned not to media professionals but rather to marketing professionals to plot a strategy for maintaining audience share.

As a consequence, the marketing and consumer research departments of news organizations increased in size during the 1980s. Editors and reporters—media professionals—were encouraged by upper management to learn from their advertising and marketing colleagues, whose departments previously had been assumed to engage in completely separate and legitimate missions of their own. One of the consequences of the melding of marketing and newsgathering is that journalists' personal influence on news content is reduced, which results in more homogeneous news content across media organizations.[44]

In addition, new (and with some resistance, many "old") media executives reconceptualized the role of the audience (the consumer) in the newsgathering process. Most newspapers became more "reader-friendly" at different stages of the newsgathering process by

- Assessing the needs of the news audience by using more market research
- Publishing more articles that are helpful to readers
- Adding more personal touches to articles
- Writing articles in such a way that they can be read quickly
- Increasing news content that is relevant to readers residing in the suburbs

- Using more graphics and pictures with articles
- Publishing more "good" news

A third, and completely different, type of managerial influence on the news is the organization of individual journalists so that deadlines for the daily newspaper or newscast can be met. That is, a story written by a journalist might require the work of a photographer and a graphic designer, who must typically cooperate to produce a story that is the approximate size (or length) that the news editor (or newscast producer) planned earlier in the day, in conjunction with planning dozens of other stories of predictable length and character. While newsroom coordination has long been a hallmark of the newsgathering process, especially for television, which relies on the filming of live events as a fundamental feature of the news show, marketing strategies have actually made planning and coordination all the more important. This planning process has substantive consequences for the news. Stories must be predictable, arrive on time, and "fit the preconceptions that have already been discussed in editorial meetings."[45]

Finally, journalists' career paths systematically weed out those who act independently of their corporate managers.[46] This weeding out occurs at several key points. First, most individuals are trained in journalism schools, which often socialize future journalists to adopt the new managerial values. Second, only individuals who appear to be sympathetic to corporate goals are hired into reporting positions. Third, journalists are further socialized into the corporate perspective on the job as they learn what they must do to get the best assignments, receive raises, and eventually be promoted. "A few independent thinkers survive, tolerated as illustrations of the 'true independence' of the media. Others give up the battle."[47]

News Routines, Deadlines, and Beats

Newspapers are delivered about the same time every morning, and the evening network news comes on promptly at thirty minutes past the hour, regardless of what there is to report, or when it occurred, or how important it is. Editors start their workdays knowing that, whatever happens in the world, the nation, or their city, a certain number of column-inches of text must be written by a deadline. The challenge is how to come up with a news product on a regular basis despite the fact that newsworthy events and issues occur only sporadically.

News organizations respond to such uncertainty by looking for news in "predictable" places, or at least in places that systematically provide news material.[48] Thus, newspapers and television news programs are organized by **beats,** in which reporters are assigned a set of (usually related) offices, topics, or contacts to monitor for newsworthy happenings, such as the White House, the Pentagon, city hall, or the city jail and courts. This "implicitly adjusts" the definition of news, "so that things that are known to happen on a regular basis become news."[49] It also provides incentives to established political and social organizations to provide a steady stream of information to reporters, in the hope that some of it will surface as free publicity. In this respect, the use of beats advantages groups and interests that are well-organized, and may thus legitimize those in power.

The organization of news staffs has additional consequences for the news organization. Assigning reporters to independent beats sets up potential turf wars between them.[50] Each beat typically has a steady stream of news, and it is up to each reporter to place as many stories as possible, largely based on arguments about newsworthiness or other journalistic norms. A common response to managing such conflict between beats (for example, between the city desk and the state desk or the domestic and the international desks) is to divide up the newshole.[51] Editors at the *New York Times* apportion space equally to different desks, partly to eliminate ongoing negotiations with reporters about the number or length of stories they might publish, thus determining newsworthiness before actual news occurrences.[52]

Planning for the day's news coverage typically begins with morning staff meetings at which each reporter or editor, depending on the size of the paper, discusses the events or issues (both new and ongoing) that are on the agenda. Because reporters and editors know they must file their stories by a certain time, it is common for these "discuss lists" to include a high proportion of "planned events" that the newspaper has been informed of prior to their occurrence. Scheduled events like meetings of Congress and the local school board provide solid potential stories for reporters, as do news conferences, which are planned for the explicit purpose of eliciting media coverage. An event that is staged solely to generate media coverage is referred to as a **pseudo-event**.

Another important implication of the reliance on news beats is that they change the nature of the newsgathering process by requiring news reporters to maintain regular contact with officials who might provide news. The result of these routine interactions is often the development of enhanced professional respect, or at least familiarity, and possibly the establishment of more personal relationships. The reporter may sympathize with government officials who have to deal with difficult situations, and this might change his or her approach to news from that beat. Reporters who cover government beats positively might be treated as insiders or be given better access and off-the-record information. Not surprisingly, the news coverage that follows may favor the interests of the officials.

Investigative Reporting

An alternative approach to making news more predictable is the use of **investigative reporting**. This type of reporting blends nicely with the adversarial and public advocacy models of the press, in that it requires reporters to rely primarily on their investigative skills to develop stories about government and politics. It contrasts dramatically with the use of the beat system, relying as little as possible on routine sources and ongoing contacts. Its origins might be the "muckraking" journalism of the Progressive Era. Investigative journalism gained new respect in the late 1970s as a consequence of revelations by two *Washington Post* reporters, Carl Bernstein and Bob Woodward, about the involvement of Richard Nixon's political operatives in a burglary of Democratic headquarters (see Chapter 3).

Investigative reporting is used less often now, partly because of the public's increasingly negative perception of news reporters, and partly because of the concern that reporters were "creating" rather than just reporting the news when they chose events or individuals to investigate. Reporters were accused of becoming political actors with their own agendas and of using their professional roles to forward such agendas.

In its place, a new type of investigative reporting has emerged, in which reporters use information leaked from ongoing governmental investigations rather than identifying their own subjects for investigation. For example, the political scandals of the Reagan administration were uncovered by government investigators rather than by newspaper or television reporters.[53] Likewise, most of the coverage of the scandal concerning Monica Lewinsky's affair with Bill Clinton (see Chapter 1) used information derived from the independent prosecutor's office, sources in the White House, or other sources involved with the investigation. One of the concerns about this shift in investigative reporting is that, when official sources (whether identified or anonymous) provide information for their stories, reporters may become the tool of government rather than a watchdog over it.[54]

The high costs associated with investigative journalism may be another reason it appears less frequently on daily news programs.[55] On the other hand, the success of investigative reporting in attracting an audience has not been lost on news corporations. The 1990s witnessed an explosion of news shows using the *60 Minutes* format. These programs reach a wider audience in prime time (and thus garner higher advertising dollars) than they would on traditional evening newscasts. At the same time, they are less expensive to produce than typical drama or comedy entertainment shows.

ON THE MEDIA BUSINESS AND MODELS OF THE PRESS

Much of the evidence presented in this chapter is consistent, at a minimum, with the profit-seeker model and, at most, with the propagandist model. As discussed in Chapter 1, the propagandist model consisted of five news filters: the size, concentrated ownership, owner wealth, and profit orientation of the dominant mass media firms; advertising as the primary income source of the mass media; the reliance of the media on information provided by government, business, and experts funded and approved by these primary sources and agents of power; flak as a means of disciplining the media; and anticommunism as a national religion and control mechanism. We have reviewed evidence consistent with each of the first four filters, and their influence seems to have strengthened since 1980.

Just as striking, however, is the enduring importance of journalists' professional values in the news process. To the extent that news production is dependent on reporters, these values likely provide at least some resistance to the news filters. Aspiring reporters will seek to satisfy their editors and publishers, and they may anticipate what is acceptable to write and how it should be written. But the essential nature of the news will nonetheless continue to be defined in part by journalism professionals, and this is of critical importance.

Moreover, a second point of resistance to the propagandist and profit-seeker models are the personal values of reporters, routinely identified as being more liberal than those of the U.S. public in general. Given the array of evidence regarding overwhelming corporate influences on the news today, these personal values may provide some balance. In this sense, critics concerned about the extent to which the news is profit- or propaganda-driven might take heart from knowing that journalists' personal beliefs may compel them to challenge corporate influences on their professional contributions.

Although this argument seems to weaken evidence for the profit-seeker and propagandist models, it does not necessarily strengthen the neutral adversary or public advocacy models. It is difficult to imagine that professional and personal values can completely overcome the organizational (financial) constraints faced by reporters seeking to play a neutral adversary role. Reporters and news organizations depend on government institutions for relatively cost-free information, so playing a neutral adversary role could be costly. News organizations are not likely to put extra resources into reporting when stories are available for free. Hence, the neutral adversary model does not fare well against the business aspects of the newsgathering process.

It is perhaps more likely that reporters' values could overcome the business constraints on newsgathering in a manner consistent with the public advocacy model. Reporters could continue to rely on government officials for information but also actively solicit citizens as news sources. Moreover, reporters could ask government officials and citizens different sets of questions, thus developing different perspectives on the news.

To be consistent with the evidence in this chapter, the public advocacy approach would have to attract a larger news audience. To the extent that the private sector and those in public power refrain from trying to manage the news product, news corporations might see an increase in profits if they provided a different type of news product. But it would be risky. Critics already point to the influence of reporters' political values on the news product. The media would risk losing their legitimacy among liberals and conservatives (and progressives and libertarians and . . .) if their news were viewed as defined solely by journalists' personal values.

CONCLUSION

The main goal of this chapter was to describe how economic constraints, the personal and political values of journalists, and organizational routines influence the newsgathering process. Although the evidence regarding economic influences on the news is overwhelming, it must be considered in light of the professionalism of journalists and the centrality of their judgments in the newsgathering process.

The findings, however, do not bode well for the ability of the media to perform a linkage function between citizens and government. One of the major trends of the past two decades has been the reduction of resources to newsrooms, and the decline of reporting hard events. Without the latter, it may be impossible for a citizen to judge his or her own interests, or to evaluate government officials accordingly. The use of soft news stories places the responsibility of evaluating the self-interest of citizens in the hands of journalists. Yet the corporate push to reduce the expenses associated with newsgathering suggests that the information provided in the mass media is likely to be that which is easiest to gather, which also tends to be that provided by government officials themselves. More details on that appear in Chapter 5, where we consider how reporters do their work and what type of news they produce as they cover the institutions of government.

Key Terms

beats	cross-media ownership	pseudo-event
competitive news	investigative reporting	ratings
markets	market-driven	reader-oriented
concentration of	news monopolies	shares
ownership	newshole	soft news
corporatization	objectivity	

Exercises

1. Investigate the ownership of the local news media in your community or in selected communities across the state. To whom does the local newspaper or television outlet report? What is the nature of the relationship in terms of shared news, editorial content, and profits?

2. Conduct an informal survey of three to five acquaintances, focusing on what interests them in the news and what news outlets they use. (Consider specific questions about their news interests carefully.) Do these responses match those discussed in the chapter?
3. What news outlets and programs did you consult yesterday? What were the topics? Call or e-mail your parents, and ask them the same questions. Are your reasons for using the news outlets similar to their reasons?
4. Write a commentary on a news program that you watch. Identify the biased nature of the news reports.

Notes

1. Ben H. Bagdikian, *The Media Monopoly*, 5th ed. (Boston: Beacon Press, 1997), p. x.
2. Ben H. Bagdikian, *The Media Monopoly*, 6th ed. (Boston: Beacon Press, 2000), p. xix.
3. Bagdikian, *The Media Monopoly*, 5th ed., p. xix.
4. Doug Underwood, *When MBAs Rule the Newsroom: How the Marketers and Managers Are Reshaping Today's Media* (New York: Columbia University Press, 1993), p. 190.
5. Ibid., p. 194.
6. Kathleen Hall Jamieson and Karlyn Kohrs Campbell, *The Interplay of Influence: News, Advertising, Politics and the Mass Media*, 5th ed. (Belmont, CA: Wadsworth, 2001), p. 156; italics in original.
7. Ibid., p. 164.
8. Ibid., p. 167.
9. Bagdikian, *The Media Monopoly*, 5th ed., p. xxii.
10. Richard Davis and Diana Owen, *New Media and American Politics* (New York: Oxford University Press, 1998), p. 35.
11. See also Philip Gaunt, *Choosing the News: The Profit Factor in News Selection* (New York: Greenwood Press, 1990).
12. Davis and Owen, *New Media and American Politics*.
13. Underwood, *When MBAs Rule the Newsroom*, p. 176.
14. Pew Research Center for the People & the Press, "Public's News Habits Little Changed by September 11." Available from http://people-press.org/reports/display.php3?PageID=616 (accessed March 18, 2003).
15. Ibid.
16. Staci Rhine, Stephen Bennett, and Richard Flickinger, "Americans' Exposure and Attention to Electronic and Print Media and Their Impact on Democratic Citizenship." Paper presented at the meeting of the Midwest Political Science Association, April 23–25, 1998, Chicago, IL.
17. See Leo Bogart, "The State of the Industry" in Philip S. Cook, Douglas Gomery, and Lawrence W. Lichty, eds., *The Future of News: Television-Newspapers-Wire Services-Newsmagazines* (Washington, DC: The Woodrow Wilson Center Press, and Baltimore: The Johns Hopkins University Press, 1992), pp. 85–103.

18. Pew Research Center for the People & the Press, "Public's News Habits Little Changed by September 11." Available from http://people-press.org/reports/display.php3?PageID=614 (accessed March 18, 2003).

19. Pew Research Center for the People & the Press, "Internet Sapping Broadcast News Audience." Available from http://people-press.org/reports/display.php3?PageID=36 (accessed March 18, 2003).

20. Pew Research Center for the People & the Press, "Public's News Habits Little Changed by September 11." Available from http://people-press.org/reports/display.php3?PageID=614 (accessed March 18, 2003).

21. Pew Research Center for the People & the Press, "Internet Election News Audience Seeks Convenience, Familiar Names," released December 3, 2000. Available from http://people-press.org/reports/display.php3?ReportID=21 (accessed March 18, 2003).

22. Bagdikian, *The Media Monopoly*, 5th ed., p. xxii, and Bagdikian, *The Media Monopoly*, 6th ed., p. xxx.

23. "Big 3 Networks Forced to Revise News-Gathering Methods," *New York Times*, October 12, 1998, pp. C1, C6.

24. Bagdikian, *The Media Monopoly*, 5th ed., pp. xxii–xxiii.

25. Underwood, *When MBAs Rule the Newsroom*, p. 140.

26. "Big 3 Networks," *New York Times*.

27. Bagdikian, *The Media Monopoly*, 5th ed., pp. xxii–xxiii.

28. Ibid., p. xx.

29. Ibid.

30. Oscar W. Alexander, *Media in the 20th Century* (San Mateo, CA: Bluewood Books, 1997), p. 181.

31. Underwood, *When MBAs Rule the Newsroom*, pp. 146–147.

32. David Weaver and G. Cleveland Wilhoit, *The American Journalist in the 1990s* (Mahwah, NJ: Lawrence Erlbaum Associates, 1996).

33. Ibid., p. 15.

34. Ibid.

35. Weaver and Wilhoit, *The American Journalist*, p. 18.

36. Ibid., p. 135.

37. Ibid., pp. 149–151.

38. Ibid., p. 217.

39. Gaunt, *Choosing the News*, p. 111.

40. Weaver and Wilhoit, *The American Journalist*, p. 225.

41. John Soloski, "News Reporting and Professionalism: Some Constraints on the Reporting of the News," in Dan Berkowitz, *Social Meanings of News: A Text-Reader* (Thousand Oaks, CA: Sage Publications, 1997), chap. 11. Originally published in *Media, Culture and Society* 11: 207–228.

42. W. Lance Bennett, *News: The Politics of Illusion*, 4th ed. (New York: Longman, 2001).

43. Ibid., pp. 184–185.

44. Gaunt, *Choosing the News*, p. 132.

45. Underwood, *When MBAs Rule the Newsroom*, p. 163.

46. J. Herbert Altschull, "Boundaries of Journalistic Autonomy," in Dan Berkowitz, *Social Meanings of News: A Text-Reader* (Thousand Oaks, CA: Sage Publications, 1997), Chap. 17. Originally published in *Agents of Power*, 2nd ed. (New York: Longman, 1995).

47. Ibid.

48. W. Lance Bennett, *News: The Politics of Illusion*, 5th ed. (New York: Longman, 2003), p. 173.

49. Ibid.

50. Gaye Tuchman, *Making News: A Study in Construction of Reality* (New York: The Free Press, 1978).

51. Leon V. Sigal, *Reporters and Officials: The Organization of Politics in Newsmaking* (Lexington, MA: D.C. Heath, 1973).

52. James S. Ettema and D. Charles Whitney, with Daniel B. Wackman, "Professional Mass Communications," in Dan Berkowitz, *Social Meanings of News: A Text-Reader* (Thousand Oaks, CA: Sage Publications, 1997), pp. 31–50.

53. Underwood, *When MBAs Rule the Newsroom*, p. 52.

54. Bill Kovach and Tom Rosenstiel, "Are Watchdogs an Endangered Species?" *Columbia Journalism Review*, May/June 2001. Available from http://www.cjr.org/year/01/3/rosenstiel.asp (accessed July 14, 2002).

55. Davis and Owen, *New Media and American Politics*, p. 36.

5 ▷ Political Institutions and the Mass Media

The Institutional Basis of Newsgathering
Accommodating the Media • Using the Media to Govern

The Presidency
What the White House Does • White House Press Coverage

Congress
What Members of Congress Do • Who Gets Covered • What Gets Covered

Federal Courts
Supreme Court and Courts of Appeal • Trial Courts

The View from Entertainment Land

Institutional Agenda-Setting
How and When Do Institutions Respond? • Responses to Crises • Responses to Exposés

On the Media as a Linkage Institution

On Models of the Press

Conclusion

ONE OF THE worst-kept national security secrets of 2002 was the Bush administration's interest in removing Iraqi ruler Saddam Hussein from power, whether through military force or some other means. "High-ranking sources" within the White House, State Department, and Pentagon were tipping off reporters about Bush's intentions. With the possibility of U.S. military attack becoming public knowledge, Hussein engaged in the theatrics, promising to bring down anyone who attacked Iraq. Administration leaks might have raised the stakes of Bush's preferred response to Hussein's continued development of proscribed weapons and his support of terrorism. Or did they instead provide Bush with a better read on public support for a military strike—or even possibly start to persuade the public that attacking was a viable, and perhaps preferred, policy option?

Whether through leaks or routine press releases, government officials are reporters' primary sources for reporting political news.[1] An analysis of the *New York Times, Washington Post,* and *Chicago Tribune,* for example, shows that government officials are the primary sources of more than half of all front-page news stories.[2] If this is the case, why are politicians so critical of the news produced by the mass media?

The previous chapters suggest some possible explanations. As noted, journalists cannot report on all issues that government officials want covered. In acting as gatekeepers, reporters' professional values of timeliness, drama, and audience interest mean that some topics receive more coverage than others, despite their objective importance or value to politicians. Moreover, the increasing economic pressures resulting from industry consolidation and a shrinking news audience suggest that journalists are now more likely to impose their professional values in choosing which news topics to report and how to report them than they were in decades past.

At the same time that reporters' gatekeeping roles have become more important, government officials and institutions have become increasingly convinced that the media play pivotal roles in the electoral success of elected government officials, the operations of government institutions, and the policies produced by these institutions. The more that government officials view the press as central to their goals, the greater the criticism of the job that the press does.

This chapter considers the nature of news coverage of the major institutions of governance in the United States, emphasizing not the adversarial relationship portrayed in popular accounts, but rather the accommodating relationships that have developed between reporters and government officials. Of critical importance is understanding how most political institutions have been redesigned to cater to the needs of reporters in an effort to garner media attention, and that these institutional changes reflect the extent to which officials believe that the press is critical to achieving their political goals.

Examining the nature of coverage of various political institutions—and the relationships between reporters and politicians within them—allows us to also consider the five models of the press introduced in Chapter 1. Chapters 2, 3, and 4 demonstrated broad support for the profit-seeker model and provided modest support for the neutral adversary, public advocacy, and propagandist models. To further identify the relative strengths and weaknesses of these models, this chapter examines the newsgathering process within the context of three major institutions of national government: the presidency, Congress, and the federal courts.

The extent to which these three institutions seek to secure media coverage varies in theoretically important ways. This variation helps us determine whether elites in political institutions control what news is, or if instead reporters independently ascertain what is newsworthy about the institutions. To the extent that elites control what (and how much) becomes news, the case for the propagandist model is strengthened relative to the profit-seeker model. Further, how elites and reporters interact in producing institutional news also reflects on the neutral adversary and public advocacy models, both of which require initiative on the part of reporters in identifying newsworthy topics.

Examining media coverage of the major institutions of government also allows us to assess how well the mass media perform as a linkage institution in our democratic society. As first noted in Chapter 1, representative democracies rely on linkage institutions to convey the preferences of citizens to government officials, as well as to provide information about the actions of government officials to citizens. The level, nature, and quality of the information provided to citizens and officials are key to understanding how effectively the mass media perform as a linkage institution. If the media provide limited information about the preferences of citizens or if that information is inaccurate, they are failing to channel citizens' opinions into the democratic process. On the other hand, if the media provide little information on the actions of government officials, citizens would be unable to exert any control over the officials.

Beyond the level of information available to citizens is the question of whether the information enhances or detracts from citizens' abilities to evaluate government officials. If the media provide only negative or only positive information, for example, citizens are not necessarily better equipped to assess whether policies are consistent with their preferences. Instead, the media are enhancing the ability of government officials to manipulate the public (in the case of only positive coverage) or may be demobilizing citizens from taking an active role in democratic politics (in the case of only negative coverage).

THE INSTITUTIONAL BASIS OF NEWSGATHERING

As early as 1920 renowned journalist and intellectual Walter Lippman wrote that the press usually reported "only what has been recorded for it by the working of institutions." "At its best," Lippman wrote, "the press is a servant and guardian of institutions; at its worst it is a means by which a few exploit social disorganization to their own ends. . . . It is like the beam of a searchlight that moves restlessly about, bringing one episode and then another out of darkness into vision."[3] Although Lippman's servant image differs dramatically from more contemporary views (which see the press as either watching government officials or operating independently according to its own political agenda), it is entirely consistent with institutional changes since the 1920s.

Institutions have been redesigned to cater to the needs of the press because government officials need press coverage to be successful, and reporters need information from government officials for their stories. This information exchange is thus necessary, but not particularly smooth, since politicians and reporters have different goals. To sustain the relationship, most political institutions must meet some basic needs of reporters as they go about doing their jobs.

Accommodating the Media

At the broadest level, government officials accommodate the media by providing a steady stream of news, which reporters need to meet their daily (or more frequent) story deadlines. Moreover, reporters' jobs are all the easier when government officials incorporate journalists' own news values. Focusing on events, for example, and providing stories in a timely and interesting fashion makes the reporter's job of developing a story (or selling it to his or her editor) even less demanding. Likewise, focusing on conflict, the unexpected, or the unusual makes for better stories, as does providing appropriately dramatic or exciting visuals.[4]

Three common institutional structures that have evolved to provide this service are press briefings and press conferences, public relations officers and offices, and production facilities and technical support. All of them represent substantial budgetary commitments by the institutions of governance in their efforts to achieve good press.

Members of Congress and presidents have responded to changes in politics and the media by adding staff whose primary responsibility is providing information to the media. Press officers are visible and important staff members of Congress, the Executive Office of the President, and the executive branch agencies. The most visible is the **White House press secretary**, who provides daily news briefings to the White House press corps (reporters assigned to the White House beat on a daily basis). The importance of the press office to the White House is underscored by the number of staff members assigned to various press functions, as shown in Figure 5-1 for the Clinton administration.

The **Office of Communications**, which has existed since the Nixon administration, focuses on managing **public relations** for the presidency. During Ronald Reagan's administration, this office introduced and became known for seemingly flawless control of the "message of the day." Once the president and his staff decided on the issue or image that was to dominate news coverage, the Office of Communications was responsible for making sure that the chosen

Ari Fleisher, former press secretary for President George W. Bush. © *AFP/CORBIS*.

message—and no other—emanated from executive branch offices and agencies. Since Reagan's administration, in consultation with the president, the office determines the messages that the administration needs to convey to gain and retain the approval of important public and private constituencies and to win support for desired policies. In this sense, the Office of Communications is less concerned with the "daily feeding" of the national press corps and more concerned with developing and implementing a broader communications strategy, which might have weekly goals and almost always involves courting the media outside of Washington. The office also coordinates the public relations activities of executive branch departments and agencies.

To secure positive **public images,** Congress makes broadcast recording facilities and technical support available to members for a small fee. Senators and representatives use these studios to produce videotapes that they send to local stations in their home districts or states.[5] The tapes range from brief segments that are issued to local news outlets as video news releases to regular broadcast programs that are used on local public affairs channels.

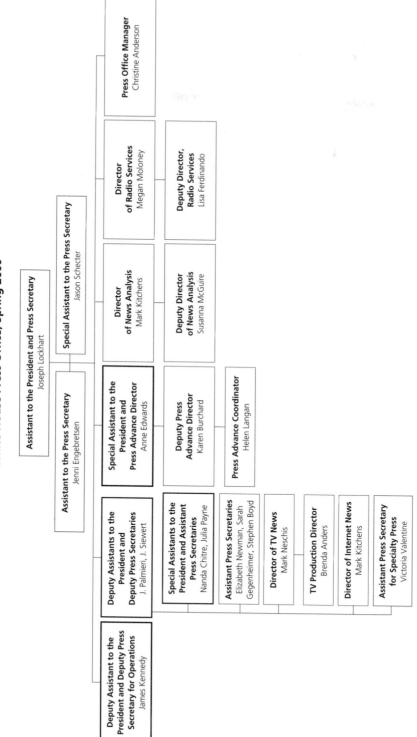

President William Clinton
White House Press Office, Spring 2000

Assistant to the President and Press Secretary
Joseph Lockhart

Special Assistant to the Press Secretary
Jason Schecter

Assistant to the Press Secretary
Jenni Engebretsen

Deputy Assistant to the President and Deputy Press Secretary for Operations
James Kennedy

Deputy Assistants to the President and Deputy Press Secretaries
J. Palmieri, J. Siewert

Special Assistant to the President and Press Advance Director
Anne Edwards

Director of News Analysis
Mark Kitchens

Director of Radio Services
Megan Moloney

Press Office Manager
Christine Anderson

Deputy Director of News Analysis
Susanna McGuire

Deputy Director, Radio Services
Lisa Ferdinando

Special Assistants to the President and Assistant Press Secretaries
Nanda Chitre, Julia Payne

Deputy Press Advance Director
Karen Burchard

Press Advance Coordinator
Helen Langan

Assistant Press Secretaries
Elizabeth Newman, Sarah Gegenheimer, Stephen Boyd

Director of TV News
Mark Neschis

TV Production Director
Brenda Anders

Director of Internet News
Mark Kitchens

Assistant Press Secretary for Specialty Press
Victoria Valentine

FIGURE 5-1 Clinton Press Office Organizational Chart

Source: White House Interview Program, whitehouse2001.org. Based on data in *The Capital Source,* Spring, 2000, National Journal Group Inc., Washington, DC.

Since newsrooms are facing shrinking budgets, these videotapes are useful, no-cost news material. Typically they provide positive media images. To the extent they are not tied to specific events, they do not need to be aired immediately. Thus, news organizations can air this packaged news when they need stories.

Using the Media to Govern

While these institutional accommodations suggest that government officials are willing to supply reporters with a steady stream of news, they do not tell the whole story. In an effort to achieve their political goals—whether to maintain a positive image among constituents, increase public support for their legislative strategies, or simply influence the public's agenda—officials are clearly choosing what type of information to provide in what format at particular times.

Government officials control the press by providing **selective access** to reporters. Similar to how reporters act as gatekeepers, sifting through a tremendous amount of "raw news" happily supplied by government officials, the government officials typically provide certain types of information in certain ways to certain reporters. Government officials rarely provide unlimited information about all issues. They are instead selective in what their press efforts deliver to reporters as news.

In light of the role that government officials play in supplying the news, Bennett has identified three types of news: fully controlled news, partially controlled news, and uncontrolled news.[6] Government officials prefer **fully controlled news,** where they are able to create events to convey politically powerful images through the media. Much fully controlled news consists of events that are planned by government officials with the express purpose of garnering media attention and providing a particular meaning to or interpretation of political reality that is to their political advantage. George W. Bush's visit to a successful charter school, for example, expresses his support for the concept of charter schools. It also conveys that primary education is an important policy priority. Yet visits like this—which were also commonly used by most presidents before Bush—are carefully scripted. A particular school was chosen that had a particular racial and class composition; the president interacted in a certain way with the students and, finally, made a speech about the administration's educational policy. Of course, if the visit had not been planned, there would have been no story on Bush's education policy that day.

The problem with **pseudo-events**, as such staged happenings are called, is that reporters are obliged to report the basics and often have little freedom to explain the strategy and meaning behind them.[7] It is news because it is an event, but its meaning is usually concealed. The press has reacted to the common use of pseudo-events by being more selective in their coverage and by accompanying stories about them with additional commentary. Nonetheless, pseudo-events typically result in highly visible and positive press coverage for presidential administrations.

In **partially controlled news** events, government officials are not completely in control of the situation and are not assured of positive coverage. The questions at press conferences, for example, are fairly predictable, but a reporter could ask an unanticipated question, or the government official could have a difficult time addressing a relatively simple question. In **uncontrolled news** situations, government officials seemingly have no control over the development and coverage of a political issue. Alternative news sources are available to the media, and the official who is making the "authoritative" statement is one voice among many. The challenge to government officials is to engage in news management techniques so as to recover their ability to define the issue and control its presentation.[8]

A notable trend associated with **presidential press conferences** is the existence of an inverse relationship between the size of the Washington press corps and the number of press conferences, which has been documented from the Roosevelt through the Reagan administrations (see Figure 5-2).[9] Paradoxically, as the demand for presidential news coverage has increased, the supply, as determined by the press office, has not responded. In general, the same has been true of prime-time television appearances by presidents, with Bill Clinton making fewer such appearances than any other presidents of the television era.[10]

The decrease in the number of prime-time television appearances likely reflects strategic calculations by the networks as well as by the press office. Be-

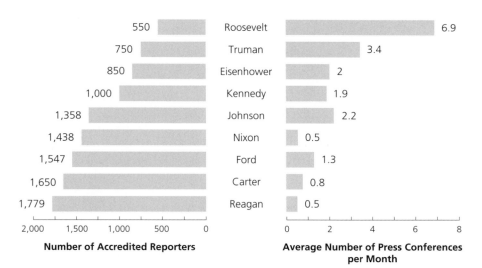

Number of Accredited Reporters — **Average Number of Press Conferences per Month**

FIGURE 5-2 National Press Corps Size and Number of Presidential Press Conferences
Source: Fredric T. Smoller, *The Six O'Clock Presidency: A Theory of Presidential Press Relations in the Age of Television* (New York: Praeger, 1990), p. 120. Number of press conferences from Samuel Kernell, *Going Public: New Strategies of Presidential Leadership* (Washington, DC: Congressional Quarterly Press, 1986), p. 69. The figures for the number of accredited reporters are from several sources. The figure for 1949 is from Cabell Phillips and others, ed., *Dateline: Washington* (New York: Doubleday, 1949), p. 148, caption to picture. The figure for 1961 comes from James E. Pollard, *Presidents and the Press, Truman Through Johnson* (Washington, DC: Public Affairs Press, 1949), p. 97. Figures for 1969 through 1984 were provided by the Secret Service, Department of Public Affairs. 1969 is the first year for which records are available.

cause the audience for telecasts of prime-time presidential press conference has also decreased over time, the networks see telecasting presidential events as less important.[11] Thus, presidential administrations probably consider traditional press conferences to be less efficient ways to secure positive national media coverage, and they have instead focused on providing access to reporters and editors beyond the **national press corps.**

Government officials also use the media to directly or indirectly gauge the public's—and other officials'—reactions to policy proposals. Sometimes this is accomplished indirectly by providing information to a reporter who agrees not to use the official's name in any stories. This kind of **leak** is also referred to as a **trial balloon.** George W. Bush's threats toward Saddam Hussein discussed in the introduction to this chapter are an example of the use of leaks and trial balloons.

A trial balloon that received a great deal of attention during the Reagan administration was the proposal to consider ketchup a vegetable in federal guidelines for food programs serving low-income children. After quite a bit of negative press attention, the proposal was not included in the guidelines. Generally, as in this case, when a potential policy move is attributed to "a high administration official," no particular individual has to take the blame if the proposal does not play positively in the media or with the public.

While using the media to float a trial balloon is clearly a conscious strategic choice by officials, in other instances information is leaked to provide an elected or appointed official with an advantage in negotiations with other executive office officials. Faced with cuts in the administration's budget, for example, appointed officials in the Department of Defense or Department of Agriculture might well decide to leak the news prematurely to prove to the administration that such cuts will face serious public opposition.

Finally, government officials use the media to provide **surveillance** of the political terrain. The federal government is so complicated that an individual (the president included, despite his large support staff) cannot be attuned to every potentially important development in various policy and electoral communities. One of the important functions of the media is to provide elected officials with reports on what other officials are doing or thinking and what the public is thinking, as indicated by public opinion surveys. This surveillance function makes particular papers, such as the *New York Times* and the *Washington Post*, "must reading" for most political elites; they are windows to the political world in which elites must operate.

One of the interesting consequences of this surveillance is that government officials become "news junkies" and assume that others likewise attend to the media in such a manner.[12] As a result, government officials might be predisposed to overestimate the power of the media over public opinion and other elites.

THE PRESIDENCY

Traditionally, the president has been portrayed as leading by bargaining with other politicians, most notably members of Congress, and as having far less power to accomplish his goals than was popularly thought. The president's power was "the power to persuade."[13] Some later evidence suggested that the president's power was "at the margins."[14] "That is, the president is not so powerful that he can dictate what types of federal policies are adopted. Instead, the president under some circumstances has the power to influence certain aspects of public policy."

Probably the most dominant model of presidential behavior today is that, due to political and technological changes, presidents in the late twentieth century have increasingly relied on **going public**—appealing to the public to gain leverage in bargaining with Congress—as a leadership strategy.[15] Going public was relatively rare until the mid to late 1900s, but it has since increased in frequency and has given some presidents an advantage in pursuing their goals. Not surprisingly, the mass media are central to going public, and numerous changes in White House organization related to the media over the past several decades confirm this.

Most scholars contend that a president's legislative success is only marginally enhanced by effective media relations and positive coverage.[16] Nevertheless, the White House devotes large financial and other resources to managing information for use by the news media, and Republican and Democratic presidents complain that the news coverage they and their policies have received has predominantly been negative. The increasing complexity and comprehensiveness of White House news operations may reflect presidents' views that some minimal amount of positive coverage of their policy proposals is needed if they are to have any chance of succeeding in governing.[17] For example, Bill Clinton entered office with a negative view of the press, saying, "When you're not in a campaign, when you have to stay there and go to work, you are at the mercy of press coverage." By his second term, however, Clinton had shifted from viewing the press as an obstacle to governing to viewing it as a means to govern. He invited weather forecasters to the White House for a briefing on the Kyoto conference on global warming, telling them that a president has to make people aware of problems and implying that the weather forecasters were experts who could help: "This is a case where people need the facts and the context."[18]

What the White House Does

Press operations in the Clinton White House, as with most recent presidential administrations, were the responsibility of several individuals: the press secretary, the Office of the Chief of Staff, and several communications clusters.[19] The press secretary is responsible for handling daily press operations and is the main point of access to the president. Mike McCurry, Clinton's White House Press Secretary, said, "I just do not think of anything beyond today as my responsibility. . . . Two-thirds of your day [as press secretary] is doing the briefing and then the rest of the one-third is just staying on top of whatever the story is."[20]

The press secretary serves a White House constituency of approximately 350 staff members and a national press corps of approximately 1,700 journalists.[21] The press secretary provides information in public settings, which include the daily press briefing and the daily **gaggle**. The gaggle begins at 9:30 A.M. and sets the scene for the day. Besides providing the president's confirmed schedule, the press secretary can provide early responses, as well as responses not attributed to anyone, on questions raised by the press—an indicator of what the press is interested in that day.

Daily press briefings are the normal channel for distributing information that the administration wants publicized. Tension between the White House that is supplying news and reporters who want to be watchdogs is evidenced in efforts to control the podium and determine who asks which questions in what order.

> A press secretary, or anyone else perched at the podium, must be prepared to establish control and not relinquish it in the face of heated exchanges. The only way he will win, though, is if reporters believe he has provided them with accurate information and that he is being straight with them in what he knows, including assuring them no more can be given at that time.[22]

There is also tension between newspapers and television. Television reporters need to be filmed while asking questions, and the major networks and CNN typically ask one-third of the questions at a briefing. Moreover, television reporters' questions differ from the questions of newspaper reporters. Policy questions are asked by journalists at the back of the room, where specialty publications and foreign news organizations are seated; questions on politics come from the television reporters and wire reporters seated up front.[23] Press briefings include appearances by other members of the administration.

The press secretary also meets with some groups and individuals privately. Reporters for *Time*, *Newsweek*, and *U.S. News and World Report* meet with the press secretary every Thursday. **Tongs** are meetings with small, specialized groups of reporters (radio reporters, for example) that are scheduled irregularly, usually with about six reporters in each. Reporters from major networks, CNN, the *Washington Post*, the *New York Times*, and the *Wall Street Journal* receive private responses to their particular inquiries—usually in a more timely fashion than other reporters.

Additional administrative responsibilities of the press secretary include coordinating department (state, defense, CIA) public information officers; scheduling the president and members of the administration on weekend events (Saturday and Sunday news shows) and providing representatives with background information; running the press office, which provides background information and other official documents to reporters; and running the Office of Media Affairs, which is oriented toward the local press and organizations outside of Washington, DC.

The press secretary's focus on daily management of the news tends to limit his or her ability to proactively manage communications messages, which is the province of the Office of the Chief of Staff.[24] The chief of staff seeks to publicize the administration's agenda and plan future events, all with an eye toward the strategy that the White House will use to accomplish its goals. The chief of staff has a series of four meetings every morning to coordinate press functions.

White House Press Coverage

A classic study of White House news operations, reporters, and coverage in the 1950s, 1960s, and 1970s noted an overemphasis on the presidency in *Time*, the *New York Times*, and CBS News.[25] More recent studies confirm the dominance of the president in national news coverage. An analysis of *CBS Evening News* transcripts from 1969 to 1985 (which included the Nixon, Ford, and Carter administrations and Ronald Reagan's first term) indicated that one-fifth of typical CBS news shows were devoted to coverage of the president.[26] From July 1999 to June 2000 the president received just over 60 percent of the time devoted to national institutions on network television.[27] Not only is the president "inherently newsworthy," but news about the president

- Is profitable
- Does not conflict with local news programs
- Fulfills FCC requirements for public affairs programming
- Is easy and cost-effective to produce
- Advances the careers of White House correspondents[28]

The tone of presidential news coverage has varied substantially over time. Between 1953 and 1965, for example, 50 percent of presidential news coverage in the *New York Times* was positive, compared to 28.5 percent in the 1966 to 1974 period and 37.5 percent in the 1974 to 1978 period.[29] This variation suggests that the press did not simply adopt a more negative stance toward the president, but rather that objective events drive the tone of coverage. The analysis of *CBS Evening News* transcripts cited above reported that most coverage between 1969 and 1985 was neutral. However, coverage toward the end of that period became more negative.[30]

In addition, presidential news coverage varies over a president's term. The pattern involves three phases—alliance, competition, and detachment—and can, for the most part, be attributed to the White House's use of different press strategies as the term proceeds.[31] In the **alliance** period at the beginning of the term, the press is interested in the new president and administration and tends to cover most stories in a very positive light. When the new administration em-

The Problem with News Coverage of the President

FREDERIC T. SMOLLER describes the problem with news coverage of the president as follows:

1. The length of the evening news programs requires stories to be short and uncompli-cated. This contributes to an abbreviated and simplistic portrayal of the president.
2. The need for pictures causes television news to exaggerate and distort the function-ing of the presidency by emphasizing those aspects that are amenable to pictures.

The need for good visuals reinforces journalism's definition of the news as the depar-ture from the norm, which often leads to unfavorable coverage. As a consequence,

> we have a complex and multifaceted office that is based on persuasion and the subtle exercise of power and influence. An office in which most significant activities are conducted in private. An institution with limited formal power that must struggle to reach and maintain consensus. An institution in which the execution of routine governing chores is offered as one measure of competence. And an institution that depends on public support for success. On the other hand we have a medium that requires simplistic, visible indicators of presidential performance. A medium that is ideally suited to the portrayal of conflict. And a medium whose purpose is to cover the unusual and atypical. The result of these conflicting needs? The organization imper-atives faced by the news bureau predispose it toward a negative portrayal of the presidency.

Source: Frederic T. Smoller, *The Six O'Clock Presidency: A Theory of Presidential Press Relations in the Age of Television* (New York: Praeger, 1990), pp. 28 ff., quotation from p. 33.

barks on getting its legislative proposals passed, the **competition** phase begins. Positive and flowing news stories are not as readily available, and the press looks to alternative sources that might provide more interesting stories, espe-cially when the White House is seeking to control the media message more tightly. **Detachment** occurs toward the end of a president's term, when most policy initiatives have been passed and the White House views positive rela-tions with the press—or positive media coverage—as unnecessary.

Why has negativity increased across presidential terms and within presiden-cies? Although "reality" is partly responsible, the media's—in particular, tele-vision's—newsgathering routines are also to blame.[32] Decisions about what will become news are determined by the need for visuals, which simplify real-ity; the need to entertain with items that are interesting; and the need for a story.

The past two decades have witnessed marked changes in news routines and values. Part of this value change is reflected in an "authority disorder" bias.[33]

Reporters have always relied on authorities to provide a sense of order and control in otherwise chaotic or unpredictable situations. In decades past, this reliance was reflected in positive stories indicating that government sources could be trusted to do, and were capable of doing, what was right or needed in difficult situations. Recently, however, the press has taken to portraying officials as "unsympathetic, scheming politicians who often fail to solve problems, leaving disorder in their wake."[34] Hence, coverage of the president and other prominent officials has become more negative, independent of the objective circumstances in which the officials finds themselves.

An alternative explanation is that increasingly negative coverage indicates changes in the president's behavior or in the context in which the president finds himself. This argument is particularly appealing to those who believe that American society as an aggregate and individual Americans no longer adhere to various social values, such as integrity, character, social connectedness, and patriotism. However, it is inconsistent with some anecdotal evidence. President Clinton's alleged sexual advances or affairs, for example, were extensively criticized in the media, whereas John F. Kennedy's affairs were ignored until many years after his death. The challenge with this explanation is the difficulty of objectively measuring reality. How does one objectively assess the character, integrity, or leadership of different presidents so as to compare this measure with press coverage over time?

Political scientists Samuel Kemell and Timothy Groelling tried to get around this problem of distinguishing between negative and biased coverage by focusing on the media's choices of stories about presidential approval.[35] The researchers tested for media bias by examining two hypotheses: (1) that news organizations are more likely to pay for polls when they have other information that the president's approval rating is dropping, and (2) that news organizations are more likely to report changes in presidential approval ratings when the changes are negative. They discovered that, despite claims to the contrary by media observers, both the commissioning of polls and the reporting of presidential approval ratings are relatively independent of changes in presidential approval, thus suggesting minimal bias on the part of the news media in general. The networks conduct polls at different levels and times, independent of negative changes in approval ratings, and the probability of reporting positive and negative changes is equal, leading the researchers to conclude that the networks are not biased against the president.

The typically negative attitude about the media held by presidents, press secretaries, and other executive branch staff members can be put into context: At the same time they perceive an increased need for and benefits of using the media to govern and devote more resources to the media, coverage of the presidency has become less positive and either more neutral or negative. Unless it is possible to show that presidents and executive branch officials are less competent, moral, honest, or capable than those who served in the past, it seems likely that the increased neutrality or negativity of reporters is driven by the

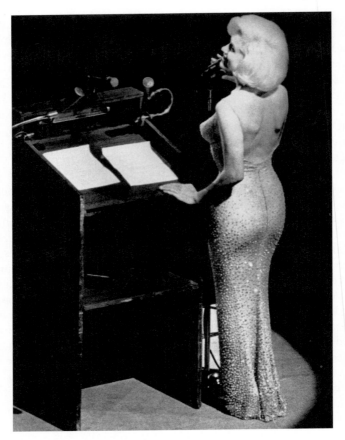

Marilyn Monroe singing "Happy Birthday" to President Kennedy. Rumors were rampant that JFK was unfaithful to his wife—and with Marilyn Monroe—but White House reporters never reported this as news. © *Bettmann/CORBIS.*

value changes discussed in earlier chapters, including increasing economic pressures on news organizations and a greater emphasis on entertainment values in news production. The relative lack of complaints by reporters about cooperation from (or manipulation by) government officials might reflect their need to maintain access for continued news stories. It might also reflect the fact that there are typically many sources for news stories (especially where entertainment values have become more important). In contrast, the president's opportunities to garner favorable, or even fair, national press coverage are much more restricted.

CONGRESS

The underlying principles, behavior, and news decisions governing coverage of Congress are generally the same as those governing coverage of the president:

> Perhaps the most accurate comparison is that of a struggle to lead a dance. . . . In short, each side holds important power—members of the House by controlling whether, when, where and how to grant access, journalists by deciding whether, when, where and how to pay attention. The movements in the tango of their relationships are constantly subject to negotiation and renegotiation.[36]

However, today the media place much more emphasis on the president as compared to Congress. An analysis of major network coverage of Congress in April of every year from 1972 through 1992 found that the level of coverage of Congress declined dramatically during that period (see Figure 5-3).[37] This has been the case despite greater routine access (floor coverage) and the tendency of congressional leaders to go public rather than directly address their colleagues in Congress. Coverage of policy issues in Congress has also declined since the late 1970s, while coverage of scandals has increased.

Not only has coverage of Congress decreased over the past several decades, but it has also become more negative. Specifically, network coverage in 1972, 1982, and 1992 shows a distinct increase in critical news coverage (see Table 5-1).[38]

As in the case of the presidency, some of these changes might reflect changes in the behavior of members of Congress. Yet they undoubtedly also relate to the changing economics of the news and reporters' considerations of newsworthiness. Perhaps the most critical difference between the two branches is

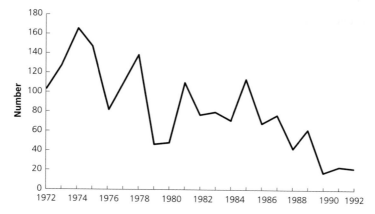

FIGURE 5-3 Portrayal of Congress in Television News
Source: S. Robert Lichter and Daniel R. Amundson, "Less News Is Worse News: Television News Coverage of Congress, 1972–92," in *Congress, the Press, and the Public,* ed. Thomas E. Mann and Norman J. Ornstein (Washington, DC: American Enterprise Institution and The Brookings Institution, 1994), p. 134.

TABLE 5-1 National Media Coverage of Congress: 1972, 1982, and 1992

Item	Positive (percent)	Negative (percent)
All statements	17	83
1972	26	74
1982	13	87
1992	11	89
Target		
Democrats	21	79
Republicans	21	79
Senate	21	79
House	17	83
Members	21	79
Institution	11	89

Source: S. Robert Lichter and Daniel R. Amundson, "Less News Is Worse News: Television News Coverage of Congress, 1972–92," in *Congress, the Press, and the Public,* ed. Thomas E. Mann and Norman J. Ornstein (Washington, DC: American Enterprise Institution and The Brookings Institution, 1994), p. 138.

that Congress is, by virtue of its structure, much more complex than the Executive Office of the President:

> The Capitol Hill beat has no agreed-upon principal newsmaker or principal news item. . . . With the wealth of hearings, markups of legislation and decisions in committees and subcommittees, the deliberations and actions on the floor in both chambers, not to mention initiatives taken in 535 members' offices, Congress has no one story, and it can be difficult to decide what to cover.[39]

What Members of Congress Do

What do members of Congress do to garner media attention? As do officials in the executive branch, virtually all members employ press secretaries, whose main responsibilities are to give the media information regarding their activities and to respond to press inquiries. Congressional press secretaries focus their public relations efforts on the local press.[40] When asked to rank press strategies, they listed local dailies, local weeklies, press releases, newsletters, local television news, targeted mail, and radio as the most effective press strategies, and studio, weekly columns, *Washington Post*, network television news, *New York Times*, and televised floor proceedings as least effective.[41] Most members of Congress do not pay much attention to national media because they expect the national media's interest to be unpredictable and short-lived.

The emphasis on local media and print rather than on television is consistent with theories of congressional behavior that emphasize the electoral needs of members of Congress. In their efforts to secure reelection, members of Congress engage in credit-claiming (for accomplishments benefiting their districts), advertising (name recognition and image-building), and position-taking (stating their policy positions).[42] About one-third of congressional press releases are primarily position-taking, compared to about one-fifth that are advertising and almost one-half that are credit-claiming.[43] About half of all press releases focused on local rather than national issues.[44] To secure reelection, then, most members of Congress seem to believe that they must provide a steady stream of news stories to local media outlets. And because local print media outlets are typically more closely aligned with their district populations than are television markets, working through the printed press is an efficient use of staff resources.

Who Gets Covered

Media coverage of Congress focuses primarily on the few members who are in formal leadership positions or who are seeking the presidency.[45] For example, in 1983 about 90 percent of senators received almost no coverage by the network evening news programs, the Sunday interview programs, and the *New York Times, Los Angeles Times, Washington Post, Christian Science Monitor,* and *Wall Street Journal.*[46]

One explanation for differences in coverage is that reporters' news routines and values determine who gets covered.[47] According to this view, gaining and maintaining access to relevant policymakers leads to coverage of formal leaders in the Senate. To simplify complex issues, reporters have also adopted a pro-and-con model of reporting, which leads to coverage of extreme senators. Their need for interesting and newsworthy stories leads them to focus on electoral strategy, scandal, and politicians who are seen as "up and coming." Analysis of stories from the Vanderbilt Television News Archive between 1972 and 1984 confirms that leadership, extreme views, opposition to the president, scandal, being from a large state, and election strategy factors are all associated with increased coverage.[48]

The media's emphasis on covering leaders—who tend to be more senior members of Congress—has been criticized for its resulting lack of coverage of two groups that have only recently been elected to Congress in large numbers: women and African Americans. An analysis of stories in major newspapers from January 1993 to October 1994 found that women candidates received more mentions in major papers than did male candidates.[49] The major theme in policy coverage of female representatives was that women members of the House were agents of change working collectively to achieve a common goal. The articles primarily focused on such "women's issues" as abortion, women's health,

health care reform, and violence; they did not acknowledge their work in other policy areas, such as crime, trade, and the budget.[50]

Media coverage of African Americans in Congress tends to emphasize the race of black, but not white, candidates and to focus on racial issues when black politicians are involved.[51] To test the hypothesis that the differences in coverage were a result of different behaviors by black members and white members, researchers interviewed press secretaries and analyzed the Web sites of black members of Congress, liberal white senators, and a group of "representative" (liberal and conservative) white senators.[52] The press secretaries for black members were significantly more likely to report stereotyping in news coverage than were press secretaries for white members of Congress. However, the press goals of the three groups were indistinguishable.

The one notable difference between African-American members' and white members' Web sites was that African Americans tended to highlight their civil rights and racial issues records and their affiliation with African-American or civil rights associations, while these rarely appeared on the white members' Web sites.[53] However, the African-American members did not emphasize their involvement with civil rights groups and issues, but merely mentioned them. Most African-American members devoted most of the space on their sites to issues other than racial concerns, and about 60 percent devoted more space to at least one other issue. There was no difference in the extent to which the three groups emphasized local issues. Hence, the researchers concluded that different media coverage of black members and white members of Congress results not from distinctive legislator behavior but instead from different news values of reporters.[54]

What Gets Covered

Lawmaking is sometimes compared to sausage: If you want to enjoy the final product, you should never watch how it is made. Not surprisingly, the nature of the legislative process—structured by the Constitution to be complex, deliberative, and, for lack of a better word, messy—does not lend itself to easy or simple news stories. In the midst of this "unpleasantness," coverage of Congress focuses on events, not processes.[55] Events provide reporters with an objective indicator of newsworthiness. The most easily identifiable, predictable event is usually the final floor vote—or, more occasionally, the final committee vote—on a bill. A historical analysis of media coverage of major legislation before Congress from 1946 through 1992 confirms that final votes on legislation indeed received the most coverage.[56] A study of media coverage of legislative initiatives of the 103rd Congress (1993–1994) found that most bills failed to receive much coverage prior to the final floor vote, regardless of the administration's marking them as legislative priorities.[57]

The same study also found that media coverage of these issues was consistently low just prior to the congressional election—the time it would be most useful to citizens. "When the media cover an issue seems to depend solely on when it is most confrontational."[58] In other words, a story about Congress becomes newsworthy when it is about winning and losing, not because of its (objective) potential implications for citizens and American society (see Table 5-2).

Reporters' focus on final votes in part reflects organizational resource constraints.[59] In essence, while Congress is in session, most news organizations do not have enough staff members to send them to committee meetings, for example. Thus, the priority is coverage on the final vote.

Despite the fact that the Founders conceived of Congress as the main deliberative policymaking body of the federal government, media coverage falls short of portraying it that way. Coverage of the president dwarfs coverage of Congress; coverage of Congress is even more negative than coverage of the president; and the little policy coverage that results focuses on strategy, not on the substance of legislative deliberation. However, because members of Congress typically view the national press as less useful for accomplishing their electoral and legislative goals, the press seems to be less of a target for them. Instead, they devote their efforts to local media, which tend to portray members of Congress much more positively. Perhaps this accounts for the well-known dictum that the mass public loves their member of Congress, but views Congress as an institution in a very negative light.[60]

TABLE 5-2 Media Coverage of Congressional Activities

Policy	Point of Peak Coverage	Reason
Crime Bill	Vote on conference report in the House of Representatives	Conference report defeated in House
NAFTA	House floor	Possible defeat in House
Health Care	Senate floor	Filibuster/dies on Senate floor
Welfare Reform	Post-1994 election	GOP surprise victory
Campaign Finance	Senate floor	2 filibusters/6 cloture votes/dies on Senate floor
Motor-Voter	Procedural motion on Senate floor	Filibuster of procedural motion
Family Leave	Senate floor	Threat to attach controversial nongermane amendment in Senate

Source: Mark D. Watts, "Media Coverage and the 103rd Congress: When to Cover Policymaking in Congress." Paper prepared for the Midwest Political Science Association, Chicago, April 23–26, 1998, p. 34.

FEDERAL COURTS

The judicial system has been perceived to be the least political branch of the U.S. government. With an avowed dedication to the principle of precedent, the Supreme Court is typically viewed as being above the political fray, largely because its members are appointed by presidents for life terms. Rather than respond to the whims of public opinion, the highest court of the land is expected to make decisions based on long-standing political values and legal traditions. In the lower courts, where local trial judges manage the disposition of conflicts between individuals and the larger society as part of the criminal legal system or between individuals as part of the civil legal system, procedural constraints are seemingly high.

Yet images are deceiving, and decades of political science research has looked at individual and systemic factors that influence judicial decision making as well as the behaviors of defense lawyers, trial attorneys, interest groups, and other individuals central to the resolution of legal disputes. The media coverage on which these (typically deceptive) images are drawn is constrained by the courts' ability, which is much greater than that of the executive and legislative branches, to control access to decision making. Ranging from the Supreme Court's secretive deliberations—decisions are drafted and redrafted in complete privacy to sustain a majority opinion—to the private negotiations between prosecutors and defense lawyers, much of what the legal system does is beyond the purview of reporters. That has significant consequences for the nature and level of media coverage of the courts.

Supreme Court and Courts of Appeal

The secrecy within which the Supreme Court operates deprives reporters "of inside information, helpful sources and the usual angles . . . editors and reporters are unlikely to find in most of the Court's activities anything that looks like news."[61] Unlike members of the executive and legislative branches, individual justices have no incentive for courting the media, other than by managing the institution's image. Hence, the main function of the Supreme Court's Public Information Office is providing reporters with information on the status of pending cases and with texts of current decisions, not seeking to enhance the status of particular justices.

With lengthy and often complex decisions being handed to reporters as the raw material of Supreme Court stories, coverage tends to be sporadic: relatively high when decisions are announced and mostly nonexistent in between. Decisions are the news event, and they become old news within twenty-four hours. That means that reporters must understand, summarize, and interpret decisions quickly, often on the same day that multiple decisions are handed down. As a result, coverage often consists of using the opinions written by the

Court to fill the newshole, with little legal, contextual, or social context provided by the reporter. Not surprisingly, most coverage of the Court is neutral rather than positive or negative.[62]

Recent analyses of media coverage of the Court suggest that the heavy focus on Court decisions does not translate to thorough coverage. In 1986–1987, for example, civil rights and First Amendment cases were covered in greater proportion than their objective importance—as determined by the number and scope of the cases—would imply.[63] Decisions on civil rights garnered one-fifth of newspaper coverage during the 1986–1987 term, but comprised only one-tenth of the cases decided by the Court.[64]

The major exception is when individuals are nominated to the Court by the president and must face Senate confirmation. While confirmation hearings were once relatively sedate events, more recently groups have mobilized against the appointments, and hearings have been contentious. Some nominees have withdrawn their names from consideration, as did Douglas Ginsberg, who admitted to smoking marijuana in law school. In other cases conflicts have erupted into more substantial political battles, as during the Senate hearing on Clarence Thomas, who was accused of sexual harassment, and Robert Bork, whose views of the Constitution and role of the Court were considered extreme by opponents.

A significant failure in media coverage relates to the impact and aftermath of Supreme Court decisions. A more thorough understanding of the Court and its societal consequences might be realized if the media chose to report "less immediate responses," such as "(t)he direct and indirect consequences of specific judicial decisions—impact—and the complex of developments subsequent to decisions, opinion, and judicial policies—aftermath."[65] Hence, not only by choosing to focus on decisions but also in failing to report on longer-term consequences, the media likely provide citizens with a biased and superficial view of the Supreme Court.

Trial Courts

Failure to cover the impact and aftermath of court decisions is not restricted to coverage of the Supreme Court. It is also a hallmark of coverage of trial courts. Based on a sample of court stories from four days in 1993, 40.7 percent of stories focused on pretrial events such as arrests, indictments, and arraignments; 23.6 percent focused on the trial (jury selection, testimony, motions, rulings, and arguments); and 27.8 percent focused on court decisions (verdicts, holdings, and sentences).[66] Coverage of the dominant mode of case disposition—plea bargains—is lacking, which gives citizens the impression that extraordinary cases are the norm: "Extensively covered trials may seem normal to lay observers who have been conditioned by television and movies to believe that criminal trials are the norm. . . . In sum, we may hypothesize that news media dramatize abnormal cases until, over time, they have normalized dramatic cases."[67]

There is even less coverage of civil cases than of criminal cases, and it is probably of even lower quality. A content analysis of coverage of cases in national and regional papers on four days in 1993 found that civil cases represented around 39 percent of all cases reported.[68] In essence, civil cases tend to be less dramatic, less visual, and more complex, which makes it all the more difficult for reporters to find cases that are "newsworthy."

Changing perceptions of newsworthiness likely help explain a recent shift in news coverage of the judicial system away from routine, to more sensationalistic, cases.[69] An examination of coverage of three lurid murder cases—the trials of Charles Manson in 1970, Claus von Bulow in 1982, and O. J. Simpson in 1995–1996—on three network evening broadcasts found that the Simpson trial received eight times the amount of coverage as the Manson trial and ten times the coverage of the von Bulow trial.[70] Consistent with this increased emphasis on sensationalistic crime, Table 5-3 presents the percentage of television newsmagazine broadcasts that contained a tabloid-style crime story between 1991 and 1998. The table shows a dramatic increase in such stories for *48 Hours* (CBS) and *Dateline* (NBC).

THE VIEW FROM ENTERTAINMENT LAND

One of the dramatic trends over the past several decades has been the decreasing size of traditional audiences for both network evening newscasts and major daily papers. At the same time, several new types of programs dealing with

TABLE 5-3 Tabloid "News" Coverage in Television Newsmagazine Broadcasts, 1991–1998

Year	*60 Minutes* (CBS)	*48 Hours* (CBS)	*Dateline* (NBC)	*20/20* (ABC)
1991	22	n/a	16	21
1992	14	n/a	15	12
1993	10	20	18	22
1994	14	24	31	21
1995	12	24	45	23
1996	19	23	35	21
1997	16	48	29	23
1998	20	47	36	19

Note: "n/a" means data not available for that year.

Source: Richard L. Fox and Robert W. Van Sickel, *Tabloid Justice: Criminal Justice in an Age of Media Frenzy* (Boulder, CO: Lynne Reiner Publishers, 2001), p. 79.

politics have been very successful. The number of televised newsmagazine shows has expanded dramatically, and such shows are now available most nights of the week. One of their central themes is investigative reporting, quite often focusing on government officials as culprits or as nonresponsive to citizens' needs. Entertainment shows focusing on the criminal justice system—police officers, judges, and attorneys—have increased in number, and "reality shows" featuring judges and cops continue to rank highly. Politicians have also begun using nontraditional media as outlets to publicize their agendas, such as presidential candidates appearing on daytime talk shows.

These shows share many of the characteristics of traditional news shows, in particular, their focus on the dramatic, sensational, and unusual. Because of their explicitly political (and typically nonpartisan) content, they might influence individuals who do not tune into evening news shows, and this influence could be unique to the extent that they differ from the traditional shows.

A recent study of television's portrayal of elected officials and civil servants from the mid-1950s through the mid-1980s found that government officials were portrayed more negatively than any other occupational group, except businessmen. More specifically, 51 percent of government officials were portrayed negatively, 40 percent were portrayed positively, and the portrayal of 9 percent was neutral. Characters who were government officials were also more likely than private-sector characters to commit crimes.[71] Prior to 1975, the political system was portrayed positively twice as much as negatively, but by the 1980s, positive portrayals had all but disappeared. As shown in Figure 5-4, in the 1990s public officials were portrayed much more negatively than were law enforcers, civil servants, and all other types of characters.

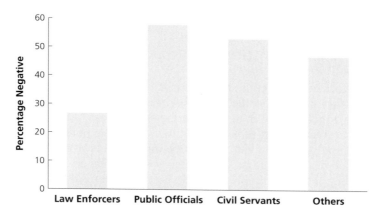

FIGURE 5-4 Portrayal of Public Officials in Entertainment Shows
Source: Data from S. Robert Lichter, Linda Lichter, and Daniel R. Amundson, "Government Goes Down the Tube: Images of Government in TV Entertainment, 1955–1998." *The Harvard International Journal of Press/Politics* 5 (2000): 99.

As discussed in Chapter 6, this shift in the portrayal of government officials coincides with notable changes in mass opinion about government—which became more negative—as well as with a possible decline in voter turnout. The question, of course, is whether the shift in prime-time television politics was the cause or an effect: Were more negative portrayals of government officials provided by the networks because the audience had become more negative, or did the audience become more negative because they were exposed to increasingly negative portrayals of government officials?

INSTITUTIONAL AGENDA-SETTING

Everyone agrees that media coverage influences the way various institutions—religion, family, Congress—operate, but identifying the unique effects of media, independent of other factors, is a challenge. This is particularly true in the case of **institutional agenda-setting,** which refers to how and when political issues are formally addressed by government institutions. The fact that political elites agree that the media influence institutional agenda-setting makes the task of identifying the specific effects all the more difficult. One reason politicians emphasize the power of the media is that they are news junkies.[72] For example, the inability of a member of Congress to move a bill out of committee may have something to do with a lack of media coverage, but it might just as well reflect the member's limited legislative skills or lack of influence with party leaders. Hence, assessing whether the media set the agenda for government institutions requires assessing other factors known to influence the policy process. This section considers the role of the media in setting the agenda primarily for Congress. Some of the factors, however, likely apply to other decision-making bodies, such as state legislatures and city councils.

How and When Do Institutions Respond?

Based on numerous in-depth interviews of appointed and elected officials, scholar Martin Linsky concluded that the press has likely affected the congressional policy *process* more than actual policy *outcomes.*[73] Linsky's conclusion is probably correct in light of what we know about the policy process in general. Substantial scholarly evidence, for example, points to the critical role of the partisanship and ideology of members of Congress in determining their votes on policy. In addition, lobbying activities by organized interests are often associated with influencing members of Congress who are undecided on issues. On particular types of issues, members of Congress have also been responsive to public opinion in their electoral districts.[74] These strong structural features make representatives' roll call votes fairly predictable. It is hard to imagine that the media somehow transcend these fundamental political constraints.

On the other hand, routine news coverage—especially the dramatic sort—has been established as a key factor in the agenda-setting process, lifting the status of some policy problems to a higher level of urgency than others. According to Downs, successful issues follow an **issue attention cycle**.[75] An unknown number of issues or problems exist in society and compete for government decision makers' attention. What draws both political elites and the mass public to attend to any one objectively important issue over others is an unusual or dramatic **triggering event** that uniquely symbolizes the critical importance of the problem. When such events are portrayed in the media as news, both the public and elected officials suddenly become aware of the problem, and the latter may choose to address it. In this respect, the mass media determine which issues will be addressed by government.

One model of the policy process proposes that the media magnify **focusing events** (triggering events) by covering particularly dramatic events and thus elevating certain objective problems over others. These are the issues that government addresses because the media coverage either enhances communication among policymakers or influences public opinion. Both mechanisms work indirectly—the media do not originate the issue but rather enhance it.[76]

An important limitation on the media's power is that placing an issue on the agenda does not mean that any particular proposal will be enacted. "The pitfall for House members is that media strategies can work to call attention to their issues without ensuring the successes they seek."[77] The relative improbability of media attention alone determining a policy action or particular outcome is echoed in interviews with House press secretaries, only fifteen out of forty of whom noted the usefulness of news coverage in the legislative process.[78]

Instead, press secretaries and House members distinguish between the advantages and disadvantages of insider and outsider strategies. The traditional **insider strategy** of getting bills passed into law is relatively immune from reporters' attention and the media's definition of the issue. Members of Congress who use an insider strategy draw on their substantive expertise, knowledge of the rules, and contacts in various party caucuses, agencies, and interest groups to persuade others to support their legislation. Those who choose an **outsider strategy** seek to pressure the major actors by acquiring sympathetic media coverage and subsequent public support for their legislation. These legislators must accommodate the media's values in news reporting, typically by taking firmer, more distinctive stands, often early enough in the legislative process that their stands are symbolic and don't have substantive results. While the outsider strategy might be a more democratic process in that it mobilizes the public, anecdotal accounts suggest that this is not common.[79]

Responses to Crises

If media agenda-setting is constrained by other structural features of routine lawmaking, are such effects more pronounced in nonroutine decision making, such as during **crises**? What happens when something unexpected, with potentially dire consequences, enters the public consciousness? Are government officials forced to respond to media coverage in ways they otherwise would not?

Children in protective custody of the state and state protective agencies unable to locate them; spring flooding of major rivers such as the Mississippi; military families earning below the poverty level: Each of these stories has received notable attention from the mass media over the past several years. Yet the reality of the circumstances—a large, underfunded administrative operation, a natural flooding cycle, years of federal budget cutting—most certainly developed slowly over time, not "suddenly" and thus deserving of news attention. While there are few systematic studies of media coverage of crises, the evidence points to one central insight: What may seem to be a crisis—due to sudden and saturated media coverage—is not necessarily new to government officials. To the extent that media suddenly cover a situation, the coverage may play into the hands of government officials who are ready to respond. In that case, government's response to the crisis is actually more like routine lawmaking.

This finding reflects on earlier observations that media coverage probably has more of an effect on the speed and timing of the policy process and on the nature of communication among government officials than on the substantive policy decisions that result. Some media observers refer to the "power" of dramatic foreign affairs crisis coverage as the **CNN effect**. Their contention is that, if no pictures were provided by CNN or another world news organization, U.S. public officials and citizens would be less likely to be aware of or concerned about, or consider responding to, the crisis.

Case studies of mass starvation, macroeconomic collapse, and ethnic and religious violence, as well as of U.S. humanitarian intervention in Somalia, challenge the notion that government decision makers are forced to respond to media coverage of crises.[80] Typically, government officials are likely to be aware of potential or actual conditions that could become crisis situations sooner than media organizations, especially given the reduction in foreign news bureaus over the past decade or two. Decision makers' awareness of and responses to the crisis is likely driven by their beliefs about whether the crisis threatens the sociopolitical security of the United States.[81] If so, there will be a response regardless of media coverage. Where sociopolitical interests are marginal, relief will be provided; if resources are plentiful, sustained relief might be enhanced by extended media coverage. Where U.S. interests are not clear, responses will be opposed by career civil servants and military officials, regardless of media coverage.

In the end, then, television's effect on these types of crises is viewed as marginal. In some ways the media limit their own power.[82] The potential power of the CNN effect comes from powerful and dramatic visuals of individuals in crisis, indisputable evidence of societal disorder that seems to beg for governmental response. These visuals conform to the news media's values of newsworthiness—great pictures, great drama, great emotion. But continued coverage of the crisis is far less appealing: There are no new pictures; not much changes from day to day; and investigating government responses to the problem is costly. Hence, there is little sustained coverage of crises. By definition, a crisis is a short-term event, not a long-standing social, economic, or political condition. So while the initial coverage seems to beg for a governmental response, the lack of sustained coverage likely limits the long-term influence on decision makers. Why should they respond to a situation that no one is paying attention to?

Nowhere is this point better illustrated than in a case study of the famine in Ethiopia in 1984.[83] Objective conditions were well known both before and after the media's, public's, and U.S. government's "discovery" of famine in 1984, and the "crisis" was entirely predictable, given food shortages in that country since the mid-1970s. Late in 1982 the Ethiopian government's request for Western aid to help feed 2 million people met with a minimal response on the part of the Reagan administration. One senior administration official was quoted as saying, "To give food to countries just because people are starving is a pretty weak reason."[84] The administration's view that the famine was a direct result of Ethiopia's own policies and mismanagement was reflected in their elimination of all food assistance to Ethiopia in the 1984 budget.

Famine continues in Ethiopia. This photo was taken in December 2002, yet the American news media and the American public have paid little attention to the continuing problem. *AP Photo/ Anthony Mitchell.*

Continued appeals for aid, along with a *Washington Post* series on famine relief in June 1983, kept officials in both the executive and congressional branches aware of the situation, and ultimately kept the administration from completely eliminating all food relief in the final appropriations bill. Partly due to more "newsworthy" events—apartheid in South Africa and war in Chad—the Ethiopian famine was not considered newsworthy, even as objective conditions worsened. This suddenly changed in October 1984, when *NBC News*

> aired stunning footage of starving Ethiopians massed together in immense government feeding stations. NBC anchor Tom Brokaw reported that some 6 million were endangered, while about 500,000 probably would die within a year. The graphic pictures had an immediate impact: UNICEF, the international children's relief agency, reported over 5,000 telephone calls during the next four days. The Save the Children Fund received over 12,000 calls in the same period, plus pledges of close to $75,000. . . . But such film had existed a long time before Brokaw decided to air it.[85]

U.S. government food aid increased by about $95 million, and much of that increase took place after the news broadcasts—and even after Ethiopia's famine was replaced in the news by the assassination of Indian Prime Minister Indira Gandhi on October 31.[86] Early in 1985 a new crisis—the plight of the American family farm—took center stage, and amendments providing financial support for American farmers were added to the bill promising famine relief for Ethiopia. The Ethiopian famine is a classic example of government officials' responding quickly to a crisis, but in the end having the substantive details of that response constrained by other political factors.

Nevertheless, media coverage seemed to weaken the administration's effort to define the problem in Ethiopia as governmental malfeasance or mismanagement and provided an opportunity for those in favor of famine relief to push their preferred policy alternatives. Thus, media coverage triggered lawmakers' and the public's attention, consistent with the issue attention cycle. The seeming lack of a substantive response affirms that the media had more of an effect on the process than on the policy outcome.

Despite the limited policy expectations suggested by systematic studies of the CNN effect, political leaders can use media coverage as a vehicle of diplomacy. In other words, officials communicate indirectly via the media. While some scholars view this as an increasingly important instrument of foreign policy, there is little systematic evidence about its prevalence or effects.[87]

Responses to Exposés

It is often assumed that institutional responses to crises and **exposés** are similar—that government officials directly respond to a sudden, dramatic report of a problem about which they are expected to do something. Unlike coverage of a crisis, however, an exposé involves devoting resources to something that fits the media's notion of a suitable investigative news story—something beyond the typical news values of drama and timeliness. In fact, those typical values are actually manipulated by the press in the case of exposés, and journalists actually have considerable control over both the dramatic presentation and the timeliness of investigative reports.

Media coverage of an issue may elicit a direct response from government officials, but may also cause an indirect one through the public. Government officials may view the outpouring of calls and donations to nonprofit organizations, as in the case of the Ethiopian famine, as evidence of widespread concern or public demand that they "do something." Citizens may also write or phone government officials with requests for action. This indirect linkage of the media and government officials through the mass public is typically viewed as a distinctive element of investigative reporting, and it seems to be the motivation (aside from audience ratings and profitability) for news organizations to devote resources to such reporting.

Some members of the press believe they have a social responsibility to provide news that enhances civic and social life, that informs citizens about public affairs, and that can be used to make society better.[88] Consistent with this **mobilization model**, investigative reporting is seen as bringing about political change by changing public opinion about an issue; government officials then respond by changing public policy. Journalists' professional and personal values come into play in that investigative reporting maintains their independence from government officials and brings about an enlightened public and changes in policy that are consistent with the public interest.[89]

However, Protess and his colleagues find that the effects of investigative reporting might be overstated.[90] Investigative stories often result in policy changes, but not as a result of public mobilization. Instead, policy changes typically did involve changes in public opinion, and sometimes occurred without changes in public opinion. Their case study evidence demonstrates the high level of interaction between journalists and government officials in developing the investigative story. In some cases, government officials actually provide the original "tip." In others, journalists consult with government officials in the earliest stage of investigations and often maintain contact with them throughout, sometimes in an effort to boost the policy impact once the story hits the news.

Moreover, although some policy responses are affected by political or electoral considerations, the dominant factor is a public official's desire to use the investigative story as leverage to promote programs to which he or she has always been committed. In this respect, investigative journalism (more than crisis coverage) might provide an advantage to particular problem definitions and therefore affect the final substantive outcome.[91]

ON THE MEDIA AS A LINKAGE INSTITUTION

The essential nature of a linkage institution is to link citizens and government officials to each other by providing information in both directions; citizens are informed of the government's actions, and government officials are informed of citizens' preferences. This chapter focuses primarily on the nature of information conveyed to citizens about government.

Reporters are constrained in what they report by economic considerations, such as the expense of foreign affairs coverage, and by organizational routines. Despite the tremendous effort that government officials put into media relations, the level and nature of media coverage of national institutions also reflects the news values of drama and simplicity. Focusing on the president simply makes for "better" news stories, despite the centrality of Congress to the policymaking process. Moreover, the increasingly negative tone of news stories—resulting either from changing news values of reporters or increased economic pressures on news organizations—likely contributes to a more cynical and disgusted public (the evidence for this is examined in Chapter 7).

This does not mean that citizens cannot find more suitable information if they seek it out. But rational citizens will seek out relatively free information in evaluating policy or party alternatives.[92] If the relatively free information available in the mass media is all that citizens rely on, and if other political and social institutions do not seek to subsidize the costs of more accurate, useful, or detailed information, the quality of democratic decision making is compromised.

Further compromising the media as a linkage institution are the findings on institutional agenda-setting, which suggest that even when government officials seem to respond to media coverage of events, the public has at best an indirect influence on their actions. Government officials are often the initial sources of the stories, and they use such stories to advance their policy interests. If this is the best, or most efficient, or only way for government officials to affect policy change or garner public support for their policies, policymakers will certainly use it. But an unintended consequence is that it results in an inaccurate portrayal of the policy process as well as of the nature of the media and the relationships between reporters and officials.

ON MODELS OF THE PRESS

This assessment of the success of the media as a linkage institution has clear implications for the models introduced in Chapter 1. As anticipated, the reporters of objective fact model cannot be sustained in light of findings about the importance of news values such as dramatization and simplification, as well as those relating to the nature of coverage. Perhaps the latter limitation is the most damaging. If coverage of policy decisions of Congress is focused at the endpoint of the policymaking process instead of being distributed across the policymaking period, as the reporters of objective fact model would require, citizens do not have the information they need when they need it to be effective participants in the political process. Moreover, the increasingly negative tone of coverage despite numerous accomplishments by various institutions of government suggests a bias that again violates the basic assumptions of the reporters of objective fact model.

The neutral adversary model likewise fails to receive broad support. If this model focused solely on being adversarial, it would do better: The increasingly negative nature of media coverage of most institutions of government seems to support the adversarial role. But the model calls for a neutral adversary, which suggests more fairness or balance than current reporting practices seem to entail. In short, the negative, cynical, and increasingly tabloid-like nature of media coverage of government officials seems to violate the basic claims of the neutral adversary model. These claims are also violated by the findings on government officials' roles in exposé and crisis coverage: Government officials are as likely to initiate these stories as they are to respond to them.

The findings suggest that institutional coverage of government is clearly inconsistent with our broad understanding of the propagandist model of the press. The timing, tone, and resources devoted to media coverage seem to delegitimize the government rather than legitimize it. One might argue that negative, biased coverage of government institutions does not delegitimize the system, but rather the particular individuals holding elected or appointed government positions. But negative and sensationalized coverage of government in the news and in entertainment are such fundamental features of what citizens are told about government that they must, at some point, threaten the integrity of the system; at some level of sensationalized coverage of individuals, the system itself has to be drawn into question.

From time to time, issues that are not propagandist in nature lend themselves to short-term or long-term coverage. Foreign conflicts are perhaps most likely to fall in this category; the visual and other symbols and lack of information sources result in reporters' conveying news that tends to legitimize the interests of the state.

Probably the strongest evidence in support of the media as public advocates relates to the increasing number of newsmagazine programs. However, even this aspect of public advocacy is determined more by news routines and entertainment values than by the desire to provide an alternative news product.

By default, then, the evidence presented in this chapter seems to support—or at least not refute—the profit-seeker model. The increased tabloid-style coverage of crime and the increasingly negative portrayal of government institutions seem to reflect changing news values that likely reflect increased pressure on news programs to produce large audiences.

CONCLUSION

A question posed earlier in this chapter was why politicians seem to be so critical of the news produced by the mass media. Most of the evidence suggests that their negative response in part reflects the increasingly negative, sensationalized nature of news coverage of political institutions. Politicians cannot be satisfied with this, especially since they are devoting more resources than ever to managing media relations. At the same time, one of the enduring principles of the relationship between the media and elected officials is that they both still need each other to do their jobs. While media coverage is increasingly negative, government officials remain their primary source of information, and in many cases the trend toward more negative news must be understood in the context of the broader finding that most news coverage is neutral rather than negative or positive. It is possible that the norm of neutrality continues to provide government officials with some ability to determine the broad contours of news coverage, even if particular details or contexts of the news are not to their liking.

Finally, we should put the question of why government officials seem so critical of the press into a broader context. There is no systematic evidence of how government officials assess the press. The question is motivated by the complaints of particular officials about particular stories or particular media outlets at particular times. The extent to which all government officials hold similar opinions of the performance of the media is unknown, as is the extent to which an official's unhappiness might be motivated by factors other than the nature of media coverage. In effect, are politicians who are not achieving their goals, or whose political efforts have been challenged by unfavorable news coverage, using the media as scapegoats? For every politician charging the media with bias, there is likely one or more who are pleased with the way the media are used to publicize an issue or enhance an image.

Key Terms

alliance
CNN effect
competition
crises
detachment
exposés
focusing event
fully controlled
    news
gaggle
going public
insider strategy

institutional agenda-
    setting
issue attention cycle
leak
mobilization model
national press corps
Office of
    Communications
outsider strategy
partially controlled news
presidential press
    conferences

pseudo-event
public image
public relations
selective access
surveillance
tongs
trial balloon
triggering event
uncontrolled news
White House press
    secretary

Exercises

1. Access the White House Web site, and review the proceedings from a recent press conference. What types of issues are raised by reporters? What types of information did the administration provide?
2. Locate the memoirs of a White House reporter or former White House press secretary, and read the portrayal of the reporter-official relationship. What were the official's frustrations and pleasures in the job?
3. Pick out a lead news story from the local newspaper, and identify the sources used by the reporter. To what extent did the reporter rely on official sources? To what extent did he or she exclude some alternative points of view by not seeking other possible sources?
4. Private companies use public relations techniques, as do foreign countries. Should government agencies, local governments, and public programs do the same? Why? Where is the line between providing information to the press so that reporters can cover government affairs and using the press to manipulate the public?

Notes

1. Leon V. Sigal, *Reporters and Officials: The Organization and Politics of News-making* (Lexington, MA: D.C. Heath, 1973).
2. Doris A. Graber, *Mass Media and American Politics* (Washington, DC: CQ Press, 2001), p. 102.
3. Walter Lippman, *Public Opinion* (New York: Macmillan, 1922).
4. Richard Davis, *The Press and American Politics*, 3rd ed. (New York: Prentice Hall, 2001), pp. 154–157.
5. Ibid., p. 264.
6. W. Lance Bennett, *News: The Politics of Illusion*, 4th ed. (New York: Longman, 2001), pp. 129–134.
7. Ibid.; Daniel Boorstein first popularized the term in *The Image: A Guide to Pseudo-Events* (New York: Atheneum, 1971).
8. Ibid.,
9. Frederic T. Smoller, *The Six O'Clock Presidency: A Theory of Presidential Press Relations in the Age of Television* (New York: Praeger, 1990), p. 120.
10. Matthew A. Baum and Samuel Kernell, "Has Cable Ended the Golden Age of Presidential Television?" *American Political Science Review* 93 (1999): 99–114.
11. Ibid.
12. Bennett, *News*.
13. Richard Neustadt, *Presidential Power and the Modern Presidents* (New York: The Free Press, 1991).

14. Jon R. Bond and Richard Fleisher, *The President in the Congressional Arena* (Chicago: University of Chicago Press, 1990); George C. Edwards III, *At the Margins: Presidential Leadership of Congress* (New Haven, CT: Yale University Press, 1989).

15. Samuel Kernell, *New Strategies of Presidential Leadership* (Washington, DC: CQ Press, 1997).

16. Bond and Fleisher, *The President in the Congressional Arena;* Edwards, *At the Margins;* Martha Joynt Kumar, "Presidential Publicity in the Clinton Era: The White House Communications Quartet." Paper delivered at the annual meeting of the Midwest Political Science Association, Palmer House, Chicago, April 23–26, 1998.

17. Kumar, "Presidential Publicity in the Clinton Era."

18. Ibid., p. 6.

19. Ibid.

20. Ibid., p. 8.

21. Ibid.

22. Ibid., p. 15.

23. Ibid.

24. Ibid.

25. Michael Baruch Grossman and Martha Joynt Kumar, *Portraying the President: The White House and the News Media* (Baltimore, MD: Johns Hopkins University Press, 1981), p. 265.

26. Smoller, *The Six O'Clock Presidency.*

27. Graber, *Mass Media and American Politics*, p. 275.

28. Smoller, *The Six O'Clock Presidency*, pp. 17–26.

29. Grossman and Kumar, *Portraying the President.*

30. Smoller, *The Six O'Clock Presidency*, pp. 47–51.

31. Grossman and Kumar, *Portraying the President.*

32. Smoller, *The Six O'Clock Presidency.*

33. Bennett, *News*, pp. 48–50.

34. Ibid., p. 49.

35. Tim Groelling and Samuel Kernell, "Is Network News Coverage of the President Biased?" *Journal of Politics* 60 (1998): 1063–1087.

36. Timothy E. Cook, *Making Laws and Making News: Media Strategies in the U.S. House of Representatives* (Washington, DC: The Brookings Institution, 1989), p. 30.

37. S. Robert Lichter and Daniel R. Amundson, "Less News Is Worse News: Television News Coverage of Congress, 1972–92," in *Congress, the Press, and the Public,* ed. Thomas E. Mann and Norman J. Ornstein (Washington, DC: American Enterprise Institute and The Brookings Institution, 1994), pp. 131–140.

38. Mark J. Rozell, "Press Coverage of Congress, 1946–92," in *Congress, the Press, and the Public,* ed. Thomas E. Mann and Norman J. Ornstein (Washington, DC: American Enterprise Institute and The Brookings Institution, 1994), pp. 109–112.

39. Cook, *Making Laws and Making News*, p. 34.

40. Timothy E. Cook, *Governing with the News: The News Media as a Political Institution* (Chicago: University of Chicago Press, 1998).

41. Cook, *Making Laws and Making News*, p. 83.

42. David Mayhew, *Congress: The Electoral Connection* (New Haven, CT: Yale University Press, 1986).

43. Stephen Hess, *The Washington Reporters* (Washington, DC: The Brookings Institution, 1981), p. 86.

44. Ibid.

45. See also Cook, *Making Laws and Making News*, p. 60.

46. Stephen Hess, *The Ultimate Insiders* (Washington, DC: The Brookings Institution, 1986), p. 5.

47. James H. Kuklinski and Lee Sigelman, "When Objectivity Is Not Objective: Network Television News Coverage of U.S. Senators and the 'Paradox of Objectivity,'" *Journal of Politics* 54 (1992): 810–833.

48. Ibid.

49. Susan J. Carroll and Ronnee Schreiber, "Media Coverage of Women in the 103rd Congress," in Pippa Norris, ed., *Women, Media and Politics* (New York: Oxford University Press, 1997), p. 135.

50. Ibid.

51. Jeremy Zilber and David Niven, "Stereotypes in the News: Media Coverage of African-Americans in Congress," *The Harvard International Journal of Press/Politics* 5 (2001): 70.

52. Ibid.

53. Ibid

54. Ibid.

55. Stephen Hess, "The Decline and Fall of Congressional News," in *Congress, the Press, and the Public*, ed. Thomas E. Mann and Norman J. Ornstein (Washington, DC: American Enterprise Institute and The Brookings Institution, 1994), pp. 141–156.

56. Rozell, "Press Coverage of Congress, 1946–92."

57. Mark D. Watts, "Media Coverage and the 103rd Congress: When to Cover Policymaking in Congress." Prepared for the Midwest Political Science Association, Chicago, April 23–26, 1998.

58. Ibid., p. 34.

59. Hess, *The Ultimate Insiders*, p. 33.

60. Jon R. Bond, Richard A. Watson, and Kevin B. Smith, *Promise and Performance of American Democracy*, 6th ed. (Itasca, IL: F. E. Peacock Publishers, 2001).

61. William Haltom, *Reporting on the Courts: How the Mass Media Cover Judicial Actions* (Chicago: Nelson-Hall, 1998), p. 98.

62. Stephanie Greco Larson, "The Content of Supreme Court Coverage: Making Sense of the Relationship Between the Media and Public Confidence," *Southeastern Political Review* 23 (1995): 231–244.

63. Jerome O'Callaghan and James O. Dukes, "Media Coverage of the Supreme Court's Caseload," *Journalism Quarterly* 69 (Spring 1992): 195–203.

64. Ibid. See also the analysis of newsmagazines during the Reagan administration in Dorothy A. Bowles and Rebekah V. Bromley, "Newsmagazine Coverage of the Supreme Court During the Reagan Administration," *Journalism Quarterly* 69 (Winter 1992): 948–959.

65. Haltom, *Reporting on the Courts*, p. 100.

66. Ibid., p. 177.

67. Ibid., p. 186.

68. Ibid., pp. 202–203.

69. Richard L. Fox and Robert W. Van Sickel, *Tabloid Justice: Criminal Justice in an Age of Media Frenzy* (Boulder, CO: Lynne Reinner Publishers, 2001), p. 3.

70. Ibid.

71. S. Robert Lichter, Linda S. Lichter, and Daniel R. Amundson, "Government Goes Down the Tube: Images of Government in TV Entertainment, 1955–1998," *The Harvard International Journal of Press/Politics* 5 (2000): 96–103.

72. Hess, *The Ultimate Insiders*, chap. 7.

73. Martin Linsky, *Impact: How the Press Affects Federal Policymaking* (New York: Norton, 1986).

74. Kim Quaile Hill and Patricia A. Hurley, "Dyadic Representation Reappraised," *American Journal of Political Science* 43 (1999): 109–141; John W. Kingdon, *Agendas, Alternatives, and Public Policies* (Boston: Little, Brown, 1984); Benjamin I. Page and Robert Y. Shapiro, *The Rational Public: Fifty Years of Trends in Americans' Policy Preferences* (Chicago: University of Chicago Press, 1992).

75. Anthony Downs, *An Economic Theory of Democracy* (New York: Harper & Row, 1957).

76. Kingdon, *Agendas, Alternatives and Public Policy.*

77. Cook, *Making Laws and Making News*, p. 119.

78. Ibid., p. 124.

79. Ibid.

80. Andrew Natsios, "Illusions of Influence: The CNN Effect in Complex Emergencies," in *From Massacres to Genocide: The Media, Public Policy and Humanitarian Crises*, ed. Robert I. Rotberg and Thomas G. Weiss (Washington, DC: The Brookings Institution, 1996), pp. 149–168; Steven Livingston and Todd Eachus, "Humanitarian Crises and U.S. Foreign Policy: Somalia and the CNN Effect Reconsidered," *Political Communication* 12 (1995): 413–429.

81. Natsios, "Illusions of Influence."

82. Ibid.

83. Christopher J. Bosso, "Setting the Agenda: Mass Media and the Discovery of Famine in Ethiopia," in *Manipulating Public Opinion: Essays on Public Opinion as a Dependent Variable*, ed. Michael Margolis and Gary A. Mauser (Pacific Grove, CA: Brooks/Cole Publishing, 1989), pp. 153–174.

84. Jack Shephard, "Ethiopia: The Use of Food as an Instrument of U.S. Foreign Policy," *Issue: A Journal of Opinion* 14 (1985): 4–9; quoted in Bosso, "Setting the Agenda," p. 158.

85. Bosso, "Setting the Agenda," p. 163.

86. Ibid., pp. 168–169.

87. For a notable exception, see Royce J. Ammon, *Global Television and the Shaping of World Politics* (Jefferson, NC: McFarland, 2001).

88. See David L. Protess, Fay Lomax Cook, Jack C. Doppelt, James S. Ettema, Margaret T. Gordon, Donna R. Leff, and Peter Miller, *The Journalism of Outrage: Investigative Reporting and Agenda Building in America* (New York: The Guilford Press, 1991), chap. 2, "The Investigative Tradition," for a more detailed history of investigative reporting.

89. Ibid.

90. Ibid., pp. 18–19.

91. Ibid., p. 250.

92. Downs, *An Economic Theory of Democracy.*

6 The Media, Political Knowledge, and Political Attitudes

Theories of Media Effects
Hypodermic Needle Model • Minimal Effects Model • Contingent Effects Model

Political Knowledge as a Requisite for a Healthy Democracy
Findings from Survey and Experimental Research • Political Learning: Individual, Mode, and Message Effects

Political Socialization, Trust, and Social Capital

Political Evaluations and Policy Support

The Media, Political Knowledge, and Political Attitudes

Conclusion

THE NUMBER OF news sources available on television and through the Internet has increased dramatically over the past decade or so. Newsmagazine programs have multiplied on the major networks, while numerous cable stations are now devoted to politics and public affairs programming. News sources are ubiquitous on the Internet. Yet most Americans know very little about the basics of American government. In 1992 about two-thirds of a national sample could not identify the names or party affiliations of their members of Congress, just over 8 percent could identify William Rehnquist as Chief Justice of the Supreme Court, and about 60 percent knew the relative ideological positions of the Democratic and Republican parties.[1] In 1989 only 20 percent of the public could name two First Amendment rights.[2]

This mismatch between available information and individuals' knowledge about politics poses a problem for most theories of individual-level media effects. Conventional wisdom suggests that the media are incredibly important in shaping people's beliefs and attitudes. How can this be true if basic political information is not "getting through" to the public?

The public's supposed ignorance of politics also poses a problem for normative theories of politics that emphasize the importance of the informed, rational citizen to the functioning of democracy. Most theories of democracy assume that people are aware of their self-interest; gather information about relevant political issues; and vote for candidates whose policy positions most closely reflect their own, or engage in some other sort of political activity. Assessing political self-interest requires adequate information about relevant political issues and an understanding of the implications of these issues for individual well-being. Assuming that this is how democracy works, the media are critical to its functioning because they are the main source of political information for citizens today. Evidence of widespread ignorance of politics suggests that the media are not doing their job, citizens are not behaving the way normative theories suggest they should, or both.

Expecting the media to perform responsibly is consistent with both the neutral adversary and public advocate models. In the neutral adversary model, the media are motivated in their watchdog role to ensure that power-seeking government officials are held accountable for their actions. Thus, the media have the responsibility of providing relevant and useful information so that citizens are able to properly evaluate government officials. In the public advocate model, the media define aspects of the public interest and are responsible for educating citizens about their political interests. Here again, the media are expected to provide relevant and useful information. In contrast to the neutral adversary model, though, they have more freedom (or responsibility) to define what is relevant and useful. The media are also expected to rely less on government officials for the definition of political interests and provision of relevant information for citizens.

The other three models—reporters of objective fact, profit-seeker, and propagandist—do not assume that it is the media's job to educate the public. In the reporters of objective fact model, the media are simply reporting facts as they emerge, and are discouraged from offering any interpretation, evaluation, or other contextual information that would help citizens evaluate government officials. In the profit-seeker model, the media are to report any information, loosely defined, that allows them to make a profit—with no attendant responsibility to inform or educate. In the propagandist model, the media are assumed to influence citizens' beliefs and attitudes, but not to enhance the pursuit of their self-interest. Instead, the propagandist model leads to citizens who are ignorant of political realities and misguided about their self-interests. Put another way, in this model the media actually make it more difficult for citizens to effectively evaluate, influence, or participate in the democratic system.

This chapter focuses on the cognitive, emotional, and evaluative effects of the media on individuals, with special emphasis on the cognitive effects of media usage in nonelectoral contexts. As noted in Chapter 1, evidence about whether (or how much) the media inform the mass public must necessarily reflect the message (or content) provided as well as how members of the news audience react to that message. While Chapter 2 was devoted to the nature of news provided by the media, this chapter investigates the validity of various assumptions about the nature of the audience, such as how much citizens seek out information and whether individuals accept information that is inconsistent with their prior beliefs.

THEORIES OF MEDIA EFFECTS

It is impossible to discuss the effect of the media on individuals by merely focusing on the nature or content of media messages, for the effect has two necessary components: the media with a message, and the audience on whom the message is expected to have an effect. Political communication scholars and political scientists have made very different assumptions about the audience from one era to another, resulting in very different theoretical expectations about what citizens learn or do not learn from the media, and why. Reflecting on these assumptions, scholars have focused on different types of media effects— **dependent variables**—and have used distinctive research methodologies to evaluate them. Scholars today have labeled these different intellectual eras by the general theoretical models guiding research at the time: the hypodermic needle model (from the 1930s to the early 1960s), the minimal effects model (mid-1960s to 1970s), and the contingent effects model (1980s to the present).[3]

Hypodermic Needle Model

World War I signaled the beginning of a new type of armed conflict between nations that relied on massive armies drawn from citizen populations. The war demanded much from the newly developed industrialized economies of the belligerents as well. Previous wars had actually demanded relatively little from those not conscripted to fight, but for nations to be successful in World War I, their populations had to support their mission in numerous ways. Mindful of this, policymakers in the major powers engaged in public relations efforts designed to strengthen citizens' loyalties. Much of this **propaganda** took the form of print and radio exposés that described either exaggerated or nonexistent atrocities committed by the enemies. The propagandists "assumed that cleverly designed stimuli would reach every individual member of the mass society via the media, that each person would perceive them in the same general manner, and that they would provoke a more or less uniform response from all."[4]

These assumptions about the audience are the core of the **hypodermic needle model,** which is also known as the "magic bullet theory" and the "transmission belt theory." Buttressing these assumptions was the intellectual dominance of **mass society theory,** in which newly industrialized society was conceptualized as an undifferentiated mass of atomistic individuals who had little in common with other people, interacted with others in only insignificant ways, and were acted directly upon by political and social authority figures. With little in the way of social connections or anchors and minimal psychological resources to fend off propagandistic messages, individuals simply received the messages political leaders sent and acted accordingly.

As intriguing (and colorful and frightening) as this model seems, however, there has never been any systematic evidence to suggest that it approximated reality. The classic example of the hypodermic needle model was Orson Welles' transmission of H. G. Wells' *War of the Worlds* on October 30, 1938. The Sunday night radio broadcast of a fictional account of Martians invading the village of Grover's Mill, New Jersey, began with an appropriate introduction indicating that it was fiction, but some people who tuned in late mistook the drama for an actual event because news bulletin updates were inserted as part of the entertainment program. Songs were interrupted, for example, by a newscaster claiming to have new information about the invasion. Anecdotal accounts suggested that some families in New Jersey packed up and headed West to escape the Martians. According to other accounts, some people committed suicide or threatened to jump off the Brooklyn Bridge because of fear of the invasion. A front page headline in the *New York Times* the next day read: "Radio Listeners in Panic, Taking War Drama as Fact" (see pp. 146–147).

In retrospect, these behavioral responses to the radio broadcast make for a colorful tale, but no systematic evidence was gathered that might confirm how representative or widespread such reactions were. It was not until World War II brought about intellectual and academic changes that systematic evidence was gathered.

Selected Text from *New York Times* Article on *War of the Worlds* Broadcast

Radio Listeners in Panic, Taking War Drama as Fact (October 31, 1938)

Many Flee Homes to Escape 'Gas Raid From Mars'—Phone Calls Swamp Police at Broadcast of Wells Fantasy

A wave of mass hysteria seized thousands of radio listeners between 8:15 and 9:30 o'clock last night when a broadcast of a dramatization of H. G. Wells's fantasy, "The War of the Worlds," led thousands to believe that an interplanetary conflict had started with invading Martians spreading wide death and destruction in New Jersey and New York.

The broadcast, which disrupted households, interrupted religious services, created traffic jams and clogged communications systems, was made by Orson Welles, who as the radio character, "The Shadow," used to give "the creeps" to countless child listeners. This time at least a score of adults required medical treatment for shock and hysteria.

In Newark, in a single block at Heddon Terrace and Hawthorne Avenue, more than twenty families rushed out of their houses with wet handkerchiefs and towels over their faces to flee from what they believed was to be a gas raid. Some began moving household furniture.

Throughout New York families left their homes, some to flee to near-by parks. Thousands of persons called the police, newspapers, and radio stations here and in other cities of the United States and Canada seeking advice on protective measures against the raids.

The program was produced by Mr. Welles and the Mercury Theatre on the Air over station WABC and the Columbia Broadcasting System's coast-to-coast network, from 8 to 9 o'clock.

The radio play, as presented, was to simulate a regular radio program with a "break-in" for the material of the play. The radio listeners, apparently, missed or did not listen to the introduction, which was: "The Columbia Broadcasting System and its affiliated stations present Orson Welles and the Mercury Theatre on the Air in 'The War of the Worlds' by H. G. Wells."

They also failed to associate the program with the newspaper listing of the program, announced as "Today: 8:00–9:00—Play: H. G. Wells's 'War of the Worlds'—WABC." They ignored three additional announcements made during the broadcast emphasizing its fictional nature.

Mr. Welles opened the program with a description of the series of which it is a part. The simulated program began. A weather report was given, prosaically. An announcer remarked that the program would be continued from a hotel, with dance music. For a few moments a dance program was given in the usual manner. Then there was a "break-in" with a "flash" about a professor at an observatory noting a series of gas explosions on the planet Mars.

News bulletins and scene broadcasts followed, reporting, with the technique in which the radio had reported actual events, the landing of a "meteor" near Princeton, N.J., "killing" 1,500 persons, the discovery that the "meteor" was a "metal cylinder" containing strange creatures from Mars armed with "death rays" to open hostilities against the inhabitants of the earth.

Despite the fantastic nature of the reported "occurrences," the program, coming after the recent war scare in Europe and a period in which the radio frequently had interrupted regularly scheduled programs to report developments in the Czechoslovak situation, caused fright and panic throughout the area of the broadcast.

Telephone lines were tied up with calls from listeners or persons who had heard of the broadcasts. Many sought first to verify the reports. But large numbers, obviously in a state of terror, asked how they could follow the broadcast's advice and flee from the city, whether they would be safer in the "gas raid" in the cellar or on the roof, how they could safeguard their children, and many of the questions which had been worrying residents of London and Paris during the tense days before the Munich agreement.

So many calls came to newspapers and so many newspapers found it advisable to check on the reports despite their fantastic content that The Associated Press sent out the following at 8:48 P.M.:

"Note to Editors: Queries to newspapers from radio listeners throughout the United States tonight, regarding a reported meteor fall which killed a number of New Jerseyites, are the result of a studio dramatization. The A. P."

Similarly police teletype systems carried notices to all stationhouses, and police short-wave radio stations notified police radio cars that the event was imaginary.

. . .

Columbia Explains Broadcast

The Columbia Broadcasting System issued a statement saying that the adaptation of Mr. Wells's novel which was broadcast "followed the original closely, but to make the imaginary details more interesting to American listeners the adapter, Orson Welles, substituted an American locale for the English scenes of the story."

Pointing out that the fictional character of the broadcast had been announced four times and had been previously publicized, it continued:

"Nevertheless, the program apparently was produced with such vividness that some listeners who may have heard only fragments thought the broadcast was fact, not fiction. Hundreds of telephone calls reaching CBS stations, city authorities, newspaper offices and police headquarters in various cities testified to the mistaken belief.

"Naturally, it was neither Columbia's nor the Mercury Theatre's intention to mislead any one, and when it became evident that a part of the audience had been disturbed by the performance five announcements were read over the network later in the evening to reassure those listeners."

Expressing profound regret that his dramatic efforts should cause such consternation, Mr. Welles said: "I don't think we will choose anything like this again." He hesitated about presenting it, he disclosed, because "it was our thought that perhaps people might be bored or annoyed at hearing a tale so improbable."

Minimal Effects Model

Before World War II, no organized academic discipline was devoted to the study of mass communications. Instead, diverse scholars from sociology, political science, and psychology made the mass communication audience a focus of studies of persuasion, social interaction, and communication. Although these scholars came from different backgrounds, they shared some assumptions and values that allow us to label their work by what it had in common.

Several intellectual developments over the course of the twentieth century led to the abandonment of some of the basic assumptions of the hypodermic needle model. For example, psychology shifted from emphasizing inheritance (nature) to emphasizing learning (nurture) as a fundamental explanation of individual behavior. An important consequence was a challenge to the assumption that individuals in the mass audience would all be equally exposed to, and would all react similarly to, mass communication messages. Social psychologists abandoned the notion that instinct motivated human behavior and instead focused on the importance of individuals' attitudes.

At the same time, the field of sociology replaced the notion of a mass society with the view that newly industrialized society was more complex and interconnected than had previously been acknowledged. In particular, society was viewed as stratified, with differences in wealth, occupation, and education (rather than inheritance) that allowed individuals to identify with or be associated with groups of individuals with shared traits, beliefs, and/or status. These groups were found to be more similar than not and to have at least some attitudes that predictably affected their behavior. Hence, the social groupings provided the social interconnectedness or anchors that mass society theorists had earlier assumed away.

This emphasis on social differentiation was also convenient in the more practical fields of business and industry. If identifiable demographic groups shared certain attitudes, and if these attitudes influenced their behaviors, the soon-to-be-booming field of marketing—the goal of which was to increase sales in the expanding World War II economy—could take advantage of these social structures by targeting products in formal advertising campaigns.

The war effort also had provided support for developing the tools to identify the demographic groups and their related attitudes and behaviors. Specifically, researchers at Columbia University adapted newly refined survey sampling techniques from the field of agriculture for use in the scientific study of political attitudes and public opinion. The earliest—and now classic—study emerging from this tradition was *The People's Choice*, published in 1944, a study of the 1940 presidential campaign between Franklin Roosevelt and Wendell Willkie conducted by Paul Lazarsfeld, Bernard Berelson, and Hazel Gaudet of Columbia University.[5]

To compare the effects of mass communication with those of social interaction and influence during the campaign, the researchers interviewed the same set of residents in Erie County, Ohio, several times over a six-month period.

What they found was quite a surprise, especially in light of the prevailing hypodermic needle model. Most people knew for whom they would vote at the beginning of the campaign. Voters tended to mention personal, rather than media, influence as having a significant effect on vote decisions, and on most days individuals were more likely to report talking to others about the campaign than to report reading about it in the newspaper. Thus, the researchers concluded that the election campaign seemed to have little effect on voters.

In an effort to explain their surprising empirical findings, Lazarsfeld, Berelson, and Gaudet introduced two new, interrelated theoretical concepts to which scholars subscribed for the next several decades. First, they claimed that certain individuals, who were most interested in politics and most likely to be exposed to media messages and to engage in politics, served as **opinion leaders** because other, less-involved citizens would look to them for information. Second, the effects of the mass media were likely channeled through these opinion leaders to the mass public, and thus the mass communication process is a **two-step flow,** from the media to opinion leaders, and from opinion leaders to the mass public.

These new theoretical concepts helped Lazarsfeld, Berelson, and Gaudet make sense of their findings, especially with regard to the relatively low level of interest and knowledge displayed by most people they interviewed. These new concepts also helped these scholars and their readers "save democracy" by rationalizing the empirical findings—keeping the American public from looking so bad. They also challenged the assumptions of the hypodermic needle model.

The empirical findings of Lazarsfeld and his associates, as well as the changing models of individual behavior and social structure in psychology and sociology, were affirmed by the 1960 publication of Joseph Klapper's *The Effects of Mass Communication.*[6] Klapper reviewed the empirical findings of the previous decades' research on mass communication and concluded that the evidence was generally inconsistent with any notion that mass communication had a broad, undifferentiated, or strong effect on individuals—in other words, that mass communication was limited in its ability to persuade people to change their political beliefs. The evidence suggested instead that the effects were minimal, and that the media were more likely to reinforce or strengthen individuals' initial attitudes than to change them. This way of looking at the effects of the mass media became known as the **minimal effects model.**

Klapper argued that several psychological mechanisms—as well as group norms and social influences—account for the minimal effects of the media. **Selective exposure** refers to individuals' tendencies to expose themselves to messages that are consistent with their prior beliefs. **Selective perception** refers to their tendencies to interpret messages in a manner consistent with their beliefs. **Selective retention** refers to the tendency to retain information that is consistent with prior beliefs. According to Klapper, these mechanisms structure how individuals process information and thus tend to minimize the extent to which a message conveyed by mass communication changes an individual's opinion or belief.[7]

Sociologists' and political scientists' adoption of survey sampling to study public opinion had tremendous consequences for the study of mass communication and public opinion. In political science, for example, nearly all public opinion research funding supported the development of the American National Election Survey (NES), a nationally representative sample survey housed at the University of Michigan that has been conducted biennially since the late 1950s. An implicit acceptance of the minimal effects model likely helps account for the fact that the NES had few questions devoted to media use in the 1960s and 1970s. Accordingly, most public opinion research relying on NES data focused almost entirely on individuals' psychological predispositions toward politics, and completely ignored the potential of election campaigns or mass communication to more generally structure people's political attitudes or behaviors. In the absence of questions regarding the mass media, for example, researchers could not empirically examine the media's effectiveness, and the implicit conclusion was that the media were irrelevant to the study of public opinion.

Contingent Effects Model

The minimal effects model has been challenged on a number of bases. The most simple criticism is that the researchers' conclusion was never as broad as what the label suggests. Klapper and Lazarsfeld, Berelson, and Gaudet allowed for the *possibility* of media effects, but they noted that such effects occur only in a particular set of circumstances relating to individual and message characteristics. Hence, scholars came to recognize that their broad interpretation of the minimal effects model was exaggerated.

Some scholars have investigated how individual characteristics, message characteristics, and the informational context structure media effects—that is, determine how strongly or weakly the media influence individuals. This **contingent effects model** indicates that particular types of media delivering specific types of messages will significantly affect some individuals at particular times. With this new theoretical expectation also came a more careful consideration of an array of possible media effects, and scholars began examining effects other than political knowledge and vote choice.

Contingent effects research typically relies on **experimental research designs** rather than on survey research. The advantages of using experiments to study media effects are that they provide especially good measures of exposure to specific media content and of individuals' responses to those messages. These are appealing features of experimental research in the social sciences (for more details, see Appendix on Experimental Research Design), and features that are necessary for researchers to observe large media effects.[8] Unlike **survey research designs,** a researcher who gathers empirical evidence in an experiment has far greater confidence that individuals were exposed to the media message (the **independent variable**) as well as the ability to develop more precise measures of their responses to the message (the dependent variable). For example, media effects research using survey data typically compares media users with nonusers, rather than comparing individuals exposed to a particular message with those not exposed to it. Moreover, measures of media exposure must necessarily rely on self-reports of survey respondents, and these reports may not be entirely reliable.

At a more fundamental level, reliance on cross-sectional survey research also limits the extent to which researchers can draw inferences from the data about whether there is a correlation between media use or exposure and the dependent variable, or a truly causal relationship. As is often the case in the social sciences, distinguishing between **correlation** and **causation** depends on the quality of the theory behind the research enterprise. But research designs are also relevant, and experimental designs allow the researcher to observe the time-ordered process of communication effects. The cross-sectional survey, on the other hand, provides no information about whether the cause (media exposure) precedes the effect on individuals' attitudes.

Not surprisingly, political scientists' study of mass communication effects has recently yielded scholarship that claims not a minimal, but rather a contingent, effect of mass communications on individuals.

POLITICAL KNOWLEDGE AS A REQUISITE FOR A HEALTHY DEMOCRACY

While mass communication and public opinion studies have certainly moved toward a more empirical, scientific approach, normative concerns about the functioning of democracy nonetheless remain important. Perhaps the most stunning single finding of Lazarsfeld, Berelson, and Gaudet—essentially replicated many times over and in very recent studies as well—was the relative lack of interest and knowledge about the presidential election campaign displayed by the mass public. The findings in *The People's Choice* in essence indicated that one of the key requirements of a healthy democracy—that citizens are active and knowledgeable participants in the political system—was not being met. If modern social science findings consistently identify mass political ignorance, what are we to do? Why are the media seemingly ineffective in this regard?

Findings from Survey and Experimental Research

The fundamental importance of political knowledge in a representative democracy is reflected by the fact that most studies of direct media effects tend to focus on cognition (the magnitude and accuracy of individuals' political information, knowledge, and beliefs) rather than on attitudes (affective, emotional, or evaluative orientations toward politics) and behavior. Early studies of mass communication assumed that these three types of effects were ordered: **Cognitive effects** were assumed to be necessary for, and to precede, any potential **affective effects,** which in turn mediated any **behavioral effects.** When studies uncovered only limited levels of political information, it was assumed that the affective and behavioral effects of mass communication were minimal.

More recently, however, scholars have argued that these three types of effects are not necessarily ordered, and that one can exist without the other. Theoretically, in other words, behavioral consequences could exist without any intervening attitudinal effects of the media. Once effects were no longer assumed to be ordered, the way was paved for the development of contingent effects studies, which tend to focus on attitudes rather than knowledge.

Political scientists typically measure citizens' knowledge of political information as the number of correct responses to a series of survey questions about political leaders or public policies. Tables 6-1 through 6-4 present selected items of this type from public opinion surveys over the past several decades. While the researchers who collected this information suggest that higher levels of information would certainly be better, they nonetheless conclude that the situation is not hopeless.[9] More than half of the sample knew the correct answers on more than half of the survey items on political institutions and processes and on around 40 percent of the items on people and players and domestic politics. They conclude that what Americans know is dependent on the availability of information: The more readily and routinely the information is provided to citizens, the more likely they are to know it.

Some scholars have argued that these survey "pop quizzes" are not valid measures of political knowledge.[10] For example, what is most critical to the functioning of democratic society is not just the discrete facts that individuals can report (differentiation), but also the extent to which they can integrate these facts into more coherent views about politics (integration).[11] Similarly, individuals can act rationally in politics by using informational shortcuts to evaluate candidates and policies, even if they lack detailed knowledge about the politicians and proposed legislation.[12] Hence, reliance on "textbook quizzes" to measure the political knowledge or sophistication of the mass public may be misleading.

These quizzes are probably also misleading in assessing the extent to which the mass media educate the mass public; at least, they should not be the only evidence from which conclusions are drawn. Recall the first condition that must be met to empirically observe media effects—that the dependent variable must be properly measured.[13] To the extent that democratic governments require sophisticated or informed citizens, but not a detailed knowledge of politicians or policies, measuring ignorance with "pop quizzes" might be misleading.

TABLE 6-1 Knowledge of Institutions and Processes (Percentage Correct)

Survey Item	%	Survey Item	%
U.S. is a member of the U.N. (1985)	96	Define wiretapping (1949)	67
Warrants allow police searches (1986)	94	Need warrant to search noncitizens (1986)	66
Length of president's term (1952)	93	Define impeachment (1974)	66
What is purpose of U.N. (1976)	90	Congress can't ban opposition (1964)	65
Define presidential veto (1989)	89	English not official national language (1986)	64
United States is a democracy (1948)	88	Define foreign trade deficit (1985)	63
Define press release (1985)	85	Need Congressional approval for military aid (1986)	62
Right to trial by jury guaranteed (1986)	83	Effect of dollar's value on import prices (1978)	62
States can have a death penalty (1983)	83	President can't adjourn Congress (1986)	59
No religious test for office seekers (1986)	81	Who determines law's constitutionality (1992)	58
Convicted persons can appeal (1983)	81	Define cold war (1950)	58
Define inflation (1951)	80	How does U.N. veto work (1947)	57
Treaties need Senate approval (1986)	79	Third in line for presidency (1985)	57
Define federal deregulation (1984)	78	Free speech protected on all media (1984)	56
What Constitution says on religion (1989)	77	Convicted felon not assured vote (1986)	55
Constitution can be amended (1986)	76	Substance of *Brown* decision (1986)	55
Gulf War reports were censored (1991)	76	# of senators from each state (1945)	55
Define Dow Jones index (1984)	76	Define newsleak (1986)	55
How presidential campaign is funded (1979)	76	Define newspaper chain (1985)	55
Small papers depend on wire services (1985)	76	Who sets monetary policy (1984)	54
First Amendment protects free press/speech (1985)	75	Define farm price supports (1953)	54
President employs White House press secretary (1985)	75	Purpose of the Constitution (1986)	54
Purpose of U.N. (1951)	74	# of women on Supreme Court (1988)	53
All states have trial courts (1977)	74	Define filibuster (1963)	53
Not all cases heard by jury (1983)	74	Define federal budget deficit (1987)	52
Name a cabinet position (1960)	72	What does FCC do (1979)	52
Define party platform (1952)	71	Effect of unbalanced budget on prices (1959)	52
Define depression (1983)	69	What effect do tariffs have (1946)	51
Define a monopoly (1949)	69		
Popular votes don't determine president (1986)	69		

(continued)

TABLE 6-1 (Continued)

Survey Item	%	Survey Item	%
Congress can't require president to believe in God (1964)	51	Describe economic system in U.S. (1951)	33
Accused are presumed innocent (1983)	50	Governors don't OK court rulings (1977)	33
How presidential delegates are selected (1978)	49	Insider trading is illegal (1987)	33
		Name a U.N. agency (1975)	35
Define reciprocal trade agreement (1945)	48	Substance of *Roe v. Wade* (1986)	30
		Length of House term (1978)	30
Define certificate of deposit (1987)	48	Substance of *Webster* decision (1989)	29
No right to own handgun (1986)	48	Libel law differs for public figures (1985)	27
What is Voice of America (1951)	46		
Define liberal (1957)	46	Name two branches of government (1952)	27
Define conservative (1957)	46		
What is N.Y. Stock Exchange (1987)	46	Define bipartisan foreign policy (1950)	26
States can't legislate silent prayer (1986)	46	Define prime rate (1985)	26
		Length of senator's term (1991)	25
TV more regulated than print (1985)	45	No guarantee for high school education (1986)	23
Substance of *Miranda* decision (1989)	45		
Congress declares war (1987)	45	Define fiscal policy (1983)	21
% vote to override presidential veto (1947)	44	Define collateral damage (1991)	21
Name a branch of government (1952)	44	Name two First Amendment rights (1989)	20
Who sets interest rates (1984)	42	What is Food & Drug Administration (1979)	20
Name a U.N. agency (1976)	41		
Define Bill of Rights (1986)	41	Define the Foreign Service (1955)	19
Purpose of NATO (1988)	40	Define supply side economics (1981)	19
How are presidential candidates selected (1952)	40	Name all three branches of government (1952)	19
Define free trade (1953)	39	Define monetary policy (1983)	18
Can't force pledge of allegiance (1986)	39	Define sampling error (1987)	16
# of states choosing U.S. representatives (1954)	37	What is the Common Market (1961)	13
		Not all federal cases reviewed by Supreme Court (1986)	12
Define primary election (1952)	36		
Define welfare state (1949)	36	Define politically correct (1991)	7
Pool system used in Gulf war (1991)	36	Name two Fifth Amendment rights (1989)	2
Define electoral college (1955)	35		

Source: Michael X. Delli Carpini and Scott Keeter, *What Americans Know About Politics and Why It Matters* (New Haven, CT: Yale University Press, 1997), pp. 70–71.

TABLE 6-2 Knowledge of People and Players (Percentage Correct)

Survey Item	%	Survey Item	%
U.S. president (1986)	99	Dukakis stance on abortion (1988)	64
Douglas MacArthur (1947)	97	Winner of Nicaraguan election (1990)	63
Walter Cronkite (1975)	93	Who are the freedom riders (1961)	61
John L. Lewis (1957)	93	What is the NAACP (1985)	59
Know Nelson Mandela is free (1990)	91	John Foster Dulles (1953)	59
Name your governor (1970)	86	Is your governor a Democrat or	
Chiang Kai-shek's country (1954)	84	Republican (1985)	59
Dean Rusk (1964)	82	Franco's nation (1949)	58
Henry Kissinger (1973)	78	Republican party stance, nuclear	
Clinton's stand on gays in the		testing (1988)	58
military (1993)	77	Nehru's country (1954)	58
Joe McCarthy (1954)	77	Barry Goldwater (1963)	58
J. Edgar Hoover (1960)	75	Republican party more conservative	
Leader of Iraq (1990)	75	(1988)	57
Ralph Nadar (1976)	75	Truman's stand on taxes (1947)	57
Charles de Gaulle (1964)	73	Secretary of state (1958)	57
Dean Rusk (1967)	73	How representative voted on	
Head of China (1943)	72	Gulf War (1991)	57
Margaret Thatcher	72	Cyrus Vance (1977)	54
Bush's stance on SDI (1988)	71	Warren Burger (1984)	51
Mikhail Gorbachev (1990)	71	CIO stance on FDR (1944)	51
Party control of House (1978)	71	President of Russia (1994)	47
Walter Reuther (1957)	70	Andrew Young (1977)	48
Truman's stance on communists		Gorbachev stance on multiparty	
in U.S. government (1947)	69	system (1990)	47
George Wallace (1967)	69	Harold Stassen (1952)	46
Party supported by most blacks (1985)	69	Moral Majority's general stances (1981)	46
Know Bush reversed stand on taxes		Incumbent House candidate (1966)	46
(1990)	68	J. Birch Society stance: ERA (1979)	45
Progressive party presidential		Ed Meese (1984)	42
candidate (1948)	67	U Thant (1964)	42
Orval Faubus (1957)	67	Dukakis vetoed pledge bill (1988)	41
Carter's stand on ERA (1979)	66	Marshal Tito (1951)	40
Verdict in J. Hazelwood trial (1990)	66	Jim Wright's party (1990)	39
Tip O'Neill (1983)	66	Reagan stance on balanced budget	
		in '82 (1981)	39

(continued)

TABLE 6-2 *(Continued)*

Survey Item	%	Survey Item	%
Kurt Waldheim (1980)	39	A person critical of Gulf War (1991)	25
Anthony Eden (1952)	38	Attorney general (1970)	24
Truman's stance on war criminals (1947)	37	Gerald Ford's party (1974)	22
Gamal Nasser (1958)	37	Socialist party presidential candidate (1948)	21
Name both your senators (1985)	35	Republican party stance: pro-life amendment (1980)	21
Harold Washington (1984)	34	Louis Farrakhan (1990)	20
President of France (1986)	34	Eugene McCarthy (1967)	19
President of CIO (1944)	34	Country Pollard spying for (1990)	19
Carter's stance on defense spending (1979)	32	Julius Rosenberg (1950)	18
Superintendent of local schools (1987)	32	Zbigniew Brzezinski (1977)	17
Elizabeth Dole (1983)	32	Robert McNeil (1980)	16
RFK-LBJ differences on Vietnam (1967)	31	Robert Bork (1987)	15
Anthony Eden (1954)	31	Sukarno (1964)	15
Ted Kennedy stance on wage and price controls (1980)	30	Ross Perot (1971)	14
Jesse Helms (1984)	29	Prime minister of Canada (1989)	11
How one senator voted on Panama Canal (1978)	29	U.S.'s U.N. representative (1947)	11
County clerk (1965)	28	Vaclav Havel (1990)	10
State senator (1965)	28	Secretary general of U.N. (1953)	10
Who said "thousand points of light" (1988)	27	Charles Percy's party (1974)	9
Secretary of defense (1959)	27	Mark Hatfield (1963)	7
Name one of "Keating Five" (1991)	27	Prime minister of Italy (1986)	6
Who are the Black Muslims (1963)	27	Elmo Roper (1960)	5
Reagan's stand on ERA (1979)	27	Head of HUD (1977)	5
Ivan Boesky (1987)	26	Lane Kirkland (1980)	5
		President of Mexico (1991)	3
		Hodding Carter (1979)	3
		Prime minister of Norway (1986)	1

Source: Michael X. Delli Carpini and Scott Keeter, *What Americans Know About Politics and Why It Matters* (New Haven, CT: Yale University Press, 1997), pp. 74–75.

TABLE 6-3 Knowledge of Domestic Politics (Percentage Correct)

Survey Item	%	Survey Item	%
What is the steel dispute about (1952)	96	Effect of tax law on mortgage deductions (1987)	63
Social Security doesn't provide job training (1974)	89	Government doesn't require religious broadcasting (1945)	61
Minimum wage (1984)	86	Public school curricula vary by state (1989)	61
Budget deficit increased since 1981 (1985)	83	Who is eligible for draft pardon (1975)	61
Oil is in short supply (1974)	81	Causes of acid rain (1981)	60
Aware of recent coal strikes (1944)	81	Excise tax legislation passed (1965)	60
Industry's position in steel dispute (1952)	80	# of points Dow Jones index fell (10/20/87)	59
Who will pay for S&L bailout (1990)	79	Birth control pill—health problem link (1978)	57
Union's position in steel dispute (1952)	78	Road beautification bill passed (1965)	55
Pesticides can pollute away from source (1979)	78	What is Watergate about (1973)	54
Social Security revenue spent, not saved (1978)	78	Why nuclear plants built by water (1980)	52
There is a federal budget deficit (1984)	77	Why Hubbel telescope in news (1990)	51
Medicare legislation passed (1965)	76	Government regulates radio (1945)	51
What is national health insurance (1978)	76	Major cause of childhood death (1989)	51
Medicare part of Social Security system (1974)	75	Illiteracy rate in U.S. (1990)	51
What happened at Three Mile Island (1980)	74	Bush vetoed plant closing bill (1990)	50
		What is greenhouse effect (1988)	50
Medicare doesn't cover all medical costs (1987)	72	Size of federal budget (1989)	49
Size of oil spill off Alaska (1989)	72	Leading cause of death in U.S. (1952)	48
Farmers having economic problems (1979)	71	Current unemployment rate (1984)	48
		Likely effect of Taft-Hartley (1946)	45
There is a federal budget deficit (1983)	70	Major cause of air pollution (1980)	45
Food preservatives linked to health problem (1978)	69	Population of U.S. (1988)	43
Fresh water not unlimited (1979)	69	Current inflation rate (1985)	42
Military personnel tested for AIDS (1987)	68	Food stamps not part of Social Security (1979)	41
Electricity in short supply (1974)	68	Steel is in short supply (1974)	41
Describe Nixon economic plan (1971)	68	Government doesn't set # of radio ads (1945)	41
Voting rights legislation passed (1965)	67	College education bill passed (1965)	41
		Primary education bill passed (1965)	40

(continued)

TABLE 6-3 *(Continued)*

Survey Item	%	Survey Item	%
Value of dollar compared to 1939 (1951)	39	Government considering suit against AT&T (1975)	18
Government doesn't set radio profits (1945)	38	% of federal budget to health care (1978)	17
Not all federal employees pay Social Security (1979)	37	% of gross taxes paid by top 25% (1978)	17
# of Americans unemployed (1984)	37	Effect of tax law on capital gains (1987)	16
What are synthetic fuels (1980)	37	How are stock profits taxed (1989)	16
Black and white blood the same (1944)	36	% of poor that are black (1985)	15
Immigration legislature passed (1965)	35	% of U.S. power from nuclear (1979)	14
Average net industry profit (1969)	35	Urban affairs bill passed (1965)	14
Westmoreland suing CBS (1985)	33	Costs or wages rising faster (1958)	14
What is affirmative action (1985)	31	Required car mpg by 1985 (1979)	13
Black relative unemployment rate (1977)	31	Corporation income tax rate (1945)	13
What is the Hoover Commission (1950)	31	What is Dixon-Yates proposal (1954)	12
% U.S. citizens who are millionaires (1979)	28	Average cost per school child (1979)	12
		How is Superfund funded (1986)	12
Social Security one of top two federal budget expenses (1989)	27	% of population that is Hispanic (1990)	12
		Meese porno report conclusion (1986)	12
Average coal miner's salary (1944)	26	What are right-to-work laws (1955)	11
What is acid rain (1980)	26	% of workers employed by government (1976)	11
What does FICA deduction mean (1989)	25	% of poor who are kids (1985)	11
What is Social Security tax rate (1979)	25	What is thalidomide (1979)	10
Amount of current gasoline taxes (1984)	23	% gas cost go to oil company profits (1984)	10
% U.S. workers in unions (1944)	23	% poor who are women (1985)	9
What is Watergate about (1972)	22	Average yearly dollars to treat AIDS patient (1987)	9
Define no-fault insurance (1969)	22	% population that is Jewish (1990)	8
What happened at Love Canal (1979)	22	% population that is black (1990)	8
% of federal budget to military (1984)	21	% federal budget to Social Security (1984)	8
Helms trying to buy CBS (1985)	21	Effect of tax law on scholarships (1987)	8
Income tax on $25,000 (1944)	19	% federal spending increased since 1980 (1988)	6
Government regulates radio ownership (1945)	18	Size of federal budget (1951)	6
% of population below poverty line (1989)	18		

Source: Michael X. Delli Carpini and Scott Keeter, *What Americans Know About Politics and Why It Matters* (New Haven, CT: Yale University Press, 1997), pp. 80–81.

TABLE 6-4 Knowledge of Foreign Affairs (Percentage Correct)

Survey Item	%	Survey Item	%
Ozone damage affects whole world (1988)	94	Countries signing Camp David accord (1979)	62
Name one country with nuclear weapons (1988)	93	U.S. is a member of NATO (1964)	61
		What is the Kremlin (1957)	61
Americans held hostage in Middle East (1989)	91	Where are Contras and Sandinistas (1988)	60
U.S. has trade deficit with Japan (1988)	88	Mineral used in A-bomb (1952)	59
Volkswagen is a foreign company (1978)	87	Most Western European countries are democracies (1948)	59
U.S. has military base in Phillipines (1985)	85	% South Africans who are black (1985)	59
		Size of Japan GNP relative to U.S. (1986)	59
U.S. provides economic aid to South Korea (1985)	83	Describe unrest in Middle East (1967)	58
Cuba is communist (1988)	82	Describe goals of SALT treaty (1979)	58
Name is a country occupying Germany (1950)	82	Where is Persian Gulf (1987)	58
		Describe current problem in Iran (1951)	57
Who brought Berlin dispute to U.N. (1948)	81	Japan has free elections (1982)	57
Nixon reaction to Calley decision (1971)	80	Apartheid is policy in South Africa (1988)	55
Soviet Union is communist (1948)	78	Palestine not independent country (1946)	55
U.S. imports oil (1984)	78		
Mainland China is communist (1985)	77	East Germany is communist (1954)	55
Describe Soviet pressure on Lithuania (1990)	77	U.S. will still defend Panama Canal (1978)	54
Reagan administration to deploy MX missile (1985)	76	Taxes higher in Western Europe than U.S. (1989)	53
Iran demand for return of U.S. hostages (1980)	74	Spain not a democracy (1948)	52
		What is hydrogen bomb (1950)	52
Way fallout from Chernobyl was spread (1988)	73	Describe situation in Poland (1981)	52
Not all Indians are Hindus (1978)	72	Relation of England to India (1942)	51
England deployed troops in Saudi Arabia (1990)	72	Black South Africans can't vote (1985)	51
		Relation of England to Canada (1942)	50
Japan not known for oil reserves (1988)	72	Israel gained ground since 1948 (1973)	50
Who does U.S. government support in Nicaragua (1988)	69	West Germany a member of NATO (1989)	50
North Korea is communist (1978)	66	Cease-fire in Middle East (1948)	49
Did rebellion in Romania succeed (1990)	66	Only nation to use nuclear weapons (1986)	49
Can Soviets make A-bomb (1949)	63	What is foreign aid spent on (1958)	48
What is Marshall Plan (1950)	63	No Jordan troops in Saudi Arabia (1990)	48

(*continued*)

TABLE 6-4 *(Continued)*

Survey Item	%	Survey Item	%
Not all Soviets in Communist party (1986)	48	Poland is in Warsaw Pact (1988)	32
Has U.S. recognized Lithuania (1990)	47	Serbians conquered much of Bosnia (1994)	27
Sweden is a democracy (1948)	46	Two countries in SALT Treaty (1979)	30
U.S. supports El Salvador government (1983)	46	Argentina ruled by a dictator (1948)	29
Has U.S. approved SALT treaty (1984)	45	# of U.S. soldiers in Vietnam (1967)	29
England rules Palestine (1946)	45	% of oil in U.S. that's imported (1977)	29
% U.S. oil from Arab nations (1973)	42	Country attacking USS *Stark* (1987)	29
Who struck first in Arab-Israeli war (1973)	42	Describe Panama's government (1988)	28
Kuwait not a democracy (1991)	42	% world population: malnourished (1979)	28
Who controls Formosa (1954)	41	Reebok a foreign company (1987)	28
Soviets not in NATO (1964)	41	East Germany in Warsaw Pact (1988)	27
U.S. has no "no first strike" policy (1988)	40	Describe Saudi Arabia's government (1990)	25
Yugoslavia is communist (1948)	39	Describe neutron bomb (1977)	24
France is a member of NATO (1988)	39	% world population: underdeveloped nations (1972)	22
No collective bargaining in Russia (1945)	38	% aliens in U.S. (1940)	20
U.S. in International Court of Justice (1946)	37	Shell Oil a foreign company (1986)	19
U.S. has military base on Cuba (1977)	37	Israel gets largest % U.S. aid (1986)	18
Soviets are in Warsaw Pact (1988)	37	Describe government of El Salvador (1988)	17
Allies took land from Germany (1944)	36	% world population that controls most of money (1979)	17
When will Panama control the canal (1990)	36	# of U.S. soldiers killed in Vietnam (1965)	17
England has nuclear weapons (1988)	35	Size of U.S. trade deficit (1984)	16
Issues in Israel withdrawal from Egypt (1957)	35	Describe the Baruch Plan (1948)	15
Describe aspect of U.S. immigration policy (1965)	35	Describe the McCarran Act (1955)	14
		What is the Bricker amendment (1954)	13
Where are most immigrants coming from (1993)	35	Describe Glasnost (1987)	11
Does Japan have a military draft (1986)	34	U.S.'s largest trading partner (1991)	8
Japan imports U.S. agricultural products (1986)	33	# of U.S. soldiers killed in Vietnam (1967)	6
		% U.S. real estate foreign owned (1989)	4
Women can vote in India (1978)	33	Is U.S. a member of UNESCO (1947)	1

Source: Michael X. Delli Carpini and Scott Keeter, *What Americans Know About Politics and Why It Matters* (New Haven, CT: Yale University Press, 1997), pp. 83–84.

Many scholars now argue that these knowledge quizzes do not explicitly model the extent to which individuals have actually been exposed to particular media. Instead, it is assumed that the knowledge is freely and easily available. From a social science research design perspective, control over the independent variable (actual exposure and content of the media message) is required, as is good measurement of learning. Since learning takes place over time, multiple measures of individuals' knowledge are needed. Hence, experimental research designs might be particularly suited for the alternative evaluation of media effects. The next section provides a detailed example of this.

Political Learning: Individual, Mode, and Message Effects

In *Common Knowledge: News and the Construction of Political Meaning,* W. Russell Neuman, Marion R. Just, and Ann N. Crigler introduce a theoretical framework that emphasizes audience members as active participants in the news communication process.[14] Individuals' learning, they contend, reflects specific characteristics of the **medium** (television, newspaper, or magazine), **mode** (audio, visual, or both), and **message** (the information conveyed). Rather than assuming, as earlier researchers had, that newspapers are a superior learning medium, Neuman, Just, and Crigler empirically tested the hypothesis that individuals learn more from reading a newspaper than from watching television.

Previous research often relied on comparisons of television viewers with newspaper readers, and differences in political knowledge were attributed to differences in learning. Newspaper readers always came out on top in that comparison, and researchers concluded that newspapers were a superior medium for learning. But the comparison ignored two important differences between the groups—that newspaper readers tend to have higher levels of education and income, and that newspapers typically include more content than does television news. Hence, comparing only the political knowledge across these two groups does not indicate whether differences result from media or message differences, or from differences in prior knowledge.

To address these limitations, Neuman, Just, and Crigler controlled the specific information provided in media messages (thus equalizing the content of messages provided by television and newspapers) and also measured individuals' prior political knowledge. Further, as in all experimental designs, they randomly assigned the subjects to media groups (television, newspaper, newsmagazines) rather than letting them choose one medium over another.

To measure knowledge before and after exposure to the media messages, the researchers asked factual questions about five issues (apartheid, AIDS, the strategic defense initiative, the stock market crash of October 1987, and drug abuse). Learning from the media was defined as having more correct answers after being exposed to the media message than before. Neuman, Just, and Crigler found that the amount of information subjects gained from any one story was typically a very small proportion of the information in the story and of what individuals already knew. Their experimental results thus suggest that learning from the media is a gradual, incremental process.

The researchers also found that, in general, individuals in the television and newsmagazine groups learned significantly more about the issues than those in the newspaper group. This general conclusion varies somewhat based on issue type. For issues that individuals are likely not to experience themselves or are complex or distant, such as apartheid in South Africa, the television group learned the most. For issues that individuals are more likely to experience themselves, such as AIDS and drug abuse, television is the least, and newspapers the most, effective medium. Therefore, newspapers are superior learning devices in some, but not all, cases. Neuman, Just, and Crigler conclude that the general **print superiority thesis** suggested in previous research is simply wrong.

The arguments and evidence presented in this chapter thus far suggest two tentative conclusions about media impact. First, individuals learn basic political information from the media, but such learning is gradual and depends on both exposure to the message and individuals' cognitive skills. Second, print media are not necessarily better learning modes than visual media. In particular, visual media such as television are especially effective in getting individuals to pay attention to new and complex issues.

The real challenge lies in figuring out how to interpret these findings. They suggest a critical and central role for the media in developing an informed, sophisticated mass public. Yet if we believe these conclusions, which are based almost solely on experimental research, why do public opinion surveys suggest that the mass public is relatively uninformed about basic political facts?

As noted above, surveys of objective information may not be good measures of media impact, especially if individuals systematically synthesize (and then discard) discrete bits of information rather than retaining them separately. Political psychologists have in fact provided empirical evidence that individuals receive facts, integrate them into broader beliefs or attitudes, and then basically forget the objective information that first led them to update their broader beliefs or attitudes.[15] By measuring media impact in terms of objective knowledge, we are overlooking a substantial media impact.

What are the broader implications of believing that individuals discard objective facts after media exposure? Probably the best response is to consider more subtle effects of the media, including their effect on broader political orientations and other more affective attitudes. We do this in the remaining part of this chapter and in Chapter 7.

POLITICAL SOCIALIZATION, TRUST, AND SOCIAL CAPITAL

As in the case of political knowledge, political scientists' study of media effects on individuals' orientations toward the political system stems at least in part from normative considerations. Democratic theorists generally argue that governance in a representative democracy requires the **latent support** of citizens—that is, positive orientations of support and loyalty to the system. This "reservoir of goodwill" provides elected leaders with some expectation of support and legitimacy as they make policy decisions, whether citizens agree with the particulars of the decisions or not.

Traditionally, political scientists have focused on the nature of **political socialization**—how individuals acquire basic orientations toward the political system—as a reflection of this concern. Most of the early studies in the 1950s and 1960s focused on how social institutions such as the family and schools influenced children's earliest and most basic beliefs about politics and government. After the 1960s, most scholars have argued that, because children spend so much time watching television, the mass media have become a major influence on them. Although families may continue to have a strong impact on children's political attitudes, there is only limited systematic empirical evidence to support such claims.

The presumption in most socialization studies is that the substantive knowledge, cognitive development, and/or media habits that are established in youth are sustained at some levels in adulthood. This presumption of sustained effects is made in a study of the effects of political advertising on children's public mood—that is, their emotional reactions to the political system.[16] The evidence is drawn from an experiment that involved showing eight- to thirteen-year-old subjects either positive or negative political ads drawn from previous presidential campaigns. Public mood was measured before and after the children saw the ads by asking them how happy, sad, and angry "thinking of America" made them feel. The researchers found that exposure to negative ads was associated with a more negative public mood. Although negative political ads did not influence attitudes about concrete objects such as the flag or the president, they did influence more generalized attitudes such as feelings about government competence.

The authors cite evidence from an annual study of high school students that shows that support of the system and trust in government have significantly declined among teenagers since 1976 (see Figure 6-1). This pattern is broadly consistent with levels of trust in government among the adult mass public (see Figure 6-2). The authors suggest that television—particularly the increase in negative political advertising that occurred across the period of the study—might be one explanation for declining levels of trust.[17]

Much post-1960s research on the media's impact on attitudes focused on a **video-malaise** thesis. This thesis suggested that the nature of television news coverage, as well as the stunning effectiveness of the visuals that accompany such coverage (and are absent from more respected newspaper coverage), helped explain the growth in political cynicism observed in the 1970s. This argument was seemingly supported by public opinion polls that showed a marked decline in the mass public's support for the political system generally, as well as for various elected officials more specifically.

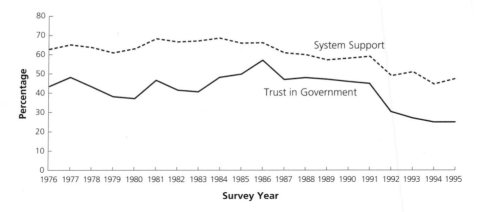

FIGURE 6-1 Diffuse System Support and Trust in Government
Source: Wendy M. Rahn and Rebecca M. Hirshorn, "Political Advertising and Public Mood: A Study of Children's Political Orientations," *Political Communication* 16 (1999): 389.

The video-malaise hypothesis was first tested empirically by Michael Robinson, partly out of concern about the numerous political scandals of the 1970s and the unknown effects of the new dominance of television as a news source for the American public.[18] Using data drawn from national surveys and experiments, Robinson concluded that occasional viewers of the typically negative evening newscasts—hosted by highly trusted and respected news anchors such as Walter Cronkite—tended to react more negatively toward government than did regular viewers. However, Robinson's research and conclusions were criticized by various scholars, and most subsequent research has failed to draw the same conclusions.[19]

More recently, television has been implicated in the decline of social capital in the United States. **Social capital** refers to "connections among individuals—social networks and the norms of reciprocity and trustworthiness that arise from them."[20] According to Robert Putnam, the advent of television has likely

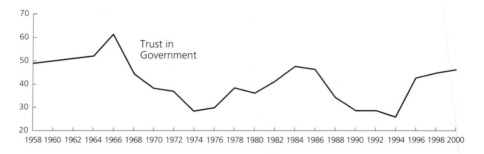

FIGURE 6-2 Trust in Government, 1958–2000
Source: The National Election Studies, August 27, 2001. Available at http://www.umich.edu/~nesguide.

decreased individuals' involvement in civic groups and has led to more passive political and social attitudes and behaviors partly because of the amount of time it takes up—the more time spent watching television, the less time available for attending political meetings or doing volunteer work. Aspects of television's entertainment and advertising content also tend to depress civic involvement, although Putnam indicates that the more that individuals watch network news programs, the more likely they are to engage in a civic activity (see Figures 6-3 and 6-4).

While Putnam acknowledges that the evidence of a causal relationship between television viewing and social capital is at best suggestive, he nonetheless concludes that

> Heavy users of these new forms of entertainment are certainly isolated, passive, and detached from their communities, but we cannot be entirely certain that they would be more sociable in the absence of television. At the very least, television and its electronic cousins are willing accomplices in the civic mystery we have been unraveling, and more likely than not, they are ringleaders.[21]

However, numerous scholars have taken issue with Putnam's claim. Pippa Norris reports that countries with greater access to newspapers, television, and the Internet also tend to have higher levels of social capital as measured by membership in voluntary associations and by how much individuals believe others can be trusted.[22] Eric Uslaner finds that television use is not associated with being less trustful (one of the reasons Putnam claims the media are associated

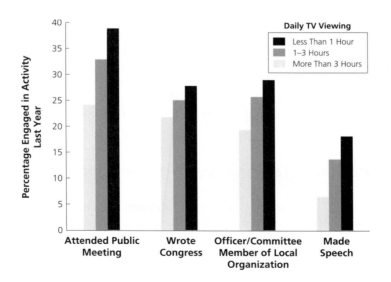

FIGURE 6-3 Television Viewing and Civic Engagement
Source: Robert D. Putnam, *Bowling Alone: The Collapse and Revival of American Community* (New York: Simon & Schuster, 2000), p. 230.

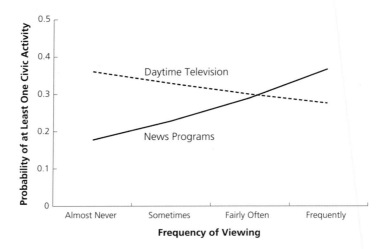

FIGURE 6-4 Types of Television Programming and Civic Engagement
Source: Robert D. Putnam, *Bowling Alone: The Collapse and Revival of American Community* (New York: Simon & Schuster, 2000), p. 244.

with lower social capital).[23] According to Dhavan Shah, some types of television exposure, such as watching news programs, actually increase civic engagement.[24]

Research on television and people's latent support for the political system is a good example of the need for carefully evaluating evidence before drawing substantive conclusions about media effects. Specifically, that supportive political attitudes (social capital) declined at the same time television exposure increased is an insufficient basis for drawing the causal inference that television viewing leads to an erosion of social support. Instead, it seems that the content of media messages is important, and that such content might have a positive or negative effect on individuals' political attitudes or civic engagement. This is a far weaker conclusion than that originally conveyed by the video-malaise thesis.

POLITICAL EVALUATIONS AND POLICY SUPPORT

According to John Zaller, scholars have erroneously concluded that the media have minimal effects because research typically fails to model the competitive nature of political communication.[25] Think of two strong and countervailing message streams to which individuals are exposed, one liberal and the other conservative. If such message streams are approximately equal in intensity, we would expect to observe very little change in public opinion. But if the two message streams were unequal—a strong liberal message and a weak conservative message, for example—we would expect to see some movement in opinion toward the liberal message. Both scenarios suggest that the media can have a strong impact, but it is difficult to observe this impact in the first instance because the two messages cancel each other out. In the right circumstances—for example, in U.S. House races or presidential primaries—the media have massive effects, but the political reality of the nature of information flows often make such effects difficult to observe. When a properly specified theoretical model is used to structure the observation of media effects, the conclusion is that such effects are far from minimal.

The news media's increasingly negative portrayal of elected political officials and candidates can be seen as a variation on Zaller's one-sided communication scenario. The fact that the public has more negative evaluations of politicians today than in decades past suggests that the message stream is effective in influencing attitudes. Ideological talk radio programs in the 1990s are examples of such one-sided information streams, and they have been seen as especially effective tools of mass persuasion. Relying on political personalities rather than professional journalists, and often targeting particular segments of the ideological market (liberals or conservatives), these shows are weakly constrained by notions of balance, fairness, or comprehensiveness in news coverage. One study found that listening to Rush Limbaugh (a one-sided conservative communication stream) had a significant effect on the audience's views of a variety of issues.[26] According to another study, listening to Rush Limbaugh was a significant predictor of voting for Republican candidates for governor, Congress, and the presidency, possibly because Limbaugh's effect on people's evaluations of President Clinton, a Democrat, led all but the most liberal to vote Republican.[27]

This evidence about the effects of listening to Limbaugh cannot be generalized to talk radio in general, where a two-sided information stream is more prevalent. One study tested whether individuals who got their news from talk radio evaluated President Clinton's character and job performance more negatively than those who did not and whether reliance on talk radio led them to view Clinton as a liberal rather than as a moderate or a conservative.[28] Controlling for sex, age, race, education, and income, the study found that exposure to talk radio was not associated with more negative evaluations of Clinton. Instead, the more negative evaluations of Clinton held by talk radio audiences reflected prior beliefs about Clinton as well as political ideology: The talk radio audience was negative about Clinton not because they listened to talk radio, but because they disapproved of Clinton in the first place.

Another one-sided communication stream had substantial effects on support for the January 1991 Gulf War. People who relied on television news were more likely to base their support for the war on emotional or affective (rather than cognitive) reactions. Television-reliant individuals were also more likely to support the intervention and to evaluate President George H. W. Bush more positively than individuals who relied on newspapers.[29]

These findings thus point to a second media effect on individuals' attitudes: changing the basis of individuals' political judgments. For example, individuals who rely on television news and those who are heavy users of the medium are more likely to have negative emotional responses to Congress than are those who do not rely on television news or are light media users. However, television-reliant individuals and heavy media users are not any more likely to evaluate Congress negatively than are those who do not rely on television or are not heavy media users.[30]

The importance of Zaller's notion of one-sided and two-sided communication flows is underscored further by the finding that the emotional effects of television coverage of the 1991 Gulf War weakened substantially during the post-conflict period, when a substantially higher level of elite disagreement emerged over whether troops had been withdrawn prematurely.[31] The study concluded that television's effect on voters' reasoning is dependent on the nature of elite discourse conveyed via television, and that a "pure" effect on how individuals' reasoned was most likely when elites were in agreement. When elites were instead portrayed as disagreeing, the same affective consequences of television exposure did not materialize.

A third way the media affect individuals' policy attitudes is related to how race is portrayed on television news. For example, individuals exposed to local news stories about crime perpetrated by African Americans are significantly more likely to support punitive (rather than rehabilitative) policies than are individuals exposed to crime stories with white perpetrators.[32] Survey data also show that frequent television news viewers are significantly more likely to support punitive policies and express more racist attitudes than are individuals who are not television-reliant. According to the researchers, local news has a "crime script" in which race plays a central and defining role, so individuals routinely exposed to these news reports are cued by suspects' race. Hence, because of the manner in which local news shows report on crime, people's nonracial policy attitudes are affected more heavily by racial considerations.[33]

The news media's portrayal of poverty has also been shown to decrease support for public welfare programs. African Americans are portrayed as poor on television and in newsmagazines much more than they actually are poor in reality; and they are less likely than whites to be portrayed as "sympathetic" (working or elderly) poor people.[34] Two-thirds of the media's poor people are black, but two-thirds of poor people in real life are white. Figure 6-5 shows this disjuncture. As a consequence of this portrayal, Americans have become increasingly opposed to welfare programs because they believe that blacks are "undeserving" poor (that is, that being poor is under their control) and therefore should not receive public assistance.[35] As in the case of the local news media's portrayal of crime, then, the news media's portrayal of poverty has primed individuals' racial attitudes.

Finally, there is some evidence (beyond that discussed above on social capital) that entertainment television may exert a significant impact on policy attitudes. A study suggested that watching "The Day After," a fictional account of the consequences of nuclear war in the Midwest, enhanced people's knowledge about nuclear war but did not affect their related political attitudes.[36] In con-

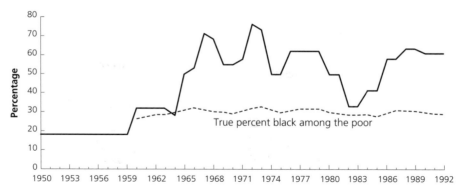

FIGURE 6-5 Racial Composition of the Poor, News Media Portrayal Versus Reality
Source: Martin Gilens, *Why Americans Hate Welfare: Race, Media, and the Politics of Antipoverty Policy* (Chicago: University of Chicago Press, 1999), p. 114.

trast, other researchers concluded that exposure to "Amerika"—a docudrama detailing life in the United States after a Soviet takeover—changed individuals' policy-related attitudes: Viewers were more likely to support strengthening the U.S. military and were less tolerant of communists than were nonviewers.[37] These one-shot studies do not clarify the extent to which individuals' political orientations were fundamentally changed, or if the observed changes were relatively short-lived. To the extent that entertainment television consistently portrays political issues using the same themes, the effects might be more lasting.

To summarize, then, under some conditions the media may have a strong effect on individuals' support for and evaluation of political candidates and particular policies. Much of this effect seems to be a reflection of the messages provided, rather than simply a mode difference between television and newspapers. Perhaps most importantly, research suggests that one of the indirect effects of relying on media for information on policies and government officials is enhancement of the role of emotion and affect in individuals' political evaluations.

THE MEDIA, POLITICAL KNOWLEDGE, AND POLITICAL ATTITUDES

What, then, does the research discussed in this chapter suggest about the media's effect on non-electoral attitudes of the mass public? Perhaps the broadest and most significant conclusion is that the media matter in more than minimal ways. Empirical evidence suggests that the direct unmediated and substantive effects of media messages are limited, as in the case of political knowledge or political trust. Most evidence suggests that learning, for example, is gradual and relatively small in magnitude. Because there is no objective standard about what is sufficient or necessary for democratic politics, even these limited effects are important.

The effects of the media are also likely to be indirect. Of special importance is the extent to which the mass media socialize generations of the mass public to politics and the extent to which such effects endure. While there is limited evidence of such socialization, the similarity of trends in political cynicism and trust over the decades is striking. Moreover, children's political orientations have been relatively stable and enduring over the decades.[38] This, too, supports the presumption that the media's socialization effects are more than fleeting.

Perhaps one of the most fundamental media effects identified in recent research is the way that television exposure alters the basis on which political evaluations are made. As noted, individuals who are reliant on television rather than newspapers tend to base evaluations more on emotional reactions to government officials and policies than on cognitive information. Moreover, to the extent that media coverage cues individuals' racial predispositions, it tends to increase their support for punitive criminal justice policies and decrease their support for public welfare programs. This suggests that the media influence the very bases of political judgment and fundamental policy preferences.

Two more discrete findings should be noted. Recent research has provided some evidence that the print superiority thesis is not generally true. This finding highlights the importance of distinguishing between medium and message in assessing communication effects. Research that simply compares television and newspaper audiences misses or confuses the point. Individuals with different cognitive abilities who are exposed to different messages demonstrate different levels of political knowledge. This merely reflects different messages, different motivation, and different cognitive abilities, nothing more. Based on this, political scientists need to consider the role of television in political learning and attitude formation in a more serious (and less value-laden) manner.

Research has confirmed that the audience is at least somewhat active in processing information. Therefore, citizens can moderate the effects of the mass media: They can choose which information to attend to and evaluate it according to their prior beliefs and some notion of the other people's beliefs. These empirical findings are notable with respect to intellectual assumptions—even conventional wisdom—about the extent to which the mass public is a victim of the media's messages, or an active participant. The latter seems to be the more appropriate characterization.

CONCLUSION

How do these findings reflect on the media models introduced in Chapter 1? The evidence of an active, rather than passive, audience suggests that it is difficult to evaluate the models based solely on the effects observed in the mass public. That the mass public displays only limited knowledge, for example, is likely to reflect the audience's lack of interest as much as it reflects the content and salience of political information provided by the media. In the case of the neutral adversary and public advocate models of the press, the active audience may choose to ignore or misinterpret information provided by the media. In the case of the profit seeker, reporters of objective fact, and propagandist models, individuals may or may not reflect the information provided, regardless of how politically relevant that information might be. In essence, when the audience is active, the significance of these models is actually minimal: Above some minimal threshold, the mass public will integrate new, although basic, political information into their prior beliefs contingent upon the nature of elite discourse in politics. To the extent that elites disagree, "pure" media effects will be limited; to the extent that elites agree, persuasive effects will be limited to those who disagree with elites but are nonetheless exposed to the new information. Hence, recent studies in mass communication suggest that political elites, rather than media elites, hold the key to understanding media effects on the mass public.

Key Terms

affective effects
behavioral effects
causation
cognitive effects
contingent effects
    model
correlation
dependent variable
experimental research
    design

hypodermic needle
    model
independent variable
latent support
mass society theory
medium
message
minimal effects
    model
mode
opinion leaders

political socialization
print superiority
    thesis
propaganda
selective exposure
selective perception
selective retention
social capital
survey research design
two-step flow
video-malaise

Exercises

1. Watch an entertainment program focusing on a political actor or institution. After the show, write down your reactions to it. How do you feel about the actors and institutions? Be sure to include both cognitive and affective reactions.
2. Your instructor will ask half of the class to watch the evening news and the other half to read a newspaper, paying particular attention to the topic that he or she indicates. Afterward, list what you learned from viewing or reading the news. Depending on the size of your class, different groups of students may watch different networks on the same night and evaluate the content of the news as well as its visual presentation.

3. Develop a set of questions for young people and elderly people about their feelings toward patriotic symbols, their support for the political system, political trust, and political efficacy. Have the interviewees explain the bases of their feelings and attitudes, and compare and contrast the different views and experiences of the younger and older generations. To what extent might media messages contribute to these attitudes? (Depending on the location of your school, you might also do the same with immigrants and native-born Americans to get at how the media help socialize immigrants to American political culture.)

4. Investigate Orson Welles' broadcast of *War of the Worlds* at http://www.war-ofthe-worlds.co.uk. Be prepared to discuss in class your reaction to the event. What do you believe happened during the original broadcast? Why?

Notes

1. Stephen Earl Bennett, "Comparing Americans' Political Information in 1988 and 1992," *Journal of Politics* 57 (1995): 521–532.

2. Michael X. Delli Carpini and Scott Keeter, *What Americans Know About Politics and Why It Matters* (New Haven, CT: Yale University Press, 1997), pp. 70–71.

3. The text that follows draws heavily on Melvin L. DeFleur and Sandra Ball-Rokeach, *Theories of Mass Communication,* 5th ed. (New York: Longman, 1989); Denis McQuail, *McQuail's Mass Communication Theory,* 4th ed. (Thousand Oaks, CA: Sage, 2000; and Richard M. Perloff, *Political Communication: Politics, Press, and Public in America* (Mahwah, NJ: Lawrence Erlbaum and Associates, 1998).

4. DeFleur and Ball-Rokeach, *Theories of Mass Communication,* p. 163.

5. Paul Lazarsfeld, Bernard Berelson, and Hazel Gaudet, *The People's Choice: How the Voter Makes Up His Mind in a Presidential Campaign* (New York: Columbia University Press, 1944).

6. Joseph Klapper, *The Effects of Mass Communication* (New York: Free Press, 1960).

7. Ibid.

8. John Zaller, "The Myth of Massive Media Impact Revived: New Support for a Discredited Idea," in *Political Persuasion and Attitude Change,* Diana C. Mutz, Paul M. Sniderman, and Richard A. Brody, eds. (Ann Arbor: University of Michigan Press, 1996), p. 18.

9. Delli Carpini and Keeter, *What Americans Know About Politics.*

10. Jeffrey J. Mondak, *Nothing to Read: Newspapers and Elections in a Social Experiment* (Ann Arbor: University of Michigan Press, 1995).

11. W. Russell Neuman, *The Paradox of Mass Politics: Knowledge and Opinion in the American Electorate* (Cambridge, MA: Harvard University Press, 1986).

12. Samuel L. Popkin, *The Reasoning Voter: Communication and Persuasion in Presidential Campaigns,* 2nd ed. (Chicago: University of Chicago, 1994).

13. Zaller, "The Myth of Massive Media Impact."

14. W. Russell Neuman, Marion R. Just, and Ann N. Crigler, *Common Knowledge: News and the Construction of Political Meaning* (Chicago: University of Chicago Press, 1992).

15. See, for example, Graber's schema theory in Doris A. Graber, *Processing the News,* 2nd ed. (New York: Longman, 1984); Milton Lodge and Kathleen McGraw, "Where Is the Schema? A Critique," *American Political Science Review* 85 (1991): 1357–1364; Popkin, *The Reasoning Voter.*

16. Wendy M. Rahn and Rebecca M. Hirshorn, "Political Advertising and Public Mood: A Study of Children's Political Orientations," *Political Communication* 16 (1999): 387–407.

17. Ibid.

18. Michael J. Robinson, "Public Affairs Television and the Growth of Political Malaise: The Case of 'The Selling of the Pentagon,'" *American Political Science Review* 70 (1976): 409–431.

19. See, for example, Garrett J. O'Keefe, "Political Malaise and Reliance on Media," *Journalism Quarterly* 57 (1980): 122–128.

20. Robert D. Putnam, *Bowling Alone: The Collapse and Revival of American Community* (New York: Simon & Schuster, 2000), p. 19.

21. Ibid., p. 246.

22. Pippa Norris, "Does Television Erode Social Capital? A Reply to Putnam," *PS: Political Science and Politics* 29 (1996): 474–480; Pippa Norris, *Digital Divide: Civic Engagement, Information, Poverty and the Internet in Democratic Societies* (New York: Cambridge University Press, 2001).

23. Eric M. Uslaner, "Social Capital, Television, and the 'Mean World': Trust, Optimism, and Civic Participation," *Political Psychology* 19 (1998): 441–467.

24. Dhavan V. Shah, "Civic Engagement, Interpersonal Trust, and Television Use: An Individual-Level Assessment of Social Capital," *Political Psychology* 19 (1998): 469–496.

25. Zaller, "The Myth of Massive Media Impact."

26. David Barker and Kathleen Knight, "Political Talk Radio and Public Opinion," *Public Opinion Quarterly* 64 (2000): 149–170.

27. David C. Barker, "*Rushed* Decisions: Political Talk Radio and Vote Choice, 1994–1996," *Journal of Politics* 61 (1999): 527–239.

28. Diana Owen, "Talk Radio and Evaluations of President Clinton," *Political Communication* 14 (1997): 333–353.

29. Zhongdang Pan and Gerald M. Kosicki, "Voters' Reasoning Processes and Media Influences During the Persian Gulf War," *Political Behavior* 16 (1994): 117–156.

30. John R. Hibbing and Elizabeth Theiss-Morse, "The Media's Role in Public Negativity Toward Congress: Distinguishing Emotional Reactions and Cognitive Evaluations," *American Journal of Political Science* 42 (1998): 475–498.

31. Pan and Kosicki, "Voter's Reasoning Processes."

32. Franklin D. Gilliam, Jr., and Shanto Iyengar, "Prime Suspects: The Influence of Local Television News on the Viewing Public," *American Journal of Political Science* 44 (2000): 560–573.

33. Ibid.

34. Martin Gilens, *Why Americans Hate Welfare: Race, Media, and the Politics of Antipoverty Policy* (Chicago: University of Chicago Press, 1999).

35. Ibid.

36. Stanley Feldman and Lee Sigelman, "The Political Impact of Prime-Time Television: 'The Day After,'" *Journal of Politics* 47 (1985): 556–578.

37. Silvo Lenart and Kathleen M. McGraw, "America Watches 'Amerika': Television Docudrama and Political Attitudes," *Journal of Politics* 51 (1989): 697–712.

38. M. Kent Jennings and Richard G. Niemi, *Generations and Politics: A Panel Study of Young Adults and Their Parents* (Princeton: Princeton University Press, 1981).

Agenda-Setting, Priming, and Framing

Psychological Foundations

Types of Agenda-Setting

Public Agenda-Setting

Priming

Framing Issues

Individual-Level Moderators

Conclusion

A T 8:45 A.M. on September 11, 2001, the first of two airliners crashed into the World Trade Center towers in New York City, resulting in several thousand deaths. Media coverage of the devastation—along with that at the Pentagon in Washington, DC, which was also hit—was almost instantaneous. The second airliner was actually filmed crashing into the towers only eighteen minutes after the first. The networks and cable news stations covered the horrifying events, and Internet news sites posted information about the crisis almost immediately. In response to the attacks, the Federal Aviation Administration stopped all air traffic in the United States; all federal buildings in Washington, DC, were closed; and U.S. embassies around the world were put on the highest security alert.

It is probably fair to say that, prior to these events, terrorist attacks on U.S. soil were not of immediate concern to most citizens. The national press provided only occasional coverage of international terrorists and paid even less attention to the possibility of domestic attacks. Few political leaders emphasized the issue of international terrorism. A month after the attacks, however, national surveys indicated that 40 percent of the public was either very or somewhat worried about terrorism.[1]

That news coverage of such dramatic and extraordinary events was reflected in individuals' concerns about terrorism seems reasonable; the objective reality of Americans being killed while peacefully going about their daily lives had an effect on the political issues individuals were thinking about. Such news coverage would seem to be a significant positive contribution of the media. But what if there is a gap between objective reality and media coverage of political issues?

Gallup public opinions surveys between 1996 and 1998 showed that a majority of Americans believed that crime had increased during the previous year, even though crime rates had dropped each year. Not until 1998, after six years of declining crime rates, did a majority of survey respondents report that crime had not increased in their area over the previous year.[2] Not surprisingly, crime was named the top national and local issue in 1994 and 2000 national public opinion surveys sponsored by the Pew Center for Civic Journalism.[3] This gap between the objective decline in crime and individuals' perceptions that crime was increasingly a problem suggests that the media were playing a critical and *independent* role in determining the political issues people were thinking about—a concept referred to as agenda-setting.

A related consequence of the media's emphasis on certain issues results from these important issues priming, or influencing, individuals' evaluations of candidates, their votes, and even their political participation. Also important is the potential for the media to frame, or define, the meaning of political issues that are brought to the public's attention. These three effects—agenda-setting, priming, and framing—are critical to understanding its impact on mass politics.

However, the international terrorism and crime examples suggest two very different implications of such influence. On the one hand, societal news can be communicated very quickly through the media. On the other hand, the media are able to convey a picture of the world that is inconsistent with reality. Aside from the normative judgments we might make about this, the more practical empirical question is this: To what extent do the media *alone* determine what individuals think about in politics, and do they do so equally for all citizens?

Answers to these questions require reviewing the empirical research evidence on agenda-setting, priming, and framing. That discussion provides an interesting example of scholars' changing views on the power of the media, in particular the shift from the minimal effects model to the contingent effects model.

The potential power of the media to alter citizens' political priorities, prime their evaluations of public officials, and frame political issues is especially important in a representative democracy, where it is assumed that citizens evaluate elected officials, at least to some extent, on whether they agree with the officials' policy positions. If the media have an independent power to determine which issues will be considered or how the issues are perceived, the media in effect are determining the basis on which elected officials are evaluated. Whether this is a good thing is not clear.

The five models introduced in Chapter 1 imply very different roles for the media in agenda-setting. Both the reporters of objective fact and neutral adversary models suggest that the media will hew fairly closely to the objective importance of a political issue. The profit-seeker model, however, suggests that the media will choose which issues to cover based on profitability concerns rather than on the objective importance of the issues. Both the public advocate and propagandist models suggest that the media will pick and choose issues to cover based on their own political priorities (which are undoubtedly different under the two models). Three of the models—neutral advocacy, public advocate, and propagandist—assume that the media have an agenda-setting capability, if not priming and framing capabilities. The reporters of objective fact and profit-seeker models are indifferent about the effects of media coverage on what or how individuals think about political issues or candidates.

Thus, in evaluating the media models, we must consider the empirical evidence in light of the extent to which people passively receive media messages and the extent to which they are active participants in processing mediated information. If they are active participants, the mass public is capable of evaluating government officials somewhat independently of the mass media and thus moderates the media's power to structure individuals' beliefs about political issues and candidates. To the extent that individuals resist or counter the effects of media messages, the neutral advocacy, public advocate, and propagandist models are necessarily constrained.

PSYCHOLOGICAL FOUNDATIONS

In an early study of public opinion and foreign policy, and writing in the shadow of the minimal effects research tradition, Bernard Cohen expressed the essence of **agenda-setting** when he claimed that the press "may not be successful much of the time in telling people *what to think,* but it is stunningly successful in telling its readers *what to think about*" [italics added].[4] More recently, scholars have focused their efforts on better understanding the concepts of priming and framing. **Priming** refers to the ability of the media to affect which issues or traits individuals use to evaluate political figures. For example, continued media coverage of terrorism might increase the importance that individuals attach to foreign affairs when evaluating the sitting president. Perhaps Republicans, who are typically viewed as "more supportive" of domestic security, will be evaluated more positively in the next congressional elections because a large amount of media attention has enhanced the importance of security against international terrorism.

While agenda-setting and priming are distinct types of media effects, the traditional view is that they share a common psychological foundation in **accessibility theory.** Social psychologists conceptualize cognitive processes as strings of information that are held in memory. Some of these strings are more readily accessible than others. When new information is received, individuals search their information "store" for preexisting information with which to process the new information, or they compute an online summary of past information, which is updated with the new information. Individuals' attitudes reflect the string or running tally of strings that are most recent, that is, most accessible.

In agenda-setting, media coverage of an issue ensures that the issue will be more salient because it is more accessible. Likewise, in priming, media coverage causes certain issues to be most accessible and therefore to be the criteria by which political actors are evaluated.[5]

Framing effects result from the media's description of an event or issue that emphasizes "a subset of potentially relevant considerations" that "cause(s) individuals to focus on these considerations when constructing their opinions."[6] The media frames thus help individuals make sense of the issue. That is, the way the media frame an issue determines how individuals perceive the issue and therefore how new information about the issue is categorized and integrated into their prior beliefs and attitudes.

Until recently, **attribution theory**—which indicates that individuals seek to understand information as they process it—has been identified as the social psychological foundation of framing effects. The idea is that people tend to attribute responsibility for social events and behaviors to either individual or societal factors. When people observe an act or event, they seek to understand it in terms of a particular frame—whether the behavior is the individual's or society's responsibility.[7] For example, are rising crime rates the result of a lack of individual responsibility in society, or are they caused by high unemployment and few social support programs for the poor? When the media emphasize the former cause, one policy response would be to combat crime, while emphasizing the latter would suggest a dramatically different policy response. Attribution theory suggests that the frame that is used makes such information more accessible for individuals, and therefore is more influential in determining their attitudes on policy responses.

TABLE 7-1 Conceptualization of Agenda-Setting, Priming, and Framing

Concept	Empirical Prediction	Political Significance
Agenda-setting	Individuals' issue priorities reflect the attention devoted to issues by the media.	The public's demand for government action on issues is determined by the media's choice of which issues to cover.
Priming	Individuals base their vote choice more on issues covered by the media than on issues not covered by the media.	Candidate vote choice is determined by which issues the media choose to cover.
Framing	Individuals view policy issues consistent with how they are portrayed by the media.	The public supports government policy responses that are consistent with the media's framing of an issue.

A challenge to this traditional notion contends that the psychological foundation of framing relates to how the media's frames shift the **belief importance** of the issue.[8] Aspects of media coverage are reflected in individuals' subsequent policy attitudes not because they are accessible, but instead because they actually shift the importance that people ascribe to particular aspects of a multidimensional issue. That is, individuals might shift from more societal to more individualistic attitudes toward crime not because the last media message was individualistic, but because beliefs about the individualistic nature of crime play a greater role in their assessment of the problem. This alternative psychological mechanism assumes an active and cognitively engaged public rather than citizens who automatically respond according to the most recent information they receive.[9]

Experimental evidence supporting this position is relatively new and has not yet been replicated. Thus, scholars are not in agreement about which psychological mechanism accounts for framing effects. However, the new argument is much more in line with recent communications research that has confirmed a more active public, one that is not equally and fully vulnerable to media effects.

The conceptual distinctions between agenda-setting, priming, and framing are summarized in Table 7-1. The table also includes examples of the political consequences of these media effects.

TYPES OF AGENDA-SETTING

The linkage between media coverage and political cognition is one of several types of agenda-setting that have potentially significant political effects. Another type is **media agenda-setting**—how the media choose stories to include in news coverage. This type of agenda-setting was indirectly addressed in the discussion of how reporters, editors, and news organizations make decisions about what becomes news in Chapter 3. While objective conditions offer some constraints on what becomes news, they are probably less important than profit considerations, the professional values of reporters, and organizational routines.

Chapter 5 covered **institutional agenda-setting**, the process in which media coverage of an issue increases the probability that government policymakers will do something about the issue. The research reported in that chapter—in particular, the quasi-experimental studies of investigative journalism—suggested that media exposés often increase the likelihood of government action or change the beliefs of government officials, but such effects are not dependent on the exposés' having a substantial effect on public attitudes. That is, the media effect is just as likely to be directly on government officials, rather than contingent on some reaction by the public to which government officials subsequently respond.

The relationships between these different types of agenda-setting are demonstrated in Figure 7-1, which emphasizes both the causal relationships and the implications of the findings that were reported in earlier chapters. Objective conditions are expected to influence the level of media coverage, the beliefs of elites, and the beliefs of the mass public about the importance and nature of an issue. Objective conditions are also expected to affect the likelihood that government officials will take action on the issue. As denoted by the dotted line, previous research suggests that these are relatively weak effects. Media coverage itself is posited to have an effect on the beliefs of political elites, on the mass public, and indirectly on the likelihood that government officials will take action on the issue. As denoted by the solid lines, research on these relationships (some of which is discussed in this chapter) suggests a stronger effect of media coverage. Finally, the relationship between public opinion and elites and between public opinion and institutional agenda-setting is documented in a broad range of studies that, cumulatively, suggests that public opinion has an independent influence on both elite beliefs and institutional agenda-setting.

It is important to remember the complex set of relationships indicated in this figure for several reasons. First, the conclusion in Chapter 5 that political

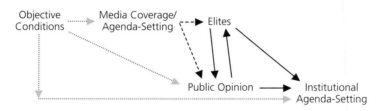

FIGURE 7-1 An Agenda-Setting Model: Media, Public, and Institutional

elites act on issues regardless of whether public opinion is affected by media coverage suggests that public agenda-setting is either nonexistent or unimportant. That would be the case only if the findings from quasi-experimental case studies were replicated in more systematic and generalizable studies of public agenda-setting. Second, in conceptualizing how to think about agenda-setting effects, it is clear that even the media are constrained, if only in part, by objective reality, and that objective reality provides an alternative explanation of what citizens are thinking about or what political elites are responding to. Third, regardless of the nature and magnitude of public agenda-setting effects by the media, Figure 7-1 is a reminder that public opinion is one factor among several that may determine whether there is an institutional response.

A few examples of how scholars typically measure the different types of agendas should help clarify the distinctions among them. Media agendas are typically based on a content analysis of media coverage over the period of interest. Researchers might videotape a major network's evening news shows for a certain period (or the news shows of three or four networks, depending on the hypotheses being investigated) and then measure the amount of time devoted to various issues. If the researcher is interested in the print media agenda, the most common measurement strategy is to do a content analysis of the front page of the *New York Times* (as an example of the best and most influential news coverage) or the front page of local dailies (chosen for a reason specific to the hypothesis being tested). In this approach, the researcher measures the number of words, number of paragraphs, or number of stories devoted to various issues. In either case, the media agenda reflects the relative amount of time or space devoted to the issues. (See Appendix A for more details on content analysis.)

The **public agenda** is what citizens as a group believe to be important. Hence, measures of the public agenda reflect the relative importance of issues to the public as a whole—to citizens nationwide or citizens of a particular state or city. This measure is typically derived from representative sample surveys (national, statewide, or citywide) in which respondents are asked, "What is the most important problem facing the country (state, city) today?" Issues or problems mentioned by a larger percentage of the public are assumed to be of greater importance than those cited by a smaller percentage. Often, these aggregate measures are taken at different points in time (preferably using the same question wording) and are compared across time with patterns of media coverage. Typical data sources include the American National Election Study, the Gallup survey, and various surveys commissioned by the major television networks.

Individual-level measures of agenda status use the same, or similar, questions from sample surveys to identify what issue each respondent in the sample thinks is most important, second-most important, and so on. Researchers then compute a dichotomous measure of agenda status, i.e., the respondent mentions the issue of interest or does not. Alternatively, surveys might ask how important a set of issues is, and respondents can answer "very important,"

"important," "somewhat important," or "not important at all" (or something similar). Researchers can then code each respondent as thinking that the issue is not important or one of the other categories, or can work with the ordinal ranking of each issue.

The institutional agenda—critical for assessing media effects on the actual behavior of political elites—is measured in numerous ways. Institutional agenda measures for legislative bodies include the number of bills introduced on a topic and the amount of floor time devoted to speeches about the issue. Institutional agendas (legislative and otherwise) might also be measured by the number of discrete acts taken on the issue, such as the number of floor votes, number of committee meetings, or level of staff resources devoted to it.

PUBLIC AGENDA-SETTING

The empirical study of agenda-setting focuses on the extent to which media coverage of an issue is associated with the issue's being on the public agenda. The typical assumption is that the causal influence goes one way, from media coverage (the independent variable) to the public agenda (the dependent variable). Initial studies of agenda-setting thus observed a correspondence between issues emphasized in the media and those emphasized by individuals as important, and concluded that a high correspondence indicated an important media effect.

For example, in an early study of agenda-setting, fourteen issues were ranked in importance by the number of articles on each that appeared in various newsmagazines during the 1960s.[10] These rankings were compared with the finding of national surveys in which respondents were asked what they thought was the most important problem facing the nation. This study suggested that even newsworthy events were covered by the media as an initial response to a stream of events associated with the issue, regardless of their objective importance. Such routine media coverage, however, disappeared before the issues reached their objective "peak" of importance.

Thus, while a high degree of correspondence between the media's and public's agendas was discovered, the association between objective conditions and media coverage was rather weak. These two substantive findings suggested that the media strongly influenced the public's beliefs about what was important, but that the media's agenda was not strongly influenced by any objective reality. This conclusion gives rise to the possibility of media manipulation: If the "big issues" in the media are not the objectively "big issues" of the day, is the public learning through exposure to the media or being manipulated?

What this researcher did not explore, and was later criticized for, was the possibility that the high correspondence between the media's agenda and the public's agenda did not reflect a causal relationship between the two, but rather indicated that both of them were affected (at least in part) by objective circumstances. That is, if the level of media coverage is even only weakly deter-mined by objective reality and the public's agenda is likewise (perhaps even strongly) influenced by objective reality, some of the high correlation between the media and public agendas is the effect of objective reality—and not of the mass media. In this case, objective reality influences both media coverage and the public, and the media do not completely determine the public's policy priorities.

This possibility is illustrated nicely in the theory of **variable news media in-fluence,**[11] which contends that news media effects on public opinion vary in strength, depending on how new the issue is and on what type of issue it is. This theory suggests that people have direct experience of **obtrusive issues,** and they will rely less on media information and interpretation. They have little or no experience of **unobtrusive issues** and will rely more on media information and interpretation. Media influence is thus variable, greater for unobtrusive than for obtrusive issues. Research comparing media effects on support for the variable influence theory is found in individuals' perceptions of the importance of the obtrusive issues (e.g., of cost of living, unemployment, and crime), com-pared to unobtrusive issues (e.g., of pollution, drug abuse, and energy).[12]

A more recent example of agenda-setting is a study of the correspondence between media coverage of the 1991 Gulf War and survey responses "about" the most important problem facing the country over the same time period.[13] As shown in Figure 7-2, prior to the start of the conflict, war-related issues were rarely mentioned as important problems. Once media coverage of the war be-gan, the aggregate survey responses referring to the Gulf War increased dra-matically; they similarly declined when news coverage decreased.

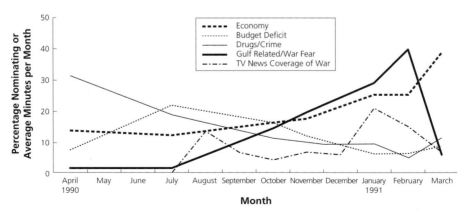

FIGURE 7-2 Agenda-Setting and the Gulf War: Changes in the "Most Important Prob-lem Facing the Nation"

Source: Shanto Iyengar and Adam Simon, "News Coverage of the Gulf Crisis and Public Opinion: A Study of Agenda-Setting, Priming and Framing." *Communication Research* 20 (1993): 375.

To summarize, then, aggregate and individual-level (survey-based) studies of public agenda-setting over the past several decades suggest that, for some issues, the media's agenda is reflected in the public's agenda. An important revision to the initial (simplistic) agenda-setting model is that objective conditions also play a role in determining individuals' agendas.

PRIMING

Empirical evidence on the priming effects of the mass media—where individuals give more weight to issues emphasized by the mass media in evaluating political figures—focuses primarily on evaluations of presidents and political candidates. Much of what we know about the priming of presidential evaluations comes from research by Jon Krosnick and his colleagues.

For example, public reactions to the Iran-Contra scandal were examined in terms of how individuals evaluated President Ronald Reagan.[14] The Iran-Contra scandal was first broadly publicized on November 25, 1986, when the attorney general announced that, as part of a covert operation associated with the National Security Council, funds obtained from illegally selling arms to Iran had been used to help support the Contra's efforts to overthrow the Sandinista government in Nicaragua.

Following this revelation of illegal activity by the administration, President Reagan's popularity level dropped substantially. Given the high level of media coverage of the scandal, the priming hypothesis would suggest that individuals' evaluations of foreign affairs would become more important, while evaluations of domestic issues would either remain as important or decline in strength. That is precisely what data from the 1986 National Election Study demonstrate. After the Iran-Contra revelation, foreign affairs became more important predictors of individuals' evaluations of President Reagan's overall performance (see Table 7-2). In addition, foreign affairs issues became significantly more important predictors of individuals' assessments of President Reagan's integrity and competence.

Similar results emerged from a study of news coverage of the Gulf War and its effect on evaluations of President George H. W. Bush.[15] Both before and after the media's coverage of the Gulf War, evaluations of the president's handling of the Gulf crisis, foreign affairs more generally, and the economy were associated with people's overall evaluations of President Bush. After the war, the weight accorded his handling of the Gulf crisis was significantly greater, while the weight accorded his performance in the other two domains remained essentially unchanged. Hence, media coverage of the Gulf War primed people's evaluations of President Bush's handling of the Gulf crisis. A shift in the importance of different issues in evaluating political figures has been confirmed in numerous experimental studies and ranges across issues, including crime, pollution, unemployment, drugs, arms control, civil rights, and immigration.

TABLE 7-2 Impact of Policy Attitudes on Evaluations of President Reagan, Before and After the Iran-Contra Affair

Opinion Domain	Unstandardized Regression Coefficients		Difference	Significance of Difference[a]
	Prerevelation Group	Postrevelation Group		
Contras–Central America	.18*	.29*	.11	.17
Isolationism	.02	.10*	.08	.02
U.S. strength	.14*	.15*	.01	.45
Economic assessments	.33*	.35*	.02	.36
Aid to blacks	.22*	.00	−.22	.05
N	607	296		

[a]Entries in this column are one-tailed *p*s.

*p < .05 (one-tailed)

Source: Joanne M. Miller and John A. Krosnick, "News Media Impact on the Ingredients of Presidential Evaluations: A Program of Research on the Priming Hypothesis," in *Political Persuasion and Attitude Change,* ed. Diana Mutz, Paul Sniderman, and Richard Brody (Ann Arbor, MI: University of Michigan Press, 1996), p. 88.

An alternative approach to the study of priming effects looked at how media coverage primed various considerations about economic conditions, and how these considerations subsequently affected evaluations of political leaders.[16] The researcher developed a general model of political evaluations from previous research on sociotropic and pocketbook voting. **Sociotropic voting** occurs when individuals' retrospective judgments about the economic condition of the nation affect their evaluations of incumbents, while **pocketbook voting** occurs when their evaluations of how well they are personally doing affect their evaluations of incumbents. Previous research suggests that individuals generally rely more heavily on sociotropic considerations in evaluating incumbents. The weaker (and inconsistent) evidence for pocketbook effects continues to puzzle scholars: Why don't individuals hold political officials accountable for their personal economic situations?

According to the model, part of this puzzle might be explained by the media's priming of economic issues. If the media tend to present coverage of economic issues as social problems rather than individual problems, individuals are more likely to rely on sociotropic considerations in evaluating public officials. The key to investigating this possibility is to consider the different sources of information about the economy available to individuals, the subjective perceptions of the economy as personal or social problems (based on that

TABLE 7-3 Impact of Domain-Specific Evaluations of President Bush, Before and After the Gulf War

Performance Domain	Unstandardized Regression Coefficients		Pre-Post Difference	Significance of Difference[a]
	Prewar	Postwar		
Gulf crisis	.21***	.30***	.09	.00
	(.02)	(.02)		
Foreign relations	.22***	.21***	−.01	.38
	(.02)	(.02)		
Economy	.26***	.27***	.01	.48
	.02*	(.02)		
Number of cases	1090	1090		

[a] Entries in this column are one-tailed *p*s.

***p < .001

Source: Joanne M. Miller and John A. Krosnick, "News Media Impact on the Ingredients of Presidential Evaluations: A Program of Research on the Priming Hypothesis," in *Political Persuasion and Attitude Change,* ed. Diana Mutz, Paul Sniderman, and Richard Brody (Ann Arbor, MI: University of Michigan Press, 1996), p. 91.

information), and how those perceptions are associated with evaluations of incumbents. In Figure 7-3, the stronger hypothesized relationships are indicated by solid lines and the weaker ones by dashed lines. The figures show that perceptions of personal economic problems are driven primarily by personal experiences; perceptions of social economic problems are based primarily on mass-mediated information; and information gained through social interaction is viewed as affecting both types of evaluations, but is expected to generally be less important than the personal or mass media information.

The research also found that regular readers of newspapers are significantly more likely to link their belief that unemployment is a state or national problem with their evaluation of the governor or president, while occasional readers and nonreaders are more likely to link their belief of a personal unemployment problem to their evaluations of incumbents.[17] This suggests that media coverage of unemployment provides individuals with an alternative basis on which to evaluate political figures. In the absence of media information, then, individuals simply rely on their personal experience.

Hence, the media operate on two levels, with potentially conflicting effects.[18] They are powerful to the extent that they are able to displace personal

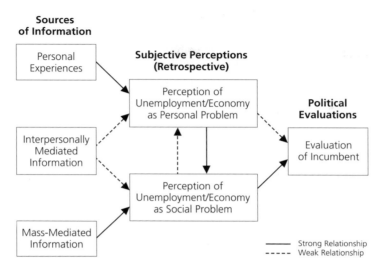

Sources of Information

Personal Experiences

Interpersonally Mediated Information

Mass-Mediated Information

Subjective Perceptions (Retrospective)

Perception of Unemployment/Economy as Personal Problem

Perception of Unemployment/Economy as Social Problem

Political Evaluations

Evaluation of Incumbent

——— Strong Relationship
- - - - - Weak Relationship

FIGURE 7-3 Relationships Between Sources of Information, Subjective Perceptions, and Evaluations of Incumbents

Source: Diana C. Mutz, "Mass Media and the Depoliticization of Personal Experience." *American Journal of Political Science* 36 (1992): 491.

experience as a basis for political evaluations. At the same time, coverage of social conditions provides a context that allows individuals to link their personal circumstances with social conditions and hence indirectly to the evaluation of political figures. In either circumstance, accuracy is important.[19] If, for example, media reports on economic conditions are biased in some way, individuals are perhaps better off basing their political evaluations on their own experiences; in the worst case, people might hold political officials accountable for economic conditions based not on reality but instead on journalistic values.[20]

FRAMING ISSUES

In what is perhaps the most exhaustive study of framing effects of the mass media, Shanto Iyengar considered how television news affects individuals' determinations of who is responsible for various social problems and what they think government should do about those problems.[21] He distinguishes between **episodic news coverage** of political issues as seemingly unrelated, discrete events and **thematic news coverage** in which issues are placed in a social or political context, and he contends that the news media's choice of which theme to present has a significant effect on individuals' beliefs about the issue. Because television is especially suited to issues that are episodic in nature, issues that cannot be presented that way are less likely to be covered. Iyengar contends

that individuals are less likely to hold government officials accountable for issues that are presented in an episodic frame, and more likely to hold them accountable for issues presented in a thematic frame. This has important political
implications: Because individuals are less likely to view government officials as
responsible for issues portrayed as episodic, television coverage in general reduces the likelihood that government officials will be viewed as responsible for
addressing these issues.

Iyengar investigated how the news media presented stories about six issues:
international terrorism, crime, poverty, unemployment, racial inequality, and
the Iran-Contra scandal. Based on content analysis of television network news,
he found that coverage of terrorism, crime, and poverty tended to be episodic;
coverage of unemployment tended to be thematic; and coverage of racial inequality was a combination of the two. Using a series of experiments, Iyengar
found that individuals' attitudes toward terrorism were strongly influenced by
the news frames. More specifically, when terrorism was presented in a thematic
frame, individuals were more likely to endorse social and political reforms as
appropriate policy responses, while when terrorism was presented in an episodic
frame, individuals were more likely to prefer punitive, individual-specific policy responses.

Similarly, episodic framing of poverty and racial inequality resulted in the
belief that individuals are the cause of such problems and should be responsible for solving them. This support for individualistic causes and policy responses was substantially reduced when the news media framed poverty and
racial inequality in thematic terms. In contrast, individuals reacted to unemployment as an economic issue regardless of news framing; much as in the case
of crime, framing effects for unemployment were minimal.

Iyengar further demonstrated the political significance of framing by showing that people's beliefs about the causes of political problems and the appropriate policy responses were associated with their policy-specific opinions. For
example, if poverty was believed to result from individuals' laziness and this
belief was enhanced by episodic framing, not only did people believe that individuals were responsible for their own economic well-being, but they also
tended to adopt more conservative policy positions (for example, they favored
less government support for poverty-related programs). This research is consistent with the variable news media theory introduced above: The media's
framing of issues sometimes affects how individuals perceive the issues, and
sometimes does not (as in the case of unemployment, an obtrusive issue).

Other scholars have also identified substantial framing effects dealing with
race-related issues. Research on support for welfare policies has consistently
pointed to the persisting importance of attitudes, in particular the importance
of prejudice or racism. One group of scholars argues that the willingness of individuals to report prejudiced or racist attitudes has declined substantially over
the past several decades, but that this does not mean that racist or prejudiced
views do not exist, just that they are harder to observe.[22] These scholars further
contend that attitudes on race-related policies—social welfare, civil rights, and

equality—are affected most strongly by underlying prejudice. By contrast, other scholars argue that what the first group sees as the result of covert racism is actually the effect of the underlying values that structure individuals' policy opinions—values such as egalitarianism, individualism, and a belief in limited government.[23]

Scholars interested in media effects have affirmed that the news media's framing of race-related issues affects individuals' policy positions. Some examine this question with respect to covert racism, others with respect to underlying values. Using aggregate data from the 1950s through the 1990s, Paul Kellstedt tested whether shifts in news media framing of racial issues in terms of egalitarianism or individualism was associated with shifts in public support for more activist government involvement in racial policies.[24] Individualism "refers to the principle that people should get ahead on their own, pull themselves up by their own bootstraps," while "Egalitarianism . . . asserts the fundamental equal value of all people. As such, every person deserves an equal opportunity to succeed in life."[25]

Kellstedt coded race-related stories appearing in *Newsweek* magazine for references to individualism or egalitarianism and found that the more that the media used egalitarian frames, the more Americans supported government intervention. This evidence demonstrates that changes in the public's attitudes on race-related policy are associated with the media's portrayal of the issues.

Race-related framing effects also go beyond the black-white divide in American public opinion.[26] David Domke, Kelley McCoy, and Marcos Torres hypothesize that racial cognitions are less likely to be associated with individuals' positions on immigration when the media emphasize **ethical news frames** that emphasize human rights or personal responsibility than when the media emphasize **material frames** (concerns about jobs or economic resources). Using an experimental research design in which subjects were given news stories about immigration either in a materialistic or an ethical frame, the authors confirmed their expectations. Specifically, when subjects were exposed to material news frames, their views about Hispanics as a group (whether they are violent, quiet, nurturing, rich, lazy) were associated more strongly with their attitudes on immigration policy and immigration's effect on the U.S. economy than when they were exposed to ethical frames.

More generally, media frames of policy issues tend to alter the factors that affect individuals' opinions on a wide range of policy attitudes.[27] Scholars have always emphasized that individuals' attitudes about groups structure their attitudes about public policies. That is, when individuals form attitudes about a policy, they consider how the policy affects various groups in society. Therefore, their attitudes about the groups that are policy targets are relevant as predictors of their policy attitudes. The more a policy is perceived to benefit a group that the individual likes, the more supportive the individual will be of that policy.

Not surprisingly, perhaps, when media frames emphasize group benefits, costs, or characteristics, individuals' attitudes about the involved groups become stronger predictors of their positions on the policy issue.[28] For example, a proposal to reduce spending on programs that assist the poor was framed in terms of the behavior or attributes of the poor (for example, "because they give away money to people who don't really need the help") and also in terms of broader economic considerations (for example, "because given the huge budget deficit, we simply can't afford it"). Attitudes about poor people were found to be stronger predictors of people's positions when subjects were shown the first frame (individual responsibility) than when subjects were shown the second frame (social responsibility).[29] Hence, when media stories provide more group-relevant frames, individuals' broader political orientations are likely to more strongly reflect their attitudes about different groups in society.

Media framing has also been shown to influence political attitudes more fundamental than policy positions. Political tolerance—"the willingness to extend civil liberties protections to ignoble and potentially dangerous groups"[30]—has traditionally been viewed as reflecting such demographic characteristics as education, attitudes about various groups, and the relative value people place on freedom of expression as opposed to public order. When the news media frame Ku Klux Klan stories as conflicts over free speech, individuals' support of the right of the Klan to demonstrate is significantly enhanced.[31] That is, when free speech frames are used to define the news story, tolerance increases; when public order values are used, tolerance decreases. As in the study of race-related policy attitudes, news media frames increase the importance accorded one value over another, and individuals' broader orientations (such as government support for minorities or political tolerance) shift in response.

To summarize, media frames in part determine how individuals define policy problems and potential solutions. These frames also affect the individuals' considerations as they determine their support for particular public policies. Further, media framing has been shown to affect individuals' nonpolicy attitudes such as political tolerance. Thus, research on agenda-setting, framing, and priming suggests numerous mass media effects on political attitudes, and these have potentially notable political consequences in terms of political support for public leaders as well as policies.

INDIVIDUAL-LEVEL MODERATORS

Although numerous agenda-setting, framing, and priming studies seem to point in the same direction—toward systematic evidence that media effects are more than minimal—other scholars have started challenging several aspects of this new evidence. The early agenda-setting studies relied on aggregate-level data, but the theory being tested was at the individual level. Confirmation of the agenda-setting hypothesis would require research focused on individuals as the unit of analysis. Once scholars considered individual-level models more explicitly, they more thoroughly investigated whether agenda-setting by the media affects all individuals equally. The expectation was that it did not.

Scholars have identified several **moderators** of media effects, factors that explain why a particular individual might be less affected than another by the media.[32] Individuals whose values differ from those of the medium or who have little confidence or trust in the outlet are likely to be less susceptible to agenda-setting effects. Liberals, for example, are probably less swayed by what they read in the *Wall Street Journal* than are conservatives. Also, individuals with access to alternative information sources, such as personal experience or interpersonal conversations that provide conflicting or distinctive messages, might also be less susceptible to agenda-setting effects. Why should someone be persuaded to change his or her opinion by a media message that runs counter to everyday experience? Individuals with a low **need for orientation**—those who already have independent knowledge or deeply held attitudes about an issue—are also less susceptible to agenda-setting effects. Lifelong Sierra Club members, for example, were likely not moved greatly in their policy priorities by the news media's discovery of global warming.

Empirical studies of public agenda-setting have examined a number of hypotheses derived from these general conditions. Scholars first relied on survey research, which includes data on survey respondents' demographic characteristics, reported media exposure, and prior beliefs, knowledge, and attitudes. Later they used experimental research designs. This research provides some evidence consistent with claims about moderators and some that is inconsistent with those claims.

An audience contingent effects model is supported by evidence that agenda-setting is greater for individuals who are susceptible to the issue.[33] Lutz Erbring, Edie Goldenberg, and Arthur Miller used survey data to test whether women and the elderly are more susceptible to (that is, agenda-setting effects are stronger for) media coverage of crime, and whether individuals whose families include union members are more susceptible to media coverage of unemployment. They found that each group is affected by objective conditions, and that agenda-setting effects are stronger for those more vulnerable to the issues.

Similarly, a series of experiments focusing on racial issues, unemployment, and Social Security funding concluded that individuals who are personally vulnerable on an issue are affected more strongly by the media.[34] The research contrasted the effects of media coverage for vulnerable and invulnerable individuals, such as African Americans and whites, the unemployed and the employed, people who are elderly and those who are not. Strong vulnerability effects were found for racial issues and Social Security funding, with African Americans and the elderly (respectively) more affected by news coverage of the issues than whites and nonelderly. Evidence about unemployment was somewhat mixed, but the researchers suggest that the unemployed are most affected by initial coverage of unemployment as an issue—when the media coverage affirms their personal experience—and that this difference is minimized as coverage is sustained over a long period of time.

Five other characteristics are possible moderators of agenda-setting: education, partisanship, political interest, media exposure, and informal political discussion.[35] Each competes with the effects of mediated information. Thus, highly educated individuals, strong partisans, highly interested individuals, individuals with high media exposure, and individuals with high levels of informal political discussion may be less influenced by the agenda-setting effects of television news coverage. A series of experiments has confirmed these hypotheses in the cases of partisanship, political interest, media exposure, and informal political discussion.

Thus, the conceptualization of the factors moderating agenda-setting influence is affirmed in every case except that of media credibility, which has not been studied systematically. It should not be assumed, however, that the same individual-level characteristics that moderate agenda-setting likewise moderate framing and priming. Although people who were more involved, such as the politically interested and strong partisans, were less susceptible to agenda-setting effects, no such differences were demonstrated for priming effects.[36] Further, partisan differences were minuscule, with Democrats no more likely than Republicans to blame the Republican president for problems. Hence, partisanship seems to provide no protection against media priming effects. Instead, the individual characteristic with the greatest potential to moderate priming effects is beliefs about problems; individuals who do not associate the president with a problem are not likely to be affected by television priming.

In contrast, political knowledge facilitates priming; individuals with greater political knowledge are more likely to be cued about what issues are important by news coverage, and to make greater use of those issues in their evaluations of presidents.[37] Further, the more individuals trust the media as a news source, the stronger the priming effect. Thus, for priming, issues covered by the media are more likely to affect candidate evaluations based on individuals' prior beliefs, knowledge, and trust in the media.

People with strong prior beliefs are less likely to be influenced by media framing. The most potent moderator is party affiliation; strong partisans are most likely to resist framing.[38] Ideology is also important; individuals identifying as strong conservatives or strong liberals are less resistant to framing effects. Demographic variables were generally ineffective as moderators of news media framing.

To summarize, research on agenda-setting, framing, and priming suggests that the mass media structure individuals' political attitudes in numerous ways, from evaluations of what is important, to conceptualizations of potential public policy issues, and to the link between particular issues or problems and evaluations of government officials. This media power is not unchecked. In terms of agenda-setting, access to alternative information sources such as objective conditions and interpersonal information limits the effects of media coverage, as does individuals' need for orientation. That is, prior political knowledge, ideological and partisan beliefs, susceptibility to issues, political interest, and cognitive skills moderate the media's agenda-setting effects. For framing and priming, however, these individual characteristics are less likely to modify media effects. Thus, while agenda-setting effects appear to be substantial, they appear to be distributed unequally across the population, while the more subtle framing and priming effects seem to be more persistent in the face of differences in political skills and interests.

CONCLUSION

Research on agenda-setting, priming, and framing provides substantial evidence that the media have more than a minimal effect on public opinion. The media's choices of which issues to cover and how to present them help structure individuals' beliefs about what issues are important, their evaluations of public figures, and their preferences about appropriate policy responses to social problems.

The potential political significance of these effects is striking. One of the assumptions of theories of representative democracy is that elected officials generally respond to citizens' policy preferences—perhaps most importantly by acting on issues that citizens believe government should act on. To the extent that the mass public's concerns structure the institutional agendas of our democracy, the ability of the media to affect what issues individuals believe to be important is fundamental.

In addition to having the ability to structure citizens' input to the representative system, the media also appear to structure the output in two ways. First, citizens tend to evaluate public figures on the basis of the issues that are emphasized in the mass media. It is but a short leap to assume that such evaluations are incorporated into individuals' decisions about which candidates to vote for. Second, the nature of media coverage helps structure individuals' beliefs about the appropriate policy responses of government. Hence, the mass media play an important role in both the choice of elected officials and the choice of public policies.

Not all members of the mass audience are equally affected by the mass media. For individuals with alternative sources of information or high levels of political involvement, media coverage is less relevant in determining issue priorities and political evaluations. Agenda-setting effects are thus strongest for those least involved in the political system. People whose prior beliefs and attitudes provide them with a strong set of political priorities and conceptualizations of problems—independent of the marginal amount of information provided by news outlets—appear to be unsusceptible to agenda-setting effects.

The normative implications depend on the quality and accuracy of media coverage.[39] Unfortunately, earlier research had suggested that objective conditions are not the most important determinant of media coverage. If the media are to link individuals' personal experiences with the broader social community in an appropriate way—a way that accurately informs individuals about the extent to which their personal concerns are shared by others—objective conditions should have some association with the media's agenda. To the extent that this occurs, the mass media might help integrate the concerns and values of the disinterested and uninvolved into the broader political system.

Individual-level characteristics are generally ineffective in moderating the priming and framing effects of media coverage. That is, most individuals seem to be about equally affected by the media's choices of which issues to cover (and therefore which issues to judge elected officials by) and of how to portray those issues.

While these findings on agenda-setting suggest that such media effects are contingent, and thus affirm an active role for the mass public audience, they nonetheless raise a critical question: Is telling people what to think *about* really any different from or less important than telling them what to think? Though it is impossible to answer this question based on empirical evidence, an answer is critical to putting this chapter's findings into perspective.

What are the implications of this research for the five models of the press? As noted at the beginning of the chapter, both the reporters of objective fact and neutral adversary models require the news media to hew fairly close to objective conditions in determining what to cover. While this is not central to the discussion in this chapter, the fact that the media's agenda is only loosely associated with objective conditions suggests that these models are not supported in the context of institutional agenda-setting (as has been noted in earlier chapters).

The assumptions of the neutral adversary, public advocate, and propagandist models, however, are supported in this chapter. The mass media can be used by reporters, elected officials, and others in positions of power to structure how the mass public thinks about and uses political issues. The profit-seeker model is indifferent to the extent to which the mass public's political beliefs are affected by media coverage. Thus, evaluating the models from these two perspectives allows the consequences for democratic politics of the public advocate, propagandist, and profit-seeker models to be considered further.

Since the profit-seeker model is indifferent to the effect of the media on public opinion, we will ignore that for now and consider only the propagandist and public advocate models. It is important to note that a major substantive conclusion of this chapter is that the audience appears to be active, not passive. This suggests that whether reporters or political elites of various stripes are setting the media agenda, at least some citizens have alternative information sources with which to counter the media messages that are intended to structure public opinion. Hence, while the three models receiving the most support in this chapter are perhaps not the most democratic, the empirical evidence suggests that the mass public is not merely a victim of any of them.

For a more detailed discussion of the extent to which the public can make rational, informed decisions within this media system—whichever model is deemed most relevant—Chapter 8 considers the role of the mass media in election campaigns. In effect, this next chapter is a case study of the mass media in

a representative democracy: the extent to which citizens can effectively participate in democratic politics and the extent to which such participation is enhanced or constrained by the nature of the mass media.

Key Terms

accessibility theory
agenda-setting
attribution theory
belief importance
episodic news
    coverage
ethical news frames
framing

institutional
    agenda-setting
material frames
media agenda-
    setting
moderators
need for orientation
obtrusive issues
pocketbook voting

priming
public agenda
sociotropic voting
thematic news
    coverage
unobtrusive issues
variable news media
    influence

Exercises

1. Identify an issue that is important to you, and document how much media
   coverage it has received. What factors might help explain why it is or is not
   on the media's agenda? Why it is on your agenda?
2. Various scholars have demonstrated that the media's priming effect influences the criteria by which government officials are evaluated. Is this good
   or bad for representative democracy? Under what conditions would this
   priming power enhance democracy? Detract from it?
3. Interview several friends or family members, asking them what they like or
   dislike about (or why they approve or disapprove of) the incumbent president or governor. Are any issues mentioned? If so, are they newsworthy issues?
4. Watch a major evening newscast, and take notes on the structure of a story
   and the specific language used by the reporters in order to document how
   one issue is framed. Rewrite the news story with a different frame (thematic
   or episodic, for example; other frames might be more useful, depending on
   the story). Bring your new story to class, and discuss how relevant policy reactions differ based on the two versions of the story.

Notes

1. Pew Research Center for the People and the Press, "Worries About Terrorism Subside
   in Mid-America: Ratings of Government Efforts Slips." Available from http://www.-
   people-press.org/reports/display.php3?ReportID=142 (accessed August 14, 2002).
2. The Sentencing Project, "Policy Brief: Crime, Punishment and Public Opinion: A
   Summary of Recent Studies and Their Implications for Sentencing Policy." Available

from http://www.sentencingproject.org/brief/pub1005.pdf.j (accessed March 29, 2003).

3. Pew Research Center for the People and the Press, "Research—Straight Talk from Americans, 2000." Available from http://www.pewcenter.org/doincj/research/r_ST2000nat1.html.

4. Bernard C. Cohen, *The Press and Foreign Policy* (Princeton, NJ: Princeton University Press, 1963), p. 13.

5. Dietram A. Scheufele, "Agenda-Setting, Priming, and Framing Revisited: Another Look at Cognitive Effects of Political Communication," *Mass Communication & Society* 3 (2000): 297–316.

    However, recent research that explicitly tests the mechanism of accessibility suggests that it does not account for priming effects. Based on several experimental studies, Miller and Krosnick find no evidence of the accessibility mechanism and instead suggest that media coverage primes individuals' evaluations of public figures because it cues them about what is important nationally, and individuals are likely to rely on this social cue (rather than the "information architecture in their minds") in forming their political evaluations. Joanne M. Miller and John A. Krosnick, "News Media Impact on the Ingredients of Presidential Evaluations: Politically Knowledgeable Citizens Are Guided by a Trusted Source," *American Journal of Political Science* 44 (2000): 301–315.

    A related argument is made by some scholars who criticize the standard measure of agenda-setting (the most important national problem question) as not indicating the salience of the issue to the individual, but rather as indicating the individual's assessment of what is important to society. Relying on media coverage as a cue about what is important nationally is thus a reasonable information shortcut, rather than something that reflects informational accessibility.

6. James N. Druckman, "On the Limits of Framing Effects: Who Can Frame?" *Journal of Politics* 63 (2001): 1042.

7. Fritz Heider, *The Psychology of Interpersonal Relations* (New York: Wiley, 1958).

8. Thomas E., Nelson, Rosalee A. Clawson, and Zoe M. Oxley, "Media Framing of a Civil Liberties Conflict and Its Effect on Tolerance," *American Political Science Review* 91 (1997): 567–584; Thomas E. Nelson and Donald R. Kinder, "Issue Frames and Group-Centrism in American Public Opinion," *Journal of Politics* 58 (1996): 1055–1078; Thomas E. Nelson, Zoe M. Oxley, and Rosalee A. Clawson, "Toward a Psychology of Framing Effects," *Political Behavior* 19 (1997): 2231–2246.

9. Ibid.

10. G. Ray Funkhouser, "The Issues of the Sixties: An Exploratory Study in the Dynamics of Public Opinion," *Public Opinion Quarterly* 37 (1973): 62–75.

11. Harold Gene Zucker, "The Variable Nature of News Media Influence," in *Communication Yearbook,* 2nd ed., ed. Brent D. Ruben (New Brunswick, NJ: Transaction Books, 1978), pp. 225–240.

12. Ibid. Zucker's study was later extended and improved upon by MacKuen, who came to the same two major conclusions: Media influence is variable over time and across issues, and this influence is independent of objective conditions. Michael B. MacKuen, "Social Communication and the Mass Policy Agenda," in *More Than News: Media Power in Public Affairs,* ed. M. B. MacKuen and Steven L. Coombs

(Beverly Hills, CA: Sage, 1981). See also Roy L. Behr and Shanto Iyengar, "Television News, Real-World Cues, and Changes in the Public Agenda." *Public Opinion Quarterly* 49 (1985): 38–57, who reach similar conclusions.

13. Shanto Iyengar and Adam Simon, "News Coverage of the Gulf Crisis and Public Opinion: A Study of Agenda-Setting, Priming and Framing," *Communication Research* 20 (1993): 365–383.

14. Jon A. Krosnick and Donald R. Kinder, "Altering Popular Support for the President Through Priming: The Iran-Contra Affair," *American Political Science Review* 84 (1990): 497–512.

15. Jon A. Krosnick and Laura A. Brannon, "The Impact of War on the Ingredients of Presidential Evaluations: Multidimensional Effects of Political Involvement," *American Political Science Review* 87 (1993): 963–975; Jon A. Krosnick and Laura A. Brannon, "News Media Influence on the Foundations of Popular Support for the President: George Bush and the Gulf Conflict," *Journal of Social Issues* 49 (1993): 167–182.

16. Diana C. Mutz, "Mass Media and the Depoliticization of Personal Experience," *American Journal of Political Science* 36 (1992): 483–508; see also Diana C. Mutz, *Impersonal Influence: How Perceptions of Mass Collectives Affect Political Attitudes* (New York: Cambridge University Press, 1998).

17. Mutz, "Mass Media and the Depoliticization of Personal Experience."

18. Ibid.

19. Ibid.

20. For an example, see Marc Hetherington, "The Media's Role in Forming Voters' National Economic Evaluations in 1992," *American Journal of Political Science* 40 (May 1996): 372–395.

21. Shanto Iyengar and Donald R. Kinder, *News That Matters* (Chicago: University of Chicago Press, 1987).

22. See, for example, Donald R. Kinder and Lynn M. Sanders, *Divided by Color: Racial Politics and Democratic Ideals* (Chicago: University of Chicago Press, 1997).

23. See, for example, Paul M. Sniderman and Edward G. Carmines, *Reaching Beyond Race* (Cambridge, MA: Harvard University Press, 1997); Paul M. Sniderman and Thomas Piazza, *The Scar of Race* (Cambridge, MA: Harvard University Press, 1993).

24. Paul M. Kellstedt, "Media Framing and the Dynamics of Racial Policy Preferences," *American Journal of Political Science* 44 (2000): 245–260.

25. Ibid., p. 249.

26. David Domke, Kelley McCoy, and Marcos Torres, "News Media, Racial Perceptions, and Political Cognition," *Communication Research* 26 (1999): 570–607.

27. Nelson and Kinder, "Issue Frames and Group-Centrism in American Public Opinion."

28. Ibid.

29. Ibid.

30. Nelson, Clawson, and Oxley, "Media Framing of a Civil Liberties Conflict," p. 576.

31. Ibid.

32. Everett M. Rogers and James W. Dearing, "Agenda-Setting Research: Where Has It Been, Where Is It Going?" *Communication Yearbook* 11 (1988): 555–594.

33. Lutz Erbring, Edie N. Goldenberg, and Arthur H. Miller, "Front-Page News and Real-World Cues: A New Look at Agenda-Setting by the Media," *American Journal of Political Science* 24 (1980): 16–49.

34. Iyengar and Kinder, *News That Matters.*

35. Ibid.

36. Ibid.

37. Joanne M. Miller and John A. Krosnick, "News Media Impact on the Ingredients of Presidential Evaluations: Politically Knowledgeable Citizens Are Guided by a Trusted Source," *American Journal of Political Science* 44 (2000): 301–315.

38. Iyengar and Kinder, *News That Matters.*

39. Diana C. Mutz, *Impersonal Influence: How Perceptions of Mass Collectives Affect Political Attitudes* (New York: Cambridge University Press, 1998).

The Mass Media and Elections

The Nature of Election Coverage: Free Media

The Substance of Campaign Coverage • Bias and Tone • Why More Negative?

Political Advertising: Paid Media

The Substance of Political Advertisements • Tone of Advertising

Media Effects: Theory and Evidence

Assumptions and Theoretical Background • Political Learning • Turnout • Agenda-Setting • Vote Choice

The Internet as a New Campaign Medium

Conclusion

T HE PREVIOUS seven chapters provided an overview of what is known about the nature of media coverage and the way it affects individual political behavior and institutional performance. This chapter draws on and extends the earlier discussions by focusing specifically on electoral politics. Elections are a central feature of democratic politics, and the substantive conclusions in this chapter about the mass media as a means of political communication are especially important. Simply put, if the current media system does not seem to be working in the case of elections, it is likely not working well enough for democratic politics to prosper.

In the U.S. system of **representative democracy,** citizens deliberate over and choose among various candidates. Elected officials are expected to adopt policies that are consistent with voters' preferences. How closely officials' policy decisions mirror the preferences of citizens is a critical feature of democratic politics. The more closely they do, the more representative the democracy, and the less likely that elected officials are enacting policies contrary to the wishes of the public.

Anthony Downs' model of the strategic behavior of political parties and individuals dominates much research on campaigns and elections today.[1] According to this framework, elections are a competition between two political parties, and the goal is to receive 50 percent plus one of the votes. To do so, parties adopt issue positions that are close to the positions of a large number of voters. Since voters choose the party (or candidate) with the closest issue position to their own, parties can win only if their issue positions appeal to the larger number of voters. To remain in power, parties try to enact the policies they campaigned on. This strategic or rational model of voting behavior can produce representative policy decisions via democratic elections.

A key assumption of the model is that voters have information about parties' and candidates' policy positions. In most elections, candidates cannot interact directly with all citizens to provide such information; the number of citizens and their geographical distribution makes it virtually impossible to do so in most races for federal and state offices, and it is prohibitively expensive for lower-level offices in many locations. The practical constraints of communicating with voters leads politicians to rely heavily on televised communications rather than traditional party organizational efforts, thus bypassing the political parties in their communications strategies. Campaigns have adapted to this new era of direct communication with voters by focusing their efforts on refining their images rather than on defining their policy positions, for the media convey images better than policy positions.[2]

Whether focusing on image or issue positions, the mass media are central to the conduct of elections, and they are used by political candidates to convey information to voters. The media may appear to have the responsibility of faithfully conveying all the information supplied by candidates to voters. On the other hand, they may be responsible for doing more than that, since candidates will likely be strategic in choosing what information to provide. For example, they may focus on image rather than policy positions.[3] In other cases, candidates may provide ambiguous information so that citizens will not be aware of their true policy positions.[4] In such situations, simply reporting the information provided by candidates will leave voters with inadequate information for decision making.

The role of the media in election campaigns is further complicated by two factors. First, reporters' behaviors are guided by a variety of incentives that might conflict with candidates' goals of selective information provision. If that is the case, what "should" be reported as election news is not obvious. Both candidates and reporters will likely want to influence the selection of campaign information to be disseminated by the mass media. The politician's goal is to get reporters to report his or her information, while the reporter's goal is to attract an audience in a way that enhances journalists' independent voice.[5] When these two goals collide, politicians react by trying to manage the media, while reporters react by creating alternative news stories (not candidate-supplied), most of which tend to be negative in nature.

Second, citizens may or may not pay attention to the information—whether candidate-supplied or reporter-supplied. If this is the case, then whether candidates and the media are doing what they should so that citizens will have adequate information may be unclear. Both candidates and reporters might be doing everything exactly right, but with little effect on citizens' information about political parties or candidates. This would be consistent with Downs' argument about **rational ignorance,** which suggests that citizens acting in their own self-interest should rely on information that is freely available to them, and not invest their own time or money to gain extra information about parties and candidates.[6]

Most of what is observed about the nature of media coverage of elections and how much individuals learn from campaigns reflects the interdependent behavior of candidates, reporters, and citizens. How reporters and candidates influence campaign coverage and how individuals react to it are the central questions addressed in this chapter. In addition, the chapter uses the empirical evidence to assess the five models of the press introduced in Chapter 1. Unlike earlier chapters, which focused on either content or effects, this chapter evaluates the models with respect to both media content and media effects. Competitive elections are a fundamental feature of a free society, and citizens need information about competing candidates and interests to make informed electoral choices. Media coverage that provides individuals with a fair and full array of information about candidates and their public policy positions, as well as evidence that such content is effective in influencing voter learning and choice, would provide much stronger evidence for the public advocate model than was seen in earlier chapters.

Earlier chapters focused almost exclusively on the nature and effects of news programs in the United States. This chapter, too, considers the content of public news programs, which are referred to as **free media** since political candidates do not directly pay for such coverage in their pursuit of public office. In the case of elections, candidates also choose to spend money to influence citizens, usually through the use of television advertising, or **paid media.** This means that during most campaigns, voters are exposed to both free and paid advertising, which may differ in both content and effect. To evaluate the consequences of media coverage for democratic elections, the chapter considers these two types of media products separately.

THE NATURE OF ELECTION COVERAGE: FREE MEDIA

Most studies of the content of election news coverage focus on two main questions about presidential news coverage: What is the substantive focus of election news, and what is the tone of coverage? The first question is motivated by the assumption that the duty of the press is to inform citizens about campaign issues so that they can make "good" decisions based on candidates' positions on important policy issues. The second question is motivated by the recognition that the reporting should not be biased so that the control or misuse of information will not prejudice electoral outcomes. An important distinction that is often made in answering these questions has to do with whether television news coverage is substantively different from print news coverage.

Studies on the focus and tone of election news coverage typically rely on content analyses of stories about particular presidential elections, although some studies provide analyses of the news content across sets of elections. Most of the social science election studies discussed in this chapter were conducted over the past few decades. Although each presidential election is unique, the nature of news coverage seems to be fairly consistent over time, with just a few interesting changes over the past few decades.

Most studies of media coverage of election campaigns focus on presidential elections. Yet presidential elections are the rarest of events in our democracy and reflect various constraints that are unlikely to be relevant in other types of elections. The chapter includes some details about nonpresidential campaign coverage as a reminder to be careful not to generalize findings in presidential contests to other election venues.

The Substance of Campaign Coverage

One of the earliest studies of media coverage of election campaigns was by Thomas Patterson, who studied television, newspaper, and newsmagazine coverage of the 1976 presidential contest.[7] His central finding was that campaign coverage focused primarily on the **game** or **horserace**—details about the strategic environment of the campaign such as who was ahead or behind and the logistics and strategy of the campaign organizations. Of network evening newscast minutes in 1976, 58 percent was devoted to the game and 29 percent to issues, policies, character traits, candidate records, and endorsements. Similarly, the media's coverage of candidate debates focused on performance and who won and lost the debate, rather than on the policy positions taken by the candidates. Studies of coverage of every presidential election since 1976 have found that the game predominates.[8]

Figure 8-1 shows the results of an analysis of local television coverage of the 2000 campaign, which also confirm Patterson's finding. However, not all television news shows focused heavily on the horserace in the 2000 campaign. A study by the Center for Media and Public Affairs, for example, showed that the PBS *Newshour with Jim Lehrer* devoted only 27 percent of its coverage to the horserace, compared to 62 percent for network television shows.[9]

Patterson found that national and regional newspapers and national newsmagazines covered the election much the same way that television news did. However, a fall 2000 campaign study by the Project for Excellence in Journalism indicated that the tendency to emphasize the horserace is likely stronger for television than for other media. The study found that 68 percent of television campaign themes was devoted to the horserace, compared to 56 percent of Internet stories and 53 percent of newspaper stories.[10]

A second important finding of Patterson's classic study is that when the media do cover issues, they cover different ones than candidates emphasize. The press, according to Patterson, prefers to focus on **clear-cut issues**—where candidates take distinctive positions—while candidates' ads and speeches focus on **diffuse issues,** about which they can make broad appeals to shore up support (rather than alienate voters by taking potentially divisive stands). Moreover, Patterson found that media coverage of issues tended to focus on **campaign issues** that typically arose because of a candidate's or campaign's miscue or blunder. These are issues only because they are created in the context of the campaign, not because they have any inherent public policy relevance.

Finally, Patterson noted that the media's focus on the game has significant consequences for how much news coverage candidates receive, particularly in the primaries. Candidates who win (**frontrunners**) or place better than expected (**dark horses**) in presidential primaries receive dramatically more coverage than

FIGURE 8-1 Horserace Coverage of the 2000 Presidential Election Campaign

	Presidential	Congress*	State**	Local***
Strategy	77%	53%	32%	39%
Issue	12%	35%	63%	51%
Adwatch, other, mixture	10%	12%	11%	10%

*Does not include stories about the death of Mel Carnahan
**Does not include state ballot initiative stories
***Does not include local ballot initiative stories

Source: USC Annenberg, The Norman Lear Center. "Local TV Coverage of the 2000 General Election." The Norman Lear Center Campaign Media Monitoring Project. Martin Kaplan, Principal Investigator and Matthew Hale, Research Director. USC Annenberg School for Communication, February 2001.

candidates who lose. Because candidates need media coverage in order to raise money during the primary season, this media tendency to cover winners more than losers tends to drain money away from losers and likely shortens the amount of time candidates remain viable, or at least significantly reduces how many viable candidates remain each week.[11]

Subsequent analyses of media coverage of presidential election campaigns expand on Patterson's findings in numerous ways. First, the emphasis on horserace coverage seems to result from reporters' norms and values, rather than from candidates' or the public's interests or efforts. An assessment of the extent to which presidential candidates in 1992 were given voice through the media found that horserace coverage dominated newspaper and television coverage of the campaign, but was far less important in political ads and interviews (see Figure 8-2). The researchers also found that local television news emphasized horserace coverage even more than national news.[12]

Second, the extent of substantive coverage varies across and within media outlets. Generally, newspapers provide more substantive information on policy issues and candidates' prior political experience. Political scientists typically view such information as more relevant than horserace information to voting decisions. A content analysis of media coverage in the 2000 presidential elec-

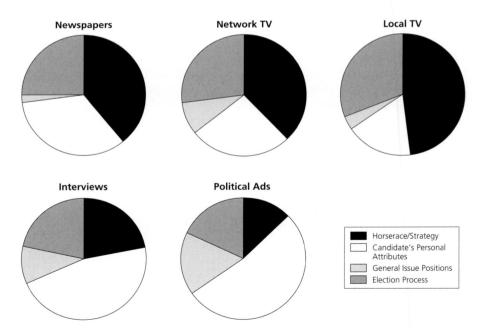

FIGURE 8-2 The Contrast Between Campaigns and Campaign Coverage

Source: Marion Just, Ann Crigler, and Tami Buhr, "Voice, Substance, and Cynicism in Presidential Campaign Media." *Political Communication* 16 (1999): 34.

tion reported that 32 percent of print news stories focused on topics that had an impact on citizens, compared to only 20 percent of television stories and 23 percent of Internet stories. In contrast, 70 percent of television stories focused on topics that impacted politicians (for example, campaign strategy and organization), compared to 59 percent of print stories and 68 percent of Internet stories.[13]

These findings suggest that newspapers generally provide better campaign coverage. There are undoubtedly exceptions to this general conclusion, for example, if one were to compare the news product provided on the *Newshour with Jim Lehrer* with coverage in many small-town newspapers. As another example, program differences on television are significant. A content analysis of the 1992 presidential election showed that campaign coverage on TV talk shows was substantive approximately 74 percent of the time, compared to 53 percent of the time for CNN's *Prime News*, 48 percent for PBS's *MacNeil-Lehrer News Hour*, 34 percent for ABC's *World News Tonight*, 29 percent for NBC *Nightly News*, and 26 percent for *CBS Evening News* (see Figure 8-3).[14]

Some of these differences might be explained by the tendency of nontraditional news shows (talk shows) to give candidates more on-air time for unscripted discussion. For example, George W. Bush had thirteen minutes of unscripted speaking during his David Letterman appearance just prior to the 2000 election, and Al Gore received more talking time in his Letterman appearance than on all networks combined in the entire month of October.[15] The findings also suggest that the focus on nonsubstantive issues is indeed controlled by the media instead of by the candidates.

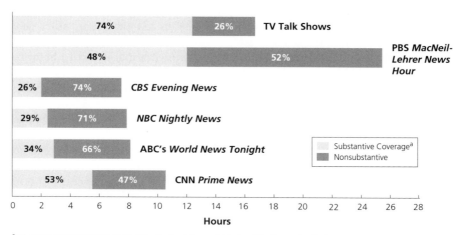

aSubstance category includes stories primarily about the candidates' qualifications and policy issues.

FIGURE 8-3 Content Differences Across Different Television Shows

Source: S. R. Lichter and R. E. Noyes, *Good Intentions Make Bad News: Why Americans Hate Campaign Journalism* (Lanham, MD: Rowman and Littlefield, 1995), p. 247.

Third, the focus on horserace journalism is greater in presidential campaigns than in other campaigns. Figure 8-1 shows that the emphasis on the horserace varied across types of elections in 2000. Campaigns for statewide office are least likely to be covered with a horserace frame. An analysis of press coverage of presidential, senatorial, and gubernatorial election campaigns in 1988 found that the horserace amounted to 55 percent of newspaper coverage of the presidential election, compared to 25 percent of coverage of Senate races and 15 percent of gubernatorial races. In contrast, only 27 percent of presidential campaign coverage was devoted to issues, compared to 65 percent of coverage of Senate campaigns and 72 percent of gubernatorial campaigns. The remainder of press coverage was devoted to personality traits (18 percent presidential, 10 percent senatorial, and 13 percent gubernatorial).[16]

Bias and Tone

Early studies of presidential elections in the 1970s and 1980s reported that **media coverage tone** in presidential elections is typically neutral, or sometimes slightly negative, rather than positive in nature. A study of the 1980 presidential campaign, for example, found that just over 50 percent of coverage on CBS and by the wire service United Press International (UPI) was neutral, about 25 percent was ambiguous, and just 20 percent was either positive or negative.[17] Recent studies indicate that press coverage has become more negative. In the 2000 presidential campaign, a majority of stories had two times more negative statements than positive statements. Even including stories that reported campaign events, which tend to be neutral or positive, negative stories outpaced positive stories three to one. The most negative portrayals were in coverage of candidate character (77 percent) and policy issues (51 percent), rather than campaign strategy and the horserace.[18]

In contrast to what one might expect from a media made up of liberal reporters, press coverage was slightly more negative for the Democrat, Al Gore, than for the Republican, George Bush; 24 percent of Bush stories and 13 percent of Gore stories were positive during the period covered by a study.[19] The study also notes that the Internet was far more likely to carry negative stories than were newspapers and television.

The importance of programming differences on television is documented in the Center for Media and Public Affair's study of the 2000 presidential campaign. This study found that PBS's *Newshour with Jim Lehrer* coverage of both candidates was predominantly positive (65 percent for Bush, 72 percent for Gore), compared to the evening network shows' predominantly negative coverage (with 33 percent and 48 percent positive, respectively).[20]

The emphasis on the tone of coverage is motivated partly by an interest in assessing whether media coverage is biased. Social scientists are very cautious in approaching questions about **media bias.**[21] How does one know biased coverage when one sees it?

One type of media bias might involve favoring one candidate over another and giving the preferred candidate more positive coverage. The problem is that some aspects of campaign reality are negative, while others are positive. If reporters respond to the differences in campaign reality in writing their stories, the amount of negative and positive coverage will not necessarily be the same for all candidates; fully accurate campaign coverage is not likely to carry the same amount of negative and positive press for all candidates. Therefore, more negative coverage of one candidate over another does not prove that media bias exists.

Assuming that candidates in a presidential race run equally visible campaigns, measuring how much media attention they receive might be a better indicator of bias. According to the Center for Media and Public Affairs, the two major party candidates in 2000 received approximately equal on-air speaking time: twenty-three minutes for Gore and twenty-two minutes for Bush.[22] The Project for Excellence in Journalism also found that Bush and Gore received about the same amount of coverage, with Bush dominating in about 24 percent of news stories and Gore dominating in about 29 percent.[23]

Another possible bias involves more accurately portraying the campaign messages of a preferred candidate. This, too, does not seem to occur. A study of the 1992 and 1996 presidential campaign compared the issue focus of campaign organizations (as measured in published speeches, press releases, and other documents) with the issue emphasis in newspaper coverage, but found no partisan bias. For example, the authors expected newspapers endorsing George H. W. Bush emphasizing Bush campaign issues more than other issues, and newspapers endorsing Bill Clinton emphasizing Clinton campaign issues. They did not find this type of issue bias in the press.[24]

Finally, a few scholars have tried to get a sense of whether the tone of coverage is driven by the nature of the campaign messages rather than by journalists. They compared candidates' campaign activities and the coverage of these activities, looking at the extent to which the negativity of candidates and their strategies is reflected in news coverage.[25] For example, the proportion of campaign discourse that focused on attacks (negative assertions without evidence) increased from 16 percent in 1960 to 25 percent in 1992. However, the proportion of oppositional statements (claims regarding the opposing candidate supported by evidence) in candidate speeches was much smaller than the proportion of oppositional statements in news coverage of candidate speeches. This holds true in every campaign year studied. Similarly, media coverage of debates contained a much higher proportion of oppositional statements than did the actual debates themselves. Both findings suggest that reporters focus on oppositional statements more than candidates do. Political campaigns thus may be somewhat more negative today than in 1960, but news reporting of the campaigns also emphasizes the negative more. The tendency of reporters to emphasize conflict and attack in covering campaigns is sometimes referred to as **negativity bias.**

Additional evidence of a negativity bias in electoral coverage is found in

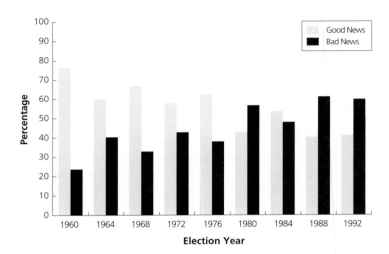

Note: Figure is based on favorable and unfavorable references to the major-party nominees in 4,263 *Time and Newsweek* paragraphs during the 1960–1992 period. "Horserace" references are excluded; all other evaluative references are included.

FIGURE 8-4 Increasing Negativity of Campaign Coverage, 1960–1992

Source: Thomas E. Patterson, *Out of Order* (New York: Knopf, 1980), p. 20.

studies on newsmagazine coverage and network news coverage. An analysis of *Time* and *Newsweek*'s coverage shows increasingly negative references to major party nominees between the 1960 and 1992 presidential elections (see Figure 8-4). In 1960 only about 25 percent of references to the nominees were negative, compared to over 60 percent in 1992.[26] Similarly, although most campaign stories on television network news are either ambiguous or neutral in tone, the proportion of positive stories has decreased since 1968, while the proportion of negative stories has increased from 10.3 percent in 1968 to 25.8 percent in 1988 (see Table 8-1).[27]

Why More Negative?

What accounts for these changes in the tone of media coverage? Most scholars contend that the news media are most directly responsible, with the increasingly negative tone of electoral coverage associated with several other content changes: decreased coverage of policy issues, increased coverage of the horserace or campaign issues, and increased reliance on **interpretive campaign stories** rather than **descriptive campaign stories.**[28]

The implication of the shift from descriptive to interpretive stories is that the desire to write more interpretation causes journalists to adopt a more critical (negative) news frame. However, the responsibility for this shift in news con-

TABLE 8-1 Increasing Negativity of Television Coverage Evaluative tone of campaign stories, 1968–1988 (number and percentage of total)

Year	Positive	Negative	Ambiguous	Neutral
1968	5	6	12	35
	(8.6)	(10.3)	(20.7)	(60.3)
1972	1	1	1	49
	(1.9)	(1.9)	(1.9)	(94.2)
1976	1	3	3	49
	(1.8)	(5.4)	(5.4)	(87.5)
1980	0	5	6	53
	(0.0)	(7.8)	(9.4)	(82.8)
1984	1	5	5	33
	(2.3)	(11.4)	(11.4)	(75.0)
1988	1	16	13	32
	(1.6)	(25.8)	(21.0)	(51.6)

Source: Daniel C. Hallin, "Sound Bite News: Television Coverage of Elections, 1968–1988." *Journal of Communication* 42 (1992): 15.

tent probably should not be placed solely on journalists; it is likely associated with the evolution of campaign management and press relations. When descriptive stories were the predominant form of journalism, campaigns typically aimed to create events that would result in positive stories based solely on the descriptive content. They were successful, and when journalists were criticized for being unwitting accomplices or dupes of campaign managers, they shifted to a more interpretive news style. Interpretation requires more of an active **journalistic voice.** Because interpretation is defined as either being critical or offering a counterpoint, the voice adopted by most journalists is negative.[29]

Another change in television news delivery is the adoption of **sound bite** news, with increasingly shorter news reports served up on a daily basis.[30] The motivation for adopting short sound bites as a feature of election news is similar to the motivation for shifting to interpretive reporting. Much longer visual clips of presidential candidates used to be used on the evening news. When these clips came to be regarded as free advertising for candidates, journalists redefined their responsibility as the provision of additional context or commentary with which the candidate's message could be understood more fully. To accomplish this, the amount of time given to candidate sound bites has been substantially reduced. For example, the average sound bite decreased from 42.3 seconds in 1968 to 7.2 seconds in 1996 (see Figure 8-5).[31] In September 2000, according to another report, sound bites averaged 7.3 seconds, down from an estimated length of 9.8 seconds in 1988 and 42 seconds in 1968.

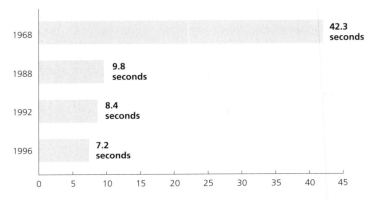

Note: ABC, CBS, NBC evening news. 1996 figure is for GOP primaries; others are for general election campaigns.

FIGURE 8-5 Sound Bites Shrinking

Source: S. Robert Lichter and Richard E. Noyes, "There They Go Again: Media Coverage of Campaign '96," in *Political Parties, Campaigns and Elections,* ed. Robert E. DeClerico (Upper Saddle River, NJ: Prentice Hall, 2000), p. 97.

Moreover, the proportion of news airtime showing candidates was estimated at 11 percent, while reporters were on air 72 percent of the time.[32]

The increased use of journalists as experts in campaign stories also seems to be associated with the increasing negativity of campaign coverage.[33] In essence, journalists are used as expert counterweights to candidates and their campaign managers or spokespersons. Almost by definition, trying to present "the other side" of the story requires critical, or more negative, commentary. Thus, changes in election coverage result at least in part from a different approach to campaign news, in which reporters tend to present more interpretive, active coverage.[34]

The increasingly negative tone of electoral coverage has also been attributed to the fact that the press has been miscast as a political institution that is expected by both the mass public and elites to play the role once occupied by strong political parties.[35] More specifically, the candidate-centered campaign process in the United States requires a consensus-building institution that organizes diverse political interests into more coherent, shared political goals.[36]

Prior to the 1970s, political parties played this role in presidential campaign politics. With fundamental changes in the presidential nominating process in the 1970s, individuals without strong party support but with strong financial backing became credible candidates, and they largely relied on mass communication to capture the major party nominations. In the old system, the press acted in its traditional role as watchdog, helping protect citizens from "bad" candidates.[37] Because the press is driven by journalistic or business values rather than by political values, it has not adapted to this new role. Hence, electoral coverage is marked by an emphasis on conflict and strategy, campaign events instead of issues, thematic news stories, reliance on experts and polling to provide a cloak of objectivity, and portrayals of character as equated with the personal failings of candidates.[38] Negative, issue-less coverage of presidential campaigns might be associated with voter cynicism or even lower voter turnout. Most of this discussion, however, typically focuses on the nature of political advertising—as opposed to free media coverage—and its deleterious effects on the mass public.

POLITICAL ADVERTISING: PAID MEDIA

Everyone seems to love to hate political advertising—except, perhaps, campaign consultants, for whom advertising is the lifeblood of the campaign. Campaigns are often remembered for their notable commercials. "Daisy Girl," for example, was a thirty-second advertisement aired only once by Lyndon Johnson's campaign in 1964. Its portrayal of the threat of nuclear war generated such a strong reaction that it has likely received more media coverage and public discussion than any other ad in the history of presidential campaign politics.

More recently, the "Willie Horton" ad about an African-American man who raped a white woman while on furlough from prison aired by the George H. W. Bush campaign in 1988 focused discussion on how election campaigns use race to their advantage. One contention is that politicians today do not use explicit racial appeals in campaign communications, but use race implicitly in campaign messages relating to such issues as welfare and crime.[39] These implicit appeals are effective in securing the votes of individuals with underlying racist attitudes. There is persuasive historical, survey research and experimental evidence supporting these claims. Interestingly, the impact of the implicit messages on whites' vote choices is weakened by elite commentary exposing the messages as appealing to racial attitudes.[40]

"Daisy Girl" and "Willie Horton" point to the two central questions raised about political advertising in presidential election campaigns: What is the content of political ads, and what effect do they have on mass political behavior? For several decades, the assumption has been that political ads focus either on trivial aspects of candidate image or on negative aspects of the opponent ("attack" ads). The first part of this assumption is driven by the development of political advertising after World War II, in which the advertising industry's principles of selling automobiles and laundry detergent were applied to "selling" political candidates. How could such ads provide the type of serious information that citizens need to make rational, informed choices between competing candidates? Also, since people are most likely to remember negative ads (whether they liked them or not), it is easy to believe that all, or even most, political ads are negative.[41]

Scholars have been somewhat slow to address these questions because of

---

Election 2000: Prominent Ads at C-SPAN.ORG

C-SPAN.ORG has archived prominent campaign advertising from the 2000 presidential election, along with selected ads from the 1960 and 1980 presidential campaigns. Access the campaign advertising Web site at http://www.cspan.org/campaign2000/advertising.asp, and consider the following the questions.

1. If voters in the 2000 presidential election had only the information provided in the ads, what would they know?
2. Do the presidential ads seem to vary across time?
3. How negative are the ads? What about the ads is negative?

---

practical difficulties in studying ads in election campaigns. In many cases, for example, there is no permanent public record of who showed which ads to whom; the ads and the information about where and when they aired belong to candidates' campaign organizations, which seemingly vanish hours after election day. While the archiving and scheduling of political ads have become more common in recent years, it is still difficult to assess their effects on individual citizens; people have a difficult time recalling whether and when they saw particular ads, or they have simply heard about them on the news or from friends or coworkers. In typical public opinion surveys, only a small percentage of respondents report having seen the ads, making statistical analyses of the effects difficult.[42] These problems present serious limitations for scholars seeking to draw general conclusions about the effects of political advertising.

The increasing amount of money spent by political campaigns on ads and the increasing resources devoted by the media in reporting about them have led to a resurgence of scholarship on political advertising. Many of the findings of early studies in the 1960s still hold today, with a few notable exceptions.

The Substance of Political Advertisements

One of the earliest studies of the content of political advertising was conducted by Robert McClure and Thomas Patterson, who did a content analysis of political ads and network evening newscasts during the 1972 presidential election.[43] Their assumption—in fact, a motivation for doing the study—was that the new medium of political advertising made it possible for political consultants to dupe voters into voting for candidates who did not represent their "true" interests. Doing a content analysis of the evening news provided a benchmark against which the expected issue-less political ads could be negatively evaluated.

To their surprise, the authors found that the political ads aired during the campaign actually provided more information about candidates and their issues than did the evening network newscasts, which tended to focus on campaign events. Of all ads aired between September 18 and November 6, 1972, 42 percent "were primarily issue communications, and another 28 percent contained substantial issue material."[44] About twelve issues received extensive coverage in these ads, and this coverage far exceeded that provided by the evening news.

Despite tremendous changes in political campaigns and the presidential nominating process since 1972, the basic conclusion that political ads provide voters with useful, as opposed to deceptive or manipulative, information still holds. An analysis of 429 prominent ads from the 1952 through 2000 presidential campaigns found that, on average, nearly a third of the ads mentioned personal qualities or domestic performance. Specific domestic or foreign policy positions were mentioned in only 22 percent and 3 percent, respectively (see Table 8-2).[45] Moreover, negative ads actually contain more issue information than positive ads, and the dominant appeal in both negative and positive ads is based on emotion, rather than logic or ethics.[46]

Interestingly, there has not been a systematic decrease in the issue emphasis of ads over time. In fact, prominent ads in the 1980s and 1990s were more substantive than those in the previous two decades.[47] This suggests that there is *not* a trend toward issue-less politics. Instead, it suggests that candidates develop and use political ads based on the strategic environment of the election, in particular, because of the competitiveness of the race and the nature of the information environment. In 2000, 43 percent of prominent ads focused on specific policy positions, compared to 33 percent that focused on the personal qualities of the two candidates.[48]

TABLE 8-2 Content of Presidential Election Advertising over Time

	1952	1956	1960	1964	1968	1972	1976	1980	1984	1988	1992	1996	2000
Domestic matters	62%	62%	24%	39%	30%	46%	38%	44%	68%	58%	68%	59%	60%
International affairs	6	0	6	19	37	21	3	11	17	10	6	0	0
Personal qualities	24	24	69	27	18	29	50	41	8	20	21	39	31
Party	6	12	0	0	0	3	3	3	0	0	0	0	0
Campaign	0	0	0	16	12	3	9	0	4	10	6	3	4

Sources: Darrell M. West, *Air Wars,* 3rd ed. (Washington, DC: CQ Press, 2001). Data from Kathleen Jamieson, *Packaging the Presidency,* 2nd ed. (New York: Oxford University Press, 1992) for 1952–1988, and *CBS Evening News* campaign tapes for 1992–2000.

Tone of Advertising

Scholars' relatively positive assessments about the informational content of political ads have been overshadowed by the perception that ads have become more negative. But this perception is incorrect in many respects. As noted earlier, people are more likely to remember attack ads because journalists are more likely to discuss them, while the more mundane, routine advertising is never discussed on network news. As a result, recent campaigns have been assessed as more negative than those in the distant past. Scholars, too, sometimes err by studying only prominent ads, rather than the complete universe or a representative sample of ads used in campaigns.

Another factor leading to incorrect inferences about negative ads is how ads are classified as negative. That is, how does a person know that an ad is negative? Researchers often code ads as "attack" or "negative" when in fact they are multidimensional—they include something negative about the opponent, but also offer some sort of affirmative statement about the sponsoring candidate.[49] Moreover, some attack ads might be truthful, while others are deceitful, and this is an important distinction as well.

In seeking to correct these deficiencies, researchers coded political ads aired in presidential elections from 1952 onward using ideas in the ads (rather than the full ads) as the units of analysis.[50] They identified three types of ideas: (1) **attack ideas** that specifically mention the candidate's opponent, (2) **advocacy ideas** that highlight the sponsoring candidate's issue positions or values, and (3) **contrast ideas** that contrast the positions of the sponsoring candidate and the opponent. The researchers found that ads that were typically seen as negative actually had a relatively high level of policy content. More specifically, across all presidential campaigns from 1952 to 1996, attack ads had the largest proportion of policy content (42 percent), followed by contrast ads (39 percent) and advocacy ads (32 percent) (see Figure 8-6). Hence, they concluded

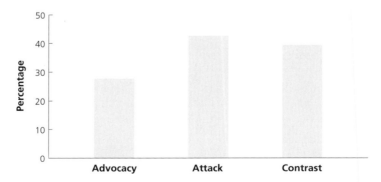

FIGURE 8-6 Issue Content of "Different Types of Negative Ads"

Source: Kathleen Hall Jamieson, Paul Waldman, and Susan Sherr, "Eliminate the Negative? Categories of Analysis for Political Advertisements," Chapter 3 in *Crowded Airwaves: Campaign Advertising in Elections,* ed. James A. Thurber, Candice J. Nelson, and David A. Dulio (Washington, DC: The Brookings Institution, 2000), p. 58.

that ads perceived to be negative are not necessarily absent of policy content.[51] Moreover, they suggested that contrast ads—used most extensively by Bill Clinton in 1992—should be given credit for highlighting differences between candidates on specific issues; they provide relevant and useful information, even if they might be described as negative.

MEDIA EFFECTS: THEORY AND EVIDENCE

Although the goal of candidates is to convince voters to vote for them, political scientists probably focus less on persuasion and more on how much citizens learn about candidates and issues from campaigns and how different aspects of the media either enhance or detract from that learning process. The more citizens learn, the more likely they are to choose a candidate who represents their interests.

Election campaigns also help determine whether individuals vote or not and influence their general orientations toward government and politics. This section reviews the theories and empirical evidence associated with each of these media effects. First some broader issues in thinking about media effects are considered.

Assumptions and Theoretical Background

Mediated campaigns (campaigns that rely heavily on mass media to reach the targeted audience) likely reach a broader audience, so they have a greater effect on the conduct of elections than do nonmediated campaigns. What would happen if presidential campaigns did not use television, the Internet, or newspapers? The only individuals exposed to the candidates would be those able to attend campaign events or who heard about campaign events from friends, neighbors, and coworkers. In this respect, mediated campaigns expand access to candidates and their campaigns, which is probably an advantage for higher-level campaigns. Even if exposure to the candidates is accidental—when quickly flipping through channels—it has few or no costs, and it might cause people to become more interested in the campaign or learn something about a candidate.

Mediated campaigns would be a disadvantage if they manipulated voters to make candidate choices that ran counter to their political interests. This concern assumes that individuals are not capable of evaluating mediated messages to determine whether they are consistent with their self-interest, or that they cannot otherwise defend themselves against the potential evils of mediated messages. As the discussion of the hypodermic model in Chapter 7 suggests, this is probably not the case.

Another point to keep in mind is the nature of the targeted audience— potential voters. Chapter 7 presented evidence that some individuals are affected more than others when exposed to mediated messages. Moreover, the magnitude and nature of the effect must be evaluated within the context of how individuals process information and how that information structures their decision-making processes.

Especially important is the amount of exposure to campaign messages and the extent to which those messages provide either new information or information that conflicts with individuals' prior beliefs. Political scientist Michael MacKuen presents a model that characterizes attitude formation as a two-step process: **Exposure** to new information is the first step, and **acceptance** (integration into preexisting attitudes) is the second.[52] Attitude change occurs when individuals both receive and accept new information.

Individuals with moderate levels of education who occasionally follow the news and have relatively weak attitudes are most likely to be affected by media exposure.[53] The acceptance step of attitude change is probably most likely to occur for weakly held attitudes, since the new information would otherwise be overwhelmed by preexisting attitudes and would have no effect. For example, there is evidence that media effects during election campaigns are likely greater for candidate image (in particular, for lesser-known candidates) than for more fundamental attitudes such as party identification.[54] Importantly, a logical necessity for opinion change (and therefore for media effects) is that individuals must be exposed to distinctive information that conflicts with their prior beliefs or opinions.[55]

These theories of political communication—each of which is supported by systematic evidence from presidential elections—provide a good perspective from which to evaluate evidence about media effects. More specifically, failure to observe one of these necessary conditions might result in the observation of limited or minimal effects.

It is also important to base the analysis of media effects on vote choice within established models of voter decision making. The predominant model of vote choice consists of three factors known to influence which candidate a voter supports: **party identification,** how closely the candidate represents the individuals' **policy positions,** and **candidate image.** In presidential elections, the empirical evidence suggests that candidate choice is most heavily influenced by party identification.[56] Among individuals who do not identify with either political party, the party that they feel most favorable toward is likely to determine which candidate gets their vote, or the candidate whose issue positions are closest to theirs or who has the most favorable image is likely to get their vote.

While it is sometimes difficult to separate these causal influences, it is still important to note that they strongly affect most decisions, especially in the case of presidential election campaigns, and that the actual effect of additional information from the mass media may often be outweighed by prior dispositions. Hence, we should generally not expect to find dramatic effects of media exposure on individuals' vote choices. The discussion that follows emphasizes this theoretical expectation, noting how most of media effects in election campaigns tend to be indirect, with an impact that varies across individuals and

Media Use During the 2000 Presidential Campaign

V OTERS GET ELECTION INFORMATION from different sources than they did several decades ago. The biggest change has been in the proportion of individuals reporting that they get campaign news from television. This change occurred at the same time readership of newspapers declined. It is probably not true that individuals who used to read newspapers now only watch television. Instead, newspaper readers are more likely to supplement their news reading with watching television news, and younger adults, who have never established the habit of reading a paper, are more likely to watch television news shows or access the Internet for campaign information (when they do so at all).

The table below presents results from a national survey of adults conducted in October and November 2000, by Princeton Survey Research Associates. Comparing the 1996 data with the 2000 results, you can see changes in the news audience's decisions about which media to use. Cable news stations seem to be enjoying larger audiences, while newspapers seem to still be losing readers. Note the small proportion of the sample that reports using the Internet as a source of election news.

Consider the following questions.

1. Why do you think the cable news audience has increased in size?
2. What are the consequences of the decline in newspaper readership for the quality of information voters have?
3. What does the reported size of the audience using the Internet for campaign news suggest about the Internet's effect on electoral politics?

Changing Sources of Campaign News

	Early Nov. 1996 %	Early Nov. 2000 %	Late Nov. 2000 %
Television	72	70	83
Network	36	22	23
Local	23	21	30
Cable	21	36	41
Newspapers	60	39	24
Radio	19	15	17
Magazines	11	4	1
Internet	3	11	10

Note: Numbers add to more than 100% because respondents could list up to two primary sources. Early November numbers are based on voters and late November numbers are based on respondents following the outcome of election.

Source: Table from "Internet Election News Audience Seeks Convenience, Familiar Names." Available from http://www.press-politics.org (accessed December 3, 2000).

Characteristics of Voters in the 2000 Election Campaign

ELOW IS A TABLE of summary findings on questions asked in exit polls after the 2000 presidential election campaign. What do these self-reported demographic and attitudinal characteristics suggest about how individuals make their vote choices? How much influence might the media have on those choices?

	Total (%)	Gore Voters (%)	Bush Voters (%)	Buchanan Voters (%)	Nader Voters (%)
Are you:					
White	81	42	54	0	3
Black	10	90	9	0	1
Hispanic/Latino	7	62	35	1	2
Asian	2	55	41	1	3
Other	1	55	39	0	4
To which age group do you belong?					
18–29	17	48	46	1	5
30–44	33	48	49	0	2
45–59	28	48	49	1	2
60+	22	51	47	0	2
No matter how you voted today, do you usually think of yourself as a:					
Democrat	39	86	11	0	2
Republican	35	8	91	0	1
Independent	27	45	47	1	6
On most political matters, do you consider yourself:					
Liberal	20	80	13	1	6
Moderate	50	52	44	0	2
Conservative	29	17	81	0	1
Do you regularly use the Internet?					
Yes	64	47	49	1	3
No	36	51	46	1	2
Do you regularly use the Internet to get political news and information?					
Yes	30	47	48	1	3
No	70	49	47	0	3
When did you finally decide who to vote for in the presidential election?					
In the last three days	11	48	46	0	5
In the last week	6	48	44	1	5
In the last month	13	49	45	1	5
Before that	69	48	50	0	1

Source: Data from ABC 2000 The Vote, "Exit Polls: State-by-State Voter Surveys." Available from http://www.abcnews.go.com (accessed August 20, 2002).

campaign contexts. This is not the same as concluding that dramatic effects never occur, only that they are likely to affect particular types of individuals in particular types of campaigns.

The campaign context is yet another point to keep in mind when considering the effect of the mass media on electoral behavior and attitudes. Most of the discussion on the content of media election coverage has focused on presidential elections because most research is on presidential elections. There are numerous reasons to believe that media coverage has far less of an effect in presidential elections than in less visible races for the Senate, the House of Representatives, a governorship, or a mayoral position, where there is often less campaign activity and media coverage.

In less visible races, individuals typically know less about the candidates and have less of a predisposition to vote on the basis of party identification (especially in nonpartisan races). There is far greater potential for information or images conveyed through the media to have an effect on vote choices. The broader conclusion is that we need to look in the right places for media effects, and we should not generalize conclusions about one campaign context to another. Where inferences from one campaign context need to be made to another, however, the most persuasive argument is that media effects are likely to decrease in magnitude as we shift from low-visibility to high-visibility races.

As noted in Chapter 7, it is important to distinguish between medium and message effects. **Medium effects** suggest that information conveyed on television has a different effect than the same information conveyed in newspapers, in newsmagazines, or on the radio. Studies that focus on medium effects typically rely on measures of media exposure (how often do you read a daily newspaper?) and attention (how much attention did you pay to campaign stories?).[57] **Message effects** suggest that the content of the message—regardless of how conveyed—influences vote choice or political attitudes. While we are typically concerned with media effects, we often do not separate out these two types of effects in research and general discussions. Rarely do television news programs convey the exact same information as newspapers, so when we observe a difference between individuals who watched a television program and those who read the newspaper, it is not clear whether the difference is a function of the different information conveyed or the nature of the medium.

For example, in the 1992 presidential campaign, candidates started to appear on both late-night and morning talk shows. Bill Clinton, for example, played his saxophone on Arsenio Hall's late-night program.[58] By 2000 the major party candidates were visiting Oprah Winfrey's daytime show. Surely they were reaching people who might not have read about the campaign in a newspaper or watched network news programs. But the candidates were also delivering different types of substantive messages via the talk shows than they were able to deliver via television news (with its reliance on sound bites, for example). Consistent with this, research found that exposure to the interview and talk show format enhanced voters' learning about the candidates.[59] Hence, enhanced access was likely the result of the use of a different medium, but more learning might also have resulted from the difference in information conveyed by the candidates.

In assessing the effects of the mass media in election campaigns, this section pays particular attention to theories of individuals' attitudes and vote choice, the distinction between medium and message effects, and whether there is evidence that effects vary across types of campaigns. The roles of both political advertising and the free media are considered for four effects—political learning, agenda-setting, turnout, and vote choice.

Political Learning

Whether voters learn about candidates and issues during election campaigns is central to determining whether they are capable of making informed choices among candidates and the policies they espouse. At least, that is what political scientists thought before the first systematic studies of voter decision making in presidential elections during the 1940 and 1948 campaigns.[60] It was widely assumed that presidential elections commanded a great deal of attention, and that the campaigns stimulated people's interest and involvement in politics. Each presidential campaign was viewed as an important means for citizens to exercise control over government and as a symbolic ritual of the strength of our democracy.

However, Bernard Berelson, Paul Lazarsfeld, and William McPhee were surprised when they repeatedly observed a sample of citizens in Elmira, New York, over the course of the 1948 presidential campaign. Citizens generally were not very interested in the campaign, knew very little about the candidates and their issue positions, and, perhaps most importantly, knew who they were going to vote for before the start of the campaign.[61] The researchers had hypothesized three possible effects of political campaigns: reinforcement, conversion, and activation.[62] **Reinforcement** meant that campaigns simply strengthened individuals' established partisan preferences. **Activation** would occur if campaigns caused individuals to relate preexisting attitudes to their vote choices. **Conversion** would occur if campaigns changed individuals' vote intentions. The evidence suggested that reinforcement was by far the most common campaign effect, with voters typically voting according to their party identification. Most deviations were highly structured by identification or interaction with social groups to which the voters belonged. Moreover, conversion was rare; the campaign did not persuade Democrats to vote for Republican candidates or vice versa.

These findings were broadly interpreted to mean that campaigns have little effect on individuals, so few studies of campaign effects were conducted over the next several decades. Yet some partisans did vote for the candidate of the other party, and the level of party loyalty varied across presidential elections. More importantly, the proportion of citizens refusing to identify with either party has increased substantially since the 1940s and 1950s. Unaffiliated individuals, referred to as **independents,** were initially believed to be more responsive to candidates' issue positions, basing their votes not on loyalty to a political party, but rather on careful assessment of which candidate represented their true interests. The rise in the number of independents occurred at about the same time that political campaigns came to rely more on the mass media, and political scientists again started thinking about how political campaigns might affect individuals in ways other than vote choice.

In some senses, political learning was the reasonable choice of scholars seeking to understand campaigns. It tied in nicely with normative concerns about rational decision making (that is, informed vote choice) and the concerns of the time about the manipulative potential of televised election campaigns, in particular the use of political advertising. It also had a lot to do with the surprise that greeted Patterson and McClure's finding (noted earlier in the chapter) that there was more issue content in political ads than in news reports.[63] Since then, scholars have continued to investigate how much citizens learn during campaigns, and whether political advertising enhances such learning. Most recently, scholars have also sought to evaluate the impact of negative advertising on individuals' political attitudes and involvement.

Kim Kahn and Patrick Kenney examined citizens' knowledge of Senate elections to test whether individuals residing in states with more negative Senate campaigns learned more than individuals residing in states with less negative campaigns.[64] They did a content analysis of a random sample of televised ads for 161 senatorial candidates in 1988, 1990, and 1992 and matched the negativity of the ads to respondents in the 1988, 1990, and 1992 American National Election Study panel.[65] Controlling for other individual characteristics such as level of education, political interest, partisanship, and attention to campaign news, these researchers found that the use of negative ads was significantly related to recognition and recall of challengers' (but not incumbents') names in Senate races. That is, the more that challengers used negative advertising, the more likely that individuals in their state either recognized or recalled their names and knew that they ran for the Senate. They also found that the higher the proportion of negative ads, the more willing people were to identify the ideological placement of the candidates, and the more successful they were at identifying the campaign themes. Both tasks are considerably more complicated than simply recognizing or recalling the names of candidates, yet reinforce the basic finding that individuals learn from political ads and, more specifically, that they learn more from negative advertising.

Similarly, Craig Brians and Martin Wattenberg found that recall of political ads as well as regular exposure and attention to network news and newspapers are associated with greater knowledge.[66] In addition, recall of political ads is associated with greater issue-based candidate evaluation—that is, attributing the reasons for voting for a candidate to particular issue positions. Neither television news exposure nor newspaper exposure is associated with greater issue-based candidate evaluation, suggesting that political ads are especially effective in stimulating individuals to use such knowledge when they make their vote choices.[67]

The campaign event that has been most extensively examined is the presidential debate. Early studies of the 1960 presidential debates were pessimistic about how much voters learned. A second generation of studies of the 1976 presidential debates, however, suggested that the debates were effective in conveying substantive details to individuals who were interested in learning about candidates' issue positions and who did not already have strong affective ties to one of them.[68]

Most recently, Thomas Patterson's Vanishing Voter project found similar effects on individuals' **issue knowledge** from debate exposure.[69] Based on a series of weekly representative national surveys, the data show that the increased issue awareness that followed the three presidential debates in 2000 was the first increase in issue knowledge since the August party conventions had been broadcast. Even then, issue knowledge across twelve different issues was low on average. Nearly half of the sample admitted that they did not know the candidates' positions; only 34 percent could correctly identify either candidate's issue positions; and about 20 percent incorrectly identified issue positions. However, the Vanishing Voter study also reported that voter involvement—being interested in the campaign, discussing it, watching the news about it—also significantly increased after the debate, suggesting an additional benefit of debates as campaign events.[70]

To summarize, scholars' assessment of learning from televised political ads and debates suggests that such learning is modest. This perhaps should be expected, given the incremental amount of information typically provided via each medium and the likely prior knowledge of individuals exposed to them. While the learning effect is not dramatic, it nonetheless meets a minimal requirement of fostering citizen learning.

Much of the research discussed above is motivated by a long-standing concern that television is inferior to newspapers as a medium for meaningful learning. Early studies of medium differences in political learning simply compared the knowledge levels of newspaper readers and television viewers, and quite likely confounded the effects of the medium with the choice of using it. That is, newspaper readers scored higher on political knowledge tests, and researchers thus concluded that they knew more because they read the newspaper, not because they had higher levels of education or political interest than television viewers.

More recently, Neuman, Just, and Crigler's study of television, newspapers, and newsmagazines concluded that television is in many ways as good as, and in some circumstances better than, newspapers in allowing individuals to learn (see Chapter 6).[71] Consistent with this argument, television exposure was found to be associated with greater learning about candidates, while newspaper exposure was associated with greater learning about issues—both possibly reflecting differences in audiences as well as in messages.[72]

Extending this line of research, political scientist Jeffrey Mondak's study of the use of newspapers during the 1992 election campaigns and compared knowledge levels, interpersonal discussion, and vote choices of individuals living in Pittsburgh, where the local paper had gone on strike, with residents of Cleveland, where the local paper continued to be published.[73] This quasi-experimental design made it possible to better answer the question of how much individuals learn from newspaper exposure during election campaigns. Mondak found few, if any, differences between the two groups. People living in an area without a local paper were not significantly less knowledgeable about the presidential campaign than were those living in an area with a local paper. Thus, Mondak concluded that newspapers do not provide a unique vehicle for learning about political events; in this case, he surmised, individuals were able to fill in the informational deficit by using national papers or television news.

In sum, individuals likely learn from both newspapers and television; and the effect of newspapers' greater detailed information might be countered by television's ability to offer different types of informational products, such as political advertisements, infomercials, and candidate debates. Learning can occur only when individuals are exposed to new information, and television might be better at causing such exposure by catching viewers unaware, or it may reach people for whom even basic political information is new.

Turnout

Over the past several decades, political scientists have repeatedly documented the fact that greater campaign spending is associated with higher voter turnout in nonpresidential contests.[74] Since media spending is by far the largest category of expenditures, a logical conclusion might be that campaign advertising mobilizes turnout. One analysis of advertising expenditures and turnout in the 1996 presidential campaign supports this assumption, demonstrating that the more advertising by candidates and by the AFL-CIO about the election, the higher the turnout.[75] Yet most research on campaign advertising has focused on whether negative advertising depresses turnout. Undoubtedly fueled by popular perceptions that campaigns are more negative than in previous decades (when turnout was higher), early research suggested that negative advertising reduces the likelihood that individuals will vote, and that such effects are especially strong among independents who do not identify with either political party.[76]

Other scholars have taken issue with these broad conclusions. Some criticism involves the experimental research design that was used and associated concerns with **external validity.** Specifically, the study of the effects of negative advertising on intended vote was conducted outside of an actual campaign context in which a candidate strategically decided to use negative advertising. Also, the research did not study "true" or "actual" turnout, but rather the experimental subjects' stated intention to vote.

Perhaps more importantly, the operationalization of negative advertising was a somewhat crude (though intuitive) categorization based on the tone of the ads. Ads that portrayed the sponsoring candidate's opponent in a negative light were considered negative ads, while those that portrayed the sponsoring candidate in a positive light were considered positive. Moreover, all ads that mentioned the opposing candidate were categorized as attack ads, regardless of their content.[77] One of the implications of this coding scheme was that anything negative that was said about an opponent was viewed as either manipulative or "overly" negative. But not all ads that attack are negative, and a political advertisement often contains both positive and negative elements.[78]

To confirm the popular claim that attack ads demobilize voters, Kathleen Hall Jamieson coded advertisements aired by presidential candidates, the AFL-CIO, and the Business Coalition as advocacy, attack, or contrast ads.[79] Advocacy ads focus on a candidate's qualifications; attack ads focus on opponents' failures; and contrast ads contain "explicit comparisons between the candidate's qualities, record, or proposals and the opponent's."[80] She found that each type of ad had a unique effect on voter turnout. Advocacy ads were weakly and positively associated with turnout; attack ads were weakly and negatively associated with turnout; and contrast ads were strongly and positively associated with turnout.

Other scholars have failed to replicate the findings from early research on negative advertising. Instead, they claim that negative advertising is positively associated with turnout. For example, when individual-level survey data from the American National Election Study were merged with a content analysis of ads and news coverage in the 1990 Senate campaigns, the finding was that negative political advertising and negative news coverage actually increased turnout.[81] But mudslinging—an excessive focus on negative and cynical topics by the candidates and the news media, as later assessed by campaign managers and consultants—depresses voter turnout. Other scholars, however, found either no effect of negative advertising or a positive (mobilizing) effect.[82]

To summarize, then, scholars have produced mixed evidence on the effects of political advertising on voter turnout. Generally, the more that candidates advertise, the higher the turnout, although the content of the ads might matter, at least in some circumstances. Overly negative *campaigns* that offend people's sense of decency or civility likely depress turnout. Whether the ads that are used in these campaigns or the news coverage of them is responsible for this effect is not clear.

Agenda-Setting

In a now-classic study of agenda-setting in election campaigns, Donald Shaw and Maxwell McCombs wanted to find out how much independence the mass media had in determining which political issues were highlighted in media coverage of election campaigns.[83] Do the mass media simply reflect the activities and interests of voters and campaigns and transmit information? Do they instead act independently in choosing which issues to cover? Shaw and McCombs hypothesized "that the press itself has some power to establish an agenda of political issues which both candidates and voters come to regard as important." They concluded that the mass media are "an independent force" in agenda-setting, and that they "both focus our attention and structure our cognitions."[84]

This study kicked off a long line of research into agenda-setting. Scholars focused on different types of media and different research settings and also sought to extend the basis of agenda-setting theory.[85] Most of these studies, however, relied primarily on cross-sectional data—survey data taken at one point in time. The evidence relied almost exclusively on whether the ordering of the issues emphasized by the media (determined by content analysis) matched (was correlated with) the ordering of issues identified as important by citizens or voters. The more coverage an issue received, the greater the proportion of the survey sample that identified it as being an important national (or local) problem.

The problem with this scholarship is that different causal structures could conceivably account for the correlation between the two sets of issues—and it is the nature of the causal structure that is of critical importance. To overcome this problem, Dalton, Beck, Huckfeldt and Kootzle tested two contrasting models of agenda-setting. In the **media-centered model,** the mass media "exercise an independent causal role in determining the public's interests. The media are seen as autonomous actors who set the agenda of both the public and political elites. . . . Through investigative reporting and news analysis, the media may also inject themes into an election separate from the events of the campaign trail."[86]

In the **transaction model,** political elites, the mass media, and the public interact with, influence, and constrain each other, and through this process the issue agendas of the media, campaigns, and likely voters are correlated with each other. "Even if the media or specific newspapers have their own agenda, their reporting of the campaign is constrained by the candidates' actions and their readers' interests. Furthermore, these social actors are responding to political events that shape the discourse of the campaign."[87] In the media-centered model, the public eventually adopts the media's view of campaign reality; in the transaction model, candidates, the media, and voters anticipate and react to each others' behaviors.

The key question the researchers sought to address was the extent to which the media control the information presented to the public. They compared the issue emphases of candidates, the mass media, and the public by conducting content analyses of campaign-generated newspaper stories and media-initiated newspaper articles and by conducting surveys in which respondents were asked to identify the most important national problem facing the country. They concluded that the media accurately reflect the issue emphases of the political campaigns. Economic issues, the federal budget, and financing issues were the dominant focus of campaign-generated stories and of media-generated articles (see Table 8-3). The biggest difference between the two types of stories was the greater emphasis in the media-generated stories on candidates' past performance. Similar results were obtained when examining editorials and other opinion pieces, by far the most likely place for journalists to identify their

TABLE 8-3 Campaign Issue Emphasis and Media Coverage

Issue Content of Narratives in Campaign-Generated Articles (in percentages)[a]

	Total		Total
Bush platform/record	9.8	Minority and rights issues	3.1
Clinton platform/record	9.0	Legal issues	2.6
Perot platform/record	1.9	Political system, institutions	2.3
Economic issues	27.9	Defense policy	1.9
Budget and finance	14.1	Education and research	0.7
Social programs	10.9	Housing/infrastructure	0.4
Foreign policy	7.5	Other domestic issues	1.1
Environment/energy	6.4	Other international issues	0.4

Issue Content of Narratives in Media-Generated Articles (in percentages)[b]

	Total		Total
Bush platform/record	8.8	Minority and rights issues	2.2
Clinton platform/record	8.4	Legal issues	4.4
Perot platform/record	3.8	Political system, institutions	3.0
Economic issues	24.1	Defense policy	2.6
Budget and finance	13.5	Education and research	1.2
Social programs	9.4	Housing/infrastructure	0.4
Foreign policy	12.7	Other domestic issues	1.2
Environment/energy	3.6	Other international issues	0.6

Issue Content of Narratives in Political Analyses, Op/Ed Columns, Cartoons, and Reader Letters (in percentages)[c]

	Total		Total
Bush platform/record	13.0	Minority and rights issues	3.9
Clinton platform/record	11.5	Legal issues	2.0
Perot platform/record	6.1	Political system, institutions	2.3
Economic issues	19.3	Defense policy	1.4
Budget and finance	15.3	Education and research	1.4
Social programs	9.0	Housing/infrastructure	0.5
Foreign policy	9.5	Other domestic issues	1.2
Environment/energy	3.5	Other international issues	0.2

[a] Table entries are the major topics discussed by each campaign in campaign-generated news articles in which the topic was an issue or policy and the main actor was a presidential candidate, vice presidential candidate, or campaign spokesperson. The unit of analysis was a narrative within an article. The numbers of narratives were as follows: Bush, 474; Clinton, 508; and Perot, 131.

[b] Table entries are the issues discussed by each campaign in media-generated news articles in which the main actor in the narrative was a presidential candidate, vice presidential candidate, or campaign spokesperson. The unit of analysis was a narrative within an article. The numbers of narratives were as follows: Bush, 234; Clinton, 197; and Perot, 67.

[c] Table entries are the issues discussed by all three campaigns combined in media-generated non-news articles in which the main actor in the narrative was a preidential candidate, vice presidential candidate, or campaign spokesperson. The unit of analysis was a narrative within an article. The numbers were as follows: new analyses, 481; op/ed columns, 1,153; cartoons, 294; and letters, 533.

Source: Russell J. Dalton, Paul Allen Beck, Robert Huckfeldt, and William Koetzle, "A Test of Media-Centered Agenda-Setting: Newspaper Content and Public Interests in a Presidential Election." *Political Communication* 15 (1998): 467, 470, 471.

Campaign Issues and Media Issues in the 2000 Presidential Campaign

THE CENTER FOR MEDIA AND PUBLIC AFFAIRS reported that, in the early stages of the fall 2000 presidential campaign, the substantive focus of television news—after the horserace—was on health care, the economy, energy, education, and foreign policy. Likewise, the Project for Excellence in Journalism (which included television, newspaper, and Internet news) reports that—after the horserace and Bush's character—foreign policy, Gore's character, health care and the elderly, other domestic issues, taxes, and energy were covered the most.

Below are exit poll data about the importance of issues in general and the voters' choices. How well does the public's agenda match up with the media's agenda? Why?

National Exit Poll Results	% of All	Gore	Bush	Buchanan
Which one issue mattered most in deciding how you voted for president?				
World affairs	12	40	54	1
Medicare	7	60	39	0
Health care	8	64	33	0
Economy/Jobs	18	59	37	0
Taxes	14	17	80	0
Education	15	52	44	0
Social Security	14	58	40	1
Which one candidate quality mattered most in deciding how you voted for president?				
He understands complex issues	13	75	19	0
He is honest and trustworthy	24	15	80	1
He cares about people like me	12	63	31	1
He has the right experience	15	82	17	0
He is a likeable person	2	38	59	0
He is a strong leader	14	34	64	0
He would have good judgment in a crisis	13	48	50	0
Which was more important in your vote for president today?				
Position on the isssues	62	55	40	1
Leadership/personal qualities	35	35	62	0

Sources: Center for Media and Public Affairs, "Press Release," October 18, 2000. Available from http://www.cmpa.com/pressrel (accessed August 20, 2002). "Project for Excellence in Journalism, Campaign 2000: Last Lap, Topline." Available from http://www.journalism.org/resources/research/reports/campaign 2000/lastlap/topline.asp (accessed March 30, 2003).

views of the important issues of the day. The authors thus conclude that the transaction model is much more consistent with the evidence generated in the 1992 presidential campaign than is the media-centered model.[88]

Vote Choice

Because the dominant theories and findings guiding research on presidential elections have minimized the importance of campaigning for decades, scholars have often assumed that the media's influence on **vote choice** is likewise minimal—or indirect. For example, Scott Keeter examined individuals' presidential candidate preferences (how much the person likes one candidate compared to how much he or she likes the other, assuming that individuals will vote for the candidate they like the most). He expected to find that the media do not directly influence vote choice, but rather alter (prime) the importance of factors that influence that choice.[89] Using American National Election Study data for 1952 through 1980, he tested whether individuals who relied on television for campaign news evaluated candidates differently than individuals who relied on newspapers for campaign news. Controlling for party identification, attitudes toward political parties, age, education, and income, he found that individuals who relied on television news gave more importance to candidates' personal qualities, that candidates' personal qualities were more important in the 1970s than in the 1950s, and that these findings did not seem to simply reflect the types of people who chose to watch television rather than read newspapers.

Keeter suggested that the increased importance of candidates' personal qualities resulted in part from the increasingly important role played by television in presidential campaigns. The personal qualities of candidates are more easily conveyed on television than are more complicated details, such as political experience or substantive expertise. He cautions the reader that he is not suggesting that television has "caused a 'politics of personality,' . . . for we do not know how important candidate traits were prior to the advent of television."[90] Moreover, we do know that campaigns have changed their strategies to use the medium of television in particular ways. Thus, the heightened impact of personal qualities results in part from the reliance on television, but only in the context of strategic choices made by campaigns to use television to their advantage.

Another way media coverage affects voter decision making is by priming the criteria that voters use in evaluating candidates. Research has shown that experimental subjects who viewed more economic news stories gave economic evaluations more weight in their overall evaluations of congressional candidates than did subjects who viewed fewer such stories.[91] Similarly, when news coverage focused more on candidates' personal qualities than on economic or party issues, individuals' feelings about the candidates mattered more in their vote choice. There is evidence that voters evaluated President Jimmy Carter more negatively in the 1980 presidential election because of the substantial proportion of news coverage devoted to the crisis in Iran that began when an anti-American mob stormed the U.S. embassy and took more than fifty Americans hostage.[92] The more negative evaluation resulted from the media's priming of the president's handling of foreign affairs as a criterion on which to evaluate him. The researchers suggest that Carter's very close loss to Ronald Reagan in 1990 was attributable at least in part to this priming effect.[93]

The notion of priming has also been investigated in the case of political advertising, with the expectation that the content of political ads primes the basis on which voters evaluate and choose to vote for candidates. However, the results are mixed. Some scholars find limited support for the notion that greater exposure to campaign ads primes the issues on which individuals make their vote choices.[94] Others provide experimental data that suggest that political advertising primes racial considerations in candidate evaluations,[95] much like implicit appeals in news media coverage do.[96]

In one of the most systematic nonexperimental studies of the effects of news coverage on presidential election outcomes, Daron Shaw looked at whether favorable media coverage of significant campaign events could influence individuals' vote choices and therefore election outcomes.[97] Using data on daily campaign events, news media coverage, and public support from August 1 through November 2 in both 1992 and 1996, Shaw found that favorable television news coverage of the Democratic candidate's campaign events decreased support for the Republican candidate in both years. Favorable newspaper coverage of campaign events was also related to changes in candidate support in 1996 (but not in 1992). The relatively weaker results for newspaper coverage were in line with his expectation that television was the more dominant source of campaign information.

In related work, Shaw tested the effect of political advertising on the electoral outcome.[98] Using data on television ad buys and candidate appearances by state in the 1988, 1992, and 1996 presidential elections, he showed that greater campaign activity in the last few weeks of the campaign—that is, television ads and candidate appearances—is associated with a larger share of the votes in the state. Further, these effects are greater in states with a larger proportion of undecided voters. While advertising in presidential elections is not likely to change the national outcome, these findings are important in the context of a very limited body of research on media effects in presidential campaigns.[99]

Beyond these general findings is the question of whether particular types of media messages affect vote choice. Here again, the relatively small amount of research points to significant, if not substantial, effects. The content of presidential election coverage varies substantially across newspaper outlets. Most importantly, the positions newspapers take in editorials—not the content of news coverage—influence how individuals vote in presidential elections.[100] The effect is not large, but it is significant. News content likely does not have an effect on individuals' vote choice because it tends to be varied, with multiple, usually conflicting, messages. Editorials therefore do a better job of persuading people in the context of electoral politics.

Though the researchers whose work is cited put their substantive findings in context and frame their results as not implying an overwhelming or dramatic effect, the research collectively suggests that campaigns are in fact buying something when they spend such a large proportion of their budgets on media expenditures. The tone of general news coverage seems to be associated with how well candidates do, but newspaper editorials and paid political advertising are also effective tools. It is important to remember, however, that these persuasive messages are most likely to influence undecided voters, and particularly in close campaigns. Moreover, the effectiveness of political advertising might also depend on the broader information environment of the election, and on the extent to which candidates are well known to begin with and distinguished from each other in free media coverage.

These results have several implications for other types of elections. In particular, if news coverage, editorials, and paid advertising influence vote choices in high-stimulus presidential campaigns, they are very likely to have similar (or even stronger) effects in low-stimulus elections. Other research supports this claim. For example, political scientist Darrell West studied the effects of political advertising and news coverage on **name recognition,** perceptions of **candidate favorability,** and **electability** and vote choice in the 1992 California Senate races.[101] State Senate races are competitive and often involve unknown candidates, so voters tend to have a greater need for orientation (information) than in presidential contests. Thus, advertising effects are likely, and are also likely to vary over the course of the campaign, playing a greater role during nomination campaigns, in which voters' party identification provides little guidance on whom to vote for. West found that political advertising had a greater effect on name recognition than did local news coverage in both the primary and general elections. Although political advertising had no effects on favorability in the general election, it was associated with favorability during the primaries— though in a rather complex manner, depending heavily on various candidate strategies. In sum, spending more money on advertising does not guarantee improved favorability ratings, even in the primaries. Media effects on candidate electability and vote choice were even weaker, with the strongest evidence demonstrated in competitive races. This latter finding suggests that media (and especially advertising effects) are most likely to be observed in competitive races.

Another study provides an example of how advertising effects are likely to vary according to the level (**high-stimulus election** or **low-stimulus election**), type (**partisan election** or **nonpartisan election**), and competitiveness of an election. Local races are particularly suited to studying advertising effects because voting decisions are expected to rely on candidate image rather than party identification (they are nonpartisan) or issues (local political issues tend to be valence issues, on which it is difficult to distinguish between candidates). Based on this logic, political scientists Patricia Hurley and Rick Wilson studied the 1985 mayoral race between Kathy Whitmire and Louie Welch in Houston,

Texas.[102] Both Whitmire and Welch previously held citywide office and were about equally financed. Moreover, their advertising strategies shifted during different stages of the campaign, and public opinion data were available to test how image affected voters' decision making.

The researchers tested the hypothesis that individuals who shifted their vote preference to Whitmire during the summer, when her campaign advertising emphasized her past performance, did so on the basis of perceptions of her competence, while those who shifted during the fall, when her advertising emphasized personal characteristics, did so on the basis of style.[103] Their analysis of data throughout the campaign affirmed these hypotheses: Switchers in the summer were more affected by their evaluations of Whitmire's experience and political style, while switchers during the fall were more affected by their evaluations of her personal style.

To summarize, media effects on vote choice are likely in electoral races that are competitive, that have one candidate who is unknown, or in which long-held political beliefs (such as party identification and issue positions) are not helpful as voting cues. Further, the general tone of news coverage and the advertising strategies of candidates are likely to generate effects. Media effects, along with political learning, agenda-setting, and priming, suggest that the media have a significant, though selective, impact on voter decision making and perhaps on electoral outcomes.

THE INTERNET AS A NEW CAMPAIGN MEDIUM

Traditional concerns about the manipulative potential of political advertising seem to be laid to rest by the various findings reported in this chapter. Political ads tend to provide relevant policy information and thus enhance voter learning during campaigns. Moreover, the media have adapted to candidates' strategic use of ads through the use of "adwatches" in which journalists evaluate the tone and substantive content of campaign ads. The overall exposure of political ads, then, is enhanced by coverage in the free media.

It is not surprising that candidates and political consultants spend a large proportion of their budgets on political advertising. Part of this is because they believe in the effectiveness of such ads, and part is that they can control media exposure in ads. Even campaign events that draw a great deal of free media coverage do not give candidates complete control over the way they are portrayed. If the idea is to get the message out, political advertising is most likely to do it.

This advantage of control is also evidenced in the use of candidate, party, and campaign Web sites. If the candidate wants to make information available, the Internet is where it can be done most easily. The problem is that the Internet can only "narrowcast" the message to people who seek out the site, and they are likely to have particular demographic features that make "Internet effects" minimal. For example, the most interested and knowledgeable people with the most highly structured political predispositions are probably most likely to seek out candidate Web sites (particularly in the case of presidential politics). Though the Internet audience is becoming increasingly diverse, it is still mostly a self-selected group, and the Internet still has minimal political effects on the mass public.

Candidates are nonetheless investing in Web sites as campaign resources, most likely to accomplish the traditional first goal of any election campaign—to shore up supporters. The 1996 presidential candidate Web sites were uniformly positive portrayals of the candidates' issue positions, experience, campaign organizations, and personal backgrounds; and the sites were technically uninspired.[104] Their most appealing aspect was that they offered the unparalleled opportunity to surf through press releases, speeches, and other campaign information. By the 2000 election, the Web sites of the major candidates had a mix of positive and negative content, were used for fundraising, and included more interactive features.[105]

If a large proportion of the electorate would access campaign information on the Web, we might see a significant increase in political learning during the campaign, or a greater conversion of independents to one candidate or the other. By 2000 less than 40 percent of the American population had access to the Internet, indicating that mass effects are unlikely.[106] That is, contrary to some of the "hype" about the Internet, not *everyone* is wired—at least at the same level that television or radio is available almost universally in the United States. Others are more positive about the audience potential. The Internet audience has exceeded the size of audiences for newsmagazines such as *Time* and *Newsweek* and the number of regular listeners of radio talk shows and elite news shows such as the *Newshour with Jim Lehrer* and programming on C-SPAN.[107]

Beyond the size of the Internet audience is the issue of whether users actually seek out political information when online. Unlike general Internet users, political activists actively seek out political discussions, specific candidate information, or contact information for elected officials. About 38 percent of Internet users report seeking out specific political information at least once a week, but more active forms of involvement such as contacting officials or engaging in political discussion are much rarer, involving about 4 percent of surfers.[108]

Consistent with the argument that individuals who seek political information online are likely to have high levels of campaign interest to begin with are findings based on 1996 American National Election Study data that Internet users are more active in campaign activities, and slightly more interested in the presidential campaign, than users of other media.[109] While this could be evidence of a mobilizing effect, it likely is the result of self-selection: People who are activists are more likely to use online resources to facilitate their involvement; online access is unlikely to increase political activity.[110]

While the size and selectivity of the Internet audience suggest that the Web is far different from television and newspapers as a *mass* medium (at least now), it is a reminder of the increasing number of mediated information sources that individuals can draw on for information about presidential candidates and elections. One of the consequences of the increasing number of sources—ranging from cable news outlets to television talk shows to the Internet to *Entertainment Tonight*—is that no single source is relied on by a majority of Americans. Although cable news and newspapers are most often cited as individuals' primary news sources for presidential election campaigns, neither is cited by more than a third of respondents in national surveys.[111]

This suggests that the Internet symbolizes a major shift in the nature of election audiences, in that they have become more fragmented.[112] Candidates can thus develop targeted messages for the distinctive audiences that each medium attracts. One of the normative concerns is whether people will use the Internet to selectively choose the information they attend to, creating an information environment that selectively reinforces their prior beliefs. Republicans, for example, might gather information only on Republican candidates, forestalling learning about Democratic or independent candidates. And Democrats might do the same.

Initial research suggests that this might not be occurring. In a recent experimental study, researchers gave some likely voters a CD with a wide range of information on George W. Bush and Al Gore, then monitored which pages were accessed. They found that individuals were selective, but not in a partisan way. Instead, people consulted only the pages that dealt with the issues they believed to be most important. Partisan self-selection was limited only to conservatives, who were significantly less likely to access the liberal and independent information sources on the CD.[113] While this research is mostly suggestive, it does suggest a more optimistic view of individuals' use of the Internet than is typically voiced.

CONCLUSION

The central questions addressed in this chapter are whether the media provide adequate information for individuals to make rational, informed decisions in elections, and whether individuals use the media product, whatever its content, to inform their vote decisions. The answers to both, unexpectedly, are positive. Diversity in substantive content across media outlets means that suitable information is provided in the media, although interested citizens likely have to look for policy-related details if that is what they want. Casual attention to the media during election campaigns is likely to provide information about campaign strategy and candidate image, which some individuals use to make "informed" decisions.

Media diversity is likely responsible for the fact that at least some citizens learn substantive details during the course of presidential campaigns. Televised presidential debates and comprehensive coverage in some daily newspapers likely account for much of this learning, while the occasional policy story on network or cable television shows might have an effect on people who are not motivated to attend to more serious media.

Moreover, the effects of political advertising appear to be far more positive than popular views suggest. Political ads tend to have at least as much policy information as televised newscasts, if not more, and hence are likely to enhance people's knowledge about political candidates. Negative ads tend to be associated with better recall of candidate names and ideological orientations as well, and may possibly increase turnout in elections. Thus, both free and paid media provide individuals with opportunities to learn and probably make better choices than if such information were unavailable.

One of the broader points demonstrated in this chapter, though, is that the extent to which the media provide substantive coverage of elections and the extent to which individuals learn from such coverage are a reflection of the strategic nature of the relationships between the media, candidates, and the mass public. Candidates need the media to run campaigns, however effective, while the media need candidates for their stories. The extent to which voters need the media to make decisions is likely more variable, depending on the nature of the campaign and the interests and attitudes of the individual. Perhaps this is why "objectively" voters know relatively little about most candidates, but what they do know seems to be enhanced via the media.

How does this reflect on the models of the press? As in earlier chapters, it is clear that the reporters of objective fact model fails in the case of election coverage. That media coverage deviates from candidates' campaign messages suggests that some facts are ignored or treated as secondary in importance. While the generally neutral to negative tone of election news indicates some support for the neutral adversary model, the focus on the horserace suggests that the media are not responding directly to candidates as adversaries, but are instead creating their own view of the campaign. Thus, neither model seems to fit the case of election news.

Also as in earlier chapters, the media message does not seem to be sufficiently monolithic to be able to portray the media as propagandist. Diversity in media outlets in terms of news coverage and editorials suggests little partisan bias. At the same time, political advertising seems to allow challengers to compete with established incumbents. Thus, it is not clear that there is a single media voice to sustain the propagandist model.

The media also seem to fail to live up to the expectations of the public advocate model. This model would fit if there were greater media coverage of the broad political issues of the day, rather than an emphasis on horserace, strategy, and image. While more serious coverage is available in particular outlets, even these outlets tend to rely on horserace stories far more than on substantive topics. Simply put, were the public advocate model accurate, voters would not have to work so hard to find basic substantive information about the candidates.

In some senses, eliminating the other models leaves us with the profit-seeker model, which does seem to be fairly well supported. The media's focus on the horserace clearly appeals to entertainment values, and is the hook to maintain a large audience. Recent decisions to cut back on coverage of party conventions and presidential debates are clearly motivated by the reduced audience size associated with these programs, while the profitability of political advertising is immense. Moreover, the fact that the media are profit-motivated does not prohibit individuals from learning from such coverage (and they do), although this is of secondary importance. Perhaps most supportive of the profit-seeker model is evidence regarding the changing nature of campaign news, with increased entertainment values, reliance on visuals, and shorter news stories and sound bites. The bigger concern is the extent to which the media, having become central to the election process, are capable of performing responsibilities other than the provision of electoral information. These broader issues are considered in the final chapter.

Key Terms

acceptance
activation
advocacy ideas
attack ideas
campaign issues
candidate
   favorability
candidate image
clear-cut issues
contrast ideas
conversion
dark horses
descriptive
   campaign stories
diffuse issues
electability
exposure
external validity

free media
frontrunners
game
high-stimulus
   elections
the horserace
independents
interpretive
   campaign stories
issue knowledge
journalistic voice
low-stimulus
   elections
media bias
media-centered
   model
media coverage
   tone

medium effects
message effects
name recognition
negativity bias
nonpartisan
   election
paid media
partisan election
party identification
party positions
policy positions
rational ignorance
reinforcement
representative
   democracy
sound bite
transaction model
vote choice

Exercises

1. Interview friends or family members who were eligible to vote in the last presidential election. Ask them what they liked and disliked about each candidate; whether they voted; why they voted; why they voted for their candidate; and where they received election information—on television, in

newspapers, on radio, from friends, etc. Does any pattern link their political responses to their source of information? Why?

2. Read one or two stories from the most recent or current presidential campaign, and evaluate the article with respect to bias. Write a brief essay, or be prepared to discuss your evaluation in class.

3. Investigate campaign coverage from a previous presidential or congressional election, and bring one example of a campaign issue to class.

4. Define what you mean by *negative advertising,* and bring a negative ad (either hypothetical or actual) to class. Do other members of the class agree with your categorization of the ad as negative? Is there anything positive about the ad?

Notes

1. Anthony Downs, *An Economic Theory of Democracy* (New York: Harper & Row, 1957).

2. John Aldrich, "Presidential Campaigns in Party- and Candidate-Centered Eras," in *Under the Watchful Eye: Managing Presidential Campaigns in the Television Era,* ed. Mathew D. McCubbins (Washington, DC: CQ Press, 1992).

3. Ibid.

4. Kenneth Shepsle, "Strategy of Ambiguity: Uncertainty and Electoral Competition," *American Political Science Review* 66 (1972): 555–568.

5. John Zaller, "The Role of Product Substitution in Presidential Campaign News," *Annals of the American Academy of Political and Social Science* 560 (1998): 111–128.

6. Downs, *An Economic Theory of Democracy;* Arthur Lupia and Mathew D. McCubbins, *The Democratic Dilemma: Can Citizens Learn What They Need to Know?* (New York: Cambridge University Press, 1998).

7. Thomas E. Patterson, *The Mass Media Election: How Americans Choose Their President* (New York: Praeger, 1980). See also Robert D. McClure and Thomas E. Patterson, *The Unseeing Eye: The Myth of Television Power in National Elections* (New York: Putnam, 1976).

8. See, for example, Michael J. Robinson and Margaret A. Sheehan, *Over the Wire and on TV: CBS and UPI in Campaign '80* (New York: Russell Sage Foundation, 1983), Chapter 6; Thomas E. Patterson, *Out of Order* (New York: Knopf, 1993); Wayne P. Steger, "Comparing News and Editorial Coverage of the 1996 Presidential Nominating Campaign," *Presidential Studies Quarterly* 29 (1999): 40–64; Robert A. Wells, "Prestige Newspaper Coverage of Foreign Affairs in the 1992 and 1996 Presidential Campaigns." Paper presented at the Southern Political Science Association annual meeting, Savannah, Georgia, November 3–6, 1999.

9. "PBS Bests Networks in Election News." Press release dated October 23, 2000. Available from http://www.cmpa.com/pressrel/electpr9.htm (accessed August 20, 2002).

10. Project for Excellence in Journalism, "The Last Lap: Differences in Medium." Available from http://www.journalism.org/publ_research/campaign7.html (accessed August 20, 2002).

11. Diana C. Mutz, "Effects of Horse-Race Coverage on Campaign Coffers: Strategic Contributing in Presidential Primaries," *Journal of Politics* 57 (1995): 1015–1042.

12. Marion Just, Ann Crigler, and Tami Buhr, "Voice, Substance, and Cynicism in Presidential Campaign Media," *Political Communication* 16 (1999): 25–44.

13. Project for Excellence in Journalism. "The Last Lap: Final Topline." Available from http://www.journalism.org/publ_research/campaign13.html (accessed August 20, 2002).

14. S. R. Lichter and R. E. Noyes, *Good Intentions Make Bad News: Why Americans Hate Campaign Journalism* (Lanham, MD: Rowman and Littlefield, 1995).

15. The Center for Media and Public Affairs, "Press Release," October 30, 2000. Available from http://www.cmpa.com/pressrel/ (accessed August 20, 2002).

16. Kim F. Kahn, "Characteristics of Press Coverage in Senate and Gubernatorial Elections: Information Available to Voters," *Legislative Studies Quarterly* 20 (1995): 23–35.

17. Robinson and Sheehan, *Over the Wire and on TV.*

18. Project for Excellence in Journalism, "The Last Lap." Research Series on Election Coverage 2000. Available from http://www.journalism.org (accessed August 20, 2002).

19. Ibid.

20. "PBS Bests Networks in Election News."

21. See the extensive discussion in Robinson and Sheehan, *Over the Wire and on TV.*

22. "Journalists Monopolize TV Election News." Press release dated October 20, 2000. Available from http://www.cmpa.com/pressrel/electpr10.html (accessed August 20, 2002).

23. "The Last Lap: Bush v. Gore." Available from http://www.journalism.org/publ_research/campaign5.html (accessed August 20, 2002).

24. R. J. Dalton, P. A. Beck, R. Huckfeldt, and W. Koetzle, "A Test of Media-Centered Agenda Setting: Newspaper Content and Public Interests in a Presidential Election," *Political Communication* 15 (1998): 463–481.

25. Annenberg Public Policy Center of the University of Pennsylvania, "Assessing the Quality of Campaign Discourse—1960, 1980, 1988, 1992." A Report of the Campaign Discourse Mapping Project of the Annenberg Public Policy Center of the University of Pennsylvania under the Direction of Kathleen Hall Jamieson, 1996. Available from http://www.asc.upenn.edu/appc/campmapp/assessing (accessed April 28, 1998).

26. Patterson, *Out of Order.*

27. Daniel C. Hallin, "Sound Bite News: Television Coverage of Elections, 1968–1988," *Journal of Communication* 42 (1992): 5–24.

28. Patterson, *Out of Order;* Hallin, "Sound Bite News." See also Just, Crigler, and Buhr, "Voice, Substance, and Cynicism in Presidential Campaign Media."

29. Patterson, *Out of Order.*

30. Hallin, "Sound Bite News."

31. Lichter and Noyes, *Good Intentions Make Bad News.*

32. "Journalists Monopolize TV Election News." Press release dated October 30, 2000. Available from http://www.cmpa.com/pressrel/electpr10.htm (accessed August 20, 2002).

33. Hallin, "Sound Bite News."

34. Ibid.; Patterson, *Out of Order.*

35. Patterson, *Out of Order.*

36. Ibid.

37. Ibid.

38. Ibid.

39. Tali Mendelberg, *The Race Card: Campaign Strategy, Implicit Messages, and the Norm of Equality* (Princeton, NJ: Princeton University Press, 2001), especially Chapter 5.

40. Ibid.

41. Michael Basil, Caroline Schooler, and Byron Reeves, "Positive and Negative Political Advertising: Effectiveness of Ads and Perceptions of Candidates," in *Television and Political Advertising*, Vol. 1: *Psychological Processes*, ed. Frank Biocca (Hillsdale, NJ: Lawrence Erlbaum, 1991); Annie Lang, "Emotion, Formal Features, and Memory for Televised Political Advertisements," in *Television and Political Advertising*, Vol. 1: *Psychological Processes,* ed. Frank Biocca (Hillsdale, NJ: Lawrence Erlbaum, 1991), pp. 221–244; John E. Newhagen and Byron Reeves, "Emotion and Memory Responses for Negative Political Advertising: A Study of Television Commercials Used in the 1988 Presidential Election," in *Television and Political Advertising*, Vol. 1: *Psychological Processes,* ed. Frank Biocca (Hillsdale, NJ: Lawrence Erlbaum, 1991), pp. 197–220; but see Richard R. Lau and Lee Sigelman, "Effectiveness of Negative Political Advertising," in *Crowded Airwaves: Campaign Advertising in Elections,* ed. James A. Thurber, Candice J. Nelson, and David A. Dulio (Washington, DC: The Brookings Institution, 2000), pp. 10–43.

42. See Darrell M. West, *Air Wars: Television Advertising in Election Campaigns 1952–2000,* 3rd ed. (Washington, DC: CQ Press, 2001), pp. 44–46, for other difficulties in studying political advertising.

43. McClure and Patterson, *The Unseeing Eye.*

44. Ibid., p. 103.

45. West, *Air Wars.*

46. Lynda Lee Kaid and Anne Johnston, "Negative versus Positive Television Advertising in U.S. Presidential Campaigns, 1960–1988," *Journal of Communication* 41 (1991): 53–64.

47. West, *Air Wars,* pp. 49–51; see also Kaid and Johnston, "Negative versus Positive Television Advertising."

48. West, *Air Wars,* pp. 49–50.

49. Kathleen Hall Jamieson, Paul Waldman, and Susan Sherr, "Eliminate the Negative? Categories of Analysis for Political Advertisements," Chap. 3, pp. 44–64, in Thurber, Nelson, and Dulio, *Crowded Airwaves: Campaign Advertising in Elections.*

50. Ibid.

51. Ibid.

52. Michael B. MacKuen, "Social Communication and the Mass Policy Agenda," in *More Than News: Media Power in Public Affairs*, ed. M. B. MacKuen and Steven L. Coombs (Beverly Hills, CA: Sage, 1981). See also the similar three-step model in John R. Zaller, *The Nature and Origins of Mass Opinion* (New York: Cambridge University Press, 1992).

53. MacKuen, "Social Communication and the Mass Policy Agenda."

54. Larry M. Bartels, "Messages Received: The Political Impact of Media Exposure," *American Political Science Review* 87 (1993): 267–285.

55. Zaller, *The Nature and Origins of Mass Opinion*.

56. See, for example, Angus Campbell, Philip E. Converse, Warren E. Miller, and Donald Stokes, *The American Voter* (New York: Wiley, 1960); Steven E. Finkel, "Reexamining the Minimal Effects Model in Recent Presidential Campaigns," *Journal of Politics* 55 (1993): 1–21; Richard Niemi and Herbert Weisberg, *Classics in American Voting Behavior* (Washington, DC: CQ Press, 1993).

57. See, for example, Charles Atkin and Gary Heald, "Effects of Political Advertising," *Public Opinion Quarterly* 40 (1976): 216–228.

58. Steven H. Chaffee, Xinshu Zhao, and Glenn Leshner, "Political Knowledge and the Campaign Media of 1992," *Communication Research* 21 (1994): 305–324; Edwin Diamond, Martha McKay, and Robert Silverman, "Pop Goes Politics: New Media, Interactive Formats, and the 1992 Presidential Campaign," *American Behavioral Scientist* 37 (1993): 257–261.

59. Steven Chafee and Xinshu Zhao, "Political Knowledge and the Campaign Media of 1992," *Communication Research* 21 (1994): 305–325.

60. Paul Lazarsfeld, Bernard Berelson, and Hazel Gaudet, *The People's Choice: How the Voter Makes Up His Mind in a Presidential Campaign* (New York: Columbia University Press, 1944); Bernard R. Berelson, Paul F. Lazarsfeld, and William N. McPhee, *Voting: A Study of Opinion Formation in a Presidential Campaign* (Chicago: University of Chicago Press, 1954).

61. Berelson, Lazarsfeld, and McPhee, *Voting*, Chapter 2.

62. Lazarsfeld, Berelson, and Gaudet, *The People's Choice*.

63. Thomas E. Patterson and Robert P. McClure, *The Unseeing Eye: The Myth of Television Power in National Elections* (New York: G. P. Putnam's Sons, 1976).

64. Kim Fridkin Kahn and Patrick J. Kenney, "How Negative Campaigning Enhances Knowledge of Senate Elections," in *Crowded Airwaves: Campaign Advertising in Elections,* ed. James A. Thurber, Candice J. Nelson, and David A. Dulio (Washington, DC: The Brookings Institution, 2000), pp. 65–95.

65. Kahn and Kenney categorized ads as either positive or negative (about 40 percent were categorized as negative) and used the proportion of negative ads to total ads in each campaign as their measure of campaign negativity.

66. Craig Brians and Martin Wattenberg, "Campaign Issue Knowledge and Salience: Comparing Perception from TV Commercials, TV News, and Newspapers," *American Journal of Political Science* 40 (1996): 172–193.

67. Chaffee, Zhao, and Leshner, "Political Knowledge and the Campaign Media of 1992," found that exposure and attention to television news as well as viewing

presidential debates, party conventions, and candidate interviews were associated with greater knowledge of candidates' issue differences during the 1992 presidential campaign. They are thus more optimistic about the positive contributions of television than are most. See also W. Russell Neuman, Marion R. Just, and Ann N. Crigler, *Common Knowledge: News and the Construction of Political Meaning* (Chicago: University of Chicago Press, 1992).

68. David O. Sears and Steven H. Chaffee, "Uses and Effects of the 1976 Debates: An Overview of Empirical Studies," in *The Great Debates: Carter vs. Ford, 1976*, ed. Sidney Kraus (Bloomington: Indiana University Press, 1979); Lee B. Becker, Idowu A. Sobowale, Robin E. Cobbey, and Chaim H. Eyal, "Debates' Effects on Voters' Understanding of Candidates and Issues," in *The Presidential Debates*, ed. George F. Bishop, Robert G. Meadow, and Marilyn Jackson-Beeck (New York: Praeger, 1978), Chapter 7, pp. 126–139; but see Doris A. Graber and Young Yun Kim, "Why John Q. Voter Did Not Learn Much from the 1976 Presidential Debates," in *Communication Yearbook 2*, ed. Brent D. Rubin (New Brunswick, NJ: Transaction Books, 1978), pp. 407–421.

69. See http://www.vanishingvoter.org or Thomas E. Patterson, *The Vanishing Voter: Public Involvement in an Age of Uncertainty* (New York: Knopf, 2002).

70. On debate effects, see also Michael X. Delli Carpini, Scott Keeter, and Sharon Webb, "The Impact of Presidential Debates," in *Politics and the Press: The News Media and Their Influences*, ed. Pippa Norris (Boulder, CO: Lynn Rienner, 1997), Chapter 6, pp. 145–164.

71. Neuman, Just, and Crigler, *Common Knowledge*.

72. Chaffee and Zhao, "Political Knowledge and the Campaign Media of 1992."

73. Jeffrey J. Mondak, *Nothing to Read: Newspapers and Elections in a Social Experiment* (Ann Arbor: University of Michigan Press, 1995).

74. See, for example, Gary Cox and M. Munger, "Closeness, Expenditures, and Turnout in the 1982 United States House Elections," *American Political Science Review* 83 (1989): 217–231; Jan E. Leighley and Jonathan Nagler, "Socioeconomic Class Bias in Turnout, 1964–1988," *American Political Science Review* 86 (1992): 725–736; Samuel C. Patterson and Gregory A. Caldeira, "Getting Out the Vote: Participation in Gubernatorial Elections," *American Political Science Review* 77 (1983): 675–689.

75. Kathleen Hall Jamieson, *Everything You Think You Know About Politics . . . and Why You're Wrong* (New York: Basic Books, 2000), Chap. 10, pp. 93–96.

76. Stephen Ansolabehere and Shanto Iyengar, *Going Negative: How Attack Ads Shrink and Polarize the Electorate* (New York: Free Press, 1995).

77. See Larry M. Bartels, "Uninformed Votes: Information Effects in Presidential Elections," *American Journal of Political Science* 40 (1996): 194–230, for additional discussion of this point as well as a more technical criticism of Ansolabehere and Iyengar's analyses.

78. Jamieson, Waldman, and Sherr, "Eliminate the Negative?"

79. Jamieson, *Everything You Think You Know About Politics,* Chap. 12, pp. 107–110.

80. Ibid., p. 99.

81. Kim Fridkin Kahn and Patrick J. Kenney, "Do Negative Campaigns Mobilize or Suppress Turnout? Clarifying the Relationship Between Negativity and Participation," *American Political Science Review* 93 (1999): pp. 877–889.

82. See, for example, S. E. Finkel and J. G. Geer, "A Spot Check: Casting Doubt on the Demobilizing Effect of Attack Advertising," *American Journal of Political Science* 42 (1998): 573–595; Paul Freedman and Ken Goldstein, "Measuring Media Exposure and the Effects of Negative Campaign Ads," *American Journal of Political Science* 43 (1999): 1189–1208; John Geer and Richard R. Lau, "A New Way to Model Campaign Effects." Paper presented at the annual meeting of the American Political Science Association, Boston, September 3–6, 1998.

83. Donald Shaw and Maxwell McCombs, *The Emergence of American Political Issues: The Agenda-Setting Function of the Press* (New York: West Publishing, 1977), p. 3.

84. Ibid., p. 151.

85. See, for example, Stephen M. Gadziala and Lee B. Becker, "A New Look at Agenda-Setting in the 1976 Election Debates," *Journalism Quarterly* 60 (1983): 122–126; Russell J. Dalton, Paul A. Beck, and Robert Huckfeldt, "Partisan Cues and the Media: Information Flows in the 1992 Presidential Election," *American Political Science Review* 92 (1998): 111–126; Leonard Tipton, Roger D. Haney, and John R. Baseheart, "Media Agenda-Setting in City and State Election Campaigns," *Journalism Quarterly* 52 (1975): 15–22; David H. Weaver, Doris A. Graber, Maxwell E. McCombs, and Chaim H. Eyal, *Media Agenda-Setting in a Presidential Election: Issues, Images and Interest* (New York: Praeger, 1981).

86. Russell J. Dalton, Paul Allen Beck, Robert Huckfeldt, and William Koetzle, "A Test of Media-Centered Agenda Setting: Newspaper Content and Public Interests in a Presidential Election," *Political Communication* 15 (1998): 463–481.

87. Ibid., p. 465.

88. Ibid.

89. Scott Keeter, "The Illusion of Intimacy: Television and the Role of Candidate Personal Qualities in Voter Choice," *Public Opinion Quarterly* 51 (1987): 344–358.

90. Ibid., p. 355.

91. Shanto Iyengar and Donald R. Kinder, *News That Matters* (Chicago: University of Chicago Press, 1987).

92. Ibid.

93. Ibid.

94. West, *Air Wars*; Robert G. Meadow and Lee Sigelman, "Some Effects and Non-effects of Campaign Commercials: An Experimental Study," *Political Behavior* 4 (1982): 163–175.

95. Nicholas A. Valentino, Vincent L. Hutchings, and Ismail K. White, "Cues That Matter: How Political Ads Prime Racial Attitudes During Campaign," *American Political Science Review* 96 (2002): 75–90.

96. Tali Mendelberg, *The Race Card: Campaign Strategy, Implicit Messages, and the Norm of Equality* (Princeton, NJ: Princeton University Press, 2001).

97. Shaw, "The Impact of News Favorability and Candidate Events in Presidential Campaigns."

98. Shaw, "The Effect of TV Ads and Candidate Appearance on Statewide Presidential Votes, 1988–96."

99. Ibid. See also Gary C. Jacobson, "The Impact of Broadcast Campaigning on Electoral Outcomes," *Journal of Politics* 37 (1975): 769–793; Richard A. Joslyn, "The Impact of Campaign Spot Advertising on Voting Defections," *Human Communication Research* 7 (1981): 47–60.

100. Dalton, Beck, and Huckfeldt, "Partisan Cues and the Media: Information Flows in the 1992 Presidential Election," 111–126.

101. Darrell M. West, "Political Advertising and News Coverage in the 1992 California U.S. Senate Campaigns," *Journal of Politics* 56 (1994): 1053–1076.

102. Patricia A. Hurley and Rick K. Wilson, "Strategic Campaigning and Voter Shifts: A Panel Analysis of Houston's 1985 Mayoral Race," *Social Science Quarterly* 68 (1987): 34–50.

103. Ibid. Hurley and Wilson report that the Welch campaign seemed to respond in an unfocused manner, or not at all, in both stages of the campaign. Hence, the expectation was that Whitmire's campaign strategy would dominate voters' decision making.

104. West, *Air Wars*. A casual review of the Bush and Gore Web sites in 2000 suggests that this description is still accurate; also see Marjorie Randon Hershey, "The Campaign and the Media," in *The Election of 2000*, ed. Gerald Pomper (New York: Chatham House, 2001), Chap. 3, pp. 46–72.

105. West, *Air Wars*.

106. Ibid., p. 61.

107. Pippa Norris, ed., "Who Surfs? New Technology, Old Voters and Virtual Democracy in the 1996 and 1998 U.S. Elections." Downloaded from http://www.ksg.harvard.edu/norrisweb/ARCHIVE/WhoSurfs2.htm. Revised draft for Elaine Kamarck, ed., *Democracy.com?* (Cambridge, MA: Hollis, 1999). See also Richard Davis and Diana Owen, *New Media and American Politics* (New York: Oxford University Press, 1998).

108. Norris, "Who Surfs?"

109. Davis and Owen, *New Media and American Politics*.

110. Ibid., pp. 180–185.

111. The Pew Research Center for the People and the Press, "The Tough Job of Communication with Voters." Press release dated February 5, 2000.

112. Ibid.

113. Shanto Iyengar, Kyu Hahn, and Markus Prior, "Has Technology Made Attention to Political Campaigns More Selective? An Experimental Study of the 2000 Presidential Campaign." Paper presented at the Annual Meeting of the American Political Science Association, San Francisco, September 2, 2001.

Media Models, Linkage Institutions, and Representative Democracy

Media Models: What Is Supported by the Evidence?

Media Models: What Should We Want?

ARLY IN 2003 news headlines were asking whether President Bush should involve the nation in a preemptive strike against Iraq. White House Press Secretary Ari Fleischer insisted that the president did not need congressional approval to attack, but that the decision needed the support of the American public. The Sunday talk shows were abuzz with debate on the issues surrounding the attack and possible aftermath.

Who was using the media in this situation? Were the media doing their job adequately in publicizing the debate? What would the consequences of the mediated public debate be?

These questions can be addressed only by recognizing the interdependence of government officials, the media, and the mass public. The White House was clearly using the media to achieve its political goals. The administration had the advantage of being the primary actor and information source upon which reporters had to rely. Its goal in using the media was not limited to persuading the American public. Leaders in numerous Middle Eastern countries were also targeted by this communication, none more than Iraq's leader, Saddam Hussein.

Disagreement among Republican elites were conveyed in the media and lent some drama to the story while exposing the mass public to competing points of view. Some citizens probably changed their opinions about whether the United States should strike Iraq, while others became even more certain of their original positions. Government leaders across the globe responded publicly or privately. The outcome seemed uncertain. Perhaps a well-publicized threat would be sufficient to force some compliant behavior on the part of the Iraqi government. Perhaps failure to gain widespread public approval would keep Bush from moving forward. Perhaps gaining it would instead allow him to move ahead more boldly.

The issue of how well the media did their job in covering the debate over attacking Iraq became a topic of conversation, at least between government officials and the press. The answer to that question depends at least in part on what role individuals believe the media should perform. These, more generally, are the questions addressed in this chapter: What kind of job is the media performing, and hence what model of the media best fits? What role should the media perform?

MEDIA MODELS: WHAT IS SUPPORTED BY THE EVIDENCE?

Chapter 1 introduced five models of the press: reporters of objective fact, neutral adversary, profit-seeker, public advocate, and propagandist. The evidence presented in subsequent chapters generally and largely supported the profit-seeker model. The weakening of the lines between the newsroom and the boardroom, the increased corporatization of the media business, budget cutbacks in news divisions, the "softening" of news content, and the topics commonly chosen for news coverage all confirm the central claim of Chapter 3—that the primary purpose of the mass media is to make a profit. That these changes have occurred at the same time that media corporations have become increasingly profitable suggests that they will not easily be undone.

Why were the other models less convincing than the profit-seeker model?

The reporters of objective fact model was fairly easily eliminated based on the nature of news content. There are systematic distortions in the view of the world presented by the media. The media do more than just report objective facts; they sift through and choose which parts of the world to present, sometimes driven by objective reality, sometimes not. Perhaps the most telling point is the increased emphasis on entertainment values in television news. Entertainment values dominate objective reality in many cases.

The neutral adversary model fails largely because the media rely on government officials as their main sources for the news. Reporters have rarely worked independently of government officials, and perhaps this is especially true today because of tight budgets. Being critical of government officials and institutions is not the same as being a neutral adversary. Unfavorable information is often provided by competing elites. It typically is not the result of investigative reporting by the press. Thus, the political and professional motives of reporters are questioned when they deliver news stories that masquerade as adversarial, but in the end are not truly neutral.

Similarly, the public advocate model fails as an approximation of reality because of the news media's reliance on government sources. The media do not put citizens in a more central role as news sources and newsmakers. The typical news product does not seek wide public understanding of issues of political importance; instead it emphasizes personality and drama. To be sure, proponents of civic journalism are promoting an alternative vision of the news profession; and the model seems to be accomplished in isolated instances. A recent survey of editors whose papers had emphasized civic journalism projects, for example, suggested that the editors were convinced of the significant contribution of this alternative news style, reporting that civic journalism "had increased public deliberation, civic problem solving, volunteerism and changed public policy."[1]

Two of the distinctive features of civic journalism projects discussed by the editors was the shift from "conflict" frames to "explanatory" frames in news stories, and in incorporating citizen perspectives. For example, the St. Paul Pioneer Press, which had developed the use of civic journalism for years, chose to develop a story relating to veiled Middle Eastern women fearful of being seen in public after the September 11, 2001, terrorist attacks in New York City. "In terms of pure, basic public journalism, we gave them back a voice," said Kate Parry, senior editor for special projects. "[Hannah] did a magnificent job of finding them and letting them tell the story of how difficult this was."[2]

As this study's investigators suggest, these findings have to be treated with caution, as one might expect that editors who had invested resources in civic journalism would likely report that there was a payoff. Yet a study of the 1996 general election in New Zealand affirms the benefits of civic journalism, concluding that election coverage was less negative, more neutral, more policy-oriented, and less likely to focus on the election as a horserace in 1996 than in the 1993 general election.[3]

The propagandist model does not quite fit either, at least not in obvious ways. Media coverage of government and government officials has become increasingly negative, and this seems to be reflected in increasingly cynical attitudes of citizens toward government. Evidence that the mass media audience is active in evaluating and processing political information also suggests that a propagandist model is inaccurate. However, supporters of the propagandist model would suggest that this is too superficial a basis on which to evaluate it. Perhaps we need more systematic evidence about the portrayal of the fundamental social cleavages of class and race in the United States, and of how that portrayal legitimizes enduring inequalities between African Americans and whites and between the rich and the poor. While some research has looked at the media's portrayal of race, not a single point has been raised about the absence of discussions of wealth inequality.

To summarize, it seems that the profit-seeker model has the most support, but aspects of the public advocate and propagandist models receive some support, too. This conclusion suggests that reporters will be at the heart of media performance in the future. To the extent that reporters in particular news outlets consciously adopt a civic journalism approach, we should see more coverage of political issues and less reliance on government officials as news sources. To the extent that reporters confront the enduring, fundamental issues of race and class, the use of the mass media as a propaganda tool could be weakened.

MEDIA MODELS: WHAT SHOULD WE WANT?

Whether you agree or disagree with this assessment, your reaction may be relief or despair, depending on your view of what the role of the press *should* be. Social science research is not the place to look for answers to "should" questions. Although my personal reaction is relief—maybe a profit-oriented media is not that bad after all—this sidesteps the question of what we, as citizens, should want the press to do.

Chapter 8 discussed the contention that the media are now being expected to play the role of a linkage institution in electoral politics, despite the fact that they were not designed to play that role.[4] This seems to be the case in coverage of nonelectoral politics as well. The media are simply not structured to give voice to citizens; the dominant direction of communication is from government officials to citizens, not the reverse.

Perhaps an alternative role is to provide a forum for public deliberation.[5] A media system that allows a large proportion of the public to be informed about and engaged in the political issues of the day is likely a good thing in a representative democracy. Evidence from case studies over several years suggests that the media do in fact provide a venue outside of formal decision-making bodies and political organizations in which elites and citizens can exchange information. The media do not perform this role flawlessly, but they often do a good job.[6]

The evidence presented in this book, too, suggests that the profit-seeking press offers a variety of outlets and programs that effectively communicate basic political information. To the extent that citizens hunt for it, it is there. When government officials seek to convey substantive policy information, they often find a way to do it.

How might the media do a better job of supporting public deliberation? The traditional answer entails three basic adjustments. First, journalists might seek to enhance news coverage of political issues rather than personality, drama, and trauma. Their personal motivations are not a concern, but the news products they turn out are. Perhaps they need to be more creative in order to overcome today's news routines. They must at least consider the possibility that substantive information about real political issues can be conveyed in a way that both engages and informs citizens. At issue is journalists' reliance on story formats. Dropping the story format might allow alternative news formats, which could convey more substantive policy and issue information, to emerge.

More details about public policies and their alternatives could improve public deliberation, although this is not to say that noncognitive decision criteria are inferior. Political scientists are examining the role of emotion in decision making, and they suggest that the use of affect sometimes produces better decisions than does the use of cognition. This point—and future research relating to it—needs to be kept in mind. In the short term, however, the relative dearth of readily available information about electoral choices and basic government policies and procedures requires additional factual information, whether or not such an emphasis reduces the emotional valence of media messages. Perhaps there are ways to present historical and contextual information that allows news consumers to make more sense of the fragmented news they currently receive.

Second, the training of reporters and their resources and professional responsibilities should encourage them to rely less on government officials as sources of routine news. For this to succeed, corporate pressures to reduce the costs of newsgathering would have to change. It is possible that our society has changed sufficiently that political elites are not the only sources of useful political information. The advent of the Internet and increased pressure for openness and representation in government decision making indicate that, while government officials may be the easiest sources for news, they are not the only ones. Perhaps the first step is a more direct and public acknowledgment of the sources for today's news stories. If news organizations were to discourage the use of vague references, such as "high administration officials," and if the officials who seek to convey news were to be more fully identified, consumers could evaluate the news more independently.

Third, the blurred distinction between entertainment news and political news should be made clearer. Would it matter if news outlets provided less space or time to political news but provided better-quality news? Redesigning news outlets to better distinguish between political news and entertainment news would allow the news audience to have clearer choices about the news they consume, and the news that was provided could be less concerned with sustaining the entertainment values so important in the business today. Who knows, maybe the audience would prefer a more focused news section to today's dramatized news product.

Such changes might also reinvigorate the interrelationships among the public, reporters, and government officials. Were citizens to learn more and recognize that they are part of a mass deliberation on public policy issues, they might evaluate government officials and the press in a different, more positive light. Government officials, on the other hand, might view a shift in the nature of the news product as an opportunity to be less concerned with headlines and entertainment values and more concerned with honest communication about the political issues and processes.

A more radical proposal is to encourage the development of a more partisan media system. That is, privately owned media outlets could adopt a partisan function to their news. In essence, this proposal would extend Fox News' current strategy of appealing to conservatives, but it would be different in that outlets would advertise that they represent a particular political or ideological cause. The professional norm of objectivity would be dropped, and each outlet would be responsible for fully conveying the political interests and claims of political elites. The personal views of reporters and editors would become irrelevant to the news product. Privately owned media could still try to maximize their audiences, whether conservative, liberal, or moderate, through variations in news packaging.

News consumers would be able to choose to attend to a partisan media outlet. Presumably, news consumers would avoid ideological news shows that became too far removed from reality. In some senses, the news media would be more of a marketplace of political ideas. As in any market, some citizens would select the types of news and information they agree with, and little persuasion might result. For citizens who are genuinely seeking political information, comparing and contrasting the news products might be both provocative and educational.

The potential negative consequences of tuning in to news that offers a narrow view of the world and simply reinforces people's prior beliefs would be countered by the fairly strong influences of social context on individuals' political attitudes and beliefs. Conversations at work or church, for example, would likely provide countervailing views of the world and moderate any "direct" effects of relying solely on a biased information source. Furthermore, more overtly political news media might result in increased demand for more educational, nonpartisan news, and such a demand could reinvigorate public television and radio stations. The public airwaves, then, could also help ameliorate the potentially negative consequences of a more partisan media, especially if public television and radio drew a larger audience than they do today. Public deliberation might be realized more effectively than in today's nonpartisan media.

Think about these two alternative scenarios. If you are especially critical of today's media system, be sure to think seriously about the second, more radical proposal. Think, too, about your habits as a news consumer and citizen of a representative democracy. The choices you make in seeking to become an informed citizen will have consequences for the success of both the media and our democracy.

Notes

1. Pew Center for Civic Journalism, "Community Impact, Journalism Shifts Cited in New Civic Journalism Study." Press release dated November 4, 2002. Available from http://www.pewcenter.org/doingcj/spotlight/index.php (accessed March 30, 2003).

2. Pew Center for Civic Journalism, Pat Ford, "Sept. 11: Helping People Get Smarter." Available from http://www.pewcenter.org/doingcj/spotlight/displaySpotlight.php?id=55 (accessed March 30, 2003).

3. Judy McGregor, Susan Fountaine, and Margie Comrie, "From Contest to Content: The Impact of Public Journalism on New Zealand Election Campaign Coverage," *Political Communication* 17 (2000): 133–148.

4. Thomas E. Patterson, *Out of Order* (New York: Knopf, 1993).

5. Benjamin I. Page, *Who Deliberates?* (Chicago: University of Chicago Press, 1996); also see Chapter 1.

6. Ibid.

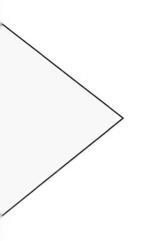

Appendix:
Content Analysis

by Christopher Owens

Content analysis is a methodological technique based on the quantitative analysis of news content. The basic procedure involves taking news stories, whether printed or televised, and systematically analyzing their content in terms of words, phrases, or related characteristics. In addition, publication details associated with each story are presented, such as total number of words or paragraphs in the story; story placement; whether a graph, illustration, or photograph accompanies the story; the length of text; and the headline. Having quantified the nature, subject, tone, length, and placement of each story on various dimensions, researchers can then compare how coverage varies across news media outlets (television, newspapers) or over time (before and after an election or crisis, for example).

Content analysis thus provides a more rigorous basis for claims like "newspapers provide more information than television," "television emphasizes the personality of candidates more than newspapers do," and "the press is biased against conservative candidates." Content analysis allows for a systematic analysis of such claims so that we do not rely on our general impressions, which are typically influenced by our own values and beliefs, about the media.

We could conduct a content analysis of a newspaper or newsmagazine over the course of a campaign or a set of campaigns and compare the length of coverage that liberal candidates receive and the length of coverage that conservative candidates receive. If there is bias against conservative candidates, we would probably expect them to receive less coverage. We could also come up with different ways to measure bias. Perhaps we could evaluate how positive the pictures of conservative candidates are compared to those of liberal candidates; or we could count the number of positive words describing conservative and liberal candidates. We might try to compare how much media coverage involves descriptive information and how much involves an evaluation of candidates' records or complaints. If the liberal press is more critical of conservative candidates, there might be more paragraphs of evaluation about a conservative candidate than about a liberal candidate.

Limitations of Content Analysis

One limitation of content analysis is that it typically focuses on written or verbal communication (printed or spoken words). One of the potentially most powerful aspects of television is its delivery of messages via visual communication—the pictures that are shown rather than words that are spoken. For example, White House officials in the Reagan era were typically unconcerned about negative stories about the president as long as positive visual images accompanied the stories.[1] After reporting on how President Reagan's decisions in office failed to live up to his campaign promises, Lesley Stahl of CBS News was shocked to receive a phone call from a White House staffer thanking her for the story. Because all the visuals were positive, the White House was thrilled to have "a four and a half minute free ad for the Ronald Reagan campaign for re-election."[2] The audience, they were convinced, pays attention only to the pictures.

Another limitation of content analysis is the possibility that researchers might allow their personal biases to influence their coding decisions. One response is to have more than one person code each story, and to assess the extent to which a diverse group of people code stories similarly. Social scientists investigating whether the press is biased against conservative candidates would need to guard against the possibility that politically conservative researchers would be more likely to "see" more negative coverage of conservative candidates. If they were, their research would suffer from measurement error: What they identified as negative might appear to be neutral or even positive to less conservative individuals. If this was the case and "negative" was in the eye of the beholder, the evidence would be bad and the substantive conclusions drawn from it would be wrong.

To guard against the influence of personal beliefs in the conduct of content analysis, social scientists typically use multiple coders. That is, they have more than one person code the same media content, taking measures of the same text. They then compare the results from several coders and determine the extent to which they agree. In social science research methods, the level of agreement is referred to as inter-coder reliability. The more coders agree, the more likely that the data are not systematically biased in any one direction, and the more confidence we can have in the results.

Using Content Analysis

Let's say we want to determine how effectively environmental interest groups have been able to garner positive media attention. The first step is to determine the population. What groups do we want to include in the study? Do we only want to look at the ideologically extreme groups such as People for the Ethical Treatment of Animals (PETA) and Greenpeace, or do we want to include all groups concerned with environmental issues? What media sources do we intend to examine? Should we look at all television, radio, and newspaper reports, or should we focus on sources within one media outlet. Often, content analyses focus on newspapers alone, partly because television news shows tend to mirror the topics covered in newspapers. In addition, there are some practical advantages to coding written text from newspapers rather than audiovisual tapes of televised news programs.

Once we have thoroughly considered our options, we determine that the population will consist of all reports involving Washington-based environmental groups in the *New York Times, Washington Post,* and *Los Angeles Times.* The next step is to decide on a suitable sample size from which to draw data. We could decide to look at all stories ever appearing in the three papers, or all stories appearing on the front page of each of the three papers. We could narrow the time frame, or randomly sample stories over a number of years or over a number of weeks occurring over a number of years. The idea is to select a sample size that can adequately answer the research question and be completed within the allotted time.

For example, the environmental movement began to gain momentum in the early 1970s, so one strategy is to sample all stories over the past thirty years; this might be especially reasonable if the content analysis is a group project. One student could take January through March of every year, the next take April through June, and so on. If the project is being done alone, however, it would make more sense to sample from the population, perhaps coding each of the newspapers for the first week of every month over the thirty-year period or choosing one of the papers and coding every third day of the month.

The next step is to choose the unit of analysis. The unit of analysis is the actual portion of the sample we want to count or evaluate. We will probably want to focus on sentences, paragraphs, or complete stories as the units of analysis. We may want to count the number of positive or negative words used in stories over the thirty-year sample. Using the story as the unit of analysis is more typical. Then all data coding would rely on each story as a case, and the variables would reflect on the story: for example, the headline; whether there was a picture; number of words, number of positive and negative words; paragraphs about the costs or the benefits of environmental regulation. We would want to make sure to code all variables necessary for answering the question or testing the hypothesis. For example, why code whether a picture accompanied the article if we weren't specifically interested in pictures? For the environmental example, we might decide that the complete story is the best unit of analysis.

Now that we have established the population, sample size, and unit of analysis, we can begin to analyze the data. Content analysis can be either structural or substantive. Structural analysis is concerned with how something is said without paying attention to the actual words themselves. How many words or paragraphs did the newspaper devote to stories about environmental groups? Where in the paper were the stories located? Were they on the front page or buried near the back? These factors can tell us about the amount of attention environmental groups received. However, they would tell us little about how environmental groups were covered. If we are concerned with the type of coverage, which our research question suggests to be the case, we will want to perform substantive content analysis. Substantive analysis focuses on the meaning of what is being said. Was the newspaper positive or negative in its coverage?

To properly conduct analysis of the data, we must develop a "dictionary" in which we explain and define the steps for classifying the tone of stories as positive, negative, or neutral. For example, we may determine tone by taking the difference between the number of positive and negative statements in each article. If so, we will want to clearly explain in the dictionary what constitutes a positive or negative statement. For example, adjectives such as *extreme, difficult,* and *demanding* might be considered negative, while adjectives such as *balanced* and *forward-thinking* might be examples of positive attributes.

A well-developed dictionary is important for two reasons: (1) It allows everyone working on the project to understand how the coding will proceed, and (2) it makes it possible for others to duplicate the findings. The first point is especially important because we will want to ensure that our results are not biased. As discussed earlier, personal or group bias can weaken or negate findings. To guard against such mistakes, it is helpful to have group members code the same stories and to compare the results across coders. This comparison, when formalized mathematically, is referred to as inter-coder reliability. Even an informal comparison of how different individuals code the same stories ensures that any differences observed across time or across media outlets are the result of true differences in the media, not just differences in who coded the story content across the media outlets.

For a more detailed discussion of content analysis, consult the following sources: Jarol B Manheim, Richard C. Rich, and Lars Willnat, *Empirical Political Analysis,* 4th ed. (New York: Longman, 2002); Robert Philip Weber, *Basic Content Analysis,* 2nd ed. (Newbury Park, CA: 1990); Klaus Krippendorff, *Content Analysis: An Introduction to Its Methodology* (Newbury Park, CA: Sage, 1980).

Notes

1. W. Lance Bennett, *News: The Politics of Illusion,* 4th ed. (New York: Longman, 2001), pp. 136–137.
2. Ibid.

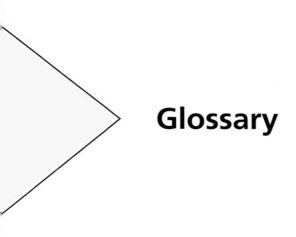

Glossary

acceptance: The second step of attitude change, in which individuals adopt an opinion consistent with a new piece of information that they have been exposed to; most likely to occur for weakly held attitudes.

accessibility: Psychological theory that poses individuals' cognitions as strings of information, where the most recent information is most accessible and therefore is used in processing new information.

activation: One of the three possible effects of political campaigns; occurs if campaigns have caused individuals to relate different preexisting attitudes to their vote choices.

advocacy ideas: Ads that highlight the sponsoring candidate's issue positions or values.

adwatches: Reporters' efforts to respond to campaign ads by providing commentary on their substance and validity.

affective effects: Changes in individuals' affective or emotional state as a result of exposure to the mass media.

agenda-setting: The process by which individuals or institutions come to acknowledge the importance of an issue or problem.

Alien and Sedition Acts of 1798: A congressional law against libel passed in an effort to regulate the printed press.

alliance: The period at the beginning of a president's term in which the press is interested in the new president and administration and tends to cover most stories in a very positive light.

altruistic democracy: Value portrayed in media coverage that suggests democracy never fails.

analyze: To consider various explanations for an occurrence or behavior.

Associated Press: News organization established in 1848 that used the telegraph to send stories nationwide to be printed by local papers.

attack ideas: Ads that specifically mention the candidate's opponent.

attribution theory: Psychological theory that argues that individuals seek to understand information as they process it.

authority-disorder bias: When news dramas or crises develop, reporters place officials at the center of the plot and portray them as uncaring, scheming politicians who fail to restore order.

beats: The organization of newspapers and television news programs in which reporters are assigned a set of (usually related) offices, topics, or contacts to monitor for newsworthy happenings, such as the White House, the Pentagon, city hall, or the city jail and courts.

behavioral effects: Changes in individuals' behavior as a result of exposure to the mass media.

belief importance: The relative weight a belief is given as an individual constucts an opinion.

campaign issues: Issues that arise during the course of a campaign, typically from a candidate's or campaign's miscue or blunder. They are issues only because they are created in the context of the campaign.

candidate favorability: How positively the candidate is viewed by the mass public.

candidate image: One of three factors known to influence which candidate a voter supports; how a voter perceives the personal characteristics and qualities of the candidate.

causation: A relationship between two variables that requires that a change in the independent variable will bring about a change in the dependent variable.

clear-cut issues: Issues on which candidates take distinctive positions in their ads and speeches.

CNN effect: The claim that dramatic television coverage forces government to respond to issues or events in foreign affairs.

cognitive effects: Changes in knowledge, beliefs, or information as a result of exposure to the mass media.

commercial newspapers: After the Revolution, newspapers that focused primarily on the publication of business and commerce news.

competition: The news phase when the new administration embarks on getting legislative proposals passed. Positive and flowing news stories are not as common as the press looks for alternative sources that might provide more interesting stories, especially if the White House is seeking to control the media message more tightly.

competitive news markets: Media markets in which multiple news outlets seek the same audience.

concentration of ownership: When an industry is controlled by only a few firms.

concrete events: Easily observable developments associated with news stories.

content analysis: A methodological technique based on the quantitative analysis of news content.

contingent effects model: The mass media are likely to influence only particular types of individuals with particular types of messages in particular political contexts. Media effects are contingent upon audience, message, and social system characteristics.

contrast ideas: Ads that contrast the positions of the sponsoring candidate and of the opponent.

conversion: One of the three possible effects of political campaigns; occurs if campaigns change individuals' vote intentions.

corporatization: The growing emphasis on business incentives in developing the news product, exemplified by the blurring of the line between the boardroom and the newsroom.

correlation: A pattern of association between two variables.

crises: An unanticipated event out of the control of individuals or governments.

cross-media ownership: Corporations owning newspapers, television stations, radio stations, newsmagazines, and news and entertainment production companies rather than owning just one type.

dark horses: Candidates who do better than expected.

dependent variable: An event or occurrence that depends on something else to occur; in social science research, the phenomenon we are trying to explain.

describe: To provide details as to observable features of an event.

descriptive campaign stories: Generally positive stories resulting from the description of campaign events.

detachment: The news phase toward the end of a president's term, when most policy initiatives are passed and the White House views positive relations with the press—or positive media coverage—as unnecessary.

diffuse issues: Issues about which a candidate can make broad appeals to shore up support instead of possibly alienating voters by taking a potentially divisive stand.

domestic news coverage: Media attention to internal political matters focusing on federal, state, and local government in the United States.

dramatic events: Incidents that can be portrayed as exciting or emotional; usually in story format with sympathetic characters, conflict, and vivid visual symbols.

dramatized news: News stories that focus on crisis, personality, and scandal having a convenient beginning, interesting middle, and satisfying end.

electability: The likelihood that a candidate can be elected.

elite press: Newspapers purchased and read by political and economic elites rather than by the mass public.

episodic news coverage: News presentation of political issues that are seemingly unrelated, discrete events.

equal time rule: Part of the Federal Communications Act of 1934; requires stations to make broadcast time "equally" available to all "similarly qualified" candidates for political office.

ethical news frames: News stories that emphasize commonly shared values such as human rights or personal responsibility.

ethnocentrism: The belief in the superiority of the U.S. political and social system over all others.

experimental research design: Research in which the researcher randomly assigns subjects to control or experimental groups and exposes only the experimental group to the stimuli (i.e., independent variable).

exposés: A story that fits the press' notion of a suitable investigative news story; something beyond the typical news values of drama and timeliness.

exposure: Whether individuals actually see or hear or read campaign messages; the first of two steps in attitude change.

external validity: The extent to which the findings of experimental research hold outside the context of the experiment.

fairness doctrine: Initially implemented by the FCC in 1949; requires stations to devote a "reasonable" amount of attention to public issues and include contrasting views.

Federal Communications Act of 1934: Established the Federal Communications Commission.

Federal Communications Commission (FCC): An independent regulatory commission established by the Federal Communications Act of 1934; its primary regulatory tool is the granting of broadcast licenses.

focusing event: A particularly dramatic event on which the media choose to focus, thus elevating certain "objective" problems over others.

foreign affairs coverage: Media attention to external political matters, focusing on events in other countries and the United States's relationships with other countries.

fragmented news: News in which chronic problems become newsworthy because they reach exceptional levels or are associated with some other type of crisis characteristic; since they are reported only occasionally, the problems and issues appear to be fragmented.

framing: Presenting or conceptualizing an issue, event, or idea as associated with other beliefs or values; guides individuals' processing of information.

free media: Media coverage presented in public news programs that is "freely" available to political candidates in their pursuit of public office.

frontrunners: Candidates who win or who place better than expected.

fully controlled news: News that is triggered by an event that is created to convey politically powerful images through the media.

gaggle: Daily meeting of the press secretary with the White House press corps to set the scene for what will occur during the day and provide early responses to reporters' questions.

game: Details about the strategic environment of the campaign, such as who is ahead or behind, and the logistics and strategy of campaign organizations.

going public: A president's appeal to the public to gain leverage in bargaining relationships with Congress.

hard news: News stories that focus on the details of concrete events.

high-stimulus elections: Elections that receive a lot of free media coverage and in which there is a high level of candidate spending.

horserace: The media's focus on the race between two candidates; who is ahead and who is behind, and what strategies the candidates are using.

human interest: The tendency to report negative developments and dramatic events rather than less personalized or emotional events in an effort to secure a large audience.

hypodermic needle model: Assumes that media messages will reach every individual member of the mass society, that each person will perceive them in the same general manner, and that they will provoke a more or less uniform response.

hypotheses: Relationships that should be observed if the theory they are based on is correct.

independents: Citizens who refuse to identify as Republicans or Democrats.

independent variable: The factor, event, or phenomenon that helps explain variation in the dependent variable.

individualism: Value expressed in media coverage that suggests that politics is about individuals seeking to survive threats from the political and social environment.

insider strategy: The traditional strategy of getting bills passed into law by working with colleagues within the legislature, behind the scenes.

institutional agenda-setting: How and when political issues are formally addressed by government institutions; the process by which media coverage of an issue increases the probability that government policymakers will do something about it.

interpretation: One of the functions of the media in mass society by their very appearance in mass communication, people, events, or issues are given legitimacy, saliency, or stature. The mass media also provide a political and/or social context within which the person, event, or issue can be understood.

interpretive campaign stories: Stories that seek to interpret the meaning and context of campaign events; they typically result in more critical content.

investigative reporting: Use of reporters' extensive and extended investigative skills to develop stories about government and politics, with as little reliance as possible on routine sources and ongoing contacts.

issue attention cycle: A predictable pattern of attention associated with a political issue, including such phases as discovery, public alarm, elite response, and decay of public support, independent of the "objective" seriousness of an issue.

issue knowledge: The ability of individuals to identify candidates' positions on public policy issues.

journalistic voice: The inclusion of journalists' opinions or beliefs in news stories.

latent support: Positive orientations of support and loyalty to a representative democracy, that provide elected leaders with some expectation of legitimacy as they make policy decisions, whether individuals agree with the particulars of the decisions or not.

leak: Information that a government official provides to a reporter with the agreement that the official's name will not be used.

linkage institution: An institution that connects citizens with their elected representatives by conveying information and providing a means of communication; traditional linkage institutions include political parties and interest groups.

low-stimulus elections: Elections that receive little free media coverage and in which candidates spend much less money; typically, the lower the race on the ballot, the lower the stimulus that the election provides to voters.

market-driven news: News developed in response to reader surveys that ask what topics are of interest.

mass media for news: Media used in the process of political communication to create and distribute news to a mass audience; consist primarily of widely circulated newspapers and national broadcast and cable television networks.

mass medium: Media outlet that creates and distributes content to a mass audience.

mass society theory: Society conceptualized as an undifferentiated mass, comprised of atomistic individuals who had little in common with others, interacted with others in only insignificant ways, and were directly acted upon by political and social authority figures. With few social connections and minimal psychological resources to fend off propagandist messages, individuals received the messages political leaders sent and acted in accordance with leaders' wishes.

material frames: News stories that emphasize economic aspects of issues or events.

media agenda-setting: How the media choose stories to include in news coverage.

media bias: Some deviation from a campaign reality that is evidenced in the nature of campaign coverage.

media-centered model: Agenda-setting process that implies that the correlation between public interests and media content comes about because the public is adopting the media's view of politics.

media coverage tone: How positive, negative, or neutral campaign coverage is.

medium: The means by which information is delivered, e.g., television, newspapers, radio, Internet, or magazines.

medium effects: Difference in the effects of the same information conveyed on television, in newspapers, in newsmagazines, and on the radio.

message: The content delivered by a news medium.

message effects: The influence that the content of the message—regardless of how conveyed—has on individuals' vote choice or political attitudes.

minimal effects model: Model of media effects that suggests that media messages have little effect on most individuals most of the time.

mobilization model: A model in which the public is viewed as a critical link between investigative news stories and officials' responses. Investigative reporting is viewed as effective in bringing about political change because it leads to a change in public opinion, to which government officials respond by changing public policy.

mode: Whether information is conveyed through hearing (audio) or seeing (visual).

moderatism: Discourages excess or extremism in behavior or attitude.

moderators: Personal characteristics that strengthen or weaken the effects of the media on individuals.

modern press: Era that began around the start of the twentieth century, when the media system became established as big business and ownership of media outlets became concentrated in the hands of a relatively small number of corporations.

name recognition: The ability of individuals to recognize the names of candidates in a campaign.

narrowcasting: The development of media targeting more specialized or fragmented audiences.

national leadership: Value expressed in media coverage that suggests that political and social authorities are responsible for restoring order.

national press corps: The reporters and editors who are assigned the presidency and other branches of government on a full-time basis in Washington, DC.

need for orientation: The extent to which individuals have independent knowledge about an issue; individuals with a low need for orientation are less susceptible to agenda-setting effects.

negativity bias: Tendency of news stories about presidential campaigns to be more negative today than in previous decades.

neutral adversary model: The primary role of the press is to discover the truth and act as a check on the government; assumes that citizens will use information to effectively control, influence, or communicate with their elected officials.

news: "The report of what a news organization has recently learned about matters of some significance or interest to the specific community that news organization serves" (Fuller, *News Values*, p. 6).

newshole: The space devoted to stories, rather than to advertising.

news monopoly: When a single firm controls a media market.

Newspaper Preservation Act of 1990: A law that allowed newspapers facing bankruptcy to share some aspects of the production process, which would previously have been a violation of antitrust regulations.

newsworthy: Journalists' assessments of what stories are most important and necessary to report.

nonpartisan elections: Elections in which candidates take no party affiliation.

objectivity: Presenting only the facts by not inserting political beliefs into the content of a news story.

obtrusive issues: Issues about which individuals have direct experience and rely less on media information and interpretation.

Office of Communications: Focuses on long-range public relationships management of the presidency. In consultation with the president, it determines the images that the administration needs to convey to gain and retain the approval of important constituencies in the public and private sectors so as to win support for desired policies.

opinion leaders: Individuals who are most interested in politics and most likely to be exposed to media messages and engage in politics, and are also most likely to convey media information to the less involved, less interested mass public.

outsider strategy: A strategy of getting bills passed that depends on getting good media coverage at the right time; lawmakers using this strategy must accommodate the media's values in news reporting, typically by taking firmer, more distinctive stands, often early enough in the legislative process that such stands become merely symbolic.

paid media: The use of television or other paid advertising by candidates.

panel design: Researchers interview the same set of residents multiple times over a period of time.

papers of record: News outlets that seek to provide comprehensive coverage of national and local events.

partially controlled news: News that is triggered in part by the actions of government officials who do not completely control the focus or nature of the coverage.

partisan elections: Elections in which candidates run with a party label.

party identification: One of the three factors known to influence which candidate a voter supports; identifying oneself as belonging to a particular political party.

party positions: What a political party believes about a political issue.

party press: The media-government relationship during the American Revolution, when newspapers were the organs of competing political factions.

penny press: Newspapers that sold for a penny, a much lower price than that charged by the elite press.

personalized news: News that focuses on personalities, to which individuals can attach emotional meaning.

pocketbook voting: Individuals' evaluations about how they are personally doing that affect their evaluations of incumbents.

political socialization: How individuals acquire basic orientations toward the political system.

postmodern campaign: Era in which campaigning has become permanent as it has become part of the governance process, with political consultants and media strategists having important roles in the offices of elected officials.

presidential press conferences: Official events in which the president takes questions from the media; while seeming to be uncontrolled, they are more likely partially controlled, and the administration has some control over who asks which questions, etc.

priming: The ability of the media to affect which issues or traits are most used in individuals' evaluations of political figures.

print superiority thesis: The assumption that people learn more from newspapers because they are a better news outlet than television.

prior restraint: State laws banning the publication of certain types of stories.

profit-seeker model: The mass media have no responsibilities other than to make profits for their owners; individuals are consumers foremost and the target for market-like competition.

propaganda: Information campaigns typically sponsored by governments in an effort to strengthen citizens' loyalties to their nations.

propagandist model: The chief purpose of the media is to support and advance the interests of those in positions of power; the media serve the state by legitimizing its policies and interests.

pseudo-event: Events that occur only because they were created to secure (positive) media coverage.

public advocate model: Journalists have a social responsibility to use the newsgathering process to engage newsmakers and newsreaders in debate over issues of political importance; this model places citizens more prominently as sources and subjects of news coverage.

public agenda-setting: The process by which the public comes to view some topics or issues as more important and politically relevant than others; often thought to be determined by the amount of attention devoted to a topic by the media.

public broadcasting: In the U.S., programming that is a mixture of public and private ownership and programming.

Public Broadcasting Act of 1967: Established public broadcasting in the United States.

public image: The general reaction of the public to a country, program, or official; typically relies on the extent of positive and negative feelings toward the object of interest.

public relations: Efforts devoted to enhancing the image of government officials, offices, or programs.

ratings: An estimate of the number of homes in the Nielson sample that are viewing a program.

rational ignorance: Anthony Downs's argument that citizens acting in their own self-interest should rely on information about the candidates that is freely available, and not invest their own resources (time, money) to gain extra information about parties and candidates.

reader-oriented news: News developed in response to reader surveys that ask what topics are of interest.

regulation: Legislation that determines how the media operate.

regulatory policy: Policy determined by Supreme Court decisions, congressional statutes, and administrative rule-making.

reinforcement: One of the three possible effects of political campaigns; occurs when campaigns strengthen individuals' preexisting attitudes.

reporters of objective fact model: The mass media act as a mirror of what is happening in the world and present a perfect reflection of that world.

representative democracy: A democratic system in which citizens choose from among various candidates who are then elected with the expectation that they will adopt policies that are consistent with voters' preferences. How closely their policy decisions mirror citizens' preferences is a critical feature of democratic politics.

research design: How one goes about collecting systematic evidence in doing research; major types include survey research, experiments, and aggregate data analysis.

responsible capitalism: Valued expressed in media coverage that suggests that capitalism benefits everyone, fully and equally.

selective access: When government officials reward some reporters with greater information or contact, usually as a reward or bribe for past or future favorable coverage.

selective exposure: Individuals' tendencies to expose themselves to messages that are consistent with their prior beliefs.

selective perception: Individuals' tendencies to interpret messages in a manner consistent with their beliefs.

selective retention: The tendency of individuals to retain information that is consistent with their prior beliefs.

self-selection: Individuals' personal selection of the group they desire to be in when participating in an experiment; or when research does not account for how individuals choose to engage in one behavior or another as it relates to the independent variable. Good research experiments randomly assign individuals to groups, rather than allowing them to self-select one group or another.

share: The percentage of households watching television that are tuned into a program.

small-town pastoralism: Valued expressed in media coverage that suggests that large cities dehumanize, while small towns and the values they represent are ideal.

social capital: An aggregate-level phenomenon; individuals in a society trust others and are willing to invest in others, and such positive attitudinal and behavioral characteristics are essential to a successful democracy.

socialization: The process by which individuals acquire the values and norms of the broader social system.

social order: Valued expressed in media coverage that suggests that society survives because of the capability to restore order in the face of crisis or conflict.

social science: Distinct from historical or journalistic approaches to learning or knowing, it relies on procedures associated with the scientific method.

sociotropic voting: The effect of individuals' judgments about how the nation is doing economically on their evaluation of incumbents.

soft news: News stories that are not keyed to specific events of the day, but are usually tied to popular opinion and emphasize entertainment values.

sound bites: Edited portions of candidate speeches and comments that are presented in news stories; they have decreased significantly in length over the past several decades.

specialized news outlets: Media that serve relatively small, self-selected audiences.

surveillance: The function of the media in viewing distant events and relaying them to help make a complex and changing world more predictable, and therefore more livable.

survey research: Research based on interviewing a random sample of adults; the results are usually good estimates of the beliefs or behaviors of the much larger population.

survey research design: Research in which individuals in a sample are asked a variety of questions, which are used as measures of the dependent variable, independent variable, and various control variables.

tabloid journalism: Journalism that focuses on sex, scandal, and corruption.

Telecommunications Act of 1996: An act that incorporated a wide range of provisions regarding telephone services, cable television, and the Internet. A key provision eliminated numerous restrictions on ownership of television, radio, and cable stations.

thematic news coverage: News presentation of political issues that are placed in a particular social or political context.

theory: A set of propositions that explains the how and why of what is being studied.

timeliness: The conveyance of information as soon as it is learned; requires recency, immediacy, and currency.

tongs: Meetings with small, specialized groups of reporters that are scheduled irregularly; usually with about six reporters in each group.

transaction model: Political elites, the mass media, and the public interact with, influence, and constrain each other; through this process the issue agendas of the media, campaigns, and likely voters are correlated with each other.

trial balloon: Idea given to reporters for use in news stories in an effort to assess the reaction of political elites and sometimes the mass public.

triggering event: An event of unusual or dramatic nature that uniquely symbolizes the critical importance of the problem.

two-step flow: The operation of the mass communication process with information going from the media to opinion leaders and from their opinion leaders to the mass public.

uncontrolled news: News that is triggered independently of government officials, who have no control over its development and coverage.

unobtrusive issues: Issues about which individuals have little or no experience, so they rely on media information and interpretation.

values: Deeply held, abstract beliefs that affect what journalists think is important and how they view the world.

variable news media influence: The argument that the correspondence between the media and the public agenda should vary over time, with the media's provision of new information resulting in stronger public agenda-setting effects earlier in the coverage of an issue rather than later.

video malaise: The theory that the nature of television news coverage, as well as the stunning effectiveness of the visuals that accompany it, help explain the growing political cynicism observed in the 1970s.

vote choice: Individuals' decisions as to whom to vote for in an election.

White House press secretary: An executive branch official who works out of the Press Office and provides daily briefings to the White House press corps.

yellow journalism: Sensationalizing news stories in pursuit of more readers; a period that lasted from around 1905 to 1920.

Bibliography

ABCNews.com. "Exit Polls: State-by-State Voter Surveys. Available from http://www.abcnews.go.com/sections/politics/2000vote/general/exitpoll_hub.html (accessed August 20, 2002).

Aldrich, John. "Presidential Campaigns in Party- and Candidate-Centered Eras." In *Under the Watchful Eye: Managing Presidential Campaigns in the Television Era,* ed. Mathew D. McCubbins. Washington, DC: CQ Press, 1992.

Alexander, Oscar W. *Media in the 20th Century.* San Mateo, CA: Bluewood Books, 1997.

Alleyne, Mark D. *News Revolution: Political and Economic Decisions About Global Information.* New York: St. Martin's Press, 1997.

Althaus, Scott L., and David Tewksbury. "Patterns of Internet and Traditional Media Use in a Networked Community." *Political Communication* 17 (1998): 21–45.

American Society of Newspaper Editors. "'Generation X' Examined in Major Study: Media Habits, Beliefs About Morality, Religion, Work, Technology Revealed," 1996. Available from http://www.asne.org/kiosk/news/genx.htm (accessed October 13, 1999).

Ammon, Royce J. *Global Television and the Shaping of World Politics.* Jefferson, NC: McFarland, 2001.

Annenberg Public Policy Center of the University of Pennsylvania. "Assessing the Quality of Campaign Discourse—1960, 1980, 1988, 1992." A Report of the Campaign Discourse Mapping Project of the Annenberg Public Policy Center of the University of Pennsylvania Under the Direction of Kathleen Hall Jamieson, 1996. Available from http://www.asc.upenn.edu/appc/campmapp/assessing (accessed April 28, 1998).

Ansolabehere, Stephen, Roy Behr, and Shanto Iyengar. *The Media Game: American Politics in the Television Age.* New York: Macmillan, 1993.

Ansolabehere, Stephen, and Shanto Iyengar. "Riding the Wave and Claiming Ownership over Issues: The Joint Effects of Advertising and News Coverage in Campaigns." *Public Opinion Quarterly* 58 (1994): 335–357.

————. *Going Negative: How Attack Ads Shrink and Polarize the Electorate*. New York: The Free Press, 1995.

Ansolabehere, Stephen, Shanto Iyengar, Adam Simon, and Nicholas Valentino. "Does Attack Advertising Demobilize the Electorate?" *American Political Science Review* 88 (1994): 829–838.

Atkin, Charles, and Gary Heald. "Effects of Political Advertising." *Public Opinion Quarterly* 40 (1976): 216–228.

Aufderheide, Patricia. "After the Fairness Doctrine: Controversial Broadcast Programming and the Public Interest." *Journal of Communication* 40 (1990): 47–73.

————. "Cable Television and the Public Interest." *Journal of Communication* 42 (1992): 52–65.

Bagdikian, Ben H. *The Media Monopoly*, 5th ed. Boston: Beacon Press, 1997.

Ball-Rokeach, Sandra J., Milton Rokeach, and Joel W. Grube. *The Great American Values Test: Influencing Behavior and Belief Through Television*. New York: The Free Press, 1984.

Barker, David C. "Rushed Decisions: Political Talk Radio and Vote Choice, 1994–1996." *Journal of Politics* 61 (1999): 527–539.

Barker, David, and Kathleen Knight. "Political Talk Radio and Public Opinion." *Public Opinion Quarterly* 64 (2000): 149–170.

Barnhurst, Kevin G., and Diana Mutz. "American Journalism and the Decline in Event-Centered Reporting." *Journal of Communication* 4 (1997): 27–53.

Bartels, Larry M. "Messages Received: The Political Impact of Media Exposure." *American Political Science Review* 87 (1993): 267–285.

————. "Uninformed Votes: Information Effects in Presidential Elections." *American Journal of Political Science* 40 (1996): 194–230.

————. Review of *Going Negative: How Attack Ads Shrink and Polarize the Electorate*, by Stephen Ansolabehere and Shanto Iyengar. *Public Opinion Quarterly* 60 (1996): 456–460.

Basil, Michael, Caroline Schooler, and Byron Reeves. "Positive and Negative Political Advertising: Effectiveness of Ads and Perceptions of Candidates." In *Television and Political Advertising*. Vol. 1: *Psychological Processes*, ed. Frank Biocca. Hillsdale, NJ: Lawrence Erlbaum, 1991.

Baum, Matthew A. "Sex, Lies, and War: How Soft News Brings Foreign Policy to the Inattentive Public." *American Political Science Review* 96 (2002): 91–110.

Baum, Matthew A., and Samuel Kernell. "Has Cable Ended the Golden Age of Presidential Television?" *American Political Science Review* 93 (1999): 99–114.

Beck, Paul Allen. "Voters' Intermediation Environments in the 1988 Presidential Contest." *Public Opinion Quarterly* 55 (1991): 371–394.

Beck, Paul Allen, Russell J. Dalton, Steven Greene, and Robert Huckfeldt. "The Social Calculus of Voting: Interpersonal, Media and Organizational Influences on Presidential Choices." *American Political Science Review* 96 (2002): 57–74.

Becker, Lee B. "The Mass Media and Citizen Assessment of Issue Importance: A Reflection on Agenda-Setting Research." In *Mass Communication Review Yearbook* (1982): 521–535.

Becker, Lee B., Idowu A. Sobowale, Robin E. Cobbey, and Chaim H. Eyal. "Debates' Effects on Voters' Understanding of Candidates and Issues." In *The Presidential Debates*, ed. George F. Bishop, Robert G. Meadow, and Marilyn Jackson-Beeck, pp. 126–139. New York: Praeger, 1978.

Behr, Roy L., and Shanto Iyengar. "Television News, Real-World Cues, and Changes in the Public Agenda." *Public Opinion Quarterly* 49 (1985): 38–57.

Bennett, Stephen Earl. "Changing Levels of Political Information in 1988 and 1990." *Political Behavior* 16 (1994): 1–20.

———. "Comparing Americans' Political Information in 1988 and 1992." *Journal of Politics* 57 (1995): 521–532.

———. "Predicting Americans' Exposure to Political Talk Radio in 1996, 1998 and 2000." *Harvard International Journal of Press/Politics* 7 (2002): 9–22.

Bennett, Stephen Earl, Staci L. Rhine, and Richard S. Flickinger. "Change and Continuity of American's Interest in the News." Paper presented at the annual meeting of the Southern Political Science Association, Savannah, Georgia, November 4–7, 1999.

Bennett, Stephen Earl, Staci L. Rhine, Richard S. Flickinger, and Linda L. M. Bennett. "'Video-malaise' Revisited: Reconsidering the Relation Between the Public's Views of the Media and Trust in Government." Paper presented at the annual meeting of the Midwest Political Science Association, Chicago, Illinois, April 15–17, 1999.

Bennett, W. Lance. *News: The Politics of Illusion,* 5th ed. New York: Longman, 2003.

Bentivegna, Sara. "Talking Politics on the Net." The Joan Shorenstein Center for Press, Politics and Public Policy, Research Paper R-20. Cambridge, MA: Harvard University, 1998.

Benton Foundation. "The Telecommunications Act of 1996 and the Changing Communications Landscape," 1996. Available from http://www.benton.org/Library/Landscape/landscape.html (accessed July 13, 2002).

Berelson, Bernard R., Paul F. Lazarsfeld, and William N. McPhee. *Voting: A Study of Opinion Formation in a Presidential Campaign.* Chicago: University of Chicago Press, 1954.

Berkowitz, Dan. "Routine Newswork and the What-a-Story: A Case Study of Organizational Adaptation." *Journal of Broadcasting and Electronic Media* (1992): 45–60.

———. *Social Meanings of News: A Text-Reader.* Thousand Oaks, CA: Sage, 1997.

Bernstein, James M., and Stephen Lacy. "Contextual Coverage of Government by Local Television News." *Journalism Quarterly* 69 (1992): 329–340.

Beville, Hugh Malcolm, Jr. *Audience Ratings: Radio, Television, Cable,* rev. ed. Hillsdale, NJ: Lawrence Erlbaum, 1988.

"Big 3 Networks Forced to Revise News-Gathering Methods," *New York Times,* October 12, 1998.

Biocca, Frank. *Television and Political Advertising.* Hillsdale, NJ: Lawrence Erlbaum, 1991.

Black, Jay, ed. *Mixed News: The Public/Civic/Communitarian Journalism Debate.* Mahwah, NJ: Lawrence Erlbaum, 1997.

Bloom, Sol. *The Story of the Constitution.* Washington, DC: National Archives and Record Administration, 1986; originally published 1937.

Bond, Jon R., and Richard Fleisher. *The President in the Congressional Arena.* Chicago: University of Chicago Press, 1990.

Boorstin, Daniel. *The Image: A Guide to Pseudo-Events.* New York: Atheneum, 1971.

Borden, Diane L., and Kerric Harvey, eds. *The Electronic Grapevine: Rumor, Reputation and Reporting in the New On-Line Environment.* Mahwah, NJ: Lawrence Erlbaum, 1998.

Bosso, Christopher J. "Setting the Agenda: Mass Media and the Discovery of Famine in Ethiopia." In *Manipulating Public Opinion: Essays on Public Opinion as a Dependent*

Variable, ed. Michael Margolis and Gary A. Mauser, pp. 153–174. Pacific Grove, CA: Brooks/Cole, 1989.

Bowles, Dorothy A., and Rebekah V. Bromley. "Newsmagazine Coverage of the Supreme Court During the Reagan Administration." *Journalism Quarterly* 69 (1992): 948–959.

Brewer, Paul R., and Lee Sigelman. "Political Scientists as Color Commentators: Framing and Expert Commentary in Media Campaign Coverage." *Harvard International Journal of Press/Politics* 7 (2002): 23–35.

Brians, Craig L., and Martin P. Wattenberg. "Campaign Issue Knowledge and Salience: Comparing Perception from TV Commercials, TV News, and Newspapers." *American Journal of Political Science* 40 (1996): 172–193.

Bureau of Labor Statistics, U.S. Department of Labor. "Occupational Employment Statistics: 2000 National Occupational Employment and Wage Estimates." Available from http://www.bls.gov/oes/2000/oes_27Ar.htm (accessed April 21, 2002).

Campbell, Angus, Philip E. Converse, Warren E. Miller, and Donald Stokes. *The American Voter.* New York: Wiley, 1960.

Campbell, James E. "When Have Presidential Campaigns Decided Election Outcomes?" *American Politics Research* 29 (2001): 437–460.

Cantril, Hadley. *The Invasion from Mars: A Study in the Psychology of Panic.* Princeton, NJ: Princeton University Press, 1940.

Cappella, Joseph N., and Kathleen Hall Jamieson. "Broadcast Adwatch Effects: A Field Experiment." *Communication Research* 21 (1994): 342–365.

———. *Spiral of Cynicism: The Press and the Public Good.* New York: Oxford University Press, 1997.

Carroll, Raymond L., C. A. Tuggle, James F. McCollum, Michael A. Mitrook, Kevin J. Arlington, and John M. Hoerner, Jr. "Consonance in Local Television News Program Content: An Examination of Intermarket Diversity." *Journal of Broadcasting and Electronic Media* 41 (1997): 132–144.

Carroll, Susan J., and Ronnee Schreiber. "Media Coverage of Women in the 103rd Congress." In *Women, Media and Politics,* ed. Pippa Norris, pp. 131–148. New York: Oxford University Press, 1997.

Carter, Richard F., and Keith R. Stamm. "The 1992 Presidential Campaign and Debates." *Communication Research* 21 (1994): 380–395.

"Cautious Newsweek Reaps Much of the Credit," *New York Times,* January 26, 1998.

Center for Media and Public Affairs. Press Releases. September 21, September 28, October 5, October 18, October 23, October 30, November 22, December 20, 2000. Available from http://www.cmpa.com/pressrel/ (accessed August 20, 2002).

Chaffee, Steven H., and Jack Dennis. "Presidential Debates: An Empirical Assessment," *The Past and Future of Presidential Debates,* ed. Austin Ranney (Washington, DC: American Enterprise Institute, 1979), pp. 75–101.

Chaffee, Steven H., Xinshu Zhao, and Glenn Leshner. "Political Knowledge and the Campaign Media of 1992." *Communication Research* 21 (1994): 305–324.

Chard, Richard E., and Cristina M. Ling. "Media Priming of the Health Security Act: How Harry and Louise Affected Presidential Vote Intentions." Paper presented at the annual meeting of the Midwest Political Science Association, Chicago, Illinois, April 16, 1999.

Charity, Arthur. *Doing Public Journalism.* New York: Guilford Press, 1995.

"Clinton Pursuers Question Selves," *New York Times,* April 5, 1998.

CNN.COM. "New Survey Finds Internet Use Is Surging." Available from http://www.cnn.com/TECH9601/internet_use/index.htm (accessed July 8, 1998).

Cohen, Bernard C. *The Press and Foreign Policy*. Princeton, NJ: Princeton University Press, 1963.

Columbia Journalism Review. "The Myth of the Minority Reader," 1994. Available from http://www.cjr.org/year/94/1/minority.as.htm (accessed October 13, 1999).

Committee of Concerned Journalists. "ePolitics: A Study of the 2000 Presidential Campaign on the Internet." Available from http://www.journalism.org/ccj/resources/ (accessed August 20, 2002).

Cook, Philip S., Douglas Gomery, and Lawrence W. Lichty, eds. *The Future of News: Television-Newspapers-Wire Services-Newsmagazines*. Washington, DC: The Woodrow Wilson Center Press, and Baltimore: The Johns Hopkins University Press, 1992.

Cook, Timothy E. *Governing with the News: The News Media as a Political Institution*. Chicago: University of Chicago Press, 1998.

———. *Making Laws and Making News: Media Strategies in the U.S. House of Representatives*. Washington, DC: The Brookings Institution, 1989.

Covington, Cary R., Kent Kroeger, Glenn Richardson, and J. David Woodard. "Shaping a Candidate's Image in the Press: Ronald Reagan and the 1980 Presidential Campaign." *Political Research Quarterly* 46 (1993): 783–798.

Cox, Gary, and Michael Munger. "Closeness, Expenditures, and Turnout in the 1982 United States House Elections." *American Political Science Review* 83 (1989): 217–231.

C-SPAN.ORG. "Campaign Advertising." Available from http://www.c-span.org/campaign2000/advertising.asp (accessed August 20, 2002).

Cunningham, Brent. "Missing the DUI Story." *Columbia Journalism Review* (January/February 2001). Available from http:www.cjr.org/year/01/1/cunningham.asp (accessed July 14, 2002).

Dalager, Jon K. "Voters, Issues, and Elections: Are the Candidates' Messages Getting Through?" *Journal of Politics* 58 (1996): 486–515.

Dalton, Russell J., Paul A. Beck, and Robert Huckfeldt. "Partisan Cues and the Media: Information Flows in the 1992 Presidential Election." *American Political Science Review* 92 (1998): 111–126.

Dalton, Russell J., Paul Allen Beck, Robert Huckfeldt, and William Koetzle. "A Test of Media-Centered Agenda Setting: Newspaper Content and Public Interests in a Presidential Election." *Political Communication* 15 (1998): 463–481.

Danielian, Lucig H., and Benjamin I. Page. "The Heavenly Chorus: Interest Group Voices on TV News." *American Journal of Political Science* 38 (1994): 1056–1078.

Dautrich, Ken. "Improving Campaign Coverage." *Media Studies Journal* 14 (2000): 124–130.

Davis, Richard. "Lifting the Shroud: News Media Portrayal of the US Supreme Court." *Communications and the Law* (October 1987): 43–59.

———. *The Press and American Politics: The New Mediator*, 2nd ed. New York: Longman, 1996.

———. *The Press and American Politics*, 3rd ed. New York: Prentice Hall, 2001.

Davis, Richard, and Diana Owen. *New Media and American Politics*. New York: Oxford University Press, 1998.

Dayan, Daniel, and Elihu Katz. *Media Events: The Live Broadcasting of History*. Cambridge, MA: Harvard University Press, 1992.

Dearing, James W., and Everett M. Rogers. *Agenda-Setting.* Thousand Oaks, CA: Sage, 1996.

DeFleur, Melvin L. *Theories of Mass Communication,* 2nd ed. New York: David McKay, 1970.

DeFleur, Melvin L., and Sandra Ball-Rokeach. *Theories of Mass Communication,* 5th ed. New York: Longman, 1989.

DeFleur, Melvin L., and Everette E. Dennis. *Understanding Mass Communication.* Boston: Houghton Mifflin, 1985.

Delli Carpini, Michael X., and Scott Keeter. *What Americans Know About Politics and Why It Matters.* New Haven, CT: Yale University Press, 1997.

Delli Carpini, Michael X., Scott Keeter, and Sharon Webb. "The Impact of Presidential Debates," In *Politics and the Press: The News Media and Their Influences,* ed. Pippa Norris, 145–164. Boulder, CO: Lynn Rienner, 1997.

Denton, Frank, and Howard Kurtz. *Reinventing the Newspaper.* New York: The Twentieth Century Fund Press, 1993.

Denton, Robert E., Jr., and Gary C. Woodward. *Political Communication in America,* 2nd ed. New York: Praeger, 1990.

Deppa, Joan. *The Media and Disasters: Pan Am 103.* New York: New York University Press, 1994.

Diamond, Edwin, Martha McKay, and Robert Silverman. "Pop Goes Politics: New Media, Interactive Formats, and the 1992 Presidential Campaign." *American Behavioral Scientist* 37 (1993): 257–261.

Dodd, Lawrence C., and Bruce I. Oppenheimer. *Congress Reconsidered.* New York: Praeger, 2000.

Domke, David, Kelley McCoy, and Marcos Torres. "News Media, Racial Perceptions, and Political Cognition." *Communication Research* 26 (1999): 570–607.

Donahue, Hugh Carter. *The Battle to Control Broadcast News: Who Owns the First Amendment?* Cambridge, MA: MIT Press, 1989.

Donovan, Robert J., and Ray Scherer. *Unsilent Revolution: Television News and American Public Life, 1948–1991.* Cambridge, England: Cambridge University Press, 1992.

Downs, Anthony. *An Economic Theory of Democracy.* New York: Harper & Row, 1957.

Drechsel, Robert E. *News Making in the Trial Courts.* New York: Longman, 1983.

Druckman, James N. "On the Limits of Framing Effects: Who Can Frame?" *Journal of Politics* 63 (2001): 1041–1067.

Edwards, George C. III. *At the Margins: Presidential Leadership of Congress.* New Haven, CT: Yale University Press, 1989.

Emery, Michael, and Edwin Emery. *The Press and America: An Interpretive History of the Mass Media,* 6th ed. Englewood Cliffs, NJ: Prentice Hall, 1988.

Erbring, Lutz, Edie N. Goldenberg, and Arthur H. Miller. "Front-Page News and Real-World Cues: A New Look at Agenda-Setting by the Media." *American Journal of Political Science* 24 (1980): 16–49.

Ericson, Richard V., Patricia M. Baranek, and Janet B. L. Chan. *Representing Order: Crime, Law, and Justice in the News Media.* Toronto: University of Toronto Press, 1991.

Eveland, William P., Jr., and Dietram A. Scheufele. "Connecting News Media Use with Gaps in Knowledge and Participation." *Political Communication* 17 (2000): 215–237.

Exoo, Calvin F. *The Politics of the Mass Media*. St. Paul, MN: West, 1994.

Eyal, Chaim H., James P. Winter, and William F. DeGeorge. "The Concept of Time Frame in Agenda-Setting." In *Mass Communication Review Yearbook* 2, Beverly Hills, CA: Sage, 1981, 212–243.

Feldman, Stanley, and Lee Sigelman. "The Political Impact of Prime-Time Television: 'The Day After.'" *Journal of Politics* 47 (1985): 556–578.

Fico, Frederick, and William Cote. "Fairness and Balance in the Structural Characteristics of Newspaper Stories on the 1996 Presidential Election." Paper presented at the annual meeting of the Midwest Political Science Association, Chicago, Illinois, April 23–25, 1998.

Fico, Frederick, and Stan Soffin. "Fairness and Balance of Selected Newspaper Coverage of Controversial National, State, and Local Issues." *Journalism and Mass Communication Quarterly* 72 (1992): 621–633.

Finkel, Steven E. "Reexamining the Minimal Effects Model in Recent Presidential Campaigns." *Journal of Politics* 55 (1993): 1–21.

Finkel, Steven E., and J. G. Geer. "A Spot Check: Casting Doubt on the Demobilizing Effect of Attack Advertising." *American Journal of Political Science* 42 (1998): 573–595.

Fox, Richard L., and Robert W. Van Sickel. *Tabloid Justice: Criminal Justice in an Age of Media Frenzy*. Boulder, CO: Lynne Reinner Publishers, 2001.

Fox, William John. "Junk News: Can Public Broadcasters Buck the Tabloid Tendencies of Market-Driven Journalism? A Canadian Experience." The Joan Shorenstein Center for Press, Politics and Public Policy, Discussion Paper D-26. Cambridge, MA: Harvard University, 1997.

Freedman, Paul, and Ken Goldstein. "Measuring Media Exposure and the Effects of Negative Campaign Ads." *American Journal of Political Science* 43 (1999): 1189–1208.

Freedman, Paul, William Wood, and Dale Lawton. "Do's and Don't's of Negative Ads: What Voters Say." *Campaigns & Elections* 20 (October/November 1999): 20–25. Response articles follow.

Fuller, Jack. *News Values: Ideas for an Information Age*. Chicago: University of Chicago Press, 1996.

Funkhouser, G. Ray. "The Issues of the Sixties: An Exploratory Study in the Dynamics of Public Opinion." *Public Opinion Quarterly* 37 (1973): 62–75.

Gadziala, Stephen M., and Lee B. Becker. "A New Look at Agenda-Setting in the 1976 Election Debates." *Journalism Quarterly* 60 (1983): 122–126.

Gallup, George, Jr. *The Gallup Poll: Public Opinion 1995*. Wilmington, DE: Scholarly Resources, 1996.

Gans, Herbert. *Deciding What's News: A Study of CBS Evening News, NBC Nightly News, Newsweek and Time*. New York: Random House, 1979.

Gantz, Walter. "The Diffusion of News About the Attempted Reagan Assassination." *Journal of Communication* 33 (1983): 56–65.

Ganzert, Charles, and Don M. Flournoy. "The Weekly 'World Report' on CNN, An Analysis." *Journalism Quarterly* 69 (1992): 188–194.

Garramone, Gina M. "Voter Responses to Negative Political Ads." *Journalism Quarterly* 61 (1984): 250–259.

———. "Effects of Negative Political Advertising: The Roles of Sponsor and Rebuttal." *Journal of Broadcasting & Electronic Media* 29 (1985): 147–159.

Garramone, Gina M., and Charles K. Atkin. "Mass Communication and Political Socialization: Specifying the Effects." *Public Opinion Quarterly* 50 (1986): 76–86.

Garramone, Gina M., Charles K. Atkin, Bruce E. Pinkleton, and Richard T. Cole. "Effects of Negative Political Advertising on the Political Process." *Journal of Broadcasting and Electronic Media* 34 (1990): 299–311.

Gaunt, Philip. *Choosing the News: The Profit Factor in News Selection.* New York: Greenwood Press, 1990.

Geer, John, and Richard R. Lau. "A New Way to Model Campaign Effects." Paper presented at the annual meeting of the American Political Science Association, Boston, Massachusetts, September 3–6, 1998.

Gilens, Martin. *Why Americans Hate Welfare: Race, Media, and the Politics of Antipoverty Policy.* Chicago: University of Chicago Press, 1999.

Gilliam, Franklin D., Jr., and Shanto Iyengar. "Prime Suspects: The Influence of Local Television News on the Viewing Public. *American Journal of Political Science* 44 (2000): 560–573.

Glynn, Carroll J., Susan Herbst, Garrett J. O'Keefe, and Robert Y. Shapiro. *Public Opinion.* Boulder, CO: Westview, 1999.

Glynn, Carroll J., Susan Herbst, Garrett J. O'Keefe, and Robert Y. Shapiro, with Mark Lindeman. "Public Opinion and Democratic Competence." In *Public Opinion,* ed. Carroll Glynn et al., pp. 249–298. Boulder, CO: Westview, 1999.

Goidel, Robert K., and Ronald E. Langly. "Media Coverage of the Economy and Aggregate Economic Evaluations: Uncovering Evidence of Indirect Media Effects." *Political Research Quarterly* 48 (1995): 313–328.

Goidel, Robert K., and Todd G. Shields. "Vanishing Marginals, the Bandwagon, and the Mass Media." *Journal of Politics* 56 (1994): 802–810.

Gomery, Douglas. "The FCC's Newspaper-Broadcast Cross-Ownership Rule: An Analysis." Washington, DC: Economic Policy Institute, 2002.

Graber, Doris A. *Processing the News,* 2nd ed. New York: Longman, 1984.

———. *Mass Media and American Politics.* Washington, DC: CQ Press, 2002.

Graber, Doris A., and Young Yun Kim. "Why John Q. Voter Did Not Learn Much from the 1976 Presidential Debates." In *Communication Yearbook 2,* ed. Brent D. Rubin, 407–421. New Brunswick, NJ: Transaction Books. 1978.

Green, John O. *The New Age of Communications.* New York: Henry Holt and Company, 1997.

Groeling, Timothy, and Samuel Kernell. "Is Network News Coverage of the President Biased?" *Journal of Politics* 60 (1998): 1063–1087.

Grossman, Lawrence K. *The Electronic Republic.* New York: Viking, 1995.

Grossman, Michael Baruch, and Martha Joynt Kumar. *Portraying the President: The White House and the News Media.* Baltimore, MD: Johns Hopkins University Press, 1981.

Gunter, Barrie. *Poor Reception: Misunderstanding and Forgetting Broadcast News.* Hillsdale, NJ: Lawrence Erlbaum, 1987.

Gwiasda, Gregory. "Network News Coverage of Campaign Advertisements: Media's Ability to Reinforce Campaign Messages." *American Politics Research* 29 (2001): 461–482.

Hachten, William A. *The World News Prism: Changing Media of International Communication,* 4th ed. Ames: Iowa State University Press, 1996.

Hallin, Daniel C. "Sound Bite News: Television Coverage of Elections, 1968–1988." *Journal of Communication* 42 (1992): 5–24.

Haltom, William. *Reporting on the Courts: How the Mass Media Cover Judicial Actions.* Chicago: Nelson-Hall, 1998.

Hamilton, John Maxwell, and George A. Krimsky. *Hold the Press: The Inside Story on Newspapers.* Baton Rouge: Louisiana State University Press, 1996.

Hardt, Hanno. *Social Theories of the Press: Early German and American Perspectives.* Beverly Hills, CA: Sage, 1979.

Harper, Christopher. "Online Newspapers: Going Somewhere or Going Nowhere?" *Newspaper Research Journal* 17 (1996): 2–13.

Heider, Fritz. *The Psychology of Interpersonal Relations.* New York: Wiley, 1958.

Herbst, Susan. "On Electronic Public Sphere: Talk Shows in Theoretical Perspective." *Political Communication* 12 (1995): 263–274.

Herman, Edward S., and Noam Chomsky. *Manufacturing Consent: The Political Economy of the Mass Media.* New York: Pantheon, 1988.

Herrnson, Paul S., Ronald G. Shaiko, and Clyde Wilcox. *The Interest Group Connection: Electioneering, Lobbying, and Policymaking in Washington.* Chatham, NJ: Chatham House, 1998.

Hershey, Marjorie Randon. "The Campaign and the Media." In *The Election of 2000,* ed. Gerald Pomper, pp. 46–72. New York: Chatham House, 2001.

Hess, Stephen. *The Washington Reporters.* Washington, DC: The Brookings Institution, 1981.

———. *The Ultimate Insiders.* Washington, DC: The Brookings Institution, 1986.

———. *Live from Capitol Hill: Studies of Congress and the Media.* Washington, DC: The Brookings Institution, 1991.

———. "The Decline and Fall of Congressional News." In *Congress, the Press, and the Public,* ed. Thomas E. Mann and Norman J. Ornstein, pp. 141–156. Washington, DC: American Enterprise Institute and The Brookings Institution, 1994.

———. *International News and Foreign Correspondents.* Washington, DC: The Brookings Institution, 1996.

Hetherington, Marc J. "The Media's Role in Forming Voters' National Economic Evaluations in 1992." *American Journal of Political Science* 40 (1996): 372–395.

Hibbing, John R., and Elizabeth Theiss-Morse. "The Media's Role in Public Negativity Toward Congress: Distinguishing Emotional Reactions and Cognitive Evaluations." *American Journal of Political Science* 42 (1998): 475–498.

Hill, David B. "Viewer Characteristics and Agenda Setting by Television News." *Public Opinion Quarterly* 49 (1985): 340–350.

Hill, Kim Quaile, and Patricia A. Hurley. "Dyadic Representation Reappraised." *American Journal of Political Science* 43 (1999): 109–141.

Hill, Ronald Paul. "An Exploration of Voter Responses to Political Advertisements." *Journal of Advertising* 18 (1989): 14–22.

Hoffmann-Riem, Wolfgang. *Regulating Media: The Licensing and Supervision of Broadcasting in Six Countries.* New York: Guilford Press, 1996.

Hofstetter, C. Richard, Mark C. Donovan, Melville R. Klauber, Alexander Cole, Carolyn J. Huie, and Toshiyuki Yuasa. "Political Talk Radio: A Stereotype Reconsidered." *Political Research Quarterly* 47 (1994): 467–476.

Hoge, James F., Jr. "Media Pervasiveness." *Foreign Affairs* (July/August 1994): 136–144.

Hohenberg, John. *Foreign Correspondence: The Great Reporters and Their Times,* 2nd ed. Syracuse, NY: Syracuse University Press, 1995.

Holbrook, Thomas M. "The Behavioral Consequences of Vice-Presidential Debates:

Does the Undercard Have Any Punch?" *American Politics Quarterly* 22 (1994): 469–482.

Horwitz, Robert Britt. *The Irony of Regulatory Reform: The Deregulation of American Telecommunications.* New York: Oxford University Press, 1989.

Howitt, Dennis. *Mass Media and Social Problems.* Oxford, England: Pergamon Press, 1982.

Hurley, Patricia A., and Rick K. Wilson. "Strategic Campaigning and Voter Shifts: A Panel Analysis of Houston's 1985 Mayoral Race." *Social Science Quarterly* 68 (1987): 34–50.

Iggers, Jeremy. *Good News, Bad News: Journalism Ethics and the Public Interest.* Boulder, CO: Westview, 1998.

Iyengar, Shanto. "Television News and Issue Salience: A Reexamination of the Agenda-Setting Hypothesis." *American Politics Quarterly* 7 (1979): 395–416.

———. "Framing Responsibility for Political Issues: The Case of Poverty." *Political Behavior* 12 (1990): 19–40.

———. *Is Anyone Responsible? How Television Frames Political Issues.* Chicago: University of Chicago Press, 1991.

Iyengar, Shanto, Kyu Hahn, and Markus Prior. "Has Technology Made Attention to Political Campaigns More Selective? An Experimental Study of the 2000 Presidential Campaign." Paper presented at the annual meeting of the American Political Science Association, San Francisco, September 2, 2001.

Iyengar, Shanto, and Donald R. Kinder. *News That Matters.* Chicago: University of Chicago Press, 1987.

Iyengar, Shanto, Mark D. Peters, and Donald R. Kinder. "Experimental Demonstrations of the 'Not-So-Minimal' Consequences of Television News Programs." *American Political Science Review* 76 (1982): 848–858.

Iyengar, Shanto, and Adam Simon. "News Coverage of the Gulf Crisis and Public Opinion: A Study of Agenda-Setting, Priming and Framing." *Communication Research* 20 (1993): 365–383.

Jacobs, Lawrence R., and Robert Y. Shapiro. "Issues, Candidate Image, and Priming: The Use of Private Polls in Kennedy's 1960 Presidential Campaign." *American Political Science Review* 88 (1994): 527–541.

Jacobson, Gary C. "The Impact of Broadcast Campaigning on Electoral Outcomes." *Journal of Politics* 37 (1975): 769–793.

Jacques, Wayne, Frank Meilinger, Michael Balmoris, Cynthia Gerns, and Steven Denby. "Some Aspects of Major Newspaper Coverage of the 1992 Presidential Debates." *American Behavioral Scientist* 37 (1993): 252–256.

Jamieson, Kathleen Hall. *Everything You Think You Know About Politics . . . and Why You're Wrong.* New York: Basic Books, 2000.

Jamieson, Kathleen Hall, and Karlyn Kohrs Campbell. *The Interplay of Influence: News, Advertising, Politics and the Mass Media,* 5th ed. Belmont, CA: Wadsworth, 2001.

Jamieson, Kathleen Hall, Paul Waldman, and Susan Sherr. "Eliminate the Negative? Categories of Analysis for Political Advertisements." In *Crowded Airwaves: Campaign Advertising in Elections,* ed. James A. Thurber, Candice J. Nelson, and David A. Dulio, pp. 44–64. Washington, DC: The Brookings Institution, 2000.

Jasperson, Amy E., Dhavan V. Shah, Mark Watts, Ronald J. Faber, and David P. Fan. "Framing and the Public Agenda: Media Effects on the Importance of the Public Budget Deficit." *Political Communication* 15 (1998): 205–224.

Jennings, M. Kent, and Richard G. Niemi. *Generations and Politics: A Panel Study of Young Adults and Their Parents.* Princeton, NJ: Princeton University Press, 1981.

Johnson, Thomas J., Mahmoud A. M. Braima, and Jayanthi Sothirajah. "Doing the Traditional Media Sidestep: Comparing the Effects of the Internet and Other Non-traditional Media with Traditional Media in the 1996 Presidential Campaign." *Journalism and Mass Communication Quarterly* 76 (1999): 99–123.

Johnson, Thomas J., Carol E. Hays, and Scott P. Hays. *Engaging the Public: How Government and the Media Can Reinvigorate American Democracy.* Lanham, MD: Rowman and Littlefield, 1998.

Johnson-Cartee, Karen S., and Gary Copeland. "Southern Voters' Reaction to Negative Political Ads in the 1986 Election." *Journalism Quarterly* 66 (1989) 888–893, 986.

Jordan, Donal L. "Newspaper Effects on Policy Preferences." *Public Opinion Quarterly* 57 (1993): 191–204.

Joslyn, Mark R., and Steve Ceccoli. "Attentiveness to Television News and Opinion Change in the Fall 1992 Presidential Campaign." *Political Behavior* 18 (1996): 141–170.

Joslyn, Richard A. "The Impact of Campaign Spot Advertising on Voting Defections." *Human Communication Research* 7 (1981): 47–60.

"Journalists Monopolize TV Election News." Press Release. October 30, 2000. Available from http://www.cmpa.com/pressrel/electpr10.htm (accessed August 20, 2002).

Jung, Donald J. *The Federal Communications Commission, the Broadcast Industry, and the Fairness Doctrine, 1981–1987.* Lanham, MD: University Press of America, 1996.

Just, Marion, Ann Crigler, and Tami Buhr. "Voice, Substance, and Cynicism in Presidential Campaign Media." *Political Communication* 16 (1999): 25–44.

Just, Marion, Ann Crigler, and Lori Wallach. "Thirty Seconds or Thirty Minutes: What Viewers Learn from Spot Advertisements and Candidate Debates." *Journal of Communication* 40 (1990): 120–133.

Kahn, Kim F. "Gender Differences in Campaign Messages: The Political Advertisements of Women and Men Candidates for the U.S. Senate." *Political Research Quarterly* 46 (1993): 481–502.

———. "Incumbency and the News Media in U.S. Senate Elections: An Experimental Investigation." *Political Research Quarterly* 46 (1993): 715–740.

———. "Does Gender Make a Difference? An Experimental Examination of Sex Stereotypes and Press Patterns in Statewide Campaigns." *American Journal of Political Science* 38 (1994): 162–195.

———. "Characteristics of Press Coverage in Senate and Gubernatorial Elections: Information Available to Voters." *Legislative Studies Quarterly* 20 (1995): 23–35.

Kahn, Kim F., and John G. Geer. "Creating Impressions: An Experimental Investigation of Political Advertising on Television." *Political Behavior* 16 (1994): 93–116.

Kahn, Kim Fridkin, and Patrick J. Kenney. *The Spectacle of U.S. Senate Campaigns.* Princeton, NJ: Princeton University Press, 1999.

———. "Do Negative Campaigns Mobilize or Suppress Turnout? Clarifying the Relationship Between Negativity and Participation." *American Political Science Review* 93 (1999): 877–889.

———. "How Negative Campaigning Enhances Knowledge of Senate Elections." In *Crowded Airwaves: Campaign Advertising in Elections,* ed. James A. Thurber, Candice J. Nelson, and David A. Dulio, pp. 65–95. Washington, DC: The Brookings Institution, 2000.

————. "The Slant of the News: How Editorial Endorsements Influence Campaign Coverage and Citizens' Views of Candidates." *American Political Science Review* 96 (2002): 381–394.

Kaid, Lynda Lee, and John Boydston. "An Experimental Study of the Effectiveness of Negative Political Advertisements." *Communication Quarterly* 35 (1987): 193–201.

Kaid, Lynda Lee, and Anne Johnston. "Negative versus Positive Television Advertising in U.S. Presidential Campaigns, 1960–1988." *Journal of Communication* 41 (1991): 53–64.

Kaid, Lynda Lee, Chris M. Leland, and Susan Whitney. "The Impact of Televised Political Ads: Evoking Viewer Responses in the 1988 Presidential Campaign." *The Southern Communication Journal* 57 (1991): 285–295.

Kaid, Lynda Lee, Sandra L. Myers, Val Pipps, and Jan Hunter. "Sex Role Perceptions and Televised Political Advertising: Comparing Male and Female Candidates." *Women and Politics* 4 (1984): 41–53.

Kaniss, Phyllis. *Making Local News.* Chicago: University of Chicago Press, 1991.

Kaplan, Martin, and Matthew Hale. "Local TV Coverage of the 2000 General Election." The Norman Lear Center Campaign Media Monitoring Project. Los Angeles: USC Annenberg, Norman Lear Center, 2001.

Keeter, Scott. "The Illusion of Intimacy: Television and the Role of Candidate Personal Qualities in Voter Choice." *Public Opinion Quarterly* 51 (1987): 344–358.

Kellstedt, Paul M. "Media Framing and the Dynamics of Racial Policy Preferences." *American Journal of Political Science* 44 (2000): 245–260.

Kerbel, Matthew R. "Cable and Network Television Coverage of the 1992 Presidential Primaries: Some Preliminary Findings." Paper presented at the annual meeting of the American Political Science Association, Chicago, Illinois, September 3–6. 1992.

Kernell, Samuel. *New Strategies of Presidential Leadership.* Washington, DC: CQ Press, 1997.

Kinder, Donald R., and Lynn M. Sanders. *Divided by Color: Racial Politics and Democratic Ideals.* Chicago: University of Chicago Press, 1997.

Kingdon, John W. *Agendas, Alternatives, and Public Policies.* Boston: Little, Brown, 1984.

Kolodny, Robin, and David A. Dulio. "Where the Money Goes: Party Spending in Congressional Elections." Paper presented at the annual meeting of the Midwest Political Science Association, Chicago, Illinois, April 19–22, 2001.

Kovach, Bill, and Tom Rosenstiel. "Are Watchdogs an Endangered Species?" *Columbia Journalism Review* (May/June 2002). Available from http://www.cjr.org/year/01/3/rosenstiel.asp (accessed July 14, 2002).

Krasnow, Erwin G., Lawrence G. Longley, and Herbert A. Terry. *The Politics of Broadcast Regulation,* 3rd ed. New York: St. Martin's Press, 1982.

Krosnick, Jon A., and Laura A. Brannon. "The Impact of War on the Ingredients of Presidential Evaluations: Multidimensional Effects of Political Involvement." *American Political Science Review* 87 (1993): 963–975.

————. "News Media Influence on the Foundations of Popular Support for the President: George Bush and the Gulf Conflict." *Journal of Social Issues* 49 (1993): 167–182.

Krosnick, Jon A., and Donald R. Kinder. "Altering the Foundation of Support for the President Through Priming: The Iran-Contra Affair." *American Political Science Review* 84 (1991): 497–452.

Kuklinski, James H., and Lee Sigelman. "When Objectivity Is Not Objective: Network

Television News Coverage of U.S. Senators and the 'Paradox of Objectivity.'" *Journal of Politics* 54 (1992): 810–833.

Kumar, Martha Joynt. "Presidential Publicity in the Clinton Era: The White House Communications Quartet." Paper delivered at the annual meeting of the Midwest Political Science Association, Chicago, Illinois, April 23–26, 1998.

———. "The Office of the Press Secretary." The White House 2001 Project, White House Interview Program, Report No. 31. Released December 5, 2000. Available from http://whitehouse2001.org.

Lake, Ronald La Due, and Robert Huckfeldt. "Social Capital, Social Networks, and Political Participation." *Political Psychology* 19 (1998): 567–584.

Lang, Annie. "Emotion, Formal Features, and Memory for Televised Political Advertisements." In *Television and Political Advertising,* Vol. 1, ed. Frank Biocca, pp. 221–244. Hillsdale, NJ: Lawrence Erlbaum, 1991.

Lanoue, David J. "Voters' Reactions to Televised Presidential Debates: Measurement of the Source and Magnitude of Opinion Change." *Political Psychology* 10 (1989): 275–285.

———. "Cognitive Consistency, Political Knowledge and the 1980 Presidential Debate." Paper presented at the annual meeting of the Midwest Political Science Association, Chicago, Illinois, 1990.

LaPlant, James T. "The Mass Media and Adolescent Political Socialization: Is Television the Vast Wasteland?" Paper presented at the annual meeting of the Southwestern Political Science Association, Corpus Christi, Texas, March 18–21, 1998.

Larson, Stephanie Greco. "How the New York Times Covered Discrimination Cases." *Journalism Quarterly* 62 (1985): 894–896.

———. *Creating Consent of the Governed: A Member of Congress and the Local Media.* Carbondale, IL: Southern Illinois University Press, 1992.

———. "The Content of Supreme Court Coverage: Making Sense of the Relationship Between the Media and Public Confidence." *Southeastern Political Review* 23 (1995): 231–244.

———. "Public Opinion in Television Election News: Beyond Polls." *Political Communication* 16 (1999): 133–145.

———. "Network Differences in Public Opinion Coverage During the 1996 Presidential Campaign." *Journal of Broadcasting & Electronic Media* 44 (2000): 16–26.

Larson, Stephanie Greco, and Martha Bailey. "ABC's 'Person of the Week': American Values in Television News." *Journalism and Mass Communication Quarterly* 75 (1998): 487–499.

Lasswell, Harold D. "The Structure and Function of Communication in Society," in *The Communication of Ideas,* ed. Lyman Bryson. New York: Harper & Bros., 1948.

Latimer, Margaret K. "Policy Issues and Personal Images in Political Advertising in a State Election." *Journalism Quarterly* 61 (1984): 776–784, 852.

Lau, Richard R., and Lee Sigelman. "Effectiveness of Negative Political Advertising." In *Crowded Airwaves: Campaign Advertising in Elections,* ed. James A. Thurber, Candice J. Nelson, and David A. Dulio, pp. 10–43. Washington, DC: The Brookings Institution, 2000.

Lawrence, Regina G. "Game-Framing the Issues: Tracking the Strategy Frame in Public Policy News." *Political Communication* 17 (2000): 93–144.

Lazarsfeld, Paul, Bernard Berelson, and Hazel Gaudet. *The People's Choice: How the Voter Makes Up His Mind in a Presidential Campaign.* New York: Columbia University Press, 1944.

Ledbetter, James. *Made Possible by . . . : The Death of Public Broadcasting in the United States.* New York: Verso, 1997.

Leff, Donna R., David L. Protess, and Stephen C. Brooks. "Crusading Journalism: Changing Public Attitudes and Policy-Making Agendas." *Public Opinion Quarterly* 50 (1986): 300–315.

Leighley, Jan E., and Jonathan Nagler. "Socioeconomic Class Bias in Turnout, 1964–1988." *American Political Science Review* 86 (1992): 725–736.

Lenart, Silvo, and Kathleen M. McGraw. "America Watches 'Amerika': Television Docudrama and Political Attitudes." *Journal of Politics* 51 (1989): 697–712.

Leonard, Thomas C. *News for All: America's Coming of Age with the Press.* New York: Oxford University Press, 1995.

Lichtenberg, Judith. *Democracy and the Mass Media.* Cambridge, England: Cambridge University Press, 1990.

Lichter, S. Robert, and Daniel R. Amundson. "Less News Is Worse News: Television News Coverage of Congress, 1972–92." In *Congress, the Press, and the Public,* ed. Thomas E. Mann and Norman J. Ornstein, pp. 131–140. Washington, DC: American Enterprise Institute and The Brookings Institution, 1994.

Lichter, Robert, Linda Lichter, and Daniel R. Amundson. *Images of Governments in TV Entertainment.* Washington, DC: Center for Media and Public Affairs, 1999.

———. "Government Goes Down the Tube: Images of Government in TV Entertainment, 1955–1998." *The Harvard International Journal of Press/Politics* 5 (2000): 96–103.

Lichter, Robert, Linda Lichter, and Stanley Rothman. *Prime Time.* Washington, DC: Regnery, 1994.

Lin, Carolyn A. "Audience Selectivity of Local Television Newscasts." *Journalism Quarterly* 69 (1992): 373–382.

Linsky, Martin. *Impact: How the Press Affects Federal Policymaking.* New York: Norton, 1986.

Lippman, Walter. *Public Opinion.* New York: Macmillan, 1922.

Livingston, Steven, and Todd Eachus. "Humanitarian Crisis and U.S. Foreign Policy: Somalia and the CNN Effect Reconsidered." *Political Communication* 12 (1995): 413–429.

Lodge, Milton, and Kathleen McGraw. "Where Is the Schema? A Critique." *American Political Science Review* 85 (1991): 1357–1364.

Lorimer, Rowland. *Mass Communications: A Comparative Introduction.* Manchester, England: Manchester University Press, 1994.

Lowery, Sharon A., and Melvin L. DeFleur. *Milestones in Mass Communication Research.* New York: Longman, 1988.

Lupia, Arthur, and Mathew D. McCubbins. *The Democratic Dilemma: Can Citizens Learn What They Need to Know?* New York: Cambridge University Press, 1998.

MacKuen, Michael B. "Social Communication and the Mass Policy Agenda." In *More Than News: Media Power in Public Affairs,* ed. M. B. MacKuen and Steven L. Coombs. Beverly Hills, CA: Sage, 1981.

Maltese, John Anthony. *Spin Control: The White House Office of Communications and the Management of Presidential News,* 2nd ed. Chapel Hill: University of North Carolina Press, 1994.

Manheim, Jarol B. "Strategic Public Diplomacy: Managing Kuwait's Image During the Gulf Conflict." In *Taken by Storm: The Media, Public Opinion, and U.S. Foreign*

Policy in the Gulf War, ed. W. Lance Bennett and David L. Paletz, pp. 131–148. Chicago: University of Chicago Press, 1994.

Manheim, Jarol B., and Robert B. Albritton. "Changing National Images: International Public Relations and Media Agenda Setting." *American Political Science Review* 78 (1984): 641–657.

Mann, Thomas E., and Norman J. Ornstein, eds. *Congress, the Press, and the Public.* Washington, DC: American Enterprise Institute and The Brookings Institution, 1994.

Mann, Thomas E., and Gary R. Orren, eds. *Media Polls in American Politics.* Washington, DC: American Enterprise Institute and The Brookings Institution, 1992.

Mayhew, David. *Congress: The Electoral Connection.* New Haven, CT: Yale University Press, 1986.

Mazzocco, Dennis W. *Networks of Power: Corporate TV's Threat to Democracy.* Boston: South End Press, 1994.

McChesney, Robert W. *Rich Media, Poor Democracy: Communication Politics in Dubious Times.* Urbana: University of Illinois Press, 1999.

McClure, Robert D., and Thomas E. Patterson. "Television News and Political Advertising: The Impact of Exposure on Voter Beliefs." *Communication Research* 1 (1974): 3–31.

———. *The Unseeing Eye: The Myth of Television Power in National Elections.* New York: Putnam, 1976.

McCombs, Maxwell E. "The Agenda-Setting Approach." In *Handbook of Political Communication,* ed. Dan D. Nimmo and Keith R. Sanders, pp. 121–140. Beverly Hills, CA: Sage, 1981.

McCombs, Maxwell E., and Donald L. Shaw. "The Agenda-Setting Function of the Mass Media." *Public Opinion Quarterly* 36 (1972): 176–187.

McCombs, Maxwell E., and David H. Weaver. "Toward a Merger of Gratifications and Agenda-Setting Research." In *Media Gratifications Research: Current Perspectives,* ed. Karl Erik Rosengren, Lawrence A. Wenner, and Philip Palmgreen, pp. 95–108. Beverly Hills, CA: Sage, 1985.

McGregor, Judy, Susan Fountaine, and Margie Comrie. "From Contest to Content: The Impact of Public Journalism on New Zealand Election Campaign Coverage." *Political Communication* 17 (2000): 133–148.

McQuail, Denis. *McQuail's Mass Communication Theory,* 4th ed. Thousand Oaks, CA: Sage, 2000.

Meadow, Robert G., and Lee Sigelman. "Some Effects and Noneffects of Campaign Commercials: An Experimental Study." *Political Behavior* 4 (1982): 163–175.

Media Central. Circulation Figures, 1997. Available from http://www.mediacentral.com/Magazines/Folio/5001996/a.htm (accessed July 10, 1998).

Media Institute. *CNN vs. the Networks: Is More News Better News?* Washington DC: The Media Institute, 1983.

Media Studies Journal. Special Issue on the 2000 Presidential Campaign. *Media Studies Journal* 14 (2000).

Medvic, Stephen K., and David A. Jones. "The CNN Effect: A Conceptual Analysis." Paper presented at the annual meeting of the Southern Political Science Association, Savannah, Georgia, November 3–7, 1999.

Mendelberg, Tali. *The Race Card: Campaign Strategy, Implicit Messages, and the Norm of Equality.* Princeton, NJ: Princeton University Press, 2001.

Mendelsohn, Matthew. "The Media and Interpersonal Communications: The Priming of Issues, Leaders, and Party Identification." *Journal of Politics* 58 (1996): 112–125.

———. "The Construction of Electoral Mandates: Media Coverage of Election Results in Canada." *Political Communication* 15 (1998): 239–253.

Merritt, Davis. *Public Journalism and Public Life: Why Telling the News Is Not Enough*. Hillsdale, NJ: Lawrence Erlbaum, 1995.

Merritt, Sharyne. "Negative Political Advertising: Some Empirical Findings." *Journal of Advertising* 13 (1984): 27–37.

Meyer, Eric K. "An Unexpectedly Wider Web for the World's Newspapers," June 23–29, 1998. Available from http://www.newslink.org/emcol10.htm (accessed June 28, 1998).

Meyers, Marian. *News Coverage of Violence Against Women: Engendering Blame*. Thousand Oaks, CA: Sage, 1997.

Meyorwitz, Joshua. "Visible and Invisible Candidates: A Case Study in 'Competing Logics' of Campaign Coverage." *Political Communication* 11 (1994): 145–164.

Milburn, Michael A., and Justin Brown. "Busted by the Ad Police: Journalists' Coverage of Political Campaign Ads in the 1992 Presidential Campaign." The Joan Shorenstein Center, Research Paper R-15. Cambridge, MA: Harvard University, 1995.

Miller, Joanne M., and John A. Krosnick. "News Media Impact on the Ingredients of Presidential Evaluations: A Program of Research on the Priming Hypothesis." In *Political Persuasion and Attitude Change*, ed. Diana Mutz, Paul Sniderman, and Richard Brody, pp. 79–99. Ann Arbor: University of Michigan Press, 1996.

———. "News Media Impact on the Ingredients of Presidential Evaluations: Politically Knowledgeable Citizens Are Guided by a Trusted Source." *American Journal of Political Science* 44 (2000): 301–315.

Mondak, Jeffery J. *Nothing to Read: Newspapers and Elections in a Social Experiment*. Ann Arbor: University of Michigan Press, 1995.

———. "Newspapers and Political Awareness." *American Journal of Political Science* 39 (1995): 513–527.

———. "Media Exposure and Political Discussion in U.S. Elections." *Journal of Politics* 57 (1995): 62–85.

Montgomery, Kathryn C. *Target: Prime Time*. New York: Oxford University Press, 1989.

Moon, David. "What You Use Still Depends on What You Have: Information Effects in Presidential Elections." *American Politics Quarterly* 20 (1992): 427–441.

Mutz, Diana C. "Impersonal Influence: Effects of Representations of Public Opinion on Political Attitudes." *Political Behavior* 14 (1992): 89–122.

———. "Mass Media and the Depoliticization of Personal Experience." *American Journal of Political Science* 36 (1992): 483–508.

———. "Contextualizing Personal Experience: The Role of Mass Media." *Journal of Politics* 56 (1994): 689–714.

———. "Effects of Horse-Race Coverage on Campaign Coffers: Strategic Contributing in Presidential Primaries." *Journal of Politics* 57 (1995): 1015–1042.

———. *Impersonal Influence: How Perceptions of Mass Collectives Affect Political Attitudes*. New York: Cambridge University Press, 1998.

Mutz, Diana C., and Paul S. Martin. "Facilitating Communication Across Lines of Political Difference: The Role of the Mass Media." *American Political Science Review* 95 (2001): 97–114.

Nadeau, Richard, Richard G. Niemi, and Timothy Amato. "Emotions, Issue Importance, and Political Learning." *American Journal of Political Science* 39 (1995): 513–527.

Natsios, Andrew. "Illusions of Influence: The CNN Effect in Complex Emergencies." In *From Massacres to Genocide: The Media, Public Policy and Humanitarian Crises,* ed. Robert I. Rotberg and Thomas G. Weiss, pp. 149–168. Washington, DC: The Brookings Institution, 1996.

Nelson, Thomas E., Rosalee A. Clawson, and Zoe M. Oxley. "Media Framing of a Civil Liberties Conflict and Its Effect on Tolerance." *American Political Science Review* 91 (1997): 567–584.

Nelson, Thomas E., and Donald R. Kinder. "Issue Frames and Group-Centrism in American Public Opinion." *Journal of Politics* 58 (1996): 1055–1078.

Nelson, Thomas E., Zoe M. Oxley, and Rosalee A. Clawson. "Toward a Psychology of Framing Effects." *Political Behavior* 19 (1997): 2231–2246.

Neuman, W. Russell. *The Paradox of Mass Politics: Knowledge and Opinion in the American Electorate.* Cambridge, MA: Harvard University Press, 1986.

———. "The Threshold of Public Attention." *Public Opinion Quarterly* 54 (1990): 159–176.

Neuman, W. Russell, Marion R. Just, and Ann N. Crigler. *Common Knowledge: News and the Construction of Political Meaning.* Chicago: University of Chicago Press, 1992.

Neustadt, Richard. *Presidential Power and the Modern Presidents.* New York: The Free Press, 1991.

Newhagen, John E., and Byron Reeves. "Emotion and Memory Responses for Negative Political Advertising: A Study of Television Commercials Used in the 1988 Presidential Election." In *Television and Political Advertising,* Vol. 1, ed. Frank Biocca, pp. 197–220. Hillsdale, NJ: Lawrence Erlbaum, 1991.

Niemi, Richard, and Herbert Weisberg. *Classics in American Voting Behavior.* Washington, DC: CQ Press, 1993.

Norris, Pippa. "The Restless Searchlight: Network News Framing of the Post–Cold War World." *Political Communication* 12 (1995): 357–370.

———. "Does Television Erode Social Capital? A Reply to Putnam." *PS: Political Science and Politics* 29 (1996): 474–480.

———. "Women Leaders Worldwide: A Splash of Color in the Photo Op." In *Women, Media and Politics,* ed. Pippa Norris. New York: Oxford University Press, 1997.

———, ed. *Politics and the Press: The News Media and Their Influences.* Boulder, CO: Lynne Rienner, 1997.

———, ed. *Women, Media and Politics.* New York: Oxford University Press, 1997.

———, ed. "Who Surfs? New Technology, Old Voters and Virtual Democracy in the 1996 and 1998 U.S. Elections." Revised draft for *Democracy.com?* ed. Elaine Kamarck. Cambridge, MA: Hollis, 1999. Available from http://www.ksg.harvard. edu/norrisweb/ARCHIVE/WhoSurfs2.htm.

———. "Social Capital and the News Media." *Harvard International Journal of Press/Politics* 7 (2001): 3–8.

Norris, Pippa, John Curtice, David Sanders, Margaret Scammell, and Holli A. Semetko, eds. *On Message: Communicating the Campaign.* Thousand Oaks, CA: Sage, 1999.

Norris, Pippa, and David Jones. "Editorial: Virtual Democracy." *Harvard International Journal of Press/Politics* 3 (1998): 1–4.

Norris, Pippa, and David Sanders. "You've Got to Ac-cent-tchu-ate the Positive: The

Effects of Television News on Party Images in the 1997 British Election." Paper presented at the annual meeting of the Midwest Political Science Association, Chicago, Illinois, April 23–25, 1998.

O'Brien, Erin. "Are the Consultants Depressing? Negative Advertising, Electoral Demobilization, and Political Consultants." Paper presented at the annual meeting of the Southern Political Science Association, Savannah, Georgia, November 3–6, 1999.

O'Callaghan, Jerome, and James O. Dukes. "Media Coverage of the Supreme Court's Caseload." *Journalism Quarterly* 69 (1992): 195–203.

O'Keefe, Garrett J. "Political Malaise and Reliance on Media." *Journalism Quarterly* 57 (1980): 122–128.

Ovisiovitch, Jay S. "News Coverage and Human Rights." *Political Research Quarterly* 46 (1993): 671–689.

Owen, Diana. "Talk Radio and Evaluations of President Clinton." *Political Communication* 14 (1997): 333–353.

Page, Benjamin I. *Who Deliberates?* Chicago: University of Chicago Press, 1996.

Page, Benjamin I., and Robert Y. Shapiro. *The Rational Public: Fifty Years of Trends in Americans' Policy Preferences*. Chicago: University of Chicago Press, 1992.

Paletz, David L. *The Media in American Politics: Contents and Consequences*. New York: Longman, 1999.

Paletz, David L., and Richard J. Vinegar. "Presidents on Television: The Effects of Instant Analysis." *Public Opinion Quarterly* 41 (1977–1978): 488–497.

Pan, Zhongdang, and Gerald M. Kosicki. "Voters' Reasoning Processes and Media Influences During the Persian Gulf War." *Political Behavior* 16 (1994): 117–156.

Parenti, Michael. *Make-Believe Media: The Politics of Entertainment*. New York: St. Martin's Press, 1992.

Parker, Kimberly Coursen. "How the Press Views Congress." In *Congress, the Press, and the Public,* ed. Thomas E., Mann and Norman J. Ornstein, pp. 157–170. Washington, DC: American Enterprise Institute and The Brookings Institution, 1994.

Patterson, Samuel C., and Gregory A. Caldeira. "Getting Out the Vote: Participation in Gubernatorial Elections." *American Political Science Review* 77 (1983): 675–689.

Patterson, Thomas E. *The Mass Media Election: How Americans Choose Their President*. New York: Praeger, 1980.

———. *Out of Order*. New York: Knopf, 1993.

———. *The Vanishing Voter: Public Involvement in an Age of Uncertainty*. New York: Knopf, 2002.

Patterson, Thomas E., and Robert P. McClure. *The Unseeing Eye: The Myth of Television Power in National Elections*. New York: G. P. Putnam's Sons, 1976.

"PBS Bests Networks in Election News." Press Release. October 23, 2000. Available from http://www.cmpa.com/pressrel/electpr9.htm (accessed August 20, 2002).

Peake, Jeffrey S. "Setting the Agenda in Foreign Policy: The President, the Congress and the Media." Paper presented at the annual meeting of the Southern Political Science Association, Norfolk, Virginia, November 6–8, 1997.

Perloff, Richard M. *Political Communication: Politics, Press, and Public in America*. Mahwah, NJ: Lawrence Erlbaum, 1998.

Pew Research Center for the People and the Press. "Americans Going Online . . . Explosive Growth, Uncertain Destinations." Times Mirror/Pew, October 1995.

———. "Audiences Fragmented and Skeptical: The Tough Job of Communicating with

Voters." News Release. Available from http://people-press.org/reports/print.php3?PageID=415 (accessed February 5, 2000).

———. "Event Driven News Audiences: Internet News Takes Off." Available from http://www.people-press.org/med98rpthtm (accessed October 11, 1998).

———. "Internet Election News Audience Seeks Convenience, Familiar Names." News Release. December 3, 2000. Available from http://www.people-press.org/reports/print.php3?PageID=137 (accessed August 23, 2002).

———. "The Internet News Audience Goes Ordinary." News Release. January 14, 1999. Available from http://www.people-press.org/reports/display.php3?ReportID=72 (accessed July 13, 2002).

———. "One-in-Ten Voters Online for Campaign '96." Available from http://www.people-press.org/tec96sum.html (accessed May 1, 1998).

———. "Pew Research Center Database: Public Attentiveness to Major News Stories (1986–1998)." Available from http://www.people-press.org/niidata.htm (accessed May 1, 1998).

———. "The Times Mirror News Interest Index: 1989–1995." Available from http://www.people-press.org/niidata.htm (accessed May 1, 1998).

———. "TV News Viewership Declines." Available from http://www.people-press.org/mediarpt.htm (accessed May 1, 1998).

———. "Worries About Terrorism Subside in Mid-America: Ratings of Government Efforts Slips." News Release. November 8, 2001. Available from http://www.people-press.org/reports/display.php3?ReportID=142 (accessed August 14, 2002).

Pfau, Michael, and Michael Burgoon. "The Efficacy of Issue and Character Attack Message Strategies in Political Campaign Communication." *Communication Reports* 2 (1989): 53–60.

Pfau, Michael, and Allan Louden. "Effectiveness of Adwatch Formats in Deflecting Political Attack Ads." *Communication Research* 2 (1994): 325–341.

Popkin, Samuel L. *The Reasoning Voter: Communication and Persuasion in Presidential Campaigns,* 2nd ed. Chicago: University of Chicago Press, 1994.

Powell, Richard J.. "Presidential Candidates and Nonverbal Imagery: Photographic Coverage of the 1992 and 1996 Presidential Election Campaigns." Paper presented at the annual meeting of the Midwest Political Science Association, Chicago, Illinois, April 23–25, 1998.

Press, Charles, and Kenneth Verburg. *American Politicians and Journalists.* Glenview, IL: Scott, Foresman, 1988.

Project for Excellence in Journalism. "A Content Analysis of Early Press Coverage of the 2000 Presidential Campaign." Research Series on Election Coverage 2000. Available from http://www.journalism.org (accessed August 20, 2002).

———. "The Last Lap." Research Series on Election Coverage 2000. Available from http://www.journalism.org (accessed August 20, 2002).

———. "Campaign 2000: Last Lap, Topline." Available from http://www.journalism.org/resources/research/reports/campaign2000/lastlap/topline.asp (accessed March 30, 2003).

———. "The Last Lap: Final Topline." Available from http://www.journalism.org/publ_research/campaign13.html (accessed August 20, 2002).

———. "The Last Lap: Differences in Medium." Available from http://www.journalism.org/publ_research/campaign7.html (accessed August 20, 2002).

———. "A Question of Character." Research Series on Election Coverage 2000. Available from http://www.journalism.org (accessed August 20, 2002).

Protess, David L., Fay Lomax Cook, Jack C. Doppelt, James S. Ettema, Margaret T. Gordon, Donna R. Leff, and Peter Miller. *The Journalism of Outrage: Investigative Reporting and Agenda Building in America.* New York: Guilford Press, 1991.

Putnam, Robert D. *Bowling Alone: The Collapse and Revival of American Community.* New York: Simon & Schuster, 2000.

Rahn, Wendy M., and Rebecca M. Hirshorn. "Political Advertising and Public Mood: A Study of Children's Political Orientations." *Political Communication* 16 (1999): 387–407.

Ranney, Austin. *Channels of Power: The Impact of Television on American Politics.* New York: Basic, 1983.

Rhee, June Woong. "How Polls Drive Campaign Coverage: The Gallup/CNN/*USA Today* Tracking Poll and *USA Today*'s Coverage of the 1992 Presidential Campaign." *Political Communication* 13 (1996): 213–229.

Rhine, Staci, Stephen Bennett, and Richard Flickinger. "Americans' Exposure and Attention to Electronic and Print Media and Their Impact on Democratic Citizenship." Paper presented at the annual meeting of the Midwest Political Science Association, Chicago, Illinois, April 23–25, 1998.

Robinson, Michael J. "Public Affairs Television and the Growth of Political Malaise: The Case of 'The Selling of the Pentagon.'" *American Political Science Review* 70 (1976): 409–431.

Robinson, Michael J., and Margaret A. Sheehan. *Over the Wire and on TV: CBS and UPI in Campaign '80.* New York: Russell Sage Foundation, 1983.

Roddy, Brian L., and Gina M. Garramone. "Appeals and Strategies of Negative Political Advertising." *Journal of Broadcasting and Electronic Media* 32 (1988): 415–427.

Rogers, Everett M., and James W. Dearing. "Agenda-Setting Research: Where Has It Been, Where Is It Going?" In *Communication Yearbook* 11 (1988): 555–594.

Rosen, Jay, and Paul Taylor. *The New News v. The Old News: The Press and Politics in the 1990s.* New York: The Twentieth Century Fund Press, 1992.

Rosenberg, Shawn W., Shulamit Kahn, and Thuy Tran. "Creating a Political Image: Shaping Appearance and Manipulating the Vote." *Political Behavior* 13 (1991): 345–368.

Roshco, Bernard. *Newsmaking.* Chicago: University of Chicago Press, 1975.

Ross, Marc H. "Television News and Candidate Fortunes in Presidential Nomination Campaigns: The Case of 1984." *American Politics Quarterly* 20 (1992): 69–98.

Rotberg, Robert I., and Thomas G. Weiss, eds. *From Massacres to Genocide: The Media, Public Policy and Humanitarian Crises.* Washington, DC: The Brookings Institution, 1996.

Rozell, Mark J. "Press Coverage of Congress, 1946–92." In *Congress, the Press, and the Public,* ed. Thomas E. Mann and Norman J. Ornstein, pp. 59–130. Washington, DC: American Enterprise Institute and The Brookings Institution, 1994.

Rudd, Robert. "Issues as Image in Political Campaign Commercials." *The Western Journal of Speech Communication* 50 (1986): 102–118.

"Rules in Flux: News Organizations Face Tough Calls on Unverified 'Facts,'" *New York Times,* January 27, 1998.

Sableman, Mark. *More Speech, Not Less: Communications Law in the Information Age.* Carbondale, IL: Southern Illinois University Press, 1997.

Scheufele, Dietram A. "Agenda-Setting, Priming, and Framing Revisited: Another Look at Cognitive Effects of Political Communication." *Mass Communication & Society* 3 (2000): 297–316.

Sears, David O., and Steven H. Chaffee. "Uses and Effects of the 1976 Debates: An Overview of Empirical Studies." In *The Great Debates: Carter vs. Ford, 1976*, ed. Sidney Kraus. Bloomington: Indiana University Press, 1979.

Seaton, Jean, and Ben Pimlott. *The Media in British Politics*. Aldershot, England: Dartmouth Publishing Company, 1987.

Shaw, Daron R. "The Effect of TV Ads and Candidate Appearances on Statewide Presidential Votes, 1988–96." *American Political Science Review* 9 (1999): 345–362.

———."The Impact of News Media Favorability and Candidate Events in Presidential Campaigns." *Political Communication* 16 (1999): 183–202.

Shah, Dhavan V. "Civic Engagement, Interpersonal Trust, and Television Use: An Individual-Level Assessment of Social Capital." *Political Psychology* 19 (1998): 469–496.

Shah, Dhavan V., Mark D. Watts, David Domke, David P. Fan, and Michael Fibison. "News Coverage, Economic Cues, and the Public's Presidential Preferences, 1984–1996." *Journal of Politics* 61 (1999): 914–943.

Shaw, Donald L., Maxwell E. McCombs, and associates. *The Emergence of American Political Issues: The Agenda-Setting Function of the Press*. New York: West Publishing, 1977.

Shephard, Jack. "Ethiopia: The Use of Food as an Instrument of U.S. Foreign Policy." *Issue: A Journal of Opinion* 14 (1985): 4–9.

Shepsle, Kenneth. "Strategy of Ambiguity: Uncertainty and Electoral Competition." *American Political Science Review* 66 (1972): 555–568.

Shoemaker, Pamela J., Lucig H. Danielian, and Nancy Brendlinger. "Deviant Acts, Risky Business and U.S. Interests: The Newsworthiness of World Events." *Journalism Quarterly* 68 (1991): 781–795.

Sigal, Leon V. *Reporters and Officials: The Organization and Politics of Newsmaking*. Lexington, MA: Heath, 1973.

Siune, Karen, and Ole Borre. "Setting the Agenda for a Danish Election." *Journal of Communication* 25 (1975): 66–73.

Smith, Tom W. "America's Most Important Problem—A Trend Analysis, 1946–1976." *Public Opinion Quarterly* 20 (1980): 164–180.

Smoller, Fredric T. "The Six O'Clock Presidency: Patterns of Network News Coverage of the President." *Presidential Studies Quarterly* 16 (1986): 31–49.

———. *The Six O'Clock Presidency: A Theory of Presidential Press Relations in the Age of Television*. New York: Praeger, 1990.

Sniderman, Paul M., and Edward G. Carmines. *Reaching Beyond Race*. Cambridge, MA: Harvard University Press, 1997.

Sniderman, Paul M., and Thomas Piazza. *The Scar of Race*. Cambridge, MA: Harvard University Press, 1993.

Solimine, Michael E. "Newsmagazine Coverage of the Supreme Court." *Journalism Quarterly* 57 (1980): 661–663.

Steger, Wayne P. "Comparing News and Editorial Coverage of the 1996 Presidential Nominating Campaign." *Presidential Studies Quarterly* 29 (1999): 40–64.

Stone, Gerald C., and Maxwell E. McCombs. "Tracing the Time Lag in Agenda-Setting." *Journalism Quarterly* 58 (1981): 51–55.

Tan, Alexis S. "Mass Media Use, Issue Knowledge and Political Involvement." *Public Opinion Quarterly* 44 (1980): 241–248

Tewksbury, David, and Scott L. Althaus. "Differences in Knowledge Acquisition

Among Readers of the Paper and Online Versions of a National Newspaper." *Journalism and Mass Communication Quarterly* 77 (2000): 457–479.

Thelan, David. *Becoming Citizens in the Age of Television: How Americans Challenged the Media and Seized Political Initiative During the Iran-Contra Debate.* Chicago: University of Chicago Press, 1996.

Thomas, Don, Craig McCoy, and Allan McBride. "Deconstructing the Political Spectacle: Sex, Race, and Subjectivity in Public Responses to Clarence Thomas/Anita Hill Sexual Harassment Hearings." *American Journal of Political Science* 37 (1993): 699–726.

Thorson, Esther, William G. Christ, and Clarke Caywood. "Effects of Issue-Image Strategies, Attack and Support Appeals, Music, and Visual Content in Political Commercials." *Journal of Broadcasting & Electronic Media* 35 (1991): 465–486.

Thurber, James A., Candice J. Nelson, and David A. Dulio, eds. *Crowded Airwaves: Campaign Advertising in Elections.* Washington, DC: The Brookings Institution, 2000.

Tidmarch, Charles M., and John J. Pitney, Jr. "Covering Congress: An Analysis of Reportage and Commentary in Ten Metropolitan Newspapers." *Polity* 17 (1985): 463–483.

Tipton, Leonard, Roger D. Haney, and John R. Baseheart. "Media Agenda-Setting in City and State Election Campaigns." *Journalism Quarterly* 52 (1975): 15–22.

Underwood, Doug. *When MBAs Rule the Newsroom: How the Marketers and Managers Are Reshaping Today's Media.* New York: Columbia University Press, 1993.

Uslaner, Eric M. "Social Capital, Television, and the 'Mean World': Trust, Optimism, and Civic Participation." *Political Psychology* 19 (1998): 441–467.

Valentino, Nicholas A., Vincent L. Hutchings, and Ismail K. White. "Cues That Matter: How Political Ads Prime Racial Attitudes During Campaigns." *American Political Science Review* 96 (2002): 75–90.

Vavreck, Lynn. "The Reasoning Voter Meets the Strategic Candidate: Signals and Specificity in Campaign Advertising, 1998." *American Politics Research* 29 (2001): 507–529.

Wanta, Wayne. *The Public and The National Agenda.* Mahwah, NJ: Lawrence Erlbaum, 1997.

Wattenberg, Martin P. *The Decline of American Political Parties, 1952–1996.* Cambridge, MA: Harvard University Press, 1998

Watts, Mark D. "Media Coverage and the 103rd Congress: When to Cover Policymaking in Congress." Paper presented at the annual meeting of the Midwest Political Science Association, Chicago, Illinois, April 23–26, 1998.

Weaver, David H.. "Media Agenda-Setting and Media Manipulation." In *Mass Communication Review Yearbook* (1981): 537–554.

Weaver, David H., Doris A. Graber, Maxwell E. McCombs, and Chaim H. Eyal. *Media Agenda-Setting in a Presidential Election: Issues, Images and Interest.* New York: Praeger, 1981.

Weaver, David, and G. Cleveland Wilhoit. *The American Journalist in the 1990s.* Mahwah, NJ: Lawrence Erlbaum, 1996.

Wells, Robert A. "Prestige Newspaper Coverage of Foreign Affairs in the 1992 and 1996 Presidential Campaigns." Paper presented at the annual meeting of the Southern Political Science Association, Savannah, Georgia, November 3–6, 1999.

West, Darrell M. "Polling Effects in Election Campaigns." *Political Behavior* 13 (1991): 151–164.

————."Political Advertising and News Coverage in the 1992 California U.S. Senate Campaigns." *Journal of Politics* 56 (1994): 1053–1076.

————. *Air Wars: Television Advertising in Election Campaigns 1952–2000*, 3rd ed. Washington, DC: CQ Press, 2001.

"A Whiff of Sexual Scandal Has Everybody Talking," *New York Times,* January 23, 1998.

Williams, Wenmouth, Jr., and David C. Larsen. "Agenda-Setting in an Off-Election Year." *Journalism Quarterly* 54 (1977): 744–749.

Wlezien, Christopher, and Robert S. Erikson. "Campaign Effects in Theory and Practice." *American Politics Research* 29 (2001): 419–436.

Wood, B. Dan, and Jeffrey S. Peake. "The Dynamics of Foreign Policy Agenda Setting." *American Political Science Review* 92 (1998): 173–184.

Yagade, Ailenn, and David M. Dozier. "The Media Agenda-Setting Effect of Concrete versus Abstract Issues." *Journalism Quarterly* 67 (Spring 1990): 3–10.

Zakon, Robert. "Hobbes' Internet Timeline v5.6." Available from http://www.zakon.org/robert/internet/timeline (accessed July 13, 2002).

Zaller, John R. *The Nature and Origins of Mass Opinion.* New York: Cambridge University Press, 1992.

————. "The Myth of Massive Media Impact Revived: New Support for a Discredited Idea." In *Political Persuasion and Attitude Change,* ed. Diana C. Mutz, Paul M. Sniderman, and Richard A. Brody, pp. 17–78. Ann Arbor: University of Michigan Press, 1996.

————. "Monica Lewinsky's Contribution to Political Science." *PS: Political Science & Politics* 31 (1998): 182–189.

————. "The Rule of Product Substitution in Presidential Campaign News." *Annals of the American Academy of Political and Social Science* 560 (1998): 111–128.

Zilber, Jeremy, and David Niven. "Stereotypes in the News: Media Coverage of African-Americans in Congress." *The Harvard International Journal of Press/Politics* 5 (2000): 32–49.

Zucker, Harold Gene. "The Variable Nature of News Media Influence." In *Communication Yearbook 2,* ed. Brent D. Ruben, pp. 225–240. New Brunswick, NJ: Transaction Books, 1978.

Acknowledgments

Table 4.1: Created by Aaron J. Moore, Ph.D., Assistant Professor of Sports Media at Ithaca College. As published by the *Columbia Journalism Review*. Reprinted with permission.

Table 4.2: Richard Davis and Diana Owen, *New Media and American Politics*, table 6.1. Copyright © 1998. Reprinted by permission of the publisher, Oxford University Press.

Box, "Changes in News Content Over Time," Copyright © 1998 by the *New York Times*. Reprinted with permission.

Table 5.1: From Robert S. Lichter and Daniel R. Amundson, "Less News Is Worse News: Television News Coverage of Congress, 1972–92," in *Congress, the Press, and the Public*. Ed. Thomas E. Mann and Norman J. Ornstein (Washington, DC: American Enterprise Institution and the Brookings Institution, 1994), p. 138. Reprinted with permission.

Figure 5.2: Frederic T. Smoller, "The Six O'Clock Presidency: A Theory of Presidential Press Relations in the Age of Television," figure 9.1. Copyright © 1990 by Greenwood Publishing Group. Reproduced with permission of Greenwood Publishing Group, Inc., Westport, CT.

Figure 5.3: From Robert S. Lichter and Daniel R. Amundson, "Less News Is Worse News: Television News Coverage of Congress, 1972–92," in *Congress, the Press, and the Public*. Ed. Thomas E. Mann and Norman J. Ornstein (Washington, DC: American Enterprise Institution and the Brookings Institution, 1994), p. 134. Reprinted by permission.

Table 5.3: From *Tabloid Justice: Criminal Justice in an Age of Media Frenzy* by Richard L. Fox and Robert W. Van Sickel. Copyright © 2001 by Lynne Rienner Publishers. Reprinted with permission.

Box, "Radio Listeners in Panic, Taking War Drama as Fact." Copyright © 1938 by the *New York Times*. Reprinted with permission.

Figure 6.1: Copyright © 1999 from "Political Advertising and Public Mood: A Study of Children's Political Orientations," by Wendy M. Rahn and Rebecca M. Hirshhorn. Reproduced by permission of Taylor & Francis, Inc., http://www.routledge-ny.com.

Table 6.1: From Michael X. Delli Carpini and Scott Keeter, *What Americans Know About Politics and Why It Matters*, pp. 70–71. Copyright © 1997. Reprinted by permission of the publisher, Yale University Press.

Figure 6.2: Reprinted by permission of the National Election Studies.

Table 6.2: From Michael X. Delli Carpini and Scott Keeter, *What Americans Know About Politics and Why It Matters*, pp. 74–75. Copyright © 1997. Reprinted by permission of the publisher, Yale University Press.

Figure 6.3: Reprinted with the permission of Simon & Schuster Adult Publishing Group. From *Bowling Alone: The Collapse and Revival of the American Community*, by Robert D. Putnam. Copyright © 2000 by Robert D. Putnam.

Table 6.3: From Michael X. Delli Carpini and Scott Keeter, *What Americans Know About Politics and Why It Matters*, pp. 80–81. Copyright © 1997. Reprinted by permission of the publisher, Yale University Press.

Figure 6.4: Reprinted with the permission of Simon & Schuster Adult Publishing Group. From *Bowling Alone: The Collapse and Revival of the American Community*, by Robert D. Putnam. Copyright © 2000 by Robert D. Putnam.

Table 6.4: From Michael X. Delli Carpini and Scott Keeter, *What Americans Know About Politics and Why It Matters*, pp. 83–84. Copyright © 1997. Reprinted by permission of the publisher, Yale University Press.

Figure 7.2: Shanto Iyengar and Adam Simon, "News Coverage of the Gulf Crisis and Public Opinion: A Study of Agenda Setting, Priming and Framing," in *Communication Research* 20 (1993), p. 375. Copyright © 1993 by Sage Publications. Reprinted by permission of Sage Publications, Inc.

Table 7.2: From Joanne M. Miller and John A. Krosnick, "News Media Impact on the Ingredients of Presidential Evaluations: A Program of Research on the Priming Hypothesis," as appeared in *Political Persuasions and Attitude Change*, ed. Diana Mutz, Paul Sniderman, and Richard Brody, pp 79–99. Copyright © 1996. Reprinted with permission.

Figure 7.3: From Diane C. Mutz, "Mass Media and the Depoliticization of Personal Experience," in *American Journal of Political Science* 36 (1992), p. 491. Reprinted by permission of the Midwest Political Science Association.

Table 7.3: From Joanne M. Miller and John A. Krosnick, "News Media Impact on the Ingredients of Presidential Evaluations: A Program of Research on the Priming Hypothesis," as appeared in *Political Persuasions and Attitude Change*, ed. Diana Mutz, Paul Sniderman, and Richard Brody, pp. 79–99. Copyright © 1996. Reprinted with permission.

Figure 8.1: From "Local TV Coverage of the 2000 General Election." The University of Southern California at Annenberg, Norman Lear Center Campaign Media Monitoring Project. Martin Kaplan, Principal Investigator, © 2001. Reprinted with permission.

Table 8.1: Reprinted with permission of Oxford University Press from Daniel C. Hallin, "Sound Bite News: Television Coverage of Elections, 1968–1998," *Journal of Communication* 42 (1992), p. 15.

Figure 8.2: Copyright © 1999 from "Voice, Substance, and Cynicism in Presidential Campaign Media," by Marion Just, Ann Crigler, and Tami Buhr. Reproduced by permission of Taylor & Francis, Inc., http://www.routledge-ny.com.

Figure 8.4: From *Out of Order* by Bonnie MacDougal, p. 20, © 1993. Copyright © 1999 by Bonnie MacDougal. Used by permission of Ballantine Books, a division of Random House, Inc.

Box, "Changing Sources of Campaign News." Reprinted by permission of the Pew Research Center for the People and the Press.

Figure 8.5: Robert S. Lichter and Richard E. Noyes, "There They Go Again: Media Coverage of Campaign '96." Reprinted by permission of the author and the Center for Media and Public Affairs.

Figure 8.6: From Kathleen Hall Jamieson, Paul Waldman, and Susan Sherr, "Eliminate the Negative? Categories of Analysis for Political Advertisements," in James A. Thurber et al., *Crowded Airwaves, Campaign Advertising in Elections*, pg. 58. Reprinted by permission of the Brookings Institution Press.

Index

ABC, 40, 73, 86, 205
   "Person of the Week" feature, 65–66
acceptance, 216
accessibility theory, 178
activation, in election campaigns, 220
advertising
   and advent of penny press, 23
   influence on news coverage, 90–91
   mass media system's reliance on, 24,
      25, 78–80
   as news filter, 12
   and newspaper circulation, 25
   on public broadcasting, 42, 91
   See also political advertising
advocacy ideas, 214, 224
"adwatches," 231
affective effects, 152. *See also* emotional
   media effects
AFL-CIO, 223, 224
African Americans, political coverage of,
   121–122
agenda-setting
   defined, 177–178
   in election campaigns, 224–228
   individual-level moderators of, 190–
      193

   measures of, 181–182
   media-centered model of, 225–228
   and objective reality, 176, 180, 181,
      182–183, 193
   relationships between different types
      of, 180–181
   transaction model of, 225–228
   See also institutional agenda-setting;
      media agenda-setting; public agenda
Alien and Sedition Acts of 1798, 34
alliance phase, of presidential news
   coverage, 115–116
All the President's Men (Woodward,
   Bernstein), 48
alternative information sources
   as moderator of media effects, 191,
      192, 193
   and narrowcasting, 32–33
   new formats for political
      communications, 30–31, 205, 219
altruistic democracy, 65
Amanpour, Christiane, 49
American National Election Study, 181,
   221, 224, 228, 232
American National Election Survey
   (NES), 150

analysis and commentary
  in election campaign coverage, 208–
    210
  in news coverage, 48, 54
Asia, news coverage of, 60
Associated Press, 24
attack ads, 211. *See also* negative
    political advertising
attack ideas, 214
attitudes. *See* political attitudes
attribution theory, 178
audience demographics. *See*
    demographics
audience interest
  for different types of news, 83
  impact on news product, 52, 53–54,
    57, 66
  marketing to, 80–81, 95–96
  in negative news, 53, 54
audience knowledge. *See* political
    knowledge
audience overlap, of news sources, 84–85
audience size
  and advertising revenue, 78–80
  for different media outlets, 81–82, 232
  impact of deregulation on, 41
authority-disorder news bias, 55, 117

Bagdikian, Ben, 39, 73, 77, 79
Bailey, Martha, 66
Baumgartner, Frank, 62, 64
beats, 96–97
Beck, Paul Allen, 225
behavioral effects, 152
belief importance, 179
Bennett, W. Lance, 55, 65, 94, 110
Berelson, Bernard, 148–149, 150, 151,
    220
Bernstein, Carl, 48, 98
Bertelsmann, 73
bias. *See* media bias
Bork, Robert, 125
Boston Gazette, 22
Boston News-Letter, 22
Bradlee, Ben, 48
Brians, Craig, 221
Brinkley, David, 27, 28
Brokaw, Tom, 132
Bush, George H. W., 167, 184, 186, 211

Bush, George W., 42, 110
  presidential campaign of, 4, 31, 71,
    205, 206, 207
  war with Iraq, 105, 112, 244
Business Coalition, 224
business elites
  opposition to fairness doctrine, 37–40
  and propagandist model of mass
    media, 12
  See also media and communications
    conglomerates

cable television networks, 3, 4
  audience size for, 81, 82
  growth of, 28, 143, 217
  regulation of, 39
campaign issues, 203
campaigns. *See* election campaigns
Campbell, Karlyn Kohrs, 78
candidate character
  negative coverage of, 206
  television and importance of, 200, 228
  and vote choice, 216, 228, 231
candidate favorability, 230
candidate image
  media effects for, 216
  in televised election campaigns, 200
Carter, Jimmy, 228–229
causation, 151
CBS, 73, 86, 206, 252
CBS Evening News, 53, 56, 115, 205
Center for Media and Public Affairs,
    203, 207
Chicago Tribune, 54, 60, 105
Chomsky, Noam, 12
civic engagement, and television viewing,
    164–166
civic journalism, 245–246
civil rights, 125
clear-cut issues, 203
Clinton, Bill, 21, 215
  Lewinsky affair, 2, 5, 14, 48, 98, 117
  negative coverage of, 167
  press operations of, 109, 113–114
  television appearances of, 30–31, 111,
    219
CNN, 5, 64, 81, 86, 114, 205
  foreign affairs coverage of, 85–86,
    130–132

CNN effect, 130–132
cognitive effects, 152. *See also* political knowledge
Cohen, Bernard, 177–178
Columbia University, 148
commercial newspapers, 23
competition phase, of presidential news coverage, 116
competitive news markets, 73
concentration of ownership, 73–77. *See also* media and communications conglomerates; media ownership
concrete events, as news, 54, 57
Congress
    and FCC policy making, 37–40
    institutional agenda-setting, 128–133
    press operations of, 4, 108–110, 120–121
congressional news coverage, 57–58
    emphasis on leaders, extreme views, and scandal, 56, 121–122
    of legislative process, 122–123, 128–133
    local media focus of, 120–121, 123
    negative tone of, 119–120, 123
    vs. presidential coverage, 119, 123
    public image videotapes used as, 108–110, 121
    of women and African Americans, 121–122
Constitution, ratification of, 5, 21
consumer, mass public as, 11, 15
consumer-oriented communications technology, 38
content analysis
    defined, 16, 251–252
    example of, 253–254
    limitations of, 252
Continental Cablevision, 40
contingent effects model, 150–151, 152, 177
contrast ideas, 214–215, 224
conversion, in election campaigns, 220
corporate ownership. *See* media and communications conglomerates; media ownership
corporatization of news organizations, 80, 245
correlation, 151

cost-cutting, impact on news product, 85–90
credit-claiming, 121
Crigler, Ann N., 161–162, 222
crime
    episodic coverage of, 188
    increased coverage of, 41, 64
    mass appeal of, 24, 176
    trial court coverage, 125–126
crises, institutional responses to, 129–132
Cronkite, Walter, 9, 28, 164
cross-media ownership, 73–77
cross-sectional survey research, 151
C-SPAN, 212, 232

"Daisy Girl" advertisement, 211
Dalton, Russell J., 225
dark horses, 203–204
democracy
    elections as central feature of, 200
    importance of latent support, 163
    and political knowledge, 143, 151
demographics
    early research on, 148
    and impact of media effects, 191–192
    and Internet use, 32–33, 232
    of journalists, 92
    and media preferences, 3, 78, 79, 82, 83
    voter, in 2000 election, 218
dependent variables, 144
deregulation, 40–41. *See also* regulation
description, in news coverage, 54
descriptive campaign stories, 208–209
detachment phase, of presidential news coverage, 116
diffuse issues, 203
directionality of information, 7
domestic news
    coverage of, 56–58, 63, 64
    political knowledge of, 157–158
Downs, Anthony, 129, 200, 201
dramatic events stories, 53–54
dramatized news, 55, 66
    trial court coverage, 125–126

Eastern Europe, developing markets in, 41

economic influences
  advertising revenues and ratings, 78–80
  corporate cost-cutting, 85–90
  corporate courtship of advertisers, 90–91
  corporate ownership, 72–77
  deregulation, 38–40
  marketing to reader interest, 80–81
  on media development, 22
  profit-seeker model, 11, 22, 51
  and yellow journalism, 25–26
economic issues
  coverage of, 57, 64
  impact of media's priming of, 185–187
  thematic coverage of, 188
  vulnerability and media effects, 191
economic power, of corporate media, 4–5
editorials, impact on vote choice, 229–230
Effects of Mass Communication, The (Klapper), 149
egalitarianism, and media framing, 189
electability, 230
election campaigns
  campaign context and media effects, 219
  dominance of television use in, 28, 200
  factors in evaluating media effects of, 215–220
  free media coverage (see election news coverage)
  impact on vote choice, 149, 216, 219, 228–231
  impact on voter turnout, 223–224
  media agenda-setting in, 224–228
  media as electoral institution, 7, 200, 210, 246
  mediated vs. nonmediated, 215–216
  and models of mass media, 234–235
  paid media coverage, 202, 211–215
  political learning during, 220–223
  postmodern era, 31
  presidential debates, 222
  role of media in, 4, 200–202, 210–211, 233–234
  three possible effects of, 220
  use of alternative broadcast formats, 30–31
  use of Internet in, 231–233
  See also election news coverage; political advertising; presidential election campaigns
election news coverage, 202–211
  bias and tone of, 206–208
  changing use of sources of, 217
  focus of studies on, 202
  horserace coverage, 202–204, 206, 234
  impact on vote choice, 229–230
  media's shortcomings in, 210–211
  negativity bias in, 207–211
  shift from descriptive to interpretive stories, 208–210
  as sound bite news, 209–210
  substance of, 202–206, 233–234
electronic broadcast media
  concentration of ownership in, 73–77
  consequences of deregulation on, 40–41
  development of, 26–28
  politics of regulation, 33–34, 37–40
  public, 33–34, 41–42
  as public resource, 36–37, 42
  regulation of broadcasting content, 36–40
  regulation of ownership of, 35–36, 39–40
  See also radio broadcasting; television broadcasting
elite press, 23
Emancipation Proclamation, 5
emotional media effects, and political evaluation, 163, 168–169, 170
entertainment, news emphasis on, 63–64, 118
entertainment media outlets
  impact on policy attitudes, 168–169
  impact on social capital, 164–166
  Internet as, 32
  negative portrayal of public officials, 127–128, 135
  political news on, 248
  political use of, 3, 30–31, 205, 219
environmental interest groups, 252, 253
episodic news coverage, 187
equal time rule, 36
Erbring, Lutz, 191

ethical news frames, 189
Ethiopian famine, 131–132, 133
ethnocentrism, 64
experimental research designs, 150–151, 161
exposés, institutional responses to, 132–133, 180
exposure, 216
external validity, 223

fairness doctrine, 36–39, 41
Fear and Favor in the Newsroom, 91
Federal Communications Act of 1934, 35, 36
Federal Communications Commission (FCC)
  establishment of, 35–36
  politics surrounding policy decisions, 37–40
  regulation of broadcasting content, 36–40
  See also regulation
Federal Radio Commission, 35, 37
First Amendment, 34–35, 125
Fleischer, Ari, 108
Flowers, Gennifer, 30
focus groups, 31
focusing events, 129
foreign affairs, political knowledge of, 159–160
foreign affairs coverage, 57, 60–61, 63, 64
  and CNN effect, 130–132
  corporate cost-cutting of, 85–86
  and interests of state, 135
Fourteenth Amendment, 35
Fowler, Mark, 38–39
Fox network, 73
Fox News, 86, 248
fragmented news, 55
framing effects, 177, 187–190
  episodic vs. thematic, 187–188
  individual-level moderators of, 192, 194
  policy related, 188–190
  political consequences of, 179
  psychological foundations of, 178–179
  race-related, 188–189
Franklin, Benjamin, 22
Franklin, James, 22

freedom of the press, 34–35, 37
free media, 201, 202–211. *See also* election news coverage
Frenau, Philip, 24
frontrunners, 203–204
Fuller, Jack, 52, 53
fully controlled news, 110

gaggle, 114
Gallup public opinion surveys, 176, 181
game, campaign coverage as, 202–204
Gandhi, Indira, 132
Gannett, 35
Gans, Herbert, 53–54, 56–57, 61, 64, 93
Gaudet, Hazel, 148–149, 150, 151
Gazette of the United States, 24
gender issues, in news coverage, 66
General Electric, 73
Gingrich, Newt, 40, 42
Ginsberg, Douglas, 125
"going public" strategy, 113
Goldenberg, Edie, 191
Gore, Al, 4, 30, 31, 205, 206, 207
government
  citizen's lack of knowledge about, 143
  early sponsorship of press, 24–25, 72–73
  See also media-government relations
government officials
  critical attitudes toward media, 105, 117, 136
  historical control of media, 22–23
  impact of priming effects on, 184–187
  interdependence with media and public, 8–9, 244
  media as neutral adversary of, 10
  negative coverage of, 127–128, 167
  as news junkies, 112, 128
  and objectivity norm, 94–95
  as primary source for news, 105, 110–112, 247–248
  and propagandist model of mass media, 12
  public's political knowledge of, 155–156
  use of Internet, 29
  use of media, 21–22, 110–112
  See also political elites
Groelling, Timothy, 117

group-related framing, 189–190
gubernatorial election campaigns, 206
Gulf War, 167, 168, 183, 184

Hamilton, Alexander, 21, 25
Harding, Warren G., 26
hard news, 31
"Harry and Louise" advertisement, 21
Hearst, William Randolph, 2
Hess, Stephen, 57, 60, 66
high-stimulus elections, 230
horserace, campaign coverage as, 202–
    204, 206, 234
Huckfeldt, Robert, 225
human interest stories, 53–54
Huntley, Chet, 27
Hurley, Patricia, 230
Hussein, Saddam, 105, 112, 244
hypodermic needle model, 144–147,
    215
hypotheses, 16

ideology, as moderator of media effects,
    192
image. See candidate image
independents, 221
independent variable, 151, 161
individual characteristics, impact on
    media effects, 150, 161–162, 190–
    193, 194
individualism, 65
    and media framing, 189
informal political discussion, as
    moderator of media effects, 192
information function, of mass media, 7
insider strategy, 129
instantaneous news delivery, 5, 28
institutional agenda-setting
    in agenda-setting model, 180–181
    defined, 128
    impact of crisis coverage on, 129–132
    impact of exposés on, 132–133, 180
    limitations of media's power in, 128–
        129
    measures of, 182
    and media as linkage institution, 134
interest groups, as linkage institution,
    6–7

Internet, 4, 143
    audience size for, 232
    as campaign medium, 217, 231–233
    class and race issues in accessing, 32–
        33
    and declining television viewership,
        84–85
    as forum for public discussion, 7, 29,
        32
    growth in use of, 16, 81, 82
    and instantaneous news, 5
    negative political coverage on, 206
    origins and growth of, 29
    political consequences of, 32–33
interpretation, as media function, 13, 15
interpretive campaign stories, 208–210
investigative reporting, 97–98
    impact on policy making, 133, 180
    in television entertainment shows,
        127
Iran-Contra scandal, 184, 185
Iran hostage crisis, 229
"iron triangles," 38
issue attention cycle, 129, 132
issue-based candidate evaluation, 221–
    222
issue knowledge, 222
issue positions. See policy positions
Iyengar, Shanto, 187–188

Jackson, Andrew, 25
Jamieson, Kathleen Hall, 78, 224
Jay, John, 21
Jefferson, Thomas, 24–25
Johnson, Lyndon, 211
Jones, Bryan, 62, 64
journalistic voice, 209
journalists
    corporate socialization of, 96
    demographic characteristics of, 92
    early professionalism of, 25
    gatekeeping role of, 105
    objectivity norm of, 94–95
    political ideology of, 92–93, 99
    professional values of, 93–94, 99,
        105
    public advocacy movement among,
        10–11

reliance on government sources, 105, 110–112, 247–248
judicial system
  Supreme Court coverage, 124–125
  trial court coverage, 125–126
Just, Marion R., 161–162, 222

Kahn, Kim, 221
Kaniss, Phyllis, 58–60
Keeter, Scott, 228
Kellstedt, Paul, 189
Kemell, Samuel, 117
Kennedy, John, 28, 117, 118
Kennedy, John, Jr., 57
Kenney, Patrick, 221
Klapper, Joseph, 149, 150
Knight-Ridder, 35, 91
Kootzle, William, 225
Krosnick, Jon, 184
Ku Klux Klan, 190

Larson, Stephanie Greco, 66
latent support, 163
Lazarsfeld, Paul, 148–149, 150, 151, 220
leaks, 112
legislative process
  impact of media coverage on, 128–133
  news coverage of, 58, 122–123
  presidential coverage, 113
  using trial balloons and leaks in, 112
  See also Congress; institutional agenda-setting
Letterman, David, 31, 205
Lewinsky, Monica, 2, 5, 14, 48, 98
liberal media, 71, 92–93
Liddy, G. Gordon, 31
Limbaugh, Rush, 3, 31, 92, 167
Lincoln, Abraham, 5
linkage institution, mass media as, 6–7, 12–13, 100, 106, 134, 246
Linsky, Martin, 128
Lippman, Walter, 54, 106–107
lobbying activities
  and agenda-setting, 128
  and FCC policy making, 38–40
  of media conglomerates, 5
local news coverage, 58–60

Los Angeles Times, 60, 86, 88, 90
low-stimulus elections, 230

MacKuen, Michael, 216
Madison, James, 21
"magic bullet theory," 145
Manson, Charles, 126
market-driven, 77. See also economic influences
marketing strategies, reader interest, 80–81, 95–96
marketplace of ideas, 35, 36
mass communications theories
  media effects on public, 13–15
  post–WWII developments, 148–151
  public's effect on media, 15
  See also media effects
mass media
  audience overlap in, 84–85
  changing scope of, 4, 15
  consequences of postmodern era, 31–33
  creating support for public deliberation, 246–248
  effects on mass public, 13–15
  as electoral institution, 7, 200, 210, 246
  historical development of, 23–26
  impact of Internet on, 29
  instantaneous news delivery of, 5
  interdependence with politicians and public, 8–9, 244
  as linkage institution, 6–7, 106, 246
  models of, 9–13, 244–246
  narrowcasting of, 32–33
  objective importance of, 4–5
  as political institution, 21–26, 43
  as profit-seeking, 8, 11, 244–246
  public's effect on, 15
  regulation of, 33–41
  role in politics, 2, 3–7, 246–249
  vs. specialized news media, 3
mass media for news, 3
mass medium, 23
mass society theory, 145
material frames, 189
McClure, Robert, 212, 221
McCombs, Maxwell, 224–225

McCoy, Kelley, 189
McCurry, Mike, 114
McKinley, William H., 2, 26
McPhee, William, 220
media agenda-setting, 176–177
    in agenda-setting model, 180–181
    in election campaigns, 224–228
    individual-level moderators of, 190–193
    measures of, 181
    and models of mass media, 177, 194
    political consequences of, 179
    psychological foundations of, 177–179
    and public agenda, 182–184
    types of, 179–182
    See also institutional agenda-setting
media and communications
        conglomerates
    cost-cutting policies of, 85–90
    and courtship of advertisers, 90–91
    economic power of, 4–5
    growth of, 73–77
    impact on news product, 77, 78–81,
        245
    and modern press, 24
    newspaper, 35
    and organizational constraints on
        newsgathering, 95–98
    and profit-seeker model, 11
    and regulatory policy, 33–41
    See also business elites; media
        ownership
media bias, 49, 71
    and audience interest, 52
    "authority disorder," 117
    in campaign coverage, 206–208
    and concentration of ownership, 73
    geographical, 52
    in institutional coverage, 135, 136
    issues in measuring, 251
    of liberal media, 71, 92–93
    negativity bias, 207–208
    and objectivity norm, 94–95
    in political news coverage, 55
    in presidential coverage, 117
media-centered model, of agenda-setting,
        225–228
media coverage tone, 206
media effects
    and civic engagement, 164–166

conclusion on research findings, 169–
    171
contingent effects model, 150–151
on election campaigns, 215–231
and emotional political evaluations,
    163, 167–169, 170
framing effects, 187–190
hypodermic needle model, 144–147
individual-level moderators of, 190–193
individual, mode, and message effects,
    161–162
media agenda-setting, 179–184
medium effects vs. message effects,
    219–220
minimal effects model, 148–150
and models of mass media, 170–171
one- and two-sided communication
    streams, 166–168
on political evaluations and policy
    support, 166–169
political socialization, 162–166, 170
priming effects, 184–187
survey findings on political knowledge,
    151–161
theories of, 144–151
media exposure, as moderator of media
    effects, 192
media-government relations, 21–22
    alternative broadcast formats, 30–31
    early government sponsorship, 24–25
    early press eras, 23–24, 72–73
    and economics of mass newspaper, 25–
        26
    and electronic broadcast media, 26–28
    in high-tech era, 28–31
    historical development of, 22–26
    and Internet, 29
    and politics of regulation, 33–41
    presidential relations, 25–26, 28
media ownership
    concentration of ownership, 24, 73–77
    and government regulation, 34–36,
        39–40
    influence on newsgathering process, 77
    newspapers, 24, 35, 72, 73, 77
    private ownership, 72–73
    public broadcasting, 41–42
    See also media and communications
        conglomerates

medium, in political learning, 161–162
medium effects, 219
Meet the Press, 31
message, in political learning, 161–162
message effects, 150, 219
Middle East, news coverage of, 60–61
Miller, Arthur, 191
minimal effects model, 148–150, 177
mobilization model, 129, 133
mode, in political learning, 161–162
moderatism, 65
moderators, 191
modern press, 24
Mondak, Jeffrey, 222–223
Monroe, Marilyn, 118
Morton, John, 79
MSNBC, 86
MTV, 30
"muckraking" journalism, 98

name recognition, factors influencing,
    230, 234
narrowcasting, 32–33, 231
Nation, The, 3
national figures, news coverage of, 53,
    56, 57–58, 65–66. *See also*
    government officials
National Gazette, The, 24
national leadership, 65
national press corps, 111, 112, 114
National Public Radio, 41
NBC, 73, 86
NBC Nightly News, 53, 86, 87, 132, 205
need for orientation, 191
negative news, audience interest in, 53, 54
negative political advertising, 211
    content of, 213, 214–215
    impact on voter turnout, 223–224
    incorrect inferences about, 214–215
    and political learning, 221, 234
negative political coverage
    as bias, 49
    of Congress, 119–120, 123
    of elected officials, 134, 135, 136, 246
    of election campaigns, 206–211
    impact on political attitudes, 163–166
    one-sided communication streams, 167
    of president, 115–118
    on television newsmagazines, 127–128

negativity bias, 207–208
Neuman, W. Russell, 161–162, 222
neutral adversary model
    and agenda-setting, 194
    defined, 10
    and development of media, 22
    and election coverage, 234
    failure of, 245
    and institutional coverage, 135
    and media agenda-setting, 177
    news coverage in, 50, 66
    and newsgathering process, 99
    and political knowledge, 143
New England Courant, 22
New Orleans *Times-Picayune*, 58
New Republic, 3
news, defined, 52–54
News Corp, 73
news coverage
    advertiser influence on, 90–91
    changing nature of, 48–49
    defining what's news, 52–54, 67
    domestic news, 56–58
    focus on concrete events, 54
    foreign affairs, 60–61, 85–86
    four biases of, 55
    growth of soft news, 86–90
    human interest and drama, 53–54
    impact of corporate cost-cutting on,
        85–90
    impact of deregulation on, 41
    local news, 58–60
    and models of mass media, 50–52, 66
    of politics, 55–64
    regional variations in, 58
    studies on changing content of, 54,
        62–64, 86–89
    timeliness of, 52–53, 67
    values reflected in, 64–66
    See also election news coverage;
        political news coverage
newsgathering process, 71–72
    and corporate cost-cutting, 85–90
    and corporate newsroom coordination,
        96
    impact of advertising and ratings on,
        78–81, 90–91
    impact of marketing strategies on, 80–
        81, 95–96

newsgathering process (*cont.*)
  influence of corporate ownership on, 72–77
  institutional basis of, 106–112
  investigative reporting, 97–98
  journalist characteristics and values influencing, 92–95, 99
  and models of mass media, 98–100
  organizational constraints on, 95–98
  reliance on newsbeats, 96–97
  reliance on public relations material, 86, 90, 108–110, 121
newshole, 79, 97
Newshour with Jim Lehrer, 203, 205, 206, 232
newsmagazine coverage, 56. *See also* television newsmagazines
news monopolies, 73. *See also* media and communications conglomerates
Newspaper Preservation Act of 1970, 35
newspapers, 3
  advertising and circulation, 78, 79–80
  audience size for, 81, 82
  colonial, 22, 23, 72
  consequences of corporate ownership, 24, 35, 72, 73, 77, 79–81
  declining readership of, 28, 41, 79, 82, 84, 95, 217
  demographics of readers, 78, 79, 82
  early press eras, 23–24
  economics of mass, 25–26
  focus on campaign policy issues, 204–205
  and government regulation, 34–35
  government sponsorship of, 24–25
  impact of broadcast news on, 28
  local news coverage of, 58–60
  online, 29
  presidential coverage, 114
  as "serious" news outlets, 27
  vs. television for political learning, 161–162, 170, 222–223
news sources
  audience overlap in, 84–85
  government officials as, 105, 110–112, 247–248
  increase in, 143
Newsweek, 3, 53, 56, 114, 189, 208, 232

newsworthy, 52
New York Daily News, 52
New York Sun, 23
New York Times, 27, 29, 40, 52, 54, 60, 61, 62–64, 97, 105, 112, 114, 115, 145, 146–147, 181
Nielsen and Arbitron ratings, 78–79
Nixon, Richard, 98, 107
nonpartisan elections, 230
Norris, Pippa, 31, 165

objective importance, of mass media, 4–5
objective reality, and agenda-setting, 176, 180, 181, 182–183, 193
objectivity, as professional norm, 94–95
obtrusive issues, 183
Office of the Chief of Staff, 113, 115
Office of Communications, 107–108
Office of Media Affairs, 4, 115
opinion leaders, 149
organizational constraints, on newsgathering process, 95–98
outsider strategy, 129
ownership. *See* media ownership

paid media, 202, 211–215. *See also* political advertising
"papers of record," 27
Park, Robert E., 53
Parry, Kate, 245
partially controlled news, 110–111
partisan elections, 230
partisan media system, 248
partisanship, as moderator of media effects, 192
party identification
  decline in, 220–221
  and vote choice, 216, 219, 220
party press, 23
Patterson, Thomas, 202–204, 212, 221, 222
penny press, 23–24
People's Choice, The (Lazarsfeld, Berelson, Gaudet), 148–149, 151
personalized news, 55, 66
Pew Center survey, 83, 84, 176
pocketbook voting, 185
policy positions
  in election campaigns, 200

media's impact on public's, 168–169, 188–190
negative coverage of, 206
newspapers' focus on candidates, 204–205
and vote choice, 216, 221–222
policy process. *See* institutional agenda-setting; legislative process
political advertising, 202, 211–215
in 2000 presidential election, 4
content of, 21, 212–213, 221
for control of message, 231
impact on political attitudes, 163
impact on vote choice, 229–231
impact on voter turnout, 223–224
and political learning, 221, 222, 231, 234
priming in, 229
tone of, 214–215
political attitudes
media effects on, 162–166
two-step formation process, 216
political elites
media effects of disagreement between, 168, 171
use of media, 21–22
See also government officials
political evaluations
and emotion-based media effects, 163, 168–169, 170
impact of priming effects on, 184–187, 193
issue-based candidate, 221–222
political institutions
accommodation of media, 107–110
Congress, 119–123
and controlled and uncontrolled news, 110–112
and institutional agenda-setting, 128–133
judicial system, 124–126
media as, 21–26, 43 (*see also* media-government relations)
media as linkage institution to, 134
nature of coverage of, 105–106
negative coverage of, 115–118, 119–120, 123, 134, 135, 136
political knowledge of, 153–157
presidency, 113–118

use of media to govern, 110–112
See also institutional agenda-setting
political interest, as moderator of media effects, 192
political knowledge
and democracy, 143, 151
as gradually acquired, 162, 169–170
individual, mode, and message effects in, 161–162
lack of interest in, 143, 151, 171
and models of mass media, 143–144
and priming effect, 192
survey findings on public's, 151–161
and theories of media effects, 144–151, 169
political learning
during election campaigns, 220–223
individual, mode, and message effects in, 161–162
medium differences in, 161–162, 222–223
political news coverage, 55–64
audience interest in, 83
and audience overlap, 84–85
congressional, 119–123
creating partisan system for, 248
domestic news, 56–58
foreign affairs, 60–61
four biases of, 55
impact of corporate cost-cutting on, 85–90
local news, 58–60
need for enhancement of, 247
presidential, 115–118
values reflected in, 64–66
See also election news coverage; news coverage
political parties
declining role in election campaigns, 7, 200, 210
as linkage institution, 6–7
and party press, 23
strategic behavior of, 200
See also party identification
political socialization, media's role and impact on, 162–166, 170
political tolerance, impact of media framing on, 190

Portland Oregonian, 54
position-taking, 121
postmodern campaign era, 31
poverty
  media framing of, 188, 190
  media portrayal of, 168, 169
president
  impact of priming on evaluations of, 184–187
  relationship with press, 25–26, 28, 92
  sources of power of, 113
presidential election campaigns
  debates, 222, 234
  factors in vote choice, 216
  horserace coverage of, 203, 206
  study of 1940, 148–149, 151
  2000, 4, 31, 71, 206–207, 217–218, 226–227
  See also election campaigns
presidential news coverage
  approval ratings, 117
  emphasis on, 56, 57, 115, 119, 123, 134
  negative tone of, 115–118
  problems with, 116
  three phases of, 115–116
presidential press operations, 4
  Clinton's press office, 109, 113–114
  daily press briefings, 114
  development of, 28
  going public strategy, 113
  Office of the Chief of Staff, 115
  presidential press conferences, 111–112
  pseudo-events, 110
  role of Office of Communications, 107–108
  role of press secretary, 113–115
press briefings, 107, 114
press clubs, 25
press conferences, presidential, 111–112
press eras, historical, 23–24
Pressler, Larry, 42
press releases, used as news, 86, 90, 108–110, 121
priming, media, 177
  of economic conditions, 185–187
  impact of evaluations of political figures, 184–187
  impact on vote choice, 228–229

individual-level moderators of, 192, 193, 194
  in political advertising, 229
  political consequences of, 179
  psychological foundations of, 178
Princeton Survey Research Associates, 217
printed press. *See* newspapers
print superiority thesis, 162, 170
prior restraint laws, 35
private ownership. *See* media ownership
profit-seeker model, 106
  and agenda-setting, 194
  defined, 11
  and development of media, 22
  and election coverage, 235
  evidence supporting, 244–246
  and institutional coverage, 135
  and media agenda-setting, 177
  news coverage in, 51, 66
  and newsgathering process, 98–99
  and political knowledge, 144
Project for Excellence in Journalism, 203, 207, 226
propaganda, 145
propagandist model
  and agenda-setting, 194
  defined, 12
  and development of media, 22
  and election coverage, 234
  failure of, 246
  and institutional coverage, 135
  and linkage institutions, 12
  and media agenda-setting, 177
  news coverage in, 51–52
  and newsgathering process, 98–99
  and political knowledge, 144
Protess, David L., 133
pseudo-events, 97, 110
psychology, impact on media effects research, 148–150
public, mass
  as active participants, 151, 161, 170–171, 177, 179, 194
  as consumers, 11, 15
  effect on mass media, 15
  interdependence with politicians and media, 8–9, 244
  media effects on, 13–15
  political knowledge of, 143

public advocate model
  and agenda-setting, 194
  defined, 10–11
  and election coverage, 234
  failure of, 245–246
  and institutional coverage, 135
  and media agenda-setting, 177
  news coverage in, 50–51, 66
  and newsgathering process, 99
  and political knowledge, 143
public affairs programming, 36–37,
  108
public agenda
  in agenda-setting model, 180–181
  measures of, 181–182
  and media agenda-setting, 182–184
public broadcasting, 33–34, 41–42, 91
Public Broadcasting Act of 1967, 41
public deliberation
  creating forum for, 246–247
  impact of Internet on, 29, 32
  as marketplace of ideas, 35
  mass media as forum for, 7
  and public advocacy journalism, 10–
  11
public images, 108
public mobilization
  and investigative reporting, 133
  in outsider strategy, 129
public opinion
  impact on agenda-setting, 133, 180–181
  media's impact on policy-related, 133,
  188–190
public opinion polls, 117, 149–150. See
  also survey research
public relations
  materials, used as news, 86, 90, 108–
  110, 121
  for presidency, 107
  during WWI, 145
public resource, broadcast airways as,
  36–37, 42
Putnam, Robert, 164–165

racial issues
  in campaign advertising, 211
  in coverage of political institutions,
  121–122
  and Internet access, 32–33
  media framing of, 188–189

media impact on attitudes about, 168,
  169
  vulnerability and media effects, 191
radio broadcasting
  audience for, 28, 81–82
  development of, 24, 26
  government regulation of, 35–36
  political talk shows on, 31, 81–82,
  167, 232
  public, 33–34, 41–42
  See also electronic broadcast media
ratings
  and advertising revenue, 78–80
  presidential approval, 117
rational ignorance, 201
reader-oriented, 77
readership surveys, problems with, 80–81
Reagan, Michael, 31
Reagan, Ronald, 5, 38, 107–108, 112,
  184, 185, 229, 252
"reality" shows, 127
Red Lion Broadcasting Company v.
  Federal Communications
  Commission, 37
regional variations, in news coverage, 58
regulation
  of broadcasting content, 36–40
  of broadcast media ownership, 35–36,
  39–40
  consequences of deregulation, 40–41
  defined, 33–34
  equal time rule, 36
  fairness doctrine, 36–39
  market-oriented approach to, 38–39
  passage of Telecommunications Act of
  1996, 39–40
  politics surrounding policy decisions,
  37–40
  of printed press, 34–35
regulatory policy, 33
Rehnquist, William, 143
reinforcement, in election campaigns,
  220
reporters of objective fact model
  and agenda-setting, 194
  defined, 9–10
  and election coverage, 234
  failure of, 245
  and institutional coverage, 134–135
  and linkage institutions, 12

reporters of objective fact model (*cont.*)
  and media agenda-setting, 177
  news coverage in, 50, 66
  and political knowledge, 143–144
representative democracy
  defined, 200
  and linkage institutions, 6–7
Republican Committee to Re-Elect the
    President (CREEP), 48
research methods, 15–16
responsible capitalism, 65
Ridge, Tom, 65
Robinson, Michael, 164
"Rock the Vote," 30
Roosevelt, Franklin, 148
Roosevelt, Theodore, 25–26
Roshco, Bernard, 53, 54

San Jose Mercury News, 91
scientific method, 15–16
Seattle Times, 58
selective access, 110
selective exposure, 149
selective perception, 149
selective retention, 149
self-selection
  and Internet use, 232–233
  and specialized news outlets, 3
Senate campaigns, 206
  impact on vote choice, 230
  political learning from, 221
September 11, 2001, terrorist attacks, 5,
    6, 48
Shah, Dhavan, 166
shares, 79
Shaw, Donald, 224–225
Simpson, O. J., 126
small-town pastoralism, 65
Smoller, Frederic T., 116
social capital, and television viewing,
    164–166
socialization, as media function, 13–14,
    15. *See also* political socialization
social order, 65
social science research, 15–16
socioeconomic status. *See* demographics
sociology, impact on media effects
    research, 148–150
sociotropic voting, 185

soft news, 31, 86–90, 100
Soloski, John, 94
sound bite, 209–210
specialized news outlets, 3. *See also*
    alternative information sources
Stahl, Lesley, 252
Stamm, Keith, 77
story format, in journalism, 13, 247
structural analysis, 254
subgovernment politics, 38
substantive analysis, 254
Supreme Court, 37
  confirmation hearings for, 125
  media coverage of, 124–125
  Public Information Office, 124
surveillance, as media function, 13, 15,
    112
survey research, 16
  findings on political knowledge, 151–
    161
  impact of adoption of, 149–151
  problems with, 80–81
  prominence of, 31

tabloid journalism, 25, 31, 41
talk radio
  audience size for, 81–82, 232
  impact on political evaluations, 167
  popularity of, 31
talk shows. *See* television talk shows
technological change
  electronic broadcast media, 26–28
  impact of telegraph, 24
  origins and growth of Internet, 29
Telecommunications Act of 1996, 37,
    39–40
telegraph, 24, 36
telephone services, regulation of, 36, 39
television broadcasting
  and decline of social capital, 164–
    166
  development of, 24, 26–28
  new political formats on, 30–31, 126–
    128, 205
  public, 33–34, 41–42
  and ratings game, 78–79
  regulation of, 36–41
  See also electronic broadcast media;
    television news

television news, 3
  audience interest in, 83
  audience size for, 81, 82
  campaign coverage on, 200, 202–203,
    205, 212–213, 217, 228
  and CNN effect, 130–132
  declining audiences of, 4, 28, 31, 41,
    95
  and emotional political evaluations,
    167–169, 170
  impact of Internet on, 84–85
  instantaneous news delivery of, 5, 28
  legitimization of, 27–28
  local news coverage of, 58–60
  vs. newspapers for political learning,
    161–162, 170, 222–223
  portrayal of Congress in, 119–120
  presidential coverage, 111–112, 114,
    115
  sound bite news, 209–210
  and video-malaise thesis, 163–166
  Web pages, 29
television newsmagazines
  audience size for, 81, 82
  negative focus on public officials, 127–
    128
  political figures appearing on, 30
  and public advocacy, 135
  tabloid news coverage on, 126
  trend in, 90, 98, 143
television talk shows
  campaign coverage on, 205, 219
  political figures appearing on, 30–
    31
terrorism, 176, 178, 188
thematic news coverage, 187
theory, 16
Thomas, Clarence, 125
timeliness, of news, 52–53, 67
Time magazine, 3, 53, 86, 89, 114, 115,
    208, 232
Times Mirror Corporation, 86, 90
Time Warner, 40, 73, 77
tongs, 114
Torres, Marcos, 189
transaction model, of agenda-setting,
    225–228
"transmission belt theory," 145
trial balloons, 112

trial courts, media coverage of, 125–
    126
Tribune Publishing Company, 52
triggering event, 129
trust in government, media impact on,
    163–164, 169
Turner Broadcasting, 40
two-step flow of, 149

uncontrolled news, 111
Underwood, Doug, 77, 91
United Press International (UPI), 206
unobtrusive issues, 183
Uslaner, Eric, 165
U.S. News and World Report, 114

values and norms
  media portrayal of, 13–14
  reflected in news coverage, 64–66
Vanderbilt Television News Archive,
    121
Vanishing Voter project, 222
variable news media influence, 183
Viacom, 73
video-malaise thesis, 163–166
violence, in foreign affairs coverage, 61
visual content, impact of, 252
von Bulow, Claus, 126
vote choice
  impact of media priming on, 228–229
  media effects on, 149, 216, 219, 228–
    231
  party identification and, 216, 219, 220
  predominant model of, 216
voter turnout, impact of campaign
  advertising on, 223–224

Wall Street Journal, 27, 40, 114, 191
Walt Disney Corporation, 4–5, 73–77
War of the Worlds (Welles), 145, 146–
    147
Washington Post, 27, 48, 98, 105, 112,
    114, 132
Watergate, 48
Wattenberg, Martin, 221
Welch, Louie, 230–231
welfare programs, media portrayal of,
    168, 188
Welles, Orson, 145, 146–147

West, Darrell, 230
Western Europe, public ownership in, 42
White House press corps, 107
White House Press Office, 4, 107, 109, 113–115
White House press secretary, 107, 113–115
Whitmire, Kathy, 230–231
"Willie Horton" advertisement, 211
Willis, Mark, 86, 90
Willkie, Wendell, 148
Wilson, Rick, 230

Winfrey, Oprah, 31
Winston-Salem Journal, 86
women
    agenda-setting effects on, 191
    political coverage of, 121–122
Woodward, Bob, 48, 98
World War I, 144–145
World War II, 148, 211

yellow journalism, 25

Zaller, John, 166–167, 168